READINGS ON EQUAL EDUCATION
(Formerly *Educating the Disadvantaged*)

READINGS ON EQUAL EDUCATION

Volume 25

DIVERSITY, MERIT, AND HIGHER EDUCATION

TOWARD A COMPREHENSIVE AGENDA FOR THE 21ST CENTURY

Series and Volume Editors
Phillip J. Bowman
Edward P. St John

Managing Editor
Phyllis Kreger Stillman

AMS Press, Inc.
New York

READINGS ON EQUAL EDUCATION
VOLUME 25

Diversity, Merit, and Higher Education
Toward a Comprehensive Agenda for the 21st Century

Copyright © 2011 by AMS Press, Inc.
All rights reserved

ISSN 0270-1448

Set ISBN-10: 0-404-10100-3
Set ISBN-13: 978-0-404-10100-8

Volume 25: ISBN-10: 0-404-10225-5
Volume 25: ISBN-13: 978-0-404-10225-8
Library of Congress Catalog Card Number 77-83137

All AMS Books are printed on acid-free paper that meets the guidelines for performance and durability of the Committee on Production Guidelines for Book Longevity of the Council on Library Resources.

AMS PRESS, INC.
BROOKLYN NAVY YARD
63 FLUSHING AVENUE – UNIT #221
BROOKLYN, NY 11205-1073, USA
www.amspressinc.com

Manufactured in the United States of America

VOLUME 25   **CONTENTS**

CONTRIBUTORS' NOTES

PHILLIP J. BOWMAN is the founding Director of the University of Michigan's *National Center for Institutional Diversity (NCID)*, which promotes national exemplars of diversity scholarship, engagement, and innovation within higher education and other major societal institutions. *NCID's* strategic partnerships bridge diversity scholarship with multilevel innovation at the institutional, local, state, national, and international levels. Bowman is also a Professor of Higher Education and Faculty Associate at the UM's Institute for Social Research. Bowman is a theoretical and applied social psychologist who has published widely on pressing diversity issues in higher education and related policy challenges including achievement gaps, health disparities, family distress, urban poverty, and racial/ethnic inequalities; his new research builds on strengths-based social psychological theory to better understand STEM (science, technology, engineering, and mathematics) pipeline interventions that improve higher education access, career opportunities, and U.S. global competitiveness. A former Rockefeller Postdoctoral Fellow and Senior Ford Foundation Postdoctoral Fellow, Professor Bowman has also had research funded by *NIGMS, NIMH, NIA, NSF, HHS*, Spencer Foundation, and others. He is an active national and international lecturer who continues to provide innovative diversity research methods training and mentoring for post-doctoral, graduate, and undergraduate scholars.

KURT BURKUM is a Senior Research Associate at *ACT, Inc.*, where he works with other experts on policy research, education and workforce research services, educational survey services, and career transitions research. He earned his PhD from Pennsylvania State University where he worked as a Research Assistant at the Center for the Study of Higher Education. His research interests include the assessment of academic readiness for college, comprehensive college admissions criteria, innovative approaches to college student retention, and diversifying the higher education pipeline. Dr. Burkum works closely with other *ACT* experts including Chapter 12 co-authors STEVE ROBBINS and RICHARD PHELPS on innovative college-readiness assessment tools and related research topics including test reliability and validity, the meaning of test-score differences, racial/ethnic achievement differences, gender bias, occupations, and interests.

JEREMY BURRUS is an Associate Research Scientist with *ETS*'s Center for New Constructs in the Research & Development (R&D) Division. He earned a Ph.D. in social psychology from the University of Illinois, Urbana–Champaign. His main research interests are in the areas of noncognitive assessments, interventions, and social judgment. Dr. Burrus has published in leading journals in the field of social psychology, including the *Personality and Social Psychology Bulletin*, *Journal of Experimental Social Psychology*, and *Journal of Consumer Psychology*. Dr. Burrus is a core member of an *ETS* research team that also includes Chapter 11 coauthors CAROLYN MACCANN, PATRICK C. KYLLONEN, and RICHARD D. ROBERTS conducting cutting-edge research on emotional intelligence, the Personal Potential Index, and other indicators with important implications for comprehensive assessment, intervention, and public policy.

ANGELA EBREO is Assistant Director for Research and Training for the *National Center for Institutional Diversity (NCID)* at the University of Michigan. The issues of diversity, equity, and social justice play a major role in her basic and engaged scholarship. Dr. Ebreo earned a PhD in social psychology from the University of Illinois, and her research focuses on cultural and psychosocial factors related to student adjustment. Her other interests include racial, ethnic, and gender disparities in health, campus–community collaborative research, and cross-cultural methods. She is Project Director and Co-Principal Investigator on a *NCID*-based, *NIH*-funded project "A Mixed-Method Study of Exemplary Research Opportunity Interventions: Bridging Theory-Driven Research with Program Innovation." Chapter 13 co-author, GLORYVEE FONSECA-BOLORIN, is a Graduate Student Research Assistant on this collaborative study and a doctoral student at the UM's Center for the Study of Higher and Postsecondary Education.

RHANA NATOUR is a researcher and documentary film producer who received a Fulbright Fellowship to research women's higher education and labor force outcomes in the United Arab Emirates after undergraduate studies at the University of Michigan. Ms. Natour coauthored Chapter 6 as an *Undergraduate Research Opportunity Program (UROP)* scholar supervised by ANGELA LOCKS at the UM's *National Center for Institutional Diversity (NCID)*. Dr. Locks is currently an Assistant Professor of Student Development in Higher Education at California State University, Long Beach. Ms. Locks supervised all *UROP* scholars at *NCID* while completing her doctorate at UM's Center for the Study of Higher and Post-secondary Education. Before her doctoral studies, she worked as Assistant Director with UM's *UROP* assisting with admissions, recruitment, retention activities, peer advising, program evaluation, and fellowship programs. Professor Locks's research interests include institutional diversity praxis and college recruitment, retention, and experiences of students of color; she explores college access, the community college student transfer process, and

African American and Latina/o retention and the institutional actions that create campus climates where students of color are successful.

MICHELE S. MOSES is Associate Professor in educational foundations, policy, and practice within the School of Education at the University of Colorado at Boulder and is affiliated with the Education and the Public Interest Center. She is a nationally prominent educational researcher; her innovative research centers on education policy issues related to equality of educational opportunity and social justice, such as affirmative action. As a scholar-activist, Professor Moses works on collaborative efforts on such pressing diversity issues bridges innovative scholarship with policy-relevant advocacy and activism along with Chapter 5 coauthors JOHN T. YUN, PATRICIA MARIN, and others.

JOHN A. POWELL is an internationally recognized authority in the areas of civil rights, civil liberties, and issues relating to race, ethnicity, poverty, and law. He is the Executive Director of the Kirwan Institute for the Study of Race and Ethnicity at the Ohio State University, where he also holds the Williams Chair in Civil Rights and Civil Liberties at the Moritz College of Law. He has written extensively on structural racism; racial justice and regionalism; concentrated poverty and urban sprawl; opportunity-based housing; voting rights; affirmative action in the United States, South Africa, and Brazil; racial and ethnic identity; spirituality and social justice; and the needs of citizens in a democratic society. Professor powell's collaborative work on such critical diversity issues at the Kirwan Institute bridges innovative scholarship with policy-relevant advocacy and activism along with many others, including Chapter 12 coauthor BECKY RENO.

CHARLES RAMOS is currently an executive consultant with Noel-Levitz. His areas of expertise include enrollment management, student success initiatives, and academic advising. He has also consulted with college and university campuses on using data and research to inform decision making. He has presented to state executive and legislative branches on current educational policies, trends, and assessment-based research to strengthen statewide educational policies. Mr. Ramos completed Chapter 7 while Director of Postsecondary/Business Services for *ACT Inc.* working with (a) postsecondary institutions in the areas of enrollment management, advising, and assessment; (b) workforce development and employers within the nine-state Midwest region; and (c) *ACT*'s educational partnerships with states, districts, postsecondary institutions, and high schools on EXPLORE, PLAN, and ACT testing.

EDWARD P. ST. JOHN is Algo D. Henderson Collegiate Professor of Higher Education at the University of Michigan's Center for the Study of Higher and Postsecondary Education and a Senior Faculty Associate at the National Center for Institutional Diversity. His extensive publications focus on the effects of public policy on equal opportunity and moral reasoning in professional practice. His recent books include *Education and the Public Interest: Education Reform, Public Finance, and Access to Higher Education* and *Action, Reflection, and Social Justice: Integrating Moral Reasoning into Professional Development*. Guided by his unique Action Inquiry Model, Professor St. John is a national expert on bridging innovative scholarship with multilevel educational policy interventions to promote diversity, equity, and college success.

KRYSTAL L. WILLIAMS is a doctoral candidate in the Center for the Study of Higher and Postsecondary Education at the University of Michigan. Ms. Williams is also a Graduate Research Assistant with the National Center for Institutional Diversity working with a Diversity Exemplar Evaluation Network initiative and an *NIH*-funded project, "A Mixed-Method Study of Exemplary Research Opportunity Interventions: Bridging Theory-Driven Research with Program Innovation." She holds an MS in pure mathematics from Clark Atlanta University. Ms. Williams's research interests focus on financial aid policy and college access for underrepresented groups; her theory-driven dissertation investigates how financial and academic barriers impede the efficacy of exemplary research opportunity interventions on STEM-related outcomes.

WILLIAM E. SEDLACEK is a Professor Emeritus of Education at the University of Maryland, College Park. He authored *Beyond the Big Test: Noncognitive Assessment in Higher Education*, the seminal publication on using noncognitive assessment as part of the selection criteria for college admission and to promote diversity in counseling, academic advising, financial aid and student affairs programs. Extensive research on his eight noncognitive variables promotes the importance of a more comprehensive, fair, and impartial assessment of a student's likelihood of success in college. Over his long and distinguished career, he has published extensively in professional journals on a wide range of topics including racism, sexism, college admissions, advising, and employee selection.

ACKNOWLEDGMENTS

The authors wish to thank several individuals and organizations for their support and contributions to this volume of **Readings in Equal Education**. Particular thanks go to Associate Director Valerie Johnson and other support staff at the University of Michigan (UM)'s *National Center for Institutional Diversity (NCID)* who helped to plan the 2008 *"National Forum on Diversity, Merit, and Higher Education: Implications for Comprehensive Admission, Pipeline, and Retention Strategies"* that provided the foundation for this volume. Thanks also go to the students in the 2009–2010 *"Graduate Seminar on Diversity and Merit in Higher Education"* in the UM's Center for the Study of Higher and Postsecondary Education. These graduate students conducted critical reviews of related literature, critiques of early drafts of the chapters in this volume, and pushed for greater clarity and coherence within and across the various chapters. The current volume also would not have been possible without the significant contributions of research groups from the Educational Testing Service; American College Testing, Inc.; and several universities. These expert teams are engaged in cutting-edge R&D activities on comprehensive assessment methods that can be used in concert with standardized SAT/ACT-type tests. In many ways, this volume represents a strategic partnership between *NCID* and these experts to promote collaborative dialogue, exchange, and innovation on more comprehensive approaches to diversity, merit, and higher education.

Work by the first author on this volume was supported by funding from the National Institutes of Health–National Institute for General Medical Sciences (1R01GM088750-01). We also want to thank the UM's Provost Office, and especially Senior Vice Provost Lester Monts, for the visionary and financial support of work on this volume and related *NCID* priority areas. Cosponsorship of the initial national forum that resulted in this volume was provided by the UM's Rackham School of Graduate Studies, School of Education, Center for the Study of Higher and Postsecondary Education, College of Architecture and Urban Planning, School of Information, School of Social Work, School of Public Health, School of Nursing, School of Dentistry, School of Pharmacy, Division of Kinesiology, Comprehensive Studies Program, Office of Academic Multicultural Initiatives, Office of the Dean of Students, and Office of Undergraduate Admissions. Finally, we wish to thank Ms. Phyllis Kreger Stillman whose diligent editing of each chapter in this volume significantly improved both the quality and clarity of the manuscript.

CHAPTER 1

NEED FOR A 21st-CENTURY MERIT AGENDA IN HIGHER EDUCATION

Phillip J. Bowman

Over the past 35 years, both public opinion and social science studies reveal a strong backlash in mainstream America against 1960s-era civil rights policies in university admissions, educational opportunity interventions, and related affirmative action efforts in employment and other public policy sectors (Bowman & Betancur, 2010; Kellough, 2006; Krysan & Lewis, 2004; Omi & Winant, 1994; Orfield & Ashkinaze, 1991; Sears, Sidanius, & Bobo, 2000). The especially strong opposition to race-targeted affirmative action in universities is deeply rooted in a problematic *mainstream merit assumption* that racial/ethnic group members with lower SAT/ACT-type test scores are *less qualified* than are Whites who face reverse discrimination if not selected with equal or higher test scores (Bobo & Kluegel, 1993; Bowman & Smith, 2002; Kluegel & Smith, 1983, 1986; Wightman, 2003). Beginning with the 1980s Reagan Revolution, the anti–affirmative action movement has successfully litigated an increasing number of reverse discrimination cases which are based on flawed but widely accepted mainstream merit ideology and arguments (Curry, 1996; Featherman, Hall, & Krislov, 2010; Glazer, 1987; Mosley & Capaldi, 1996; W. Smith, Altbach, & Lomotey, 2002).

The implicit merit assumption in many of these reverse discrimination cases that reduce the construct of merit or qualification to a single indicator—SAT/ACT-type score differences—is problematic and has become increasingly controversial (Guinier & Strum, 2001; Sedlacek, 2004; Steele, 2004). For example, critics have frequently taken issue with this broadly accepted merit assumption in reverse discrimination arguments, especially during Supreme Court cases in higher education such as *The Regents of the University of California v. Bakke* (1978) and the two University of Michigan affirmative action lawsuits, *Gratz v. Bollinger* (2003) and *Grutter v. Bollinger* (2003). Partly in response to such critics, some colleges and universities no longer use the SAT in admissions, and many more have begun to broaden the criteria of merit in more "comprehensive" and "holistic" reviews that systematically consider SAT/ ACT scores as *only one* of several criteria (e.g., Gilbert, 2008; Pusser, 2004; Sedlacek, 2004). The ongoing *experimentation*

1

with more comprehensive approaches for selecting the most qualified or deserving students seek to identify not only "prepared" applicants who can succeed academically but also those with talents and assets that best represent the university's mission, values, and goals.

Historical Context

In addition to affirmative action and mainstream merit issues, the need for a more comprehensive 21st-century merit agenda in higher education is also spurred by major historical shifts in national debates about the proper use of SAT/ACT-type testing as well as emerging global forces (i.e., Nettles, Perna, & Millett, 1998; D. G. Smith, 2009; Williams, Chapter 3 this volume). Early in the 20th century, the development of the SAT had profound, diversifying effects on admissions policies in the most selective American colleges by expanding the definition of merit beyond the qualities of elite students from wealthy families attending private schools in the Northeast (e.g., Lemann, 1999). In 1934, Harvard President James Bryant Conant utilized the SAT to broaden these early merit criteria to select for the first time a small group of talented "Harvard National Scholars" with strong academic potential from high schools all over the Midwest. During the late 1930s, this experiment was replicated and was expanded throughout the Ivy League with profound socioeconomic, regional, and intellectual diversity implications for the student population. Ironically, as we move further into the 21st century, a similar use of the SAT as the primary indicator of merit in university admissions may result in *declining numbers* of talented African American, Latina/o, low-income, male, and U.S. students—and *increasing proportions* of high-skilled immigrant, affluent, female, and international students.

Critical diversity and inequality issues associated with these projections are discussed in greater detail in the next chapter, including controversial race, class, gender, and global complexities. To better understand 21st-century challenges, it is also important to place the evolving research and policy debates on mainstream merit assumption into historical context. Despite shifts in historical framing, tensions between diversity, merit, and opportunity in higher education have been hotly debated in the USA for over a century. Table 1 briefly highlights *four* evolving themes in related debates, major historical periods for these evolving themes, and related references.

Table 1.		
Historical Debates	**Major Debate Periods**	**Selected References**
SAT as IQ	1920s–Present	Brigham (1923)
SAT vs. ACT	1959–Present	Lemann (1999)
"Big Tests" Opposition	1970s–Present	Flaxman (1980)
Comprehensive Approach	1990s–Present	Gilbert (2008)

Research and development work in the 1920s by Carl Brigham at Princeton University clearly linked prototype SAT scores to related studies on *intelligence quotients (IQ)* or innate intelligence, which were assumed to be genetics based (Brigham, 1923). In his book on *The Big Test*, Lemann (1999) shows how the Educational Testing Service (ETS) initially endorsed such *"SAT as IQ"* links under the leadership of its first president, Henry Chauncey, with an emphasis on SAT scores as valid and reliable measures of innate ability and aptitudes. Today, ETS formally cautions against such SAT–IQ links, but there remains a widespread mainstream tendency to misinterpret SAT/ACT-type scores as objective indicators of innate ability within public discourse, legal decisions, professional practice, and even scholarly studies. Moreover, since the founding of American College Testing Incorporated (ACT Inc.) in 1959, debates about the relative utility of the *"SAT vs. ACT"* have revolved around mainstream merit debates about the extent to which these two popular admissions tests reflect *innate aptitudes* or *scholastic opportunities* (Hilliard, 1994; Lemann, 1999; Peterson, 1983; Schudson, 1972). Going beyond earlier critics, *"Big Tests Opposition"* to SAT/ACT-type tests grew especially strong during the 1970s, as illustrated by various authors in *Volume 6* of *Readings in Equal Education,* with some even calling for a complete moratorium on all testing (Flaxman, 1980). These authors (e.g., Bernal, 1980; Cleary, Humphreys, Kendrick, & Wesman, 1975/1980; Jackson, 1980) engaged in intense debate about the prevalent *misuse* of SAT/ACT-type tests as indicators of IQ, natural ability, or innate aptitudes to label, track, and restrict educational opportunities among talented minority and low-income students.

Beyond Mainstream Merit Assumptions

As we move further into the 21st century, the traditional mainstream merit argument is being radically reformulated by a new trend toward "comprehensive" or "holistic" review in U.S. higher education. Especially in more selective colleges and universities, there is a growing emphasis on developing, articulating, and refining *more comprehensive strategies* that utilize SAT/ACT-type test scores as *only one* among a diverse set of individual merit criteria in admissions and related pipeline interventions. Beginning in the 1990s, this new comprehensive review era was spurred by strategic institutional responses to intense, nationwide opposition to affirmative action and mandates to eliminate what was perceived to be widespread "reverse discrimination" and "racial preferences" in Texas, California, Washington, Michigan, and beyond (Chang, Witt, Jones, & Hakuta, 2003; Featherman et al., 2010; Gurin, Lehman, & Lewis, 2004; Pusser, 2004; W. Smith et al., 2002). In addition to avoiding "racial quotas," more comprehensive approaches also go beyond the *mainstream merit assumption* that SAT/ACT scores are sufficient to conclude that a student is *more or less qualified* to systematically consider a more diverse set of merit criteria. A growing number of higher education institutions have begun to systematically *experiment* with carefully designed approaches to comprehensive assessment of merit in admissions, retention efforts, and pipeline interventions.

In addition to the impetus provided by the affirmative action debate, there are several other important reasons for current efforts to go beyond mainstream merit ideology to seek a more comprehensive agenda for the 21st century. First, in a diversifying nation any progress toward a true multicultural democracy may well depend on the successful development of a more comprehensive approach that provides fair and equal opportunities for all talented students regardless of race/ethnicity, class, gender, or national origin. Second, the best scientific evidence strongly questions the mainstream merit assumption and the related "Big Tests" view that SAT/ACT-type scores alone should be used as "the" indicator of merit, qualification, and ability (especially when comparing scores across members of diverse groups that differ on past educational opportunity). For example, existing education and social science research on the "achievement gap" strongly suggests that persistent *Black–White* test-score disparities reflect more an *"opportunity gap"* than an "ability gap" (e.g., Darling-Hammond, 2010; Oakes, 2005).

Although less often discussed, the growing salience of **"multiple achievement gaps"** facing the United States is another major reason for the current movement beyond the mainstream merit assumption and toward a more comprehensive agenda in the 21st century. Recent trends in intergroup disparities on *"Big Tests"* show not only persistent racial/ethnic differences, but also multiple achievement gaps that are growing across diverse *socioeconomic, gender, and cross-national groups* with profound public policy implications (e.g., Bowen, Chingos, & McPherson, 2009; Darling-Hammond, 2010; Friedman, 2005; Oakes, 2005; Schmidt, 2008; Takagi, 1992; Whitmire, 2009). These multiple achievement gaps have begun to *raise serious questions* about the mainstream merit assumption that *go beyond* a narrow focus on "preferences" for Black *over* White students *to emerging debates* about "preferences" for low-income *over* more affluent students, male *over* female students, non-immigrant *over* high-skilled immigrant students, and U.S. citizens *over* international students. These emerging debates raise serious questions about whether *lower* SAT/ACT-type test scores *alone* make lower-income, male, nonimmigrant minority, or domestic students *less qualified* than more affluent, female, high-skilled immigrant, or international students, especially the growing numbers from large Asian/Pacific nations.

The prospects of closing the multiple achievement gaps across diverse groups within the United States call for a ***more comprehensive merit agenda in higher education for the 21st century*** that moves beyond current diversity debates over "reverse discrimination," "racial preferences," "Black quotas," or "affirmative action" to more ***strategic national action*** in a global context. There is a growing recognition that America's future depends not only on attracting more skilled international talent, but also on closing ***cross-national achievement gaps*** between the United States and currently higher performing Asian and European nations through more comprehensive talent development strategies for ***all*** racial/ethnic, socioeconomic, and gender groups (e.g., Darling-Hammonds, 2010; Friedman, 2005; also see Committee on Prospering in the Global Economy of the 21st Century, 2005; Members of the 2005 "Rising Above the Gathering Storm" Committee, 2010). For example, the United States currently ranks only 25th among nations in mathematics and 27th in science and appears to be falling even farther behind according to a recent report by the Members of the 2005 "Rising About the Gathering Storm" Committee, *Rising Above the Gathering Storm, Revisited – Rapidly Approaching Category 5* (2010). Therefore, a more comprehensive approach to diversity and merit in higher education has strategic policy implications for both holistic college admissions and related multilevel interventions to promote more inclusive talent development, organizational excellence, sustainable prosperity, and competitiveness in a rapidly diversifying nation and global economy (e.g., Bowman & Betancur, 2010; Featherman et al., 2010; Gurin et al., 2005; Page, 2007). Bowman and Betancur (2010) suggest that a critical component of the ***race*** for sustainable economic prosperity among the United States, China, and other nations in the 21st century may well become which country can best close the striking achievement gaps between the most affluent students and the marginalized segments of their student populations that remain in extreme poverty.

In addition to attracting more global talent to the United States, there is also increasing recognition that a comprehensive approach to improving

America's competitiveness in the 21st century requires more strategic investment in talent development among *historically underrepresented students* especially in science, technology, engineering, and mathematics (STEM). For example, there is a growing collaboration among several nonprofits and governmental agencies to support more comprehensive approaches to understanding and improving interventions that promote success among minorities and women in STEM fields. This collaboration has resulted in a series of conferences, workshops, white papers, research projects, and policy initiatives supported by the National Academies, National Institutes of Health, National Science Foundation, American Association for the Advancement of Science, and other partners (DePass & Chubin, 2008; Olson & Fagen, 2007). Similarly, the U.S. Department of Education has begun to place a major priority on closing achievement gaps through more comprehensive strategies that combine the creative use of high-stakes SAT/ACT-type testing with other multilevel strategies that also consider systemic barriers, opportunities, and resources. With a focus on the multilevel social-ecology, a major exemplar of this trend is the new federal PROMISE NEIGHBORHOOD initiative that seeks to reduce the alarming achievement gaps in urban schools with a comprehensive approach that combines high-stakes SAT/ACT-type testing with collaborative efforts to *strengthen multilevel systemic resources* including teachers, classrooms, schools, families, and neighborhoods.

Strategic national action to eliminate multiple achievement gaps through a more comprehensive approach to identifying, developing, and utilizing talent may well become the pivotal factor that determines whether or not the United States remains the major world power in the 21st century. Nations with the most effective higher education strategies for reducing achievement gaps and developing talent within diverse populations may well be at a major advantage in the race for sustainable prosperity in the 21st century. There is growing evidence that such effective higher education strategies in the U.S. must include a more comprehensive approach that systematically combines SAT/ACT-type assessment with more inclusive and multifaceted merit criteria in admissions, retention, and related pipeline interventions. However, the successful development of such a comprehensive agenda in the United States must be based on a better understanding of the challenges and opportunities associated with the evolving debate over diversity, merit, and higher education.

Overview of Current Volume

The current volume of *Readings on Equal Education* includes original articles by leading national scholars, most of whom participated in a National Forum on "Diversity, Merit, and Higher Education: Implications for Comprehensive Admission, Pipeline, and Retention Strategies" sponsored by the National Center for Institutional Diversity at the University of Michigan. This volume is organized around *four major issues* to guide future research and policy discourse:

1. Critical analysis of contested constructions of merit in higher education.

2. Emerging complexities in merit and opportunity challenges in higher education.

3. Innovative approaches for expanding indicators of merit in diversifying populations.

4. The importance of a translational research approach that bridges innovative scholarship with comprehensive intervention initiatives to promote strategic policy and social change.

Together, these interrelated issues and chapters provide the foundation for a comprehensive 21st-century agenda to address the growing complexities in debates about diversity and merit in higher education.

Part I: Contested Constructions of Merit in the 21st Century: From the Big Test to the Diversity Debate in Higher Education

The three chapters in **Part I** provide a critical analysis of related literature on contested constructions of merit in higher education to better clarify emerging challenges and opportunities for the 21st century. These chapters not only trace the origins of SAT/ACT-type tests but also provide a critical analysis of their limitations as a primary indicator of merit in higher education along with alternative perspectives to guide more comprehensive strategies.

Chapter 2, "Diversity and Merit in Higher Education: Challenges and Opportunities for the 21st Century," by Phillip J. Bowman provides a conceptual framework to further clarify complex diversity and inequality issues in alternative constructs of merit. Dr. Bowman discusses how the debate over merit in the United States has centered around *three alternative* *constructs* with differential implications for the role of SAT/ACT-type tests in the admissions and intervention strategies in higher education.

Chapter 3, "The Qualified Applicant: Origins of Admissions Tests in Higher Education," by Krystal L. Williams focuses on the historical development of the SAT as the primary indicator of merit.

Chapter 4, "Critical Analysis of Merit Assumptions in Higher Education," by Edward P. St. John provides a more philosophical critique of merit assumptions, discussing several critical issues regarding standards of fairness in the merit debate and three related principles of justice with significant educational policy implications.

Part II: Merit and Opportunity in Higher Education: Complexities, Challenges, and Trends in a Diversifying Nation

The three chapters in **Part II** focus on complex merit and opportunity challenges facing higher education in a rapidly diversifying nation. Within a changing sociopolitical terrain, these chapters chart the complex effects of anti-affirmative action policies in selective universities and exemplary efforts to build K–12 partnerships to improve college readiness and reduce enrollment decline among underrepresented students.

Chapter 5, "Diversity and Opportunity in Higher Education: The Role of Affirmative Action," by Michelle S. Moses, John T. Yun, and Patricia Marin provides an in-depth analysis of affirmative action in postsecondary admissions. The penetrating analysis includes a concurrent review of recent court rulings, state legislation, higher education enrollment data, and future institutional and policy implications.

Chapter 6, "Diversity, Merit, and College Choice: Role of a Dynamic Sociopolitical Environment," by Rhana Natour, Angela Locks, and Phillip J. Bowman considers underrepresented students with exemplary SAT/ACT scores who might choose not to attend universities with affirmative action bans or ambiguous diversity commitments. This chapter provides a critical review of related literature and suggests a reformulation of traditional college choice models to consider how some underrepresented students may avoid campuses with a sociopolitical climate perceived as not diverse, non-inclusive, or hostile.

Chapter 7, "ACT's P–16 Partnerships: Expanding Opportunity for Academic Merit," by Charles Ramos highlights the importance of partnerships to develop innovative assessment, test-taking, and intervention strategies. This chapter outlines ACT Inc. strategies which have become national models for K–12 academic pipeline development efforts that remain a major higher education response to affirmative action bans.

Part III: Toward a Comprehensive Agenda

The three chapters in **Part III** focus on five innovative approaches for expanding merit indicators for diversifying populations in the 21st century.

Chapter 8, "Toward a Strengths-based Assessment System: A Comprehensive Social Psychological Approach," by Phillip J. Bowman highlights several competing models and presents an integrative theoretical framework for incorporating complementary insights from various models into a comprehensive strengths-based approach.

Chapter 9, "Using Noncognitive Variables in Assessing Readiness for Higher Education," by William E. Sedlacek builds on over 40 years of research to show how a consideration of courses, grades, and tests should be combined with measures of eight noncognitive factors to better assess college readiness in a changing world.

Chapter 10, "Admissions, Academic Readiness, and Student Success: Implications for Growing a Diverse Pipeline," by Kurt Burkum, Steve Robbins, and Richard Phelps builds on cutting-edge research-and-development work at ACT Inc. to show how a Student Readiness Inventory can help guide a more comprehensive approach to college admission, retention, and pipeline interventions, especially for underrepresented students.

Chapter 11, "Noncognitive Constructs in K–16: Assessments, Interventions, Educational and Policy Implications," by Jeremy Burrus, Carolyn MacCann, Patrick C. Kyllonen, and Richard D. Roberts highlights innovative research based at the ETS Center for New Constructs that supports the importance of a more comprehensive approach to guide admissions and K–16 academic pipeline interventions.

Chapter 12, "A Democratic Merit Agenda: An Alternative Approach," by john a. powell and Becky Reno outlines a more transformative approach that goes beyond "individualistic" concepts of merit to a range of initiatives that embrace ideals of "democratic merit" for diverse multicultural societies.

Part IV: Bridging Scholarship with Comprehensive Intervention

The final two chapters focus on the importance of bridging scholarship with comprehensive intervention strategies in higher education to promote the development of exemplary professional practice, institutional innovation, strategic public policy, social change, and movement toward a true meritocracy in the 21st century.

Chapter 13, "Diversity and Comprehensive Strategies in Higher Education," by Angela Ebreo, Gloryvee Fonseca-Bolorin, and Phillip J. Bowman reviews literature on comprehensive admissions, pipeline, and retention strategies along with highlights from interviews with campus experts on related challenges and opportunities.

Chapter 14, "Toward a 21st-Century Meritocracy: Bridging Scholarship, Intervention, and Social Change," by Phillip J. Bowman and Edward P. St. John further promotes the importance of a reciprocal translational research agenda that builds on the *reciprocal benefits* of *basic scholarship* and *intervention inquiry*. They conclude that such reciprocal translation of basic scholarship ←→ intervention inquiry is essential for the innovative design, evaluation, development, legitimization, and institution-alization of more comprehensive merit-based strategies for the 21st century.

Note

Preparation of Volume 25 of *Readings in Equal Education* was partially supported by a grant from the National Institutes of Health—National Institute for General Medical Sciences (1R01Gm088750-01), for which the first author serves as principal investigator. However, the perspectives represented in each chapter are those of the authors and are not to be attributed to the funding agency. We also extend our thanks to Phyllis Kreger Stillman for diligent editorial assistance with each chapter and to the members of the graduate seminar on Diversity and Merit in Higher Education, Center for the Study of Higher and Postsecondary Education, University of Michigan for their feedback on an earlier draft of this manuscript.

References

Bernal, E. M., Jr. (1980). A response to "Educational uses of tests with disadvantaged subjects." In E. Flaxman (Ed.), *Readings on Equal Education: Vol. 6. 1975–1976* (pp. 345–351). New York, NY: AMS Press.

Bobo, L. & Kluegel, J. R. (1993). Opposition to race-targeting: Self-interest, stratification ideology, or racial attitudes? *American Sociological Review, 58*, 443–464.

Bowen, W. G., Chingos, M. M., & McPherson, M. S. (2009). *Crossing the finish line: Completing college in America's public universities.* Princeton, NJ: Princeton University Press.

Bowman, P. J., & Betancur, J. J. (2010). Sustainable diversity and inequality: Race in the USA and beyond (pp. 55–78). In M. Janssens,

M. Bechtold, G. Prarolo, & V. Stenius (Eds.), *The sustainability of cultural diversity: Nations, cities and organizations*. Cheltenham, England: Edward Elgar.

Bowman, P. J., & Smith, W. A. (2002). Racial ideology in the campus community. In W. A. Smith, P. G. Altbach, and K. Lomotey (Eds.), *The racial crisis in higher education: Continuing challenges for the 21st century* (pp. 103–120). Albany: State University of New York Press.

Brigham, C. C. (1923). *A study of American intelligence*. Princeton, NJ: Princeton University Press.

Chang, M. J., Witt, D., Jones, J., & Hakuta, K. (2003). *Compelling interest: Examining the evidence of racial dynamics in colleges and universities*. Stanford, CA: Stanford University Press.

Cleary, T. A., Humphries, L. G., Kendrick, S. A., & Wesman, G. B. (1980). Educational uses of tests with disadvantaged students. In E. Flaxman (Ed.), *Readings on Equal Education: Vol. 6. 1975–1976* (pp. 285–333). New York, NY: AMS Press.

Committee on Prospering in the Global Economy of the 21st Century. (2005). *Rising above the gathering storm: Energizing and employing America for a brighter economic future* (Report prepared for the National Academy of Sciences, National Academy of Engineering, and Institute of Medicine of the National Academies). Washington, DC: National Academies Press.

Curry, G. (1996). *The affirmative action debate*. New York, NY: Addison Wesley.

Darling-Hammond, L. (2010). Structured for failure: Race, resources, and student achievement. In H. R. Markus & P. M. L. Moya (Eds.), *Doing race: 21 essays for the 21st century* (pp. 295–321). New York, NY: W. W. Norton.

DePass, A. L., & Chubin, D. E. (2008). *Understanding interventions that encourage minorities to pursue research careers: Building a community of research and practice*. Bethesda, MD: American Society of Cell Biology.

Featherman, D., Hall, M., & Krislov, M. (2010). *The next 25 years: affirmative action in higher education in the United States and South Africa*. Ann Arbor: University of Michigan Press.

Flaxman, E. (1980). *Readings on Equal Education: Vol. 6. 1975–1976*. New York, NY: AMS Press.

Friedman, T. (2005). *The world is flat: A brief history of the 21st century*. New York, NY: Farrar, Straus and Giroux.

Gilbert, J. (2008). Application quest: A case study on holistic diversity in admission. *Journal of College Admission, 199*, 12–18.

Glazer, N. (1987). *Affirmative discrimination: Ethnic inequality and public policy.* Cambridge, MA: Harvard University Press.

Gratz v. Bollinger, 539 U.S. 244 (2003).

Grutter v. Bollinger, 539 U.S. 306 (2003).

Guinier, L., & Strum, S. (2001). *Who's qualified?* Boston, MA: Beacon Press.

Gurin, P., Lehman, J. S., & Lewis, E. (2005). *Defending diversity: Affirmative action at the University of Michigan.* Ann Arbor: University of Michigan Press.

Hilliard, A. G. (1994). What good is this thing called intelligence and why bother to measure it? *Journal of Black Psychology, 20,* 430–444

Jackson, G. D. (1980). On the report of the ad hoc committee on educational uses of tests with disadvantaged students. In E. Flaxman (Ed.), *Readings on Equal Education: Vol. 6. 1975–1976* (pp. 333–343). New York, NY: AMS Press.

Kellough, J. E. (2006). *Understanding affirmative action: Politics, discrimination, and the search for justice.* Washington, DC: Georgetown University Press.

Kluegel, J. R., & Smith, E. R. (1983). Affirmative action attitudes: Effects of self-interest, racial affect, and stratification beliefs on whites' views. *Social Forces, 61,* 796–824.

Kluegel, J. R., & Smith, E. R. (1986). *Beliefs about inequality: Americans' views of what is and what ought to be.* New York, NY: Aldine de Gruyter.

Krysan, M., & Lewis, A. (2004). *The changing terrain of race and ethnicity.* New York, NY: Russell Sage.

Lemann, N. (1999). *The big test: The secret history of the American meritocracy.* New York, NY: Farrar, Straus and Giroux.

Members of the 2005 "Rising Above the Gathering Storm" Committee. (2010). *Rising above the gathering storm, Revisited—Rapidly approaching category 5* (Report prepared for the Presidents of the National Academy of Sciences, National Academy of Engineering, and Institute of Medicine of the National Academies). Washington, DC: National Academies Press.

Mosley, A. G., & Capaldi, N. (1996). *Affirmative action: Social justice or unfair preference?* New York, NY: Rowan & Littlefield.

Nettles, M. T., Perna, L. W., & Millett, C. M. (1998). Race and testing in college admissions. In G. Orfield & E. Miller (Eds.), *Chilling admissions* (pp. 97-100). Cambridge, MA: Harvard Education.

Oakes, J. (2005). *Keeping track: How schools structure inequality.* New Haven, CT: Yale University Press.

Olson, S., & Fagen, A. P (2007). *Understanding interventions that encourage minorities to pursue research careers: Summary of a workshop.* Washington, DC: National Academies Press.

Omi, M., & Winant, H. (1994). *Racial formation in the United States: From the 1960s to the 1990s.* New York, NY: Routledge.

Orfield, G., & Ashkinaze, C. (1991). *The closing door: Conservative policy and Black opportunity.* Chicago, IL: University of Chicago Press.

Page, S. (2007). *The difference: How the power of diversity creates better groups, firms, schools, and societies.* Princeton, NJ: Princeton University Press.

Peterson, J. J. (1983). *The Iowa Testing Programs: The first fifty years.* Iowa City: University of Iowa Press.

Pusser, B. (2004). *Burning down the house: Politics, governance, and affirmative action at the University of California.* Albany: State University of New York Press.

The Regents of the University of California v. Bakke, 434 U.S. 963 (1977).

Schmidt, P. (2008, February 20). Asians, not whites, hurt most by race-conscious admissions. *USA Today*, p. 13A.

Schudson, M. (1972). Organizing the "Meritocracy": A history of the College Entrance Examination Board. *Harvard Educational Review, 42*(1), 34–69.

Sears, D. O., Sidanius, J., & Bobo, L. (Eds.). (2000). *Racialized politics: The debate about racism in America.* Chicago, IL: University of Chicago Press.

Sedlacek, W. E. (2004). *Beyond the big test: Noncognitive assessment in higher education.* San Francisco, CA: Jossey-Bass.

Smith, D. G. (2009). *Diversity's promise for higher education: Making it work.* Baltimore, MD: John Hopkins University Press.

Smith, W., Altbach, P., & Lomotey, K. (2002). *The racial crisis in higher education.* Albany: State University of New York Press.

Steele, C. (2004). Not just a test. *The Nation, 287*(17), 38–40.

Takagi, D. Y. (1992). *The retreat from race: Asian Americans admissions and racial politics.* New Brunswick, NJ: Rutgers University Press.

Whitmire, R. (2009). *Why boys fail: Saving our sons from an educational system that's leaving them behind.* New York, NY: American Management Association.

Wightman, L. F. (2003). Standardized tests and equal access: A tutorial. In M. J. Chang, D. Witt, J. Jones, & K. Hakuta (Eds.), *Compelling interest: Examining the evidence of racial dynamics in colleges and universities* (pp. 49–96). Stanford, CA: Stanford University Press.

Section I

Contested Constructions of Merit in the 21st Century: From the Big Test to the Diversity Debate in Higher Education

CHAPTER 2

DIVERSITY AND MERIT IN HIGHER EDUCATION: CHALLENGES AND OPPORTUNITIES FOR THE 21st CENTURY

by Phillip J. Bowman

Di-ver-si-ty—**n. 1. quality, state, fact, or instance of being diverse; difference 2. variety.**
Mer-it—**n. 1. A commendable quality; worthiness. 2. (pl.) the quality by which something is evaluated or rewarded.—v.t. earn; deserve.**

There is a growing *tension* in American ideology between the concepts of *diversity*, *merit*, and *opportunity* (Bowman & Smith, 2002; Guinier, 2003–2004; Guinier & Sturm, 2001; Kluegel & Smith, 1986; Takagi, 1992; Turner, 1960). As we move further into the 21st century, this tension will continue to challenge both higher education and other major social institutions. It is especially important to better understand how *persistent inequalities* within the United States increasingly combine with *global forces* to further exacerbate this tension and shape related public policy debates (Bobo & Kluegel, 1993; Bowman & Betancur, 2010; Featherman, Hall, & Krislov, 2010). For example, this tension has played a pivotal role in intense national debate over affirmative action policies to address inequalities in education, employment and other civil rights arenas. The center of the anti–affirmative action debate in higher education has shifted from the University of Texas, University of California, and University of Washington in the 1990s to the University of Michigan and beyond in the 21st century. Indeed, related debates over merit and multilevel interventions to address discrimination based on race, class, and gender have been major sources of tension throughout the history of American higher education. However, much less understood is how this historical tension is increasingly exacerbated by the growing number of highly skilled international and non-European immigrant students who are rapidly diversifying America's most selective colleges and universities.

For most Americans, the *concept of merit* centers on the belief that people should succeed based on their ability and hard work (Simpson & Wendling, 2005; Thorngate, Dawes, & Foddy, 2008; Tierney, 2007). This concept of individual merit is in stark opposition to the inherently unfair institutional practices that have traditionally enabled people from privileged backgrounds to succeed based on who they are, their networks, or whom

17

they know (Karen, 1991; Kluegel & Smith, 1983, 1986; Schudson, 1972; Turner, 1960). Lemann (1999) and others show how access to the most selective colleges and universities in the United States traditionally depended primarily on elite social capital that reflected conventional class, racial, and gender privilege—rather than ability and hard work. Since the mid-20th century, *SAT/ACT-type tests* have been used as the *primary indicator of merit* to assess academic qualifications and broaden access to the most selective institutions. However, the college admissions process can become overly narrow and problematic when both mainstream ideology and institutional practice treat such test scores as definitive merit criteria that accurately measure innate ability, aptitude, or intelligence (e.g., Hilliard, 1994; Smith, 2009; Wightman, 2003). Movement toward a more inclusive meritocracy in higher education may well depend on institutionalizing a *comprehensive approach* that systematically combines the appropriate use of SAT/ACT-type testing with more evidence-based and multifaceted merit criteria.

Alternative Merit Constructs: Primary, Secondary, and Tertiary Factors

A better understanding of critical diversity issues in SAT/ACT-type scores and alternative constructs of merit is necessary to address related challenges and opportunities in the 21st century. As illustrated in **Figure 1**, the debate over merit in the United States has centered around *three alternative constructs* with differential implications for the role of SAT/ACT tests in the admissions process. The *Primary Construct of Merit* has focused on genetic-based intelligence, inborn cognitive ability, or innate scholastic aptitude. Historically, psychologists and early developers of the SAT emphasized this merit construct to both educators and the general public as the scientific way to interpret individual differences in IQ and SAT test scores (Brigham, 1923; Cleary, Humphries, Kendrick, & Wesman, 1980; Lemann, 1999; Williams, this volume).

For most Americans, however, the concept of merit centers on a more multifaceted belief that people should succeed based not only on innate ability but also motivation or hard work (Kluegel & Smith, 1983, 1986; Simpson & Wendling, 2005; Thorngate et al., 2008; Tierney, 2007). Therefore, motivation or hard work has long been a *Secondary Construct of Merit* and is widely considered in more comprehensive reviews of merit in selective admissions. This secondary construct is also at the center of a growing body of related research and development work on what is often called "noncognitive" predictors of college success by university-based scholars as well as experts at Educational Testing Service (ETS) and ACT Inc. (Burkem, Robins, & Phelps, this volume; Burrus, MacCann, Kyllonen, & Roberts, this volume; Sedlacek, 2004, this volume).

Finally, as **Tertiary Constructs of Merit**, sponsorship and special talents have long been considered commendable qualities which are worthy of evaluation and reward in selective college admissions (Guinier, 2003–2004; Lemann, 1999; Turner, 1960). Although not without controversy, family networks and legacies as well as gifted musicians, artists, athletes, inventors, entrepreneurs, and other special talents continue to be viewed as either earning or deserving preferential consideration in selective college admissions.

The Merit Concept in Higher Education: Diversity and Inequality Issues

Merit-based tests, considerations, or contests operate in a variety of contexts ranging from college admissions to jobs, contracts, grants, licenses, and trophies (Simpson & Wendling, 2005; Thorngate et al., 2008; Tierney, 2007; Wightman, 2003). Despite the persistence of family legacies, merit-based methods are widely accepted as more equitable than rewarding family privilege, political or social connections, wealth, bribery, or aggression (Guinier, 2003–2004; Lemann, 1999; Mosley & Capaldi, 1996; Turner, 1960). However, despite a deeply rooted American value for merit-based rewards, conventional methods for judging merit in higher education are prone to a variety of limitations, errors, and biases. Moreover, related institutional practices that often employ SAT/ACT-type assessment as the official merit criterion are deeply rooted in highly questionable assumptions and continue to fuel intense debate. Debates about these institutional practices and related public beliefs reflect conflicting assumptions about the degree to which a person's scores on such Big Tests are based on their *innate intelligence* (IQ), *scholastic opportunity*, or *socioeconomic privilege*.

In his book on *The Big Test*, Lemann (1999) suggests the ETS has tended to promote the SAT as primarily a measure of innate intelligence or aptitude since its beginning in the mid-20th century. However, even the ETS founding president Henry Chauncey emphasized in 1947 the importance of measuring a range of abilities including motivation, persistence, personality, and other factors linked to success. Carl Brigham, who developed the prototype SAT in 1926 at Princeton University, also cautioned that

> The testing movement came to this country some twenty-
> five or thirty years ago accompanied by the most glorious

Figure 1. Diversity Issues and Alternative Merit Constructs

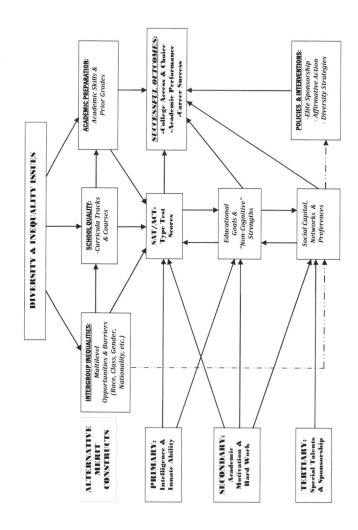

fallacies in the history of science, namely, that the tests measure native intelligence purely and simply without regard to training or schooling. I hope nobody believes that now. The test scores very definitely are a composite including schooling, family background, familiarity with English, and everything else, relevant and irrelevant. The "native intelligence" hypothesis is dead. (Lemann, 1999, p. 34)

As illustrated in **Figure 1**, it is important to better understand how critical ***diversity and inequality issues*** impinge on the merit debate through socially structured inequalities that systematically differentiate multilevel opportunities and barriers (race, class, gender, national origin). Intergroup inequalities can alter college access most clearly through school quality, standardized test scores and social capital or elite sponsors (Darling-Hammond, 2010; Oakes, 2005; Orfield & Gordon, 2000; Wightman, 2003). In this conceptual framework, tertiary constructs of merit often operate through a type of ***sponsored mobility*** where family networks, legacies, and elite social capital often reflect conventional racial, class, and gender privilege (Guinier, 2003–2004; Karen, 1991; Lemann, 1999; Turner, 1960). In a classic work, Turner (1960) notes that "under sponsored mobility, elite recruits are chosen by the established elite or their agents, and elite status is *given* on the basis of some criterion of supposed merit and cannot be taken by any amount of effort or strategy" (p. 856). By contrast, Turner posits that "contest mobility is a system in which elite status is the prize in an open contest and is taken by the aspirants' own efforts" (p. 856).

In contrast to the traditional focus on SAT/ACT-type scores as indicators of innate ability, a growing scientific and policy-relevant literature on "achievement gaps" (by race, class, gender, and national origin) systematically link test score gaps to policies, opportunities, barriers, school quality, and academic preparation (Friedman, 2005; Frierson, Wyche, & Pearson, 2009; Jencks & Phillips, 1998; Oakes, 2005; Whitmire, 2009). Therefore, a major limitation of conventional ideology and institutional practice that treat SAT/ACT scores as primarily indicators of innate ability is that they ignore compelling evidence that race and class "test score disparities" more accurately reflect "opportunity" rather than "ability" gaps. In contrast to an early emphasis on intelligence, ETS currently acknowledges this compelling scientific evidence on its website by noting that race, class, and gender disparities on their tests reflect "different educational backgrounds and opportunities." Similarly, ACT, Inc. has long promoted ACT scores as primarily a measure of scholastic opportunity closely tied to class-related factors such as school quality, curricula, courses, teachers, instructional resources, and pedagogy. Moreover, test preparation corporations such as Kaplan, Princeton Review, and elite boarding schools and college prep interventions continue to demonstrate the value of systematic opportunities for intensive exam-coaching to boost SAT/ACT-type scores.

Persistent Race and Class Complexities: Challenges and Opportunities

Ironically, early in the 20th century, the development of the SAT had a diversifying effect on admissions into selective colleges by expanding the definition of merit to be more inclusive of especially talented students from diverse socioeconomic backgrounds and regions rather than only students from wealthy families attending elite private schools in the Northeast (Lemann, 1999). However, even though SAT/ACT tests have helped diversify the college student population to a certain degree, they also continue to reinforce serious class, race, and geographic bias especially against low-income students of color from non-suburban neighborhoods (Bowen & Bok, 1998; Bowen, Chingos, & McPherson, 2009; Jencks & Phillips, 1998; Sedlacek, 2004). This systematic race and class bias and the related test score gaps are deeply rooted in persistent U.S. racial segregation and unequal opportunities, resources, environments, cross-generational capital, and pre-college preparation (Darity, Dietrich, & Guilkey, 2002; Oakes, 2005; Orfield & Gordon, 2001). Yet, test score gaps among racial/ethnic minorities are still often represented as differences in individual merit and innate ability despite evidence of differential opportunity by race and class. For example, Chang, Witt, Jones, and Hakuta (2003) note that

> Merit is usually narrowly, and exclusively, equated with test scores, and because blacks, Latinos, and Native Americans are as a group approximately one standard deviation below those of whites and Asians, these minority students are considered to be less deserving … Equating merit solely with test scores ignores the multifaceted dimensions of academic success. Those who have earned a college degree know quite well that this achievement requires more than just test scores. Other individual characteristics such as perseverance, creativity, experiences outside the classroom, demonstrated commitment to different causes, resiliency, public-speaking skills, leadership capacity, and ability to overcome challenges, to name a few, contribute to academic success. (pp. 15–16)

Major testing organizations such as the College Board, ETS, and ACT Inc. continue to caution against the "misuse" of their test scores as a definitive indicator of merit in the college admissions process. Wightman (2003) notes that these organizations have never suggested that their tests could or should serve as a surrogate for merit but have "been clear and forthcoming about the limitations of test scores and the necessity of looking at a variety of factors in making admission decisions" (p. 88). These organizations continue to provide advice and warnings to both test takers and users about the appropriate use as well as the limitations of SAT/ACT-type tests. For example, the ETS (n.d.) website notes

> no single factor should be used as the sole criterion for any important education decision. No single test can give a complete picture of an individual, and we urge score users to view a test score as simply one of the many pieces of information available about a student.

However, despite extensive evidence about limitations, test scores are still too often portrayed as "the" accurate, objective measure of merit.

Gender and Global Complexities: Challenges and Opportunities

Beyond race and class, there are also complex gender and cross-national disparities in SAT/ACT-type scores that are emerging as additional factors in the trend toward a more comprehensive merit agenda in higher education. Similar to race and class, these emerging gender and cross-national disparities also present major diversity challenges and opportunities for the United States in the 21st century.

Emerging Reverse Gender Disparities: Trends and Complexities

Women continue to lag behind men on a range of education and employment indicators, especially at the highest prestige levels and in scientific fields (Rosser, 2004; Smith, 1989; Stewart, Malley, & LaVaque-Manty, 2007; Valian, 1999). Traditional "gender gaps" have also been observed in boys performing higher than girls in math but girls performing better than boys on verbal segments of SAT/ACT-type tests. However, women continue to make impressive overall gains and "reverse gender gaps" have begun to emerge on several educational achievement indicators across the K–16 pipeline and beyond (Brown, 2005; Francis & Skelton, 2005; Frierson, Pearson, & Wyche, 2009; Frierson, Wyche, et al., 2009; Whitmire, 2009). In fact, there has been an escalating debate over the past 20 years on a growing "reverse gender gap" within both the African American (Frierson, Pearson, et al., 2009; Frierson, Wyche, et al. 2009; Rowley & Bowman, 2010) and European American (Francis & Skelton, 2005; Hoff Sommers, 2000; Whitmire, 2009) populations. The reverse gender gap generating the most intense debate continues to be widening Black female over Black male disparities; policy-relevant analyses have begun to focus on both the root causes (Frierson, Wyche, et al., 2009; Rowley & Bowman, 2009) as well as programs, interventions, and policies to address this crisis (Caldwell, 2009; Frierson, Pearson, et al., 2009). Although less well documented, a recent American Council on Education report (Philanthropy News Digest, 2010) reveals a similar trend among Latina/os, the fastest growing segment of the U.S. population, with young Latino males showing the lowest educational attainment levels of all subgroups.

In contrast to African Americans, there has been much less attention on the growing reverse gender gap among European Americans, with boys falling further behind girls on some standardized tests, K–12 achievement, and college attendance. However, the reverse gender gap on college campuses and related challenges in the K–16 pipeline have increasingly captured the attention of policy analysts, researchers, educators, and journalists in the U.S. in recent years (i.e., Francis & Skelton, 2005; Hoff Sommers, 2000; Jacobs, 2002; Whitmire, 2009). For example, in December 2009, the U.S. Commission on Civil Rights (Terris, 2009) agreed to investigate several colleges charged with discrimination against women in admissions by giving preferences and more generous financial aid to males in efforts to minimize lopsided gender mixes on campus.

Although the urgency of a reverse gender gap among Whites continues to be contested in the United States, similar test score and achievement deficits among males have been a major public policy issue for over 20 years in Australia, the United Kingdom, and other European countries. Francis and Skelton (2005) suggest that as "globalization takes an increasing hold and countries measure themselves up against each other in terms of pupil achievement . . . then it will increasingly be the case that the focus will be on those groups who are not perceived as performing at the prescribed levels" (p. 38). Despite cross-national differences in policy discourse, Hoff Sommers (2000) suggests that the United States must be much more strategic, systematic, and cross-national in its policy agenda setting to address reverse gender gaps and related concerns over male test score deficits:

> The widening education gap threatens the future of millions
> of American boys. We should be looking not to "gender

experts" and activists for guidance but to the example of other countries that are focusing on boys' problems and dealing with them constructively. Like American boys, boys in Great Britain and Australia are markedly behind girls academically, notably in reading and writing . . . The big difference is that British educators and politicians are ten years ahead of Americans in confronting and specifically addressing the problem of male underachievement. (p. 15)

Current U.S. policy discourse on the reverse gender gap has begun to center on methods other than affirmative action, which has been increasingly rejected by voters. There is growing agreement that the reverse gender gap in test scores and achievement across various groups raise complex multilevel questions (e.g., Caldwell, 2009; Francis & Skelton, 2005; Frierson, Pearson, et al., 2009; Whitmire, 2009). Educators and policymakers are being called upon to consider not only the deficiencies in individual boys themselves, but also the broader educational and social context, including possible strategies that focus on teachers, schools, districts, and states as well as national and cross-national policies.

Despite the improving test scores among women, it is also important to note that a glass ceiling and institutionalized barriers continue to restrict women's progress, especially in high-status science, technology, engineering, and mathematics (STEM) career fields (Eckel & Kezar, 2003; Rosser, 2004; Stewart, Malley, & LaVaque-Manty, 2007; Valian, 1999; Xie & Shauman, 2003). This *gap* between women's exemplary test score performance and their slower progress at advanced education and career achievement levels in STEM fields continues to raise serious questions about *merit* and *opportunity* in the 21st century. Stewart and colleagues (2007) reviewed research showing that addressing this gap and related patterns of underrepresentation requires looking beyond inadequacies within women themselves to features of the *institutional* environment:

Particular concepts that have been used to understand and study institutions include *climate, tacit knowledge* (how the institution, discipline, funding agencies work), *networks* (and exclusionary processes), *schemas* (associated both with gender and with the fields of study), *evaluation bias*, and *accumulation of disadvantage*. (p. 6, emphasis added)

Emerging Cross-National Disparities: Trends and Complexities

The traditional **tension** in American ideology between the concepts of **diversity**, **merit**, and **opportunity** may be further exacerbated by the growing number of highly skilled international and non-European immigrant students who are rapidly diversifying America's most selective colleges and universities (Bennett & Lutz, 2009; Brown, 2005; Colburn, Young, & Yellen, 2008; Deskins, 1991; Schmidt, 2008; Takagi, 1992). According to the Institute of International Education, the number of foreign students hit 671,616 in 2008–2009, an all-time high. In addition to the 283,329 graduate students, Fischer (2009) notes that the 269,874 undergraduate students studying for both bachelor's and associate's degrees accounted for the largest increase. The primary source countries continue to be China, India, and South Korea, but increases also reflect significant gains from Vietnam, Saudi Arabia, and countries in Europe and South America.

To be sure, there are a complex set of global forces behind the increasing numbers of highly skilled international and non-European immigrant students (Bennett & Lutz, 2009; Friedman, 2005; Schmidt, 2008; Takagi, 1992). However, the degree to which non-U.S.-born students often have superior scores on SAT/ACT-type tests further complicates their use as the primary indicator of merit in the college admissions process. Systematic test score gaps between college students born inside and outside the United States reflect the complexity of cross-national diversity. Within the global economy, there are complex cross-national differences in demographics as well as educational standards, school quality, opportunities for intensive exam-coaching, and noncognitive cultural, social-psychological, and/or motivational orientations. For example, Friedman (2005) noted in his widely read book *The World is Flat: A Brief History of the 21st Century* that

> a lot of those new players from India, China, and the former Soviet Empire are not just walking onto the flat-world with their enormous hunger to get ahead by out-learning their competition. What we are witnessing is a mad dash—born of fifty years of pent-up aspirations in places like India, China, and the former Soviet Empire, where for five decades young people were educated, but not given an outlet at home to really fulfill their potential. . . . That's the kind of explosion of aspirations coming out of India, China, and the former Soviet Empire today. (p. 214)

This cross-national diversity in the global economy further complicates domestic diversity challenges in U.S. higher education as increasing numbers of these highly skilled international students and their children become permanent residents, American citizens, and immigrants in the 21st century (see Committee on Prospering in the Global Economy of the 21st Century, 2005; Members of the 2005 "Rising Above the Gathering Storm" Committee, 2010).

Diversifying the Merit Construct: From Big Tests to a More Comprehensive Approach

A major challenge for the United States in the 21st century is to develop a more comprehensive and scientifically based merit approach for a diversifying nation in a competitive global economy. This more comprehensive approach must place a premium on talent development and challenge both mainstream ideology and institutional practices that currently over-rely on a narrow definition of merit highly associated with class privilege, institutional discrimination, blocked opportunities, and cross-national arrangements.

Selective institutions of higher education in the United States continue to refine more "comprehensive" admission strategies that include the use of SAT/ACT-type tests scores as only one among a diverse set of individual merit criteria. There is a growing consensus among experts that test scores and grades are necessary but not sufficient indicators of merit in the higher education admissions process. For example, Bowen and Bok (1998) clarify the value of test scores and grades for screening out applicants who are less likely to be able respond to the high academic expectations in selective institutions. However, these two former college presidents caution in their classic book *The Shape of the River: Long-Term Consequences of Considering Race in College and University Admissions* (1998)

> Yet even when combined judiciously, test scores and grades still predict academic performance imperfectly. Moreover, such measures play an even smaller role in determining which applicants will contribute to the development of fellow students or which will go on to be leaders in their chosen fields of endeavor. (p. 25)

The need for more comprehensive merit criteria that include but go beyond academic preparation is also driven by the aims of diverse institutions—private and public, academic programs and professional schools. Unfortunately, there is a widespread misconception that SAT/ACT-type scores and grades represent the only truly valid criteria in deciding whom to admit into selective colleges and universities. Noting this misconception, former university presidents Bowen and Bok (1998) state that

> one often hears that students with top scores and the highest grades should be admitted "on the merits," as if these measures were the sole legitimate basis for admission and that other considerations were somehow insubstantial or even morally suspect. This is patently false. Deciding which students have the most "merit" depends on what one is trying to achieve. (pp. 24–25)

As part of a "comprehensive review process," selective private and public institutions go beyond test scores and grades to carefully examine personal statements, letters of recommendation from multiple sources, and narrative responses to application queries to identify other noncognitive aspects of merit. Although the specific aims of selection may vary, particular emphasis is often placed on academic motivation, special talents, extracurricular activities, leadership skills, employment histories, civic involvement, diversity engagement, alumni affiliation, and other experiences that shed light on non-academic accomplishments or potential. Specific academic programs may place particular weight on intrinsic subject matter passion or specialized intellectual, artistic, and/or musical talents. Business, medical, law, or engineering programs may place differential weights on entrepreneurial, humanistic, leadership, and technological strengths.

Spurred by an intense national debate over affirmative action and diversity, selective public institutions of higher education have been especially challenged to experiment and develop more comprehensive approaches to the assessment of merit in the admissions process (Bowen, et al., 2009; Chang, et al., 2003; Gurin, Lehman, & Lewis, 2004; Pusser, 2004). For example, challenged by the 1996 *Hopwood v. Texas* decision, the University of Texas (U-Texas) Ten Percent Plan admitted the top 10% of the graduating class (based on grades) from every high school in the state to complement the traditional admission practice that relied more heavily on SAT/ACT test scores. Evaluation studies show that students admitted under the 10% standard had higher freshman-year grades at U-Texas than did those admitted under the conventional criteria of superior SAT/ACT scores. Although more research is needed, Guinier and Sturm (2001) hypothesize that the 10 percenters performed better because they "see themselves as successful, have drive and self-confidence, and are willing to seek help and ask questions when needed" (p. 99). Pusser (2004) describes how the University of California (U-C), similar to U-Texas, began to experiment with more comprehensive admissions as well as related outreach strategies in the aftermath of Proposal 209 in 1996 that prohibited the use of race and gender in admissions decisions. However, despite ongoing experimentation with more comprehensive strategies, African American and Latina/o students continue to be grossly underrepresented at U-C's two flagship campuses—UC-Berkeley and UCLA.

The University of Michigan has also been at the forefront of clarifying why race/ethnicity and other sources of diversity should be considered significant factors in the admissions process (Gurin et al., 2004). A very strong case for carefully considering diversity in admissions was reinforced in the two landmark Supreme Court cases that supported the importance of universities including race as one of many factors in admitting students (*Gratz v. Bollinger*, 2003; *Grutter v. Bollinger*, 2003). Proponents of using SAT/ACT-type scores as the primary indicators of merit have often ignored the important contributions that diversity among the student body makes to the educational experience of all students. Consequently, Wightman (2003) and others suggest that not recognizing diversity as a characteristic "meriting" consideration in admissions reduces the potential of bringing diverse perspectives and experiences to the college setting as valuable educational resources.

An unprecedented number of organizations submitted amicus briefs in support of the University of Michigan's defense of diversity as an admission criterion in selective universities and colleges. More than 75 amicus briefs were submitted representing hundreds of colleges, universities, and other major social institutions. For example, Gurin and colleagues (2004) cited support from

> more than fifty higher education associations representing virtually every college and university in the nation; sixty-eight Fortune 500 corporations; twenty-nine former high-ranking military leaders; twenty-four U.S. states and territories; labor unions; religious organizations . . . more than a dozen members of Congress; the major social science organizations within education, sociology, and psychology . . . ; civil rights organizations . . . the National Academy of Sciences and National Academy of Engineering; twenty-eight broadcast media companies and organizations; legal organizations (p. 173).

In addition to supporting more comprehensive admission criteria, U-M President Mary Sue Coleman (2004) also noted that these "briefs offer vivid insight into the value of diversity to our entire society, from universities to industry to the military" (p. 190). Hence, the briefs supported not only U-M's basic legal argument but also a core value that racial/ethnic diversity at the nation's higher education institutions is essential for producing culturally competent students for productive engagement in all societal institutions within a diverse democracy and organizational leadership roles within a global economy.

Conclusions and Implications

The growing **tension** in American higher education between the concepts of **diversity, merit,** and **opportunity** continue to spur intense debate about how to go beyond SAT/ACT scores toward a more comprehensive merit agenda for the 21st century. Future scholarship, public debate, and policy-relevant intervention strategies must be informed by a better under-standing of how persistent inequalities and growing diversity within the United States increasingly combine with global forces to provide a compelling context for a more strategic 21st-century merit agenda. Toward this end, a conceptual framework was developed in this chapter to better clarify the complex diversity and inequality issues in the use of **three alternative constructs of merit** with significant implications for developing a more comprehensive merit agenda in a rapidly diversifying nation. A more comprehensive merit agenda can move us beyond the traditional system of sponsored mobility based on the reproduction of class, race, and gender privileges to a more strategic, fair, inclusive and competitive system to develop the nation's best talent for leadership roles in a multicultural democracy and global economy.

The National Center for Institutional Diversity (NCID), based at the University of Michigan, has begun to promote strategic dialogues and collaboration between university-based, ETS, and ACT experts and a growing number of government, foundation, and other stakeholders with strong interests in cutting-edge research that informs more comprehensive approaches to merit in higher education admissions and pipeline inter-ventions. Hopefully, these NCID-based strategic exchanges can provide the foundation for ongoing collaborations and partnerships to move beyond a reactionary anti–affirmative action focus on "reverse discrimination," "racial preferences" or "Black quotas" to more **strategic national action** to develop a more comprehensive merit agenda for the 21st century. A comprehensive approach to diversity and merit in higher education not only is critical to building a multicultural democracy but also represents a compelling business case in a diversifying nation and global economy. There is growing evidence that a comprehensive merit agenda in higher education has strategic policy implications for improving fairness in admissions as well as informing multilevel interventions to promote national talent development, organizational excellence, cultural competence, and economic competitiveness within both domestic and global markets.

Future efforts to develop a more comprehensive merit agenda will be faced with both unique challenges and opportunities as discussed in greater detail by the various authors in this book. Among the most critical *challenges* are to better clarify contested constructions of merit in higher education and move beyond divisive debates about diversity, merit and opportunity. However, we also have unique *opportunities* to promote dialogue and collaboration among various stakeholders engaged in cutting-edge scholarship on more comprehensive approaches to merit to build a strategic translational research agenda that bridges innovative scholarship with policy-relevant intervention strategies to develop a more inclusive, evidence-based meritocracy in the 21st century.

References

Bennett, P., & Lutz, A. (2009). How African American is the net Black advantage? Differences in college attendance among immigrant Blacks, native Blacks, and Whites. *Sociology of Education, 82*, 70–99.

Bobo, L., & Kluegel, J. R. (1993). Opposition to race-targeting: Self-interest, stratification ideology, or racial attitudes? *American Sociological Review, 58*, 443–464.

Bowen, W. G., & Bok D. (1998). *The shape of the river: Long-term consequences of considering race in college and university admissions.* Princeton, NJ: Princeton University Press.

Bowen, W. G., Chingos, M. M., & McPherson, M. S. (2009). *Crossing the finish line: Completing college in America's public universities.* Princeton, NJ: Princeton University Press.

Bowman, P. J., & Betancur, J. J. (2010). Sustainable diversity and inequality: Race in the USA and beyond. In M. Janssens, M. Bechtold, G. Prarolo, & V. Stenius (Eds.), *The sustainability of cultural diversity: Nations, cities and organizations* (pp. 55–78). Cheltenham, England: Edward Elgar.

Bowman, P. J., & Smith, W. A. (2002). Racial ideology in the campus community. In W. A. Smith, P. G. Altbach, and K. Lomotey (Eds.), *The racial crisis in higher education: Continuing challenges for the 21st century* (pp. 103–20). Albany: State University of New York Press.

Brigham, C. (1923). *A study of American intelligence*. Princeton, NJ: Princeton University Press.

Brown, H. (2005). *Findings from the CGS International Graduate Admissions Survey III: Admissions and Enrollment*. Washington, DC: Council of Graduate Schools. Retrieved from http://www.cgsnet .org/pdf/CGS2005IntlAdmitIII_Rep.pdf

Caldwell, L. (2009). Special Issue: Academic Success for School-Age Black Males. *Journal of Negro Education, 78*(3), 1–364.

Chang, M. J., Witt, D., Jones, J., & Hakuta, K. (2003). *Compelling interest: Examining the evidence of racial dynamics in colleges and universities*. Stanford, CA: Stanford University Press.

Cleary, T. A., Humphries, L. G., Kendrick, S. A., & Wesman, G. B. (1980). Educational uses of tests with disadvantaged students. In E. Flaxman (Ed.), *Readings on Equal Education: Volume 6. 1975–1976* (pp. 285–333). New York, NY: AMS Press.

Colburn, D. P., Young, C. E., & Allen, V. M. (2008). Admissions and public higher education in California, Texas, and Florida: The post-affirmative action era. *InterActions: UCLA Journal of Education and Information Studies, 4*(1), 1–21.

Coleman, M. S. (2004). Afterword. In P. Gurin, S. Lehman, & E. Lewis (Eds.), *Defending diversity: Affirmative action at the University of Michigan* (pp. 189–195). Ann Arbor: University of Michigan Press.

Committee on Prospering in the Global Economy of the 21st Century. (2005). *Rising above the gathering storm*: *Energizing and employing America for a brighter economic future* (Report prepared for the National Academy of Sciences, National Academy of Engineering, and Institute of Medicine of the National Academies). Washington, DC: National Academies Press.

Darity, W. A., Dietrich, J., & Guilkey, D. K. (2002). Persistent advantage or disadvantage? Evidence in support of the intergenerational drag hypothesis. *The American Journal of Economics and Sociology, 60*, 435–470.

Darling-Hammond, L. (2010). Structured for failure: Race, resources, and student achievement. In H. R. Markus & P. M. L. Moya (Eds.), *Doing race: 21 essays for the 21st century* (pp. 295–321). New York, NY: W. W. Norton.

Deskins, D. (1991). Winners and losers: A regional assessment of minority enrollment and earned degrees in U.S. colleges and universities, 1974–84. In W. Allen, E. Epps, & N. Z. Haniff (Eds.), *College in black and white* (pp. 17–40). Albany: State University of New York Press.

Eckel, P., & Kezar, A. (2003). *Taking the reins: Institutional transformation in higher education.* Westport, CT: Praeger.

Educational Testing Service. (n.d.). Frequently asked questions about ETS. Retrieved from http://www.ets.org/about/faq/

Featherman, D., Hall, M., & Krislov, M. (2010). *The next twenty-five years: Affirmative action in higher education in the United States and South Africa.* Ann Arbor: University of Michigan Press.

Fischer, K. (2009). Number of foreign students in U.S. hit a new high last year. *The Chronicle of Higher Education, 49142,* 1–10.

Francis, B., & Skelton, C. (2005). *Reassessing gender and achievement: Questioning contemporary key debates.* London, England: Routledge.

Friedman, T. (2005). *The world is flat: A brief history of the 21st century.* New York, NY: Farrar, Straus and Giroux.

Frierson, H. T., Pearson, W., & Wyche, J. H. (2009). *Black American males in higher education: Diminishing proportions* (Vol. 6). New Milford, CT: Emerald.

Frierson, H. T., Wyche, J. H., & Pearson, W. (2009). *Black American males in higher education: Research, Programs and Academe* (Vol. 7). New Milford, CT: Emerald.

Gratz v. Bollinger, 539 U.S. 244 (2003).

Grutter v. Bollinger, 539 U.S. 306 (2003).

Guinier, L. (2003–2004). Admissions rituals as political acts: Guardians at the gates of our democratic ideals. *Harvard Law Review, 117,* 113–224.

Guinier, L., & Strum, S. (2001). *Who's qualified?* Boston, MA: Beacon Press.

Gurin, P., Lehman, S., & Lewis, E. (2004). *Defending diversity: Affirmative action at the University of Michigan.* Ann Arbor: University of Michigan Press.

Hilliard, A. G. (1994). What good is this thing called intelligence and why bother to measure it? *Journal of Black Psychology, 20,* 430–444.

Hoff Sommers, C (2000). *The war against boys.* New York, NY: Simon & Schuster.

Hopwood v. Texas, 78 F.3d 932 (5th Cir. 1996).

Jacobs, B. A. (2002). Where the boys aren't: Non-cognitive skills, returns to school and the gender gap in higher education. *Economics of Education Review, 21,* 589–598.

Jencks, C., & Phillips, M. (1998). *The Black-White test score gap.* Washington, DC: Brookings Institution.

Karen, D. (1991). "Achievement" and "ascription" in admission to an elite college: A political-organizational analysis. *Sociological Forum, 6,* 349–380.

Kluegel, J. R., & Smith, E. R. (1983). Affirmative action attitudes: Effects of self-interest, racial affect, and stratification beliefs on White's views. *Social Forces, 61,* 796–824.

Kluegel, J. R., & Smith, E. R. (1986). *Beliefs about inequality: Americans' views of what is and what ought to be.* New York, NY: Aldine de Gruyter.

Lemann, N. (1999). *The big test: The secret history of the American meritocracy.* New York, NY: Farrar, Straus and Giroux.

Members of the 2005 "Rising Above the Gathering Storm" Committee. (2010). *Rising above the gathering storm, Revisited—Rapidly approaching category 5* (Report prepared for the Presidents of the National Academy of Sciences, National Academy of Engineering, and Institute of Medicine of the National Academies). Washington, DC: National Academies Press.

Mosley, A. G., & Capaldi, N. (1996). *Affirmaive action: Social justice or unfair preference?* New York, NY: Rowman & Littlefield.

Oakes, J. (2005). *Keeping track: How schools structure inequality* (2nd ed.). New Haven, CT: Yale University Press.

Orfield, G., & Gordon, N. (2001). *Schools more separate: Consequences of a decade of resegregation.* Cambridge, MA: Civil Rights Project, Harvard University.

Philantrophy News Digest. (2010). Gender Gap in College Enrollment Stabilizing Except Among Hispanics, Report Finds. Posted online on January 27, 2010 at: http://foundationcenter.org/pnd/news/story.jhtml? id=282700004

Pusser, B. (2004). *Burning down the house: Politics, governance, and affirmative action at the University of California.* Albany: State University of New York Press.

Rosser, S. V. (2004). *The science glass ceiling: Academic women scientists and the struggle to succeed.* New York, NY: Routledge.

Rowley, L., & Bowman, P. J. (2009). Risk, protection, and achievement disparities among African American males: Cross-generation theory, research and comprehensive intervention. *Journal of Negro Education, 78,* 305–320.

Schmidt, P. (2008, February 20). Asians, not Whites, hurt most by race-conscious admissions. *USA Today,* p. 13A.

Schudson, M. (1972). Organizing the "Meritocracy": A history of the College Entrance Examination Board. *Harvard Educational Review, 42*(1), 34–69.

Sedlacek, W. E. (2004). *Beyond the big test: Noncognitive assessment in higher education.* San Francisco, CA: Jossey-Bass.

Simpson, E., & Wendling, K. (2005). Equality and merit: A merit-based argument for equity policies in higher education. *Education Theory, 55,* 385–398.

Smith, D. G. (1989). *The challenge of diversity: Involvement or alienation in the academy.* Washington, DC: George Washington University.

Smith, D. G. (2009). *Diversity's promise for higher education: Making it work.* Baltimore, MD: John Hopkins University Press.

Stewart, A. J., Malley, J. E., & LaVaque-Manty, D. (2007). *Transforming science and engineering: Advancing academic women.* Ann Arbor: University of Michigan Press.

Takagi, D. Y. (1992). *The retreat from race: Asian Americans admissions and racial politics.* New Brunswick, NJ: Rutgers University Press.

Terris, B. (2009). Civil-rights panel names 19 colleges it will investigate for gender bias in admissions. *The Chronicle of Higher Education,* December 16, 2009. Available online at: http://chronicle.com/article /Civil-Rights-Panel-Names-19/62613/

Thorngate, W., Dawes, R. M., & Foddy, M. (2008). *Judging merit.* London, England: Psychology Press.

Tierney, W. G. (2007). Merit and affirmative action in education: Promulgating a democratic public culture. *Urban Education, 42,* 385–402.

Turner, R. H. (1960). Sponsored and contest mobility in the school system. *American Sociological Review, 25,* 855–862.

Valian, V. (1999). *Why so slow? The advancement of women.* Cambridge, MA: MIT Press.

Whitmire, R. (2009). *Why boys fail: Saving our sons from an educational system that's leaving them behind.* New York, NY: American Management Association.

Wightman, L. F. (2003). Standardized tests and equal access: A tutorial. In M. J. Chang, D. Witt, J. Jones, & K. Hakuta (Eds.), *Compelling interest: Examining the evidence of racial dynamics in colleges and universities* (pp. 49–96). Stanford, CA: Stanford University Press.

Xie, Y., & Shauman, K. A. (2003). *Women in science: Career processes and outcomes.* Cambridge, MA: Harvard University Press.

CHAPTER 3

THE QUALIFIED APPLICANT: ORIGINS OF ADMISSIONS TESTS IN HIGHER EDUCATION

Krystal L. Williams

The use of standardized test scores in college admissions has again become a topic of heated debate within higher education as we move further into the 21st century. Similar to the authors of *Readings on Equal Education*, Volume 6 (Bernal, 1980; Cleary, Humphreys, Kendrick & Wesman, 1980; Jackson, 1980), this volume also debates the social, psychological, and ideological complexities in this critical educational policy issue. Although this topic has been contentious for some time, debate has taken on new dimensions as the anti–affirmative action movement continues to spread across the country, and test scores play the pivotal role in access to selective universities, leaving many underrepresented students with a questionable future. The advances in access that underrepresented students gained during the 1970s have eroded (Chang, Altbach, & Lomotey, 2005).

Due to legislation in places such as California, Florida, Texas, and Michigan, programs that target underrepresented minorities in each of those states (i.e., Blacks, Hispanics, and Native Americans) have been abolished. Although much of the current discourse concerning merit focuses on standardized testing, test makers and college admissions offices recognize test scores are not the only measure of achievement or predictor of college success. Accordingly, institutions have adopted broader criteria for admission including students' extracurricular activities, letters of recommendation, and leadership roles in school and/or community to help increase student diversity. Despite evidence of the usefulness of various noncognitive measures in the admissions process (Noftle & Robins, 2007; Oswald, Schmitt, Kim, Ramsay, & Gillespie, 2004; Robbins et al., 2004), many activists still argue that test scores are the fairest measure of merit, often ignoring the historical context of discrimination and inequality in education (Nettles, Perna, & Millet, 1998).

To be sure, there are two common frameworks of justice to keep in mind when examining the influence of standardized testing on college opportunities (e.g., Natour, Locks, & Bowman, this volume). While *distributive justice* emphasizes that access to resources and opportunities should be determined by merit, *procedural justice* suggests the need to apply consistent practices across groups (consistency of procedure). Many proponents of college admissions exams highlight the usefulness of the tests with regard to distributive justice. From this vantage point, students with high test scores are more deserving of college opportunities. However, evidence that admission tests are not consistent indicators of future success across all groups calls to question whether test scores are sufficient indicators of merit (Fleming, 2002; Fleming & Garcia, 1998). Also, the predictive validity of the SAT (formerly the Scholastic Admissions Test) score is most frequently examined in relation to students' freshman-year GPA (Camara & Echternacht, 2000). Hence, there is sparse evidence that the test predicts students' education and career success beyond the first year in college.

A number of recommendations have emerged to address the limitations in the predictive validity of the SAT. For example, Freedle (2003) suggests a corrective scoring method to adjust for any ethnic or social class bias. Other scholars have offered alternative approaches to better identify students who are qualified or deserving of college (powell & Reno, this volume; Sedlacek, this volume.).

Given the impact of the banning of affirmative action on minority students' higher education participation and the increased emphasis on standardized test scores as a measure of merit, it is important to review the origins of using test scores in admissions decisions. I provide a historical analysis of the emergence of uniform testing in college admissions with a particular emphasis on the development of the modern SAT. I begin the analysis by discussing the evolution of intelligence testing—the predecessor of the SAT. I then review the history of the College Board and the Educational Testing Service (ETS) and how those organizations were involved in the expansion of testing in higher education admissions. Finally, I discuss the current controversy involving the SAT along with the test's impact on admissions for minority and low-income students.

The Lineage of the Modern SAT

The Chinese are often credited with the establishment of standardized testing. As early as 200 B.C. the Chinese government required citizens to take a test in order to be employed with the Chinese Imperial Civil Service. These tests were very rigorous and covered areas including history, philosophy, literature, calligraphy, poetry, and painting (Zwick, 2002). There is disagreement about the origins of admission tests in higher education. However, the evidence suggests that the use of standardized tests was well established in Europe before their use in the United States. One account suggests that standardized testing started in Madrid in 1575

(Stewart, 1998); another highlights the use of admissions tests by the French during the 13th century (U.S. Congress, Office of Technology Assessment, 1992). However, many scholars conclude that current admissions tests in the United States are the descendents of intelligence tests that date back to the early 20th century (Owen & Doerr, 1999; Lemann, 1999).

A French psychologist, Alfred Binet, developed the first version of an intelligence test in the early 1900s (Lemann, 2004; Owen & Doerr, 1999). The French government solicited Binet to create a test to identify children with learning disabilities in hopes of using special education to help them to advance scholastically. Although Binet created the test to assess the academic abilities of children, he was reluctant to use his test beyond narrowly defined diagnostic purposes. Even at this early stage, Binet was aware of the potential for such tests to be abused (Owen & Doerr, 1999).

Despite Binet's reservations, Henry Goddard, an American psychologist who operated a school in Vinelane, New Jersey, translated Binet's study into English (Owen & Doerr, 1999; Lemann, 1999). Historical text indicates that not only was Goddard a eugenicist, he also viewed his school as a holding tank for the "feeble-minded" and a way to isolate people with inferior genes to prevent them from "contaminating prime American breeding stock" (Owen & Doerr, 1999, p. 174). Goddard advocated for the use of intelligence tests to (a) limit the reproduction of individuals deemed mentally inferior and (b) determine the distribution of goods in society. Specifically, he believed people should receive benefits and opportunities based on their inherited intellectual abilities, which he believed could be measured by a test (Owen & Doerr, 1999).

In addition to Goddard's promotion of intelligence testing, Lewis Terman, a psychology professor at Stanford who developed the Stanford-Binet Intelligence Scale, also advanced Binet's work (Lemann, 2004; Owen & Doerr, 1999). Similar to Henry Goddard, Terman hoped to use the intelligence scale as a tool to calibrate society members and determine an individual's future vocational fitness. In 1917, with the assistance of Goddard and Terman, Robert M. Yerkes, a professor of psychology at Harvard, created the Army Alpha Test, an intelligence test used to determine appropriate job assignments for army recruits (Brigham, 1923; Owen & Doerr, 1999). While traveling internationally to study the use of psychological methods in Canada's military activities, Yerkes was introduced to Carl Brigham, who eventually became recognized as the father of the SAT. Thereafter, Yerkes recruited Brigham to take part in the U.S. military intelligence testing experiment.

Carl Brigham's involvement with the army testing experiment provided him with experiences that later distinguished him as a prime candidate for developing a similar aptitude test to be used by colleges and universities. In fact, the Army Alpha test was adapted for use in college admissions (Lemann, 2004). However, Brigham's data analysis from the army experiment is quite contentious. He included the results of the study in a controversial book titled *A Study of American Intelligence* (1923). In his writings, Brigham suggested that Catholics, Greeks, Hungarians, Italians, Jews, Negroes, Poles, Russians, and Turks were naturally less intelligent than people of Nordic ancestry. He also believed that Blacks should be banned from mixing with Whites in an attempt to avoid the dilution of the superior White race and stated that Americans would become increasingly unintelligent with increases in certain immigrant groups and growth in the Black population. Brigham later recanted most of his derogatory statements about the intelligence of minority groups and immigrants (Lemann, 2004; Wechsler, 1977; Zwick, 2002), and formally retracted this work in a follow-up study (1932); however, there is some debate regarding the sincerity of the recantation (Owen & Doerr, 1999).

Despite the racist undertones implicit in Brigham's analysis, there is no evidence that his explicit intentions for developing the SAT were to keep Blacks and recent immigrants out of college; when the SAT—originally referred to as the Scholastic Aptitude Test—was invented, students from these groups did not pose a threat to the elite institutions. However, Brigham's objective was to establish a modern day meritocracy where the innate intellectual abilities of individuals would be measured and compared (Owen & Doerr, 1999). Furthermore, Brigham believed that intelligence testing would help to eliminate the external contamination of American intellect by immigrants (Brigham, 1923).

The Emergence of Uniform Testing, the College Board, and ETS

Historical text suggests that, traditionally, many individual institutions had internal entrance examinations even before the SAT was developed. For example, during the late 1800s, Harvard and Yale administered entrance exams both on- and off-campus; other campuses adopted similar policies (Crouse & Trusheim, 1988; Karabel, 2005). Additionally, Columbia University initiated the use of intelligence tests in admissions starting in 1918 when the institution's leadership became worried about the increasing Jewish presence in the student body and the potential that upper-middle-class White students would not want to attend the university because of its shift in student demographics. A comment offered by the university president, Nicholas M. Butler, described the 1917–1918 freshman class as "depressing in the extreme . . . largely made up of foreign born and children

of those but recently arrived in this country. The boys of old American stock
... have sought opportunity for military or other public service and have no
time to go to college" (cited in Crouse & Trusheim, 1988, p. 20).
Accordingly, the university's administration implemented testing in
admissions with hopes to (a) limit the number of Jews, (b) increase the
number of students from outside of New York State, and (c) attract students
with northern and western European ancestry who were assumed to have
supreme innate intelligence (Crouse & Trusheim, 1988). Despite the use of
testing at individual institutions, the idea of uniform testing was an anomaly
until the SAT was developed.

Wechsler (1977) provides a thorough historical account of how the
College Board was established. As early as the late 1800s, preceding the
emergence of uniform testing for college admission, there were concerns
about the alignment of college and secondary school curricula that echo
many of the issues presented in today's K–16 initiatives. The National
Education Association (NEA) established the Committee of Ten to address
the need to link the course work of secondary schools and higher education
institutions. This committee began as an idea at the NEA Annual Convention in 1892. Its membership included academic leaders at prestigious
institutions, secondary schoolmasters, and the U.S. Commissioner of
Education, William Harris. Well-known academics served on subcommittees
organized by discipline, and Harvard President, Charles W. Eliot, served as
the committee chairman (Wechsler, 1977).

The committee's deliberations resulted in a list of suggestions for
uniform entrance requirements at leading institutions including an expansion
of the disciplines considered in the admissions process. Several conferences
of academic leaders from Ivy League institutions were organized at
Columbia University to help advance the committee's recommendations.
Nicholas M. Butler was a leading proponent for the establishment of the
Committee of Ten, and he played a significant behind-the-scenes role at the
Columbia meetings. Using the results of the Committee of Ten as a
foundation, Butler extended the suggestion for uniform entrance
requirements to uniform entrance examinations. After failed attempts to
present his ideas to leaders at various Ivy League institutions, Butler
presented his proposal at the Middle States Association annual meeting in
1899. This time his suggestion was received favorably, and the proposal to
establish the College Entrance Examination Board was adopted (Wechsler,
1977). Colleges were not required to abandon their internal entrance
examinations, but they were obliged to accept Board certificates as proof
that a candidate met the college's entrance requirements in the subject

tested. Nevertheless, institutions still had the liberty to deny admissions as they deemed appropriate (Crouse & Trusheim, 1988; Wechsler, 1977).

Evolution of the SAT

Membership in the College Board was open to all recognized colleges—not just those in the Middle States Association. The board would grade exams, and schools would decide what examinations applicants should take (Wechsler, 1977). These tests initially covered English, history, Greek and Latin, and they laid the foundation for later development of the SAT (Zwick, 2002). Despite buy-in from colleges in the Middle States Association, colleges in the east initially resisted the examination process because of the lesser reputation of the College Board affiliated colleges, and their hesitation to experiment with something as important as testing. Membership in the College Board gradually expanded from its initial level of 11 colleges in 1900 to 27 by 1915. Overall, schools were attracted to the idea of reaching new potential students without the cost of administering a test (Wechsler, 1977).

Despite the popularity of intelligence testing in the early 1900s, by the 1920s the idea of native intelligence had already become controversial, and the claims of intelligence tests were beginning to be seriously questioned. However, institutions continued to use such testing (Wechsler, 1977). In fact, by 1920 over 200 institutions administered intelligence tests. However, at this time much of the testing was for institutional studies and did not actually play a role in admissions decisions (Crouse & Trusheim, 1988). Moreover, few attempts were made to determine what exactly the tests measured, although many were beginning to doubt if it was indeed native intelligence (Wechsler, 1977). In 1925, impressed by his work with the Army Alpha tests, the College Board hired Carl Brigham to develop an intelligence test for college admissions—the SAT. The College Board distinguished the SAT from achievement tests by suggesting that it predicted success in higher education and that it would help institutions identify students who, despite poor high school preparation, could be successful if admitted. The College Board also noted that the test freed secondary schools from teaching to meet the requirements of entrance exams for specific institutions and helped to identify the intellectual elite who would be qualified to fulfill the highest occupational strata (Crouse & Trusheim, 1988; Lemann, 1999).

The SAT was first administered in 1926. Despite the College Board's attempts to promote the SAT, buy-in from colleges remained slow for various reasons. The United States soon was in the midst of the Great Depression, which likely influenced the number of students who could afford to pay for the test. The SAT questions were not always readily available and the grading process for the exam was confusing, so institutions were more comfortable with the subject matter and essay exams that the Board also offered. There was not a consensus at colleges and universities about the usefulness of intelligence tests. However, despite early hesitation to incorporate the test in admissions decisions, the SAT's popularity increased after World War II (Crouse & Trusheim, 1988).

As was the case with World War I, during World War II, College Board representatives helped to develop tests to determine appropriate job assignments for military recruits (Lemann, 1999). After the war ended, veterans returned home and the demand for college admission grew (Crouse & Trusheim, 1988; Owen & Doerr, 1999). This growth in student applications was partly fueled by the 1944 GI Bill, which allowed thousands of veterans to go to college (Zwick, 2002). Ultimately, colleges sought a way to filter through applicants easily, which evolved into the further development of the SAT (Owen & Doerr, 1999).

As its role in higher education continued to expand, the College Board found it difficult to keep pace and partnered with the American Council on Education and the Carnegie Foundation for the Advancement of Teaching to create the Educational Testing Service (ETS), founded in Princeton, New Jersey, in 1947 (Owen & Doerr, 1999). Its first president was Henry Chauncey, a former assistant dean at Harvard. Like Brigham, Chauncey believed in the usefulness of intelligence tests in college admissions. Specifically, he envisioned standardized tests as a "tool to remake society" and to dampen the "unreasonable aspirations of the undeserving" (Zwick, 2002, p. 186). Chauncey was a firm believer in meritocracy and saw ETS as a way to determine how societal goods should be fairly distributed (Lemann, 1999; Zwick, 2002). In addition to higher education testing, ETS was granted a military contract to develop the Selective Service College Qualification Test to determine if college students drafted into military service for the Korean War should be able to defer service to attend college. This contract helped ETS to establish itself financially, bolster its reputation, and further invest in the SAT (Lemann, 1999).

ETS officially transformed into a major industry with the development of the automatic scoring machine, refinements in the SAT, and the development of a range of related tests, products, and services. Today, ETS is the largest testing organization in the United States (Zwick, 2002). Its testing services and clients span many industries ranging from national organizations such as the Central Intelligence Agency and Defense Department, to international entities such as the Malaysian Ministry of Education. However, ETS's largest and most controversial testing program remains its Admissions Testing Program, which is still centered around the SAT (Crouse & Trusheim, 1988).

The SAT Controversy

Despite the widespread use of standardized testing for college admissions across America, the use of SAT scores remains controversial. Over time, ETS has been criticized for various aspects of the SAT including limited public access to data and other information about the test (Crouse & Trusheim, 1988). However, as might be expected, the organization has remained steadfast about the usefulness of the SAT in the admissions process. With a heavy investment in research and development, ETS posits that combining students' SAT performance with high school records significantly increases predictive validity for successful college outcomes (Kobrin, Patterson, Shaw, Mattern, & Barbuti, 2008). However, some have questioned this finding because of model specifications and other contested issues (Crouse & Trusheim, 1988; Rothstein, 2004), suggesting that the predictive validity of the SAT for future student performance is overstated based on a critique of empirical evidence.

ETS also suggests that test scores help students identify colleges and universities aligned with their level of academic ability. However, critics argue that the organization has yet to discuss evidence concerning how students are using their test scores to make application decisions (Crouse & Trusheim, 1988). Moreover, ETS argues that the SAT helps to equalize access to college admissions and economic growth by circumventing opportunity structures that were once based on class and economic status. Yet, there remains intense scholarly debate and public misunderstanding of admissions testing and the appropriate use of SAT scores for minorities and low-income White students. Ironically, ETS would not make SAT scores disaggregated by race available until 1981, despite the fact that it began to compile summary data in 1971 (Crouse & Trusheim, 1988). However, the test score gap between Whites and minorities on the SAT and other standardized tests is a longstanding phenomenon that has been well documented (Hedges & Nowell, 1998; Jencks & Phillips, 1998; Vars & Bowen, 1998). With regard to the SAT in particular, a number of explanations for this discrepancy have been posed (Helms, 1992). From a qualitative perspective, Walpole and colleagues (2005) explored African American and Latino/a high school students' negative perceptions of the college admissions test and posited that these attitudes could potentially have a negative impact on student scores. A growing body of empirical research further validates the related "stereotype threat" hypothesis regarding the persistent Black–White test score gap (Steele & Aronson, 1995).

It is also important to note that there is a strong positive relationship between SAT score and family income. As the SAT minimum requirement for admission to colleges and universities increases, the number of low-income applicants who will qualify decreases. In fact, many socioeconomic status background measures are positively and more strongly correlated with SAT scores than with high school rank; hence, emphasizing rank rather than SAT score would do more to equalize opportunity despite ETS claims of the relationship between testing and equity. The use of SAT scores in admissions has an adverse impact on lower-income applicants while doing little to improve the ability to predict college success (Crouse & Trusheim, 1988).

Although ETS acknowledges the impact SAT scores have on access for students of color and those from low-income families, it currently provides institutions with little guidance for predicting freshman grades for these students. Instead, ETS argues that the SAT simply measures the real problems of inequities in educational opportunity that exist in society and that the test results help the public to be aware of that problem and, thus, press for corrections (Crouse & Trusheim, 1988).

Framing Current Discussions Concerning Standardized Tests and Merit

The historical context can help inform current discussions concerning standardized testing and merit. First, since the inception of the SAT there has always been a debate concerning its usefulness in effectively determining who should have the opportunity to go to college. The paradigm shift toward increased reliance on test scores in admissions decisions was partly a consequence of the need for a convenient way to filter through a growing list of applicants, not necessarily a realistic attempt to measure students' merit. When the SAT was initially developed, the College Board was hesitant to explicitly say what the test measured. Instead, the board suggested similarities between the SAT and intelligence tests to imply that the test measured students' innate academic abilities. Fortunately, ETS has increasingly moved away from this historical assumption by changing the name of the test from Scholastic Aptitude Test to Scholastic Assessment Test and finally to simply SAT. It is also important to note that ETS cautions against the misuse of admission tests and advises that students' test scores should always be considered *along with other factors* in the admissions decision-making process, including high school grade point average (Kobrin et al., 2008). Additionally, ETS engages in ongoing research and development efforts to investigate the influence of noncognitive factors on student achievement. As Burrus and colleagues illustrate in this volume, there is a body of literature that suggests that student characteristics such as emotional intelligence and conscientiousness can significantly affect the prediction of educational outcomes. This approach is aligned with other research in higher education that examines how non-academic student characteristics also influence a range of successful education and career outcomes (Le, Casillas, Robbins, & Langley, 2005; Sedlacek, 2004; Thomas, Kuncel, & Crede, 2007; Tracey & Sedlacek, 1987). However, there is a clear need for further research in this area.

To be sure, in the current context standardized tests are not considered indicators of general intelligence, but tests such as the SAT are the direct descendants of what are commonly referred to as intelligence quotient (IQ) tests. Alfred Binet, the founding father of IQ, warned against the potential misinterpretation and abuse of these instruments which supposedly measure a person's native intelligence (Owen & Doerr, 1999). The first IQ tests were developed to identify people in need of academic assistance and to help them achieve scholastically. The initial objective was not to give certain groups an advantage because of supposed academic superiority. However, some forefathers of the SAT disregarded this fact as they transplanted intelligence testing assumptions to the United States. Moreover, early 20th-century scientists involved with creating the SAT were socialized to accept the mainstream ideology in the racialized caste system in the United States where many marginalized groups underrepresented in higher education were deemed intellectually inferior (Owen & Doerr, 1999). In many instances, testing was introduced to the admissions process with the explicit purpose of decreasing the enrollment of immigrant students who university leaders found less desirable than more privileged American applicants.

It is important to note that not all institutions used testing with an intended purpose of exclusion. For example, former Harvard president James B. Conant cautioned against the establishment of a caste system in America and argued that merit should determine peoples' place in society (Lemann, 1999; Zwick, 2002). However, the end results of such good faith efforts are questionable, given the problematic links between SAT scores as current proxies for merit with concomitant class and race-related opportunities. In fact, research suggests that a student's competitiveness in the admissions process can be predicted simply by knowing his or her race, quality of schooling, and family background (Crouse & Trusheim, 1988). This strong relationship between social/economic opportunities and SAT scores raises serious questions about the common practice of systematically labeling certain groups of students as "less merit worthy" based on admissions test scores. The question of why certain groups of students with restricted opportunities are systematically less "merit-worthy" than others is in dire need of investigation and reformulation.

Discussion and Recommendations

Although the likelihood of selective colleges and universities completely eliminating test scores in admissions is slim, examining the historical context and evolution of uniform entrance exams can help to guide future efforts to reduce their misuse. This is increasingly critical as many of today's institutions enter an era when test scores are too often emphasized as pivotal indicators of merit without sufficient consideration of other factors in a more holistic approach to college admissions. A historical lens helps to illuminate the various issues that continue to plague tests such as the SAT.

Despite cautions by test makers, many in higher education and the broader public still believe that standardized test scores are the only fair measure by which to gauge how worthy a student is for admission to college. This popular belief and related educational practices continue to reinforce the misuse of admission tests and promote a sense of entitlement when privileged students score higher than the less privileged. Recent case history clearly illustrates this point and highlights the sense of entitlement that often accompanies high achievement on these exams (*Gratz v. Bollinger*, 2003; *Grutter v. Bollinger*, 2003). Although most selective institutions consider a number of factors when crafting an incoming cohort of students, the public debate undoubtedly oversimplifies a dynamic process by overemphasizing test scores. The salience of test scores is also reinforced because they influence college rankings and are often flaunted by colleges and universities as indicators of prestige. However, it is incumbent upon both proponents and critics of standardized testing in college admissions to allow history to inform their perspectives as they negotiate the debates of the 21st century. Institutions have a responsibility to increase public understanding of the complexities of merit and the various factors that make a student worthy of admission. A better understanding of the historical evolution of admission testing is necessary for a more in-depth analysis of the current trend toward more "comprehensive" or "holistic" consideration of other factors that make a qualified applicant. This type of in-depth analysis is also necessary to move toward a comprehensive understanding of diversity and merit in higher education.

References

Bernal, E. M., Jr. (1980). A response to "Educational uses of tests with dis-advantaged subjects." In E. Flaxman (Ed.), *Readings on Equal Education: Vol. 6. 1975–1976* (pp. 345–351). New York, NY: AMS Press.

Brigham, C. C. (1923). *A study of American intelligence.* Princeton, NJ: Princeton University Press.

Brigham, C. C. (1932). *A study of error.* New York, NY: College Entrance Examination.

Camara, W. J., & Echternacht, G. (2000). *The SAT I and high school grades: Utility in predicting success in college.* New York, NY: College Entrance Examination Board.

Chang, M. J., Altbach, P. G., & Lomotey, K. (2005). Race in higher education: Making meanings of an elusive target. In P. G. Altbach, R. O. Berdahl, & P. J. Gumport (Eds.), *American higher education in the 21st century* (2nd ed., pp. 517–536). Baltimore, MD: Johns Hopkins University Press.

Cleary, A. T., Humphreys, L. G., Kendrick, S. A., & Wesman, A. (1980). Educational uses of tests with disadvantaged subjects. In E. Flaxman (Ed.), *Readings on Equal Education: Vol. 6. 1975–1976* (pp. 285–331). New York, NY: AMS Press.

Crouse, J., & Trusheim D. (1988). *The case against the SAT.* Chicago, IL: University of Chicago Press.

Fleming, J. (2002). Who will succeed in college? When the SAT predicts Black students' performance. *Review of Higher Education, 25*, 281–296.

Fleming, J., & Garcia, N. (1998). Are standardized tests fair to African Americans? Predictive validity of the SAT in Black and White institutions. *Journal of Higher Education, 69*, 471–495.

Freedle, Roy O. (2003). Correcting the SAT's ethnic and social-class bias: A method for reestimating SAT scores. *Harvard Educational Review, 72*, 1–43.

Gratz v. Bollinger, 539 U.S. 244 (2003).

Grutter v. Bollinger, 539 U.S. 306 (2003).

Hedges, L., & Nowell, A. (1998). Black-White test score convergence since 1965. In C. Jencks & M. Phillips (Eds.), *The Black-White test score gap* (pp. 149–181).Washington, DC: Brookings Institution.

Helms, J. E. (1992). Why is there no study of cultural equivalence in standardized cognitive ability testing? *American Psychologist, 47*, 1083–1101.

Jackson, G. D. (1980). On the report of the ad hoc committee on educational uses of tests with disadvantaged students. In E. Flaxman (Ed.), *Readings on Equal Education: Vol. 6. 1975–1976* (pp. 333–343). New York, NY: AMS Press.

Jencks, C., & Phillips, M. (1998). The Black-White test scope gap: Why it persists and what can be done. *The Brookings Review, 16*(2), 24.

Karabel, J. (2005). *The chosen: The hidden history of admission and exclusion at Harvard, Yale, and Princeton*. Boston, MA: Houghton Mifflin.

Kobrin, J. L., Patterson, B. F., Shaw, E. J., Mattern, K. D., & Barbuti, S. M. (2008). *Validity of the SAT for predicting first-year college grade point average* (College Board Research Report No.2008–5). New York, NY: The College Board.

Le, H., Casillas, A., Robbins, S. B., & Langley, R. (2005). Motivational and skills, social, and self-management predictors of college outcomes: Constructing the Student Readiness Inventory. *Educational and Psychological Measurement, 65*, 482–508.

Lemann, N. (1999). *The big test*. New York, NY: Farrar, Straus and Giroux.

Lemann, N. (2004). A history of admissions testing. In R. Zwick (Ed.), *Rethinking the SAT: The future of standardized testing in university admissions* (pp. 5–14). New York, NY: RoutledgeFalmer

Nettles, M. T., Perna, L. W., & Millett, C. M. (1998). Race and testing in college admissions. In G. Orfield & E. Miller (Eds.), *Chilling Admissions* (pp. 97–110). Cambridge, MA: Harvard Education.

Noftle, E., & Robins, R. (2007). Personality predictors of academic outcomes: Big five correlates of GPA and SAT scores. *Journal of Personality and Social Psychology, 93*, 116–130.

Oswald, F., Schmitt, N., Kim, B., Ramsay, L., & Gillespie, M. (2004). Developing a biodata measure and situational judgment inventory as predictors of college student performance. *Journal of Applied Psychology, 89*, 187–207.

Owen, D., & Doerr, M. (1999). *None of the above*. New York, NY: Rowman & Littlefield.

Robbins, S. B., Lauver, K., Le, H., Davis, D., Langley, R., & Carlstrom, A. (2004). Do psychosocial and study skill factors predict college outcomes? A meta-analysis. *Psychological Bulletin, 130*, 261–288.

Rothstein, J. (2004). College performance predictions and the SAT. *Journal of Econometrics, 121*(1–2), 297–317.

Sedlacek, W. E. (2004). *Beyond the big test: Noncognitive assessment in higher education*. San Francisco, CA: Jossey-Bass.

Steele, C., & Aronson, J. (1995). Stereotype threat and the intellectual test performance of African Americans. *Journal of Personality and Social Psychology, 69*, 797–811.

Stewart, D. M. (1998).Why Hispanic students need to take the SAT. *The Education Digest, 63*(8), 33–36.

Thomas, L. L., Kuncel, N. R., & Crede, M. (2007). Noncognitive variables in college admissions: The case of the Non-Cognitive Questionnaire. *Educational and Psychological Measurement, 67*, 635–657.

Tracey, T. J., & Sedlacek, W. E. (1987). A comparison of White and Black student academic success using noncognitive variables: A LISREL analysis. *Research in Higher Education, 27*, 333–348.

U.S. Congress, Office of Technology Assessment. (1992). *Testing in American Schools: Asking the right questions* (OTA-SET-519). Washington, DC: U.S. Government Printing Office.

Vars, F. E., & Bowen, W. G. (1998). Scholastic aptitude test scores, race, and academic performance in selective colleges and universities. In C. Jencks & M. Phillips (Eds.), *The Black-White test score gap.* Washington, DC: Brookings Institution.

Walpole, M., McDonough, P. M., Bauer, C. J., Gibson, C., Kanyi, K., & Toliver, R. (2005). This test is unfair: Urban African American and Latino high school students' perceptions of standardized college admission tests. *Urban Education, 40*, 321–349.

Wechsler, H.S. (1977). *The qualified student.* New York, NY: Wiley-Interscience.

Zwick, R. (2002). *Fair game?* New York, NY: RoutledgeFalmer.

CHAPTER 4

CRITICAL ANALYSIS OF MERIT ASSUMPTIONS IN HIGHER EDUCATION

Edward P. St. John

Affirmative action has, for a number of years, provided colleges and universities with an imperfect mechanism for adjusting measures of merit in admissions for purposes of fairness. Such an adjustment was necessary because (a) hundreds of years of discrimination in higher education admissions was not corrected for between the Supreme Court's 1973 *Adams v. Richardson*, as modified in *Adams v. Califano* in 1977, and 1992 *United States v. Fordice* decision, the brief period during which systemic inequalities could be directly addressed through admissions remedies (Brown & Hendrickson, 1997; St. John, 1998), and (b) there are extreme quality differences among high schools that make it necessary to adjust admissions practices to deal with inequalities in prior opportunities to prepare for college. While the *Gratz* and *Grutter* decisions provided a window of time to adjust admissions to deal with the underlying systemic inequalities through the application of affirmative action, many institutions have had to adapt to legal challenges to or outright bans on the use of affirmative action by seeking alternative procedures that are fairer and provide workable measures of merit. The systemic problems with merit measures—how they came about and how problems with them can be remedied—are the focus of this chapter.

The notion that merit can be measured by a test and can be used fairly in college admissions decisions or the awarding of student financial aid is fundamentally flawed, unless there is means to adjust for prior inequalities. Specifically, the use of standardized tests in college admissions assumes that students have had equal opportunity to prepare for college in K–12 education. There are two reasons why test scores on the ACT and SAT should not be applied without adjustment in the college admissions process:

- College admissions decisions and analysis of college enrollment must assume equal prior preparation (Lleras, 2004). Inequalities in high schools usually make it impossible to assume equality of preparation. For example, in Michigan most minority students have been enrolled in high

51

schools that did not include curriculum that would make it possible for them to apply for the state merit grant program when it was first implemented (St. John & Chung, 2004).

- The ACT and SAT exams include the same types of questions that are used in high school accountability systems. For example, the ACT is used as the 11th-grade exam in Michigan, which means that it now legally measures the quality of high schools, which has an impact on state funding decisions. The ACT has also become a de facto measure of inequality in high schools. It is essential to adjust for any prior inequality to have a fair use of the test in the college admissions process or in decisions about student financial aid.

At the very least, public higher education should move toward alternative measures of merit that are fairer and provide methods of measuring the potential for student academic success that can work as well as or better than the tests. Given these challenges, I critique common assumptions in higher education admissions by examining the contradictory uses of standardized tests in K–16 education by describing how this distorts the use of standardized tests in college admissions by creating inequality in selection and by suggesting alternative views of merit that can guide a new generation of selection practices for college admission and merit-based student aid.

A Critical Examination of the Use of SAT and ACT for College Admission

To understand the assumptions underlying the use of merit measures, I examine how test scores have been used in U.S. K–12 and higher education, as well as the ambiguities created by these practices. A discussion of conflicting underlying assumptions about merit in the U.S. system follows the review of these practices.

The Uses of Measures of Merit in K–16 Education

Prior to the 1980s, using college admission tests was thought to be a fair method of selection for colleges and universities. However, changes in the use of standardized tests in K–12 systems coupled with research that examines the linkages between high school courses and tests scores reveal the inherent contradiction underlying the continued uncritical use of SAT or ACT scores as a basis for college admission decisions.

The use of testing differs fundamentally in the United States compared to other nations. In the United States, test scores have been used to evaluate educational systems. Schools have been penalized for having low scores or not improving their scores, an orientation toward managing outcomes rather than inputs that emerged under Ronald Reagan (Finn, 1990). In contrast, most other nations use tests to sort students into differentiated systems of high schools, with high-achieving students going to college-preparatory high schools and others to vocational high schools, although there has recently been a global trend toward the notions of accountability pioneered in the United States (Henry, Lingard, Rizvi, & Taylor, 2001).

These uses of tests need to be considered in relation to the original purpose of the tests, which was to sort military men for different jobs in the war effort (Williams, this volume). This process rested on an assumption of general intelligence (*g* factor). The same concept can be applied to the use of test scores on the SAT and ACT in college admissions, especially when test scores are used along with high school courses and high school grades as measures of preparation. When the combination is used without considering the interrelationships between them, an implicit assumption is made that the tests measure general intelligence while student achievement is measured by grades.

The diagnostic role of tests to determine relative ability, their historical role in college, is undermined by the relationship between test scores, the courses students complete in high school, and the funding of schools. Analyses of national SAT scores has found that, controlling for other factors (background, high school grades, and so forth), completing a course in Calculus in high school adds about 106 points to the SAT score, compared to Algebra II or less, and that taking Trigonometry/Pre-Calculus adds 55 points (St. John & Musoba, 2010). This relationship is complicated because not all students have access to advanced courses: African Americans are at a historical disadvantage (Trent & St. John, 2008). In addition, state school funding has a direct effect on test scores controlling for individual differences (Musoba, 2006; St. John & Musoba, 2010), meaning students in under-resourced schools are at a disadvantage.

The unequal conditions of high schools, the unequal access to advanced curriculum, and the unequal funding of schools, realities of K–12 systems, mean the strict application of tests and an ordinal scale of relative ability is inappropriate, leading to high ability students being ranked artificially low if they attend underfunded schools that did not offer advanced courses. At a minimum, this set of statistical relationships between students' school experiences and test scores should influence a more judicious analysis of test scores in college admissions—if they are to be used at all.

Several states now use the ACT as a state exit exam, requiring all high school juniors to take the test (Daun-Barnett, 2008). At a prima facie level, there are some advantages to this policy because it results in all students taking a college entrance exam, a desirable situation if tests are considered a neutral arbitrator of ability to achieve in college. However, there is a deep and troubling problem inherent in this system. The ACT and SAT were formerly intended as fair measures of college preparedness, a difficult goal to realize in itself. Now, these tests are also being used to measure the quality of schools and to fulfill federal requirements under No Child Left Behind (NCLB). Given the role of tests in measuring the quality of schools, students from low-achieving schools would be in double jeopardy if unadjusted scores were used in college admissions.

If the ACT and SAT[1] are now officially accepted as instruments to measure school quality, then doesn't this contradict their use in college admissions? If a specific test measures school quality, then using that test score for college admissions without adjusting for the quality of the high school means that students who attended poor quality schools (i.e., schools with lower average test scores) will be penalized because their scores will generally be lower as well, regardless of the student's actual potential. The fact is, the entrepreneurial ambitions of the testing industry which resulted in using admissions tests for measuring school quality has undermined the legitimacy of using them as a fair instrument in college admissions.

Conflicting Assumptions About the Meaning of "Admission" Tests

There has long been a problem with testing because it has been difficult for testing companies to separate the g factor from the content knowledge measured by tests. At the current time, courses students complete in high school predict their test scores better than their background, merit grants (another measure of ability and achievement in relation to peers), and other individual factors. Further, school funding has a substantial and significant affect on students' test scores. These conditions suggest that admissions tests may be good measures of the quality of schools students attend, but not a fair measure of student ability.

---

[1] The ACT and the SAT are highly correlated, and as a consequence, colleges and universities use a simple cross-walk to standardize scores when they accept both types of tests from applicants. If one of the tests is used for the purpose of evaluating schools, then both tests have this potential use and meaning.

The recent rush by the testing industry to use college admission tests as measures of school quality as defined by law (e.g., NCLB) indicates that the tests are generally accepted as a legal measure of school quality. In this case, it is *immoral* to assume the ACT and SAT tests provide fair measures of individual differences.[2] At the very least, in states that use either of these college entrance tests as the exit exam for accountability, it seems unethical to use an unadjusted test for college admission. This would be a form of double jeopardy that seems immoral and should be illegal: In effect, students are penalized twice for going to poor-quality schools. In these states, public universities have a moral imperative to index the test to the high school mean as part of selection. The use of exams for evaluating the quality of high schools is not the only reason for adjusting selection to school contexts, but it is the most obviously crucial. Strategies for adjusting for inequalities in public schools are examined in the following section.

Developing and Using Merit to Achieve Fairness in Selection

There is clearly a need to engage in a process of thinking through the assumptions and practices campuses use when they make decisions about admissions and merit aid. Other authors in this volume examine different methods of measuring merit and, in some instances, make recommendations about specific methods that can be used. I outline criteria that can be used to make informed judgments about merit and illustrate how different approaches might inform the development of new and fairer selection practices.

Standards for Fairness in Selection

To conceptualize the criteria for fairness, consider both John Rawls's works on principles of justice (1971, 1999, 2001) and Martha Nussbaum's concepts of human capabilities (1999, 2000, 2004). Rawls provides a frame for balancing concerns about rights and differences, while Nussbaum provides the logic of capabilities that can guide deeper consideration of means of dealing with thresholds of preparation. Both concepts are critical in constructing new measures of merit and applying them in college selection procedures for admission and merit aid.

Rawls gives us a moral lens for thinking about current education policy choices. In particular, he provides three principles critical to constructing

---

[2] In theory, one could argue that the SAT should be used in college admissions if the purpose of the ACT has shifted to being a measure of school quality. However, this argument would ignore the high correlation between the SAT and the ACT.

fairness in selection which can be used to find balance among competing interests in the education debates:

- Principle 1 relates to basic rights, which all individuals have in a democratic society (Rawls, 1971). The right to an education is nearly universally accepted (Nussbaum, 1999; Sen, 1999), and in the United States, equal access to college should be a right for those who qualify academically.

- Principle 2 argues that if there is an inequality it should favor the most disadvantaged (Rawls, 1971). The historic emphases on equal opportunity in school desegregation and student financial aid are a few of many examples of this approach in education policy.

- Principle 3 is the "just savings principle" which relates to cross-generation equity, including the use of taxation to support education. In the current context of majority concern about tax rates, it is important to balance taxpayer costs with concerns about equity and basic rights in education.

The first principle requires us to consider all people as having the same rights. With respect to admission into elite public colleges, all citizens should have the right to apply and be judged by the same criteria with selections made fairly based on individual excellence. Affirmative action that considered race as a factor provided a mechanism for altering this process within a legal process of fairness. However, the new legal context requires colleges to use different means for selection. Since inequalities in K–12 education have not been remedied and are unlikely to be remedied in the near future, higher education must consider ways of developing and using a standard set of criteria taking that fact into consideration. Thus, a first standard of fairness in admissions and selection is

- *Standard 1: Common criteria should be developed and equally administered when selecting students for admission into a college. In a system that allows affirmative action, this may include consideration of race/ethnicity.*

Rawls's second principle gives us insight into the basis for adjusting a standard set of criteria. In addition, Nussbaum (1999, 2000) argues that all women—and by extension one can argue all adults—have the right to an education to a level necessary to support a family. St. John (2006) has expanded Nussbaum's argument to assert that all citizens in the United States have the right to a high school education meeting a standard that prepares them for college and the 21st-century workplace, but recognizes this is a goal and not a reality. This poses a complicated context for admissions. Is there a minimum threshold of preparation, and, if so, how should it be applied? Our argument is that if affirmative action that considers race is not possible or desirable for college, it is necessary to (a) set thresholds of preparation (or even minimum standards for admissions) but that (b) these standards should be administered in ways that adjust for prior inequalities in preparation. The difference principle of justice requires use of a common standard to equalize unequal prior schooling alone and/or take family circumstances into consideration.

The second standard of fairness is

- *Standard 2: College selection criteria should be adjusted for prior inequalities in opportunities to prepare, especially in selective educational systems funded by public tax dollars.*

If the public uses tax dollars to fund a selective college—and any four-year college that applies admissions criteria (with a level of selectivity other than open admissions) would meet this threshold—then adjustments should be made to the admissions criteria to contend with prior inequality attributable to differences in public and private schools. Beyond that, while private K–12 schools are generally tax exempt, receiving only an indirect taxpayer subsidy, public schools receive a direct subsidy. Thus, public taxation and distribution influence inequalities prior to college application. Methods of adjusting merit criteria to prior inequality can be called merit-aware approaches (Goggin, 1999; St. John, Simmons, & Musoba, 2002). Such approaches use merit and, as part of the process, adaptations to consider issues related to inequality.

Logically, there are at least three approaches to making adjustments in selection: one primarily aimed at prior inequalities in high schools as part of the selection process for admission, one based on individual traits and characteristics such as those uncovered by using noncognitive variables (Sedlacek, 2004), and a third that would explicitly consider income and parents' education (Cabrera, Terenzini, & Bernal, 2001).

Rawls's just savings principle would require that financial resources be considered as part of the calculation of admission. His original argument (1971) about just savings was that each generation owes the next a progressively better set of basic rights, including education. However, the neoliberal argument of the late 20th century has been that a system of basic liberties requires constraint on government services and taxation (Harvey, 2005). While the Obama revolution may indicate a swing back to a more substantial public role, the constraints on public subsidies to education are abundantly evident. It is necessary to consider how to fairly administer admissions taking into account levels of state funding to both high schools and institutions of higher education.

A third standard of fairness is

> • *Standard 3: Fairness in admissions requires adapting financing schemes to maintain equity, adjusting budgeting practices as necessary. This means that funding for student aid and supplemental educational opportunities is necessary.*

This is not a simple standard for colleges to meet. It is also not an argument that the public must fund at a certain level, but rather that the admission process has implications for how funding is used within the collegiate system. For example, the argument that selective colleges should not consider financial need in admissions would require colleges to offer very substantial amounts of need-based aid, probably through higher tuition, as a means of maintaining equitable admissions, an argument frequently made (e.g., McPherson & Schapiro, 1997). Thus, part of the issue is that colleges must consider student aid costs when they set tuition, just as they consider other education-related costs. In addition, colleges must budget for the provision of services to students who meet admissions standards as adjusted for prior inequality but need remedial assistance because of those prior inequalities.

Designing a New Admissions Scheme

These standards provide a basis for rethinking the use and adaptation of admissions practices within selective colleges and universities. Table 1 uses the three standards to compare three widely known methods of selection: standardized tests, class rank, and noncognitive variables. The analysis illustrates that the decisions institutions make about selection criteria are complex and depend on local contexts and student demand.

Table 1. Application of Standards for Fairness in Selection to Common Methods

Standard	Common Criteria	Fairness	Cost
Standardized Tests Only	Can be consistently applied, but assumes sufficient demand among diverse students with high scores	May be necessary to use affirmative action (e.g., considering race/ethnicity) to maintain diversity	Educational systems that attract students with high test scores usually make substantial investments in educational programs; student aid is necessary for low-income students.
Class Rank Only	Can be consistently applied, but limits ability to admit higher numbers of students from schools with high scores	If there is racial isolation within the educational system (e.g., high schools are predominantly White or Black), diversity can be maintained.	Greater need to fund supplemental programs if some high schools lack preparatory curriculum; costs of student aid increase with increase in high-need students.
Noncognitive Variables Only	Can be consistently applied, but could limit ability to attract some high-achieving students	Provides a mechanism for attracting diverse students with high ability to overcome barriers to success	Must adjust educational strategies, support systems, and financial aid to new clientele

First, using standardized tests as the only measure of merit in selection assumes a high demand among diverse students if maintaining a reasonable standard of diversity is seen as important. It is difficult to maintain diversity without some form of affirmative action and/or need-based aid. The reason for this is that prior inequalities in the nation's education system limit the number of high-achieving students of color, especially when test scores are the primary means of selection. Private colleges find it easier to consider race in admissions and student aid, but even private colleges are prone to lawsuits if their use of race-based criteria excludes some groups (St. John, Affolter-Caine, & Chung, 2007). Some highly selective colleges find the costs of need-based admissions to be excessive and adjust admissions for ability to pay (Ehrenberg, 2002). In other words, the use of tests alone in selection can only be maintained by a few highly selective colleges, and even in those cases it is usually necessary to use some form of affirmative action to maintain the diversity demanded by excellent students from all racial/ethnic groups.

Using class rank represents a viable alternative for public colleges in states that have outlawed affirmative action. While the denial of the use of affirmative action has a nefarious aspect and seems overtly inconsistent with the U.S. Constitution as interpreted by the Supreme Court, it has still been banned in several states. It is apparent that in Florida, the implementation of the top 20% has been accompanied by increased diversity in 4-year colleges (St. John & Moronski, 2008). Yet, institutional decisions to apply class rank can be problematic. The use of class rank in selection may raise the costs of supplemental support services if some high schools lack a college preparatory curriculum. Using class rank represents a school-based adaptation of merit measures. Similar results are evident from adjusting test scores for school context, including ranking students based on how their test scores deviate from the mean score of their school (St. John, Simmons, & Musoba, 2002).

The use of noncogntive variables provides a means of achieving diversity, if there is sufficient demand among highly qualified, diverse students (Sedlacek, 2004). In fact, Oregon State actually raised its profile as a consequence of converting to noncognitive variables. It was possible for the university to advertise in new ways and heighten the appeal of the college. However, it is also conceivable that in a highly selective university the exclusive use of noncognitive variables could radically alter the yield of students over time, creating a greater demand for support services. I argue that such transformations are just.

No single method of selection is ideal for all colleges. Rather than propose a method as ideal, we suggest institutions consider these standards of fairness in the design of their own selection systems. The choice of admissions practices is and should remain a campus-level decision based on the local context, although state policy can appropriately set guidelines. For example, over several decades the California Master Plan set different admission thresholds for 2-year, comprehensive colleges (California State system) and its research university (University of California) (Smelser & Almond, 1974). Each campus adapted and adjusted admissions to yield diversity and meet the educational needs of students in the state. Subsequent policies changed that system, inserting an intrusive political ideology into admissions that is highly problematic relative to reasonable standards of justice and fairness.

Without a more comprehensive approach to college admissions guided by new standards of fairness, conventional practices based primarily on SAT/ACT test scores as the primary indicator of merit will continue to support a system of ***sponsored mobility*** (i.e., Guinier, 2002; Lemann, 1999; Turner, 1960). According to Turner (1960), sponsored mobility is characterized by elite recruits being chosen by the established elite or their agents. Thus, elite status is allocated based on criteria of supposed merit that cannot be overcome through any amount of effort or strategy. Such sponsored mobility is neither fair nor just but reproduces conventional racial, class, and gender inequalities. Rather than equality of opportunity, sponsored mobility is based on unequal access to quality K–12 schools as well as related family networks, legacies, and elite social capital (see Bowman, Chapter 2, this volume).To move beyond sponsored mobility, we need to systematically change historic admission practices in highly selective research universities guided by better research as well as the principles of fairness and justice.

Conclusion

The recent history of the use of college admission tests undermines their historical role as neutral instruments that measure the ability of students to complete college. Traditionally, standardized tests have been employed to provide an open contest where students could compete for admissions to elite institutions and gain access based upon personal responsibility and quantifiable measures of merit (Guinier, 2002; Turner, 1960). Although this historic approach allegedly advanced an agenda of fairness in student evaluations for admissions, it neglected the disadvantaged who lacked access to adequate preparation. Currently, the following problems with admissions tests undermine their historic role:

- The courses students take in high school predict more variance in ACT and SAT scores than do other individual background or achievement variables.

- Students' access to advanced courses, like Calculus, varies across states and across schools within states.

- School funding influences student achievement, even after controlling for background and grades.

These factors alone argue against using test scores as ordinal scales without adjusting for school quality. When state governments and state testing agencies use test scores as instruments to measure school quality, as instruments of state compliance under NCLB, this further undermines the moral basis of using the ACT or SAT in college admissions without adjusting for school characteristics.

For decades, affirmative action provided colleges and universities with a convenient way to overlook the contradictory meanings of tests. Since minorities attended inferior schools more frequently than did majority students, affirmative action provided a means of achieving diversity without altering the use of admissions tests. There was an inherent problem with this band-aid to admissions: It tended to result in the selection of minority students who attended suburban schools with advanced courses, increasing the unfairness for students who attended more troubled inner-city schools and under-resourced rural schools. Unfortunately, affirmative action did not mitigate the unfair use of standardized tests, even though it increased the percentage of minorities admitted.

The new legal constraints on using affirmative action, along with agitation from neoconservatives who claim this method undermines equal rights,[3] mean that many colleges and universities are seeking alternatives to the old system of using affirmative action coupled with test scores. Using noncogntive variables in admissions provides one workable alternative to using test scores coupled with affirmative action. Other authors in this volume suggest different ways of applying noncognitive criteria for this purpose. The examination of noncognitive and similar variables in a holistic review process demonstrates the use of test scores supplemented by other merit-worthy characteristics determined by university admissions committees (Guinier, 2002; Turner, 1960). In addition, colleges can adjust their achievement measures for schools by using class rank or indexing ACT scores to the school mean, a method possible in states where all high school

---

[3] The question of whether or not affirmative action actually undermined equity in admissions is highly complicated given the historical discrimination against African Americans and Hispanics in the United States (Newton, 2006). We agree with those who argue it is too early to eliminate this procedure, but colleges and universities need to increase fairness in college admissions whether or not they have used affirmative action to rectify historic racial discrimination.

students are required to take the test. Such an approach would employ a system of structural mobility in which institutions alter their admissions practices to account for criteria that inadvertently privilege students who attend well-resourced schools (Guinier, 2002; Sobel, 1980). There is no one best way to solve these critical issues because the issues facing different campuses vary, just as the context and quality of schools vary across states and locales.

Public universities have a special obligation to go beyond sponsored mobility and find creative ways to address these issues using frameworks that are fair in relation to their state's policies. While the Florida 20% plan has improved the situation in Florida, it may not be the right solution for other states where a lower percentage of students qualify for college. The elitism implicit in historical admission practices of highly selective research universities must end; these universities have a responsibility to maintain fair admissions practices for all the citizens of their states. As the dust settles after overly simplistic debates about affirmative action, it is important college and university administrators take additional steps to design, test, and refine admission practices that enhance fairness.

References

Brown, M. C., II, & Hendrickson, R. M. (1997). Public historically Black colleges at the crossroads: *United States v. Fordice* and higher education desegregation. *Journal for a Just and Caring Education, 3*(1), 95–113.

Cabrera, A. F., Terenzini, P. T., & Bernal, E. M. (2001). *Leveling the playing field: Low-income students in postsecondary education* (Report from the College Board). Washington, DC: College Board.

Daun-Barrett, N. (2008). *Preparation and access: A multi-level analysis of state policy influences on the academic antecedents to college enrollment* PhD dissertation. University of Michigan, Ann Arbor, Michigan, Available online at: http://www.airweb.org/webrecordings /forum2008/702%20-%20Preparation%20and%20Access.pdf

Ehrenberg, R. G. (2002). *Tuition rising: Why college costs so much.* Cambridge, MA: Harvard University Press.

Finn, C. (1990). Why we need choice. In W. L. Boyd & H. J. Walberg (Eds.), *Choice in education: Potential and problems* (pp. 3–20). Berkeley, CA: McCutchan Publishing.

Goggin, W. J. (1999, May). A "merit-aware" model for college admissions and affirmative action. *Postsecondary Education Opportunity Newsletter, 83*, 6–12.

Guinier, L. (2002). Admission policies as political acts: Guardian at the gates of our democratic ideal. *Harvard Law Review, 117*, 113–224.

Harvey, D. (2005). *A brief history of neoliberalism.* New York, NY: Oxford University Press.

Henry, M., Lingard, B., Rizvi, F., & Taylor, S. (2001). *The OECD, globalization and education policy.* Amsterdam, the Netherlands: Pergamon Press.

Lemann, N. (1999). *The big test: The secret history of the American meritocracy.* New York, NY: Farrar, Straus and Giroux.

Lleras, M. P. (2004). *Investing in human capital: A capital markets approach to student funding.* Cambridge, England: Cambridge University Press.

McPherson, M. S., & Schapiro, M. O. (1998). *The student aid game: Meeting need and rewarding talent in American higher education.* Princeton, NJ: Princeton University Press.

Musoba, G. D. (2006). Accountability v. adequate funding: Which policies influence adequate preparation for college? In E. P. St. John (Ed.), *Readings on Equal Education: Vol. 21. Public policy and equal educational opportunity: School reforms, postsecondary encouragement, and state policies on postsecondary education* (pp. 75–125). New York, NY: AMS Press.

Newton, J. (2006). *Justice for all: Earl Warren and the nation he made.* NY: Riverhead Books.

Nussbaum, M. C. (1999). *Sex and social justice.* Oxford, England: Oxford University Press.

Nussbaum, M. C. (2000). *Women and human development: The capabilities approach.* New York, NY: Cambridge University Press.

Nussbaum, M. C. (2004). *Hiding from humanity: Disgust, shame, and the law.* Princeton, NJ: Princeton University Press.

Rawls, J. (1971). *A theory of justice.* Cambridge, MA: Belknap Press of Harvard University Press.

Rawls, J. (1999). *The law of peoples.* Cambridge, MA: Harvard University Press.

Rawls, J. (2001). *Justice as fairness: A restatement.* Cambridge, MA: Belknap Press of Harvard University Press.

Sedlacek, W. E. (2004). *Beyond the big test: Noncognitive assessment in higher education.* San Francisco, CA: Jossey-Bass.

Sen, A. (1999). *Development as freedom.* New York, NY: Anchor Press.

Smelser, J. J., & Almond, G. (1974). *Growth, structural change, and conflict in California higher education.* Berkeley: University of California Press.

Sobel, L. (Ed.). (1980). *Quotas and affirmative action.* New York, NY: Facts on File.

St. John, E. P. (1998). Higher education desegregation in the post-Fordice legal environment: An historical perspective. In R. E. Fossey (Ed.), *Readings on Equal Education: Vol. 15. Race, the courts, and equal education: The limits of the law* (pp. 101–122). New York, NY: AMS Press.

St. John, E. P. (2006). Improving access and college success. In E. P. St. John & Associates (Eds.), *Education and the public interest: School reform, public finance, and access to higher education* (pp. 217–234). Dordrecht, the Netherlands: Springer.

St. John, E. P., Affolter-Caine, B., Chung, A. S. (2007). Race-conscious student financial aid: Constructing an agenda for research, litigation, and policy development. In, G. Orfield, P. Marin, S. M. Flores, & L. Garces, *Charting the future of college affirmative action: Legal victories, continuing attacks, and new research* (pp. 173–204). Los Angeles, CA: Civil Rights Project, UCLA School of Education. Available from___http://civilrightsproject.ucla.edu/research/college-access/affirmative-action/charting-the-future-of-college-affirmative-action-legal-victories-continuing-attacks-and-new-research

St. John, E. P., & Chung, C. G. (2004). The impact of GMS on financial access: Analyses of the 2000 cohort. In E. P. St. John (Ed.), *Readings on Equal Education: Vol. 20. Improving access and college success for diverse students: Studies of the Gates Millennium Scholars Program* (pp. 115–153). New York, NY: AMS Press.

St. John, E. P., & Moronski, K. (2008, January). *The impact of the Florida Bright Futures Scholarship Program on college preparation and access for low-income and minority students* [Special report]. *ENLACE FLORIDA, 3,* 2–36. Retrieved from http://enlacefl.usf.edu/research/Research%20Briefs/2009/The-Impact-of-FL-BrightFuturesScholarship-on-CollegePrep.pdf

St. John, E. P., & Musoba, G. D. (2010). *Pathways to academic success: Expanding opportunity for underrepresented students.* New York, NY: Routledge.

St. John, E. P., Simmons, A. B., & Musoba, G. D. (2002). Merit-aware admissions in public universities: Increasing diversity. *Thought & Action, 17*(2), 35–46.

Trent, W. T., & St. John, E. P. (Eds.) (2008). *Resources, assets, and strengths among successful diverse students: Understanding the contributions of the Gates Millennium Scholars Program.* In *Readings on Equal Education: Vol. 23.* New York, NY: AMS Press, Inc.

Turner, R. H. (1960). Sponsored and Contest Mobility and the School System. *American Sociological Review*, *25*, 855-862

Supreme Court Cases

Adams v. Califano, 430 F. Supp. 118 (D. D. C. 1977).

Adams v. Richardson, Civ. A. No. 3095-70, U.S. Dist., 356 F. Su92 (February 16, 1973).

Gratz v. Bollinger, 539 U.S. 244 (2003).

Grutter v. Bollinger, 539 U.S. 306 (2003).

United States v. Fordice, 505 U.S. 717; 112 S. Ct. 2727; 120 L. Ed. 2d 575 (June 26, 1992).

Section II

Merit and Opportunity in Higher Education: Complexities, Challenges, and Trends in a Diversifying Nation

CHAPTER 5

DIVERSITY AND OPPORTUNITY IN HIGHER EDUCATION: THE ROLE OF AFFIRMATIVE ACTION

Michele S. Moses, John T. Yun, and Patricia Marin

Despite significant legal and political challenges, affirmative action is still a legal method of increasing opportunities for higher education in 45 states.[1] The Supreme Court has ruled on four important cases since its *Regents of the University of California v. Bakke* (1978) decision and in those cases has maintained its position on the constitutionality of using race/ethnicity as *one qualifying factor* in college and university admissions. It has narrowed the use of race-conscious affirmative action in education, most recently at the K–12 level, but overall, the practice remains legal and viable. *Bakke*, therefore, has not been overturned by the U.S. Supreme Court even though two different conservative-leaning courts have had the chance to do so. Nevertheless, the debate and even confusion about affirmative action in higher education continue.

The primary aim of this chapter is to provide an overview of the current status of affirmative action in postsecondary admissions through a concurrent review of recent court rulings, state legislation, and higher education enrollment data. The authors are policy researchers whose work has centered on affirmative action and related policies, with a focus on the links between affirmative action and diversity, equality, and justice. As such, we approach this chapter from the assumption that legal affirmative action policy plays a singular role in fostering diversity and equal opportunity, and that abolishing it would have (and has had) negative results for higher education.

This is a particularly interesting time for affirmative action, over 30 years after the landmark *Bakke* (1978) ruling, less than a decade after the University of Michigan affirmative action lawsuits—*Gratz v. Bollinger* (2003) and *Grutter v. Bollinger* (2003)—and soon after additional states voted on anti–affirmative action ballot initiatives in 2008. While others have

---

[1] The five states where affirmative action in higher education admissions is illegal are California, Washington, Michigan, Nebraska, and Florida. In the first four, the affirmative action ban was the result of voter referenda; in Florida, the ban was the result of an Executive Order by the Governor. It is important to note that higher education institutions in Florida, while prohibited from using race/ethnicity in admissions decisions, may use race/ethnicity in non-admissions decisions, policies, and practices.

69

provided analyses of a single component, such as the court rulings (e.g., Greene, 2004; Korrell, 2007), analyzing each of the factors in the context of the others is important because the court decisions and state-level legislation have an effect on enrollment outcomes and, consequently, opportunities for and diversity in institutions of higher education. From a broad philosophical and legal perspective, then, we ask two questions: (a) What is the current legal and political status of race-conscious policy in higher education admissions? and, given the current status, (b) What is the likelihood that by 2028 affirmative action will no longer be needed to further the goals of diversity and opportunity on college and university campuses?[2] For the purposes of this chapter, we focus on affirmative action in education, specifically in higher education admissions, examining K–12 issues only when relevant to the higher education context.

To answer our first question, we engage in conceptual analysis centered on the following court decisions: *Regents of the University of California v. Bakke* (1978), *Hopwood v. Texas* (1996), *Smith v. University of Washington* (2000), *Johnson v. Board of Regents of the University of Georgia* (2001), *Gratz v. Bollinger* (2003), *Grutter v. Bollinger* (2003), *Parents Involved in Community Schools v. Seattle School District No. 1, et. al.* (2007). We also look at state legislation: California's Proposition 209 (1996), Washington's Initiative 200 (1998), Florida's Executive Order 99-281, the One Florida Initiative (1999), Michigan's Proposal 2 (2006), and the 2008 ballot initiative campaigns in Arizona, Colorado, Missouri, Nebraska, and Oklahoma. We incorporate research findings and analysis of institutional-level data to understand the outcomes of affirmative action case law and ballot initiatives. In addition, we use secondary sources to examine the political implications of the rulings and legislation related to affirmative action policy.

For our second research question, we use enrollment data from the Integrated Postsecondary Education Data System (IPEDS) to examine the racial/ethnic diversity across selected flagship universities and their state-level population pools. The primary comparison is between (a) racial/ethnic diversity of first-time, degree-seeking undergraduates **at several state flagship institutions** from 1994 to 2005, and (b) the racial/ethnic diversity of the same first-time, degree-seeking undergraduate students attending all 2- and 4-year degree-granting public and private institutions **in the flagship's state**. This allows us to examine the patterns of college and university

---

[2] The 2028 date stems from Justice Sandra Day O'Connor's admonition in the *Grutter* (2003) majority opinion in which she expressed the Court's hope that in 25 years— 2028—affirmative action will no longer be necessary to achieve the diversity that enriches college life and learning.

admission of racially/ethnically diverse classes in several select institutions and consider whether it seems viable that by 2028 such institutions will no longer need affirmative action in admissions decisions. In particular, for states likely to face anti–affirmative action ballot initiatives in coming years, these analyses provide one approach to examining the current need for affirmative action in admissions and the likely consequences if new ballot initiatives pass. Finally, we conclude with reflections on what the evolving legal and sociopolitical climate means for education research, policy, and practice concerned with diversity and equality of educational opportunity. Given the recent changes in affirmative action law, our analyses offer an understanding of affirmative action policies today and for the immediate future that will have both theoretical and practical uses for educators, researchers, administrators, and policy makers.

From the Court of Public Opinion to State and Federal Courts

Sandel (1991) wrote that affirmative action causes a "conflicted public mind" (p. 13) due to the simultaneous desire for racial equality and color-blind policies. The public mind has become no less conflicted in the last dozen or so years as affirmative action policy has been tested and contested in state and federal courts and through ballot initiatives that have passed in four states. Initiatives were attempted in four other states; of these, three ultimately failed prior to reaching the ballot (Arizona, Missouri, and Oklahoma), and the fourth was defeated by voters in Colorado, as we discuss later. With all the legal and political activity surrounding affirmative action, it can be difficult to tease out the race-conscious policies and programs currently allowable by law and, beyond that, which ones will be able to withstand what are sure to be future challenges. In this section, we attempt to clarify the current landscape of affirmative action policy related to admissions to colleges and universities.

Prior to the 1978 U.S. Supreme Court case *Regents of the University of California v. Bakke*, the national mood had been tilting in favor of policies and programs designed to support equality of educational opportunity (Gill, 1980). Great Society and War on Poverty programs were indicative of this mood. In the 1970s, however, the United States witnessed a change in the desire to address social inequalities characterized as "a spreading mania within American society, a mania increasingly adamant against governmental and societal efforts to help blacks, other minorities and the poor" (Gill, 1980, p. 1). For over 30 years, affirmative action programs have weathered a persistent backlash, combined with legal and political challenges (Moses, 2002). These challenges have taken the form of court cases, state-level legislation, and state ballot measures aimed at curbing or eliminating affirmative action. The landmark *Bakke* case was the first in which U.S. Supreme Court Justices ruled on affirmative action in higher education admissions.

Regents of the University of California v. Bakke

Bakke's legacy in affirmative action law is strong (Marin & Horn, 2008). Perhaps its most lasting effect was to clarify that the use of numeric quotas and set-aside places within admission programs in higher education violated the 14th Amendment to the U.S. Constitution. Even though the legal legacy of the *Bakke* case is significant, the decision itself was the result of a fractured Supreme Court. The Justices held 4–1–4 that "(a) the minority-admissions program of the University of California Medical School in Davis had discriminated illegally against a white male applicant, but (b) that universities could legally consider race as a factor in admissions" (Sobel, 1980, p. 145). Justices Warren Burger, John Paul Stevens, Potter Stewart, and William Rehnquist decided in favor of Allan Bakke on both counts; Justices William Brennan, Byron White, Thurgood Marshall, and Harry Blackmun decided in favor of the University of California at Davis Medical School on both counts, and, in the swing vote, Justice Lewis Powell decided *against* the Davis policy, but *in favor of* universities' ability to use race as a plus factor in admissions decisions. Although Powell was the only justice to use the educational benefits of diversity as his rationale in favor of race-conscious admissions policies, his became the court's controlling opinion, since he cast the deciding vote for each side. Divided though it was, the Supreme Court indicated to the nation that affirmative action programs were constitutional and could be implemented legally.

The dispute over the nature of affirmative action and its consideration of race/ethnicity did not end with the *Bakke* ruling. The next important court case regarding higher education admissions was decided in 1996 with *Hopwood v. Texas*.

Hopwood v. Texas

In deciding *Hopwood*, the 5th Circuit Court of Appeals ruled against race-conscious affirmative action policies in higher education admissions, thus nullifying the U.S. Supreme Court's *Bakke* ruling in the three states in the 5th Circuit: Texas, Louisiana, and Mississippi.[3] The White, female

---

[3] Much legal debate ensued after the 5th Circuit Court issued this opinion. Many legal scholars argued that the 5th Circuit did not have the authority to overrule the U.S. Supreme Court (Torres, 2003).

plaintiff in the case, Cheryl Hopwood, argued that she had been discriminated against by the University of Texas Law School's admissions system. *Hopwood*'s three-judge panel prohibited the use of race-conscious admissions criteria to achieve diversity at the law school, concluding that a state's interest in acquiring a diverse student body was not legally compelling enough to justify an admissions program like the one at the law school. However, even though the 5th Circuit struck down the diversity rationale for affirmative action, it maintained that a remedial justification could still serve a compelling interest. Race/ethnicity could be used in admissions decisions only when colleges and universities were trying to remedy the present effects of past institutional discrimination (Greve, 1999). The University of Texas appealed the case to the U.S. Supreme Court. Because the Justices declined to review the case, the ruling was upheld, but only in the 5th Circuit. *Hopwood* was the first successful challenge to an affirmative action admissions program since *Bakke*. One year later, then-Texas Attorney General Dan Morales offered clarification on the *Hopwood* decision for the state, maintaining that its reach extended to programs outside of admissions, including financial aid, recruitment, and scholarships. Subsequent research on the impact of the decision concluded that *Hopwood* had a chilling effect on college access for Black and Hispanic[4] high school graduates in Texas (Dickson, 2004; Kain & O'Brien, 2001).

The University of Texas at Austin put a great deal of effort into implementing various policies and programs to help mitigate the effects of losing affirmative action. In addition, the Texas legislature passed House Bill 508—the Top Ten Percent Plan—guaranteeing "admission to the top 10% of a high school graduating class to any public higher education institution in the state" (Marin & Flores, 2008, p. 226).[5] However, once the U.S. Supreme Court issued its 2003 rulings effectively overturning *Hopwood*, then-president Larry Faulkner indicated that the university would work with the Texas legislature to resume affirmative action policies (University of Texas at Austin, 2003a). Having had the experience of operating without affirmative action, President Faulkner was eager to re-institute the policy. Dr. Bruce Walker, vice provost and director of admissions at UT Austin said at the time, "We have used race-neutral policies for seven years and still do not have a critical mass of African American or Hispanic students in our classrooms"

---

[4] In this chapter, for simplicity, we use the racial identifiers Black, White, Asian/Pacific Islander (API), Hispanic, and American Indian used in our key data set—the Integrated Postsecondary Education Data System (IPEDS). Where cited research uses different identifiers, we try to use the language of the cited research.
[5] The Top Ten Percent Plan served as the model for the percent plans implemented in California and Florida.

(University of Texas at Austin, 2003b). Currently, UT Austin continues to use both race-conscious admissions policies as well as the Top Ten Percent Plan (Chapa & Horn, 2007).[6]

Smith v. University of Washington

In *Smith v. University of Washington* (2000), three White applicants who were not accepted to the University of Washington Law School sued the university. Even though Initiative 200 (passed in 1998) required the university to abandon the admissions program under question in the suit, the case moved forward. A symbolic victory came for affirmative action supporters in December 2000 when the 9th Circuit Court of Appeals ruled that the Law School's affirmative action program was constitutional. In 2001, the U.S. Supreme Court let stand the lower court's ruling in *Smith* (Gose & Schmidt, 2001).

Johnson v. Board of Regents of the University of Georgia

Another important affirmative action case is *Johnson v. Board of Regents of the University of Georgia* (2001). At the time of the ruling, 6% of the University of Georgia's students were African American in a state in which African Americans made up 25% of the state population (Walsh, 2001). In 2001, the three-judge panel of the 11th Circuit Court of Appeals[7] upheld a district court ruling in favor of three White women against University of Georgia's affirmative action plan (Firestone, 2001). The University was using a point-based system that automatically awarded "bonus" points to non-White and male applicants rather than conducting an individualized review of each application, which the 11th Circuit Court of Appeals found to be unconstitutional. The University of Georgia decided not to appeal the ruling. *Johnson* struck down the University's point-based system that awarded a fixed number of points for students of color as well as for nearly a dozen other factors such as first-generation college student status (Walsh, 2001); this seemed to pave the way for the U.S. Supreme Court's decisions in the University of Michigan cases.

---

[6] UT Austin is once again facing a court challenge to its affirmative action policy. The primary plaintiff is an 18-year-old White senior in high school from Sugar Land, Texas, who alleges that she was not accepted to UT Austin in March because of "racial preferences" (Kever, 2008, para. 1, line 2). The plaintiff's attorneys from the Project on Fair Representation argue that, per *Grutter*, UT Austin can only use affirmative action if race-neutral alternatives did not succeed in admitting a diverse student body. A U.S. District Court judge ruled in favor of UT Austin in 2009. At the time of this writing, the case remained on appeal to the 5th Circuit Court.

[7] The 11th Circuit includes Alabama, Florida, and Georgia.

Soon after *Johnson*, the U.S. Supreme Court finally agreed to hear a case about affirmative action in higher education; in fact, it heard two: *Gratz v. Bollinger* (2003) and *Grutter v. Bollinger* (2003).

Gratz v. Bollinger and *Grutter v. Bollinger*

The plaintiffs in *Gratz* and *Grutter* were White applicants who felt they would have been admitted to the University of Michigan had it not been for the consideration of race/ethnicity in the institution's admissions decisions; Jennifer Gratz sued regarding the undergraduate admissions policy and Barbara Grutter regarding the law school admissions policy. Overall, the June 2003 decisions in *Gratz* and *Grutter* reaffirmed the Court's ruling in *Bakke*, upholding the constitutionality of using race/ethnicity as a plus factor in higher education admissions decisions and emphasizing the importance of individualized, holistic reviews of applications. In *Gratz*, the Justices struck down the University of Michigan's race-conscious undergraduate admissions program and made clear that any type of quota or numerical point system that automatically awards points to minority applicants does not fall under the permissible standards regarding the use of race/ethnicity in admissions decisions. In its *Grutter* ruling, the Court affirmed that the educational benefits flowing from a diverse student body served a compelling state interest. The diversity rationale was the central justification in upholding the constitutionality of affirmative action. Writing for the majority in *Grutter*, Justice O'Connor explained: "The Law School's educational judgment that such diversity is essential to its educational mission is one to which we defer. The Law School's assessment that diversity will, in fact, yield educational benefits is substantiated by respondents and their *amici*" (*Grutter*, 2003, p. 328). In addition, the *Grutter* decision highlighted Justice O'Connor's idea that affirmative action should no longer be necessary in 25 years.[8] Ultimately, the ruling in *Grutter* invalidated the 5th Circuit's ruling in *Hopwood*. The *Grutter* decision thus underscored the importance—and legal viability—of the diversity rationale for affirmative action in college and university admissions. This justification seems to have wider appeal than the remedial justification, as even those who oppose affirmative action sometimes support the idea of diversity (see, e.g., Bush, 2003; Deardorff & Jones, 2007[9]). In fact, even the plaintiffs in *Gratz v. Bollinger* did not contest

---

[8] In O'Connor's words: "We expect that 25 years from now, the use of racial preferences will no longer be necessary to further the interest approved today" (*Grutter*, 2003, p. 343).

[9] Deardorff and Jones's (2007) survey of southern and midwestern colleges showed that among the southern schools although administrators generally did not support or agree with the University of Michigan decisions, they all agreed that race plays a significant role in our society, and administrators at all schools reported that diversity was important.

the importance of diversity to higher education. In addition, the *Grutter* court emphasized that institutions should engage in a holistic review of applicants, within which they consider both quantitative (e.g., high school grade point average) and qualitative (e.g., extracurricular activities) assessments of the applicant's qualifications for admission.

Parents Involved in Community Schools v. Seattle School District No. 1, et al.

Extending outside of higher education are several court cases involving K–12 race-conscious student assignment plans in public schools. Although these cases are important primarily for the K–12 arena, we discuss *Parents Involved in Community Schools v. Seattle School District No. 1, et al.* briefly insofar as it is relevant to higher education. In 2007 the U.S. Supreme Court took up the issue of voluntary race-conscious student assignment in public schools when it agreed to hear *Parents Involved in Community Schools v. Seattle School District No. 1* and *Meredith v. Jefferson County Board of Education.*[10] The Court had changed significantly in its composition since the 2003 University of Michigan cases. Chief Justice William Rehnquist had died and been replaced by similarly conservative Chief Justice John Roberts, who was appointed by President George W. Bush. Perhaps more significantly, Justice Sandra Day O'Connor retired, and her position was filled by Justice Samuel Alito. Justice O'Connor had been known as a moderate within a divided court and was often the swing vote in contentious cases, such as *Grutter*. By contrast, Justice Alito was expected to align with his conservative colleagues on the high court. It was not surprising, then, when the Supreme Court ruled that voluntary racial integration plans in place in school districts in Seattle and Louisville were unconstitutional (Korrell, 2007). However, it left *Grutter* standing and, in fact, supported the idea that diversity is a compelling interest in higher education. Nevertheless, efforts at the state level have been, and continue to be, undermining *Grutter*. It is to that issue the chapter now turns.

Curbing Affirmative Action State by State: Executive Orders and Ballot Measures

The state shall not discriminate against, or grant preferential treatment to, any individual or group on the basis of race, sex, color, ethnicity, or national origin in the operation of public employment, public education, or public contracting.

---

[10] These cases were combined by the U.S. Supreme Court as *Parents Involved in Community Schools v. Seattle School District No. 1, et. al.,* 127 S.Ct. 2738 (2007).

The above language formed the primary text of state ballot initiatives seeking to curb the use of affirmative action in public institutions in California (1996), Washington (1998), Michigan (2006), and Nebraska (2008). The initiative passed in all four states.[11] Similar ballot initiatives recently were proposed in four additional states. In Arizona, Missouri, and Oklahoma, the initiatives did not make it onto the 2008 ballot (Blank, 2008; Hoberock, 2008). Perhaps the most interesting development was in Colorado where the initiative was defeated by a narrow margin. Those behind these campaigns, however, intend to pursue similar ballot initiative campaigns in these and other states in the coming years (Bassett, 2008). Regardless of the official standing of these campaigns, examination of the racial representation in the state systems of higher education is important to understand the context of the battle in these targeted states.

In this section we examine how the initiatives passed in California, Washington, and Michigan, as well as the Executive Order banning affirmative action in Florida, have affected or may affect diversity and opportunity in higher education.[12] We then discuss the five states targeted by anti–affirmative action campaigns in 2008.

California
Spurred on by then University of California (UC) Regent Ward Connerly,[13] in 1995 the Regents of the University of California voted to bar the consideration of race/ethnicity in admissions decisions in the UC system by approving SP-1.[14] California's Proposition 209 soon followed. Known by proponents as the California Civil Rights Initiative (CCRI), Proposition 209 was a ballot initiative for a constitutional amendment to abolish all "preferences"[15] based on race, ethnicity, and sex. Even though the Proposition

---

[11] Once passed, such legislation is very difficult to undo. Not even the Supreme Court rulings in *Gratz* and *Grutter* overturned California's Proposition 209 or Washington's Initiative 200.

[12] We do not include Nebraska in this analysis of states with affirmative action bans; it is too soon after the vote to know what the effect will be.

[13] Ward Connerly was cofounder of the American Civil Rights Institute, a national non-profit organization that opposes affirmative action; he currently serves as the Institute's president (see www.acri.org/index.html).

[14] Because this chapter focuses on college and university admissions, we address SP-1, which eliminated affirmative action in UC admissions policy. SP-2, which eliminated affirmative action in UC hiring and contracting, was passed simultaneously, but is not relevant for our discussion.

[15] We place "preferences" in quotes because it is a controversial term used predominantly by those opposed to affirmative action. We do not interpret affirmative action as "preferences." In keeping with the ruling in *Grutter* (2003), we view race/ethnicity as one possible factor among many in the admissions process.

never mentioned affirmative action by name, its effect was to eliminate affirmative action in higher education admissions (as well as in other state programs). Proposition 209 passed with 54% of the vote (Chávez, 1998). Opponents of the amendment challenged its constitutionality in court, but in 1997 the U.S. Supreme Court let stand the ruling by the 9th Circuit Court of Appeals that upheld Proposition 209 (Lederman, 1997). The impact on California's public college student population was felt almost immediately and is visible to this day. In fall 1998, the flagship University of California campus, Berkeley, reported a 52% decrease in the number of Black and Hispanic first-year students for the first class admitted without affirmative action. Because of this, Black and Hispanic students made up only 9.9% of the first-year class, in comparison with 20.7% the previous year (Healy, 1998). At Berkeley's law school, there was only one Black student in the entering class during 1997–1998. In partial response to the negative attention given to the University of California system, in 2001 the Regents voted to rescind their ban on affirmative action (Schevitz, 2001). Because of Proposition 209, however, the Regents' change of heart was entirely symbolic and therefore did little to stem the rollback of students of color in the University of California system, especially the most selective campuses. Contreras (2005), for example, examined the effects of Proposition 209 on college access at three University of California campuses: Los Angeles, Davis, and Riverside. Using "parity" as a measure of access (a ratio comparing admissions rates to proportional representation in the K–12 system), Contreras found that although this ratio did not change for Asian American and White students, significant declines were experienced by African American, Chicano, and Latino students. That is, she found significant underrepresentation of these groups at all three campuses studied. Further, consider that UCLA's first-year class in the fall of 1997 had 221 African American students; by fall 2006, it included fewer than half that amount, only 100 (Leonhardt, 2007, p. 78).

These examples from previous research set the groundwork for our examination of the admissions patterns in the states without affirmative action. Since the state of California has had an affirmative action ban in place the longest, we can examine potential impacts of the loss of race-conscious admissions policies as well as institutional attempts to address such a loss. Examining enrollment data for first-time, degree-seeking undergraduates from 1994 to 2005 for the two most selective UC campuses—Berkeley and Los Angeles—yields trends that corroborate evidence of a clear impact in 1998, the first year the full class was admitted without considering the race/ethnicity of applicants (Figures 1 and 2). At the same time, significant decreases in UC-Berkeley Black and Hispanic enrollment were observed

Figure 1. First-Time, Degree-Seeking Undergraduates at UC-Berkeley, by Race/Ethnicity, 1994–2005

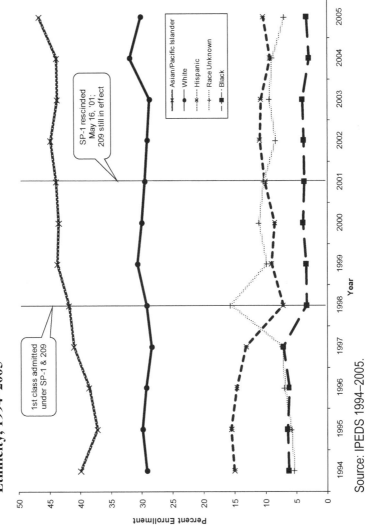

Source: IPEDS 1994–2005.

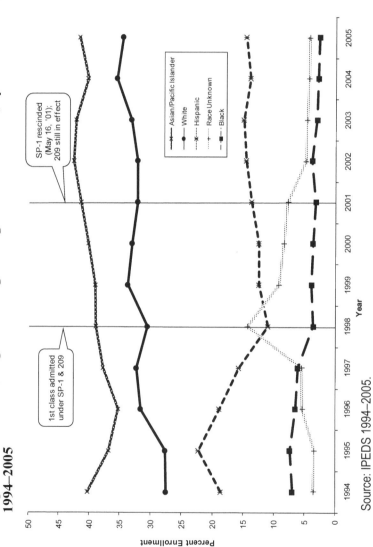

Figure 2: First-Time, Degree-Seeking Undergraduates at UCLA, by Race/Ethnicity, 1994–2005

Source: IPEDS 1994–2005.

(noted previously). White and Asian/Pacific Islander (API) student enrollment increased, but by less than 2 percentage points. Interestingly, the proportion of students declining to state their race/ethnicity more than doubled—from 7% in 1997 to 16% in 1998; by 2005 this number was back to 1997 levels. While difficult to say with absolute certainty who made up the "race unknown" group during this critical time, the increase suggests a negative impact on applicant perceptions of how race/ethnicity is viewed by the institution.[16]

At UCLA, 1998 was also a critical year, with Hispanic and Black enrollments between 1997 and 1998 decreasing by 30% and 40%, respectively. The enrollment pattern for Hispanic students at UCLA is similar to that at Berkeley. In both cases, however, the decreases in enrollment began prior to 1997, with the sharpest decreases at UCLA beginning in 1995 and at Berkeley a year later, in 1996;[17] the enrollment share for Hispanic students had dropped by 50% prior to the loss of affirmative action. White students showed a loss of fewer than 2 percentage points and the proportion of APIs increased by 1 percentage point. Once again, however, an important part of the story is the increase in the proportion of students declining to state their race/ethnicity—at UCLA, that group increased from 5.5% in 1997 to over 14% in 1998. This group was approaching 1994 levels again by 2005.

While these enrollment changes provide examples of the impact of losing race-conscious affirmative action in higher education, overall trends are also significant. Although Berkeley and UCLA have made attempts to address the loss of race-conscious admissions policies (Chapa & Horn, 2007), it is clear their efforts have not yielded significant results. At both institutions, Hispanic and Black enrollments have yet to return to the levels observed prior to the implementation of SP-1 and Proposition 209. This is in the face of both increased programmatic efforts on the part of the institutions and increases in these populations in the state.

Washington

The next state-level challenge to affirmative action policy came in Washington two years after Proposition 209 passed in California. In 1998,

---

[16] For additional research discussing the increase in "race unknown" in the UC System; see, for example, Saenz, Oseguera, and Hurtado (2007).

[17] One possible explanation for this pattern of reduced Hispanic enrollment is that the passage of SP-1 in 1995 created a "chilling effect" on applications to UC. From 1995–1997, prior to the enforcement of Proposition 209 but after the passage of SP-1, applications to UC by Chicano/Latino and Black students fell by 5.8% and 7.7%, respectively (Karabel, 1998). These drops in applicants could easily be translated into decreases in enrollment among these groups, particularly because the number of applications from White and API students grew by over 10% during this same period (Karabel, 1998).

59% of Washington's voters approved Initiative 200 (I-200), a CCRI-like referendum banning the consideration of race and sex in public hiring, contracting, and college and university admissions. In assessing the impact I-200 had on the college application and enrollment decisions of high school seniors in Washington, Brown and Hirschman (2006) found that in the year following the passage of I-200, there was a significant decrease in the number of students of color applying to and enrolling in the University of Washington (the flagship public institution which bore almost the entire brunt of the effects of the initiative). It is this political context within which White applicants to the University of Washington Law School contested their rejection in the *Smith v. University of Washington* case (discussed previously).

Our analysis of University of Washington data suggests similar results and reveals additional patterns. Figure 3 shows results from IPEDS enrollment data analysis for first-time, degree-seeking undergraduates at the University of Washington from 1994 to 2005. We observe interesting changes for Washington that are different from those at California's flagship institutions. While the fall of 1999 class was the first admitted under Initiative 200, important enrollment changes occurred as early as 1996. For example, White student enrollment during this period was at its maximum of 68% in 1995 but began to decrease as early as 1996 and has yet to return to 1995 levels. During approximately the same time, the "race unknown" category witnessed large increases that began in 1997, two years before a race-neutral admissions policy was required by the University of Washington. Interestingly, it appears that increases and decreases in the "race unknown" category since 1997 are mirrored by the changes in percent White enrollment. While it is impossible to know whether the students in the unknown category are White students, these patterns support this possibility, suggesting that, in fact, White enrollment decreases were not as large as the percent White measurements might suggest.

Similar to the patterns exhibited in California, starting in 2000 Asian/Pacific Islander student enrollment increased after the implementation of I-200 (from 25% to a high of 30%) and Black and Hispanic student shares dropped by over one-third. Black enrollment from 1999 through 2005 stayed at the 1999 levels, while the Hispanic share recovered slightly by 2003 to pre-1999 levels. What is different at the University of Washington is the consistently lower shares overall (and over time) for both Black and Hispanic students compared with the California institutions.

Florida

Florida was the next state to have an anti–affirmative action ballot campaign. Connerly and the American Civil Rights Institute (ACRI) had

Figure 3: First-Time, Degree-Seeking Undergraduates at the University of Washington, by Race/Ethnicity, 1994–2005

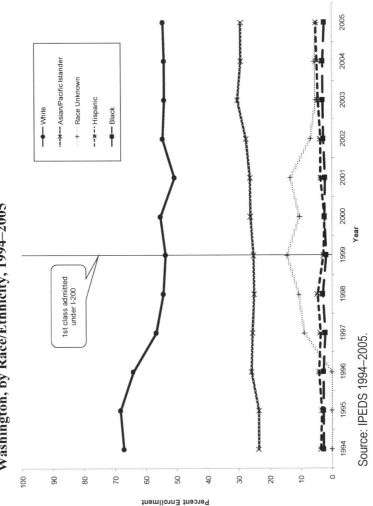

Source: IPEDS 1994–2005.

begun collecting petition signatures to get such an initiative on the 2000 ballot. However, these plans were derailed when, in November 1999, Governor Jeb Bush issued Executive Order 99-281, entitled One Florida. With regard to higher education, this order ended the consideration of race/ethnicity in state college and university admissions. As an alternative, Florida adopted the Talented 20 program, a percent plan ensuring admission of the top 20% of public high school graduates to Florida's state colleges and universities. Governor Bush's Executive Order is a state law that, like state ballot initiatives that are made into law, is unaffected by the Supreme Court rulings in *Gratz* and *Grutter*. An important distinction, however, between Florida's executive order and the ballot initiatives passed in other states is that in Florida, although public institutions of higher education cannot consider race/ethnicity in admissions decisions, they still can consider race/ethnicity in non-admissions practices and programs including recruitment, the awarding of scholarships, and outreach programs. As with California, enrollment changes were observed in Florida's flagship universities immediately following the implementation of One Florida (Marin & Lee, 2003).

Examining enrollment data for first-time, degree-seeking undergraduates from 1994 to 2005 at Florida's flagship institution—the University of Florida (UF)—we see that the first class admitted without affirmative action showed enrollment gains for White students and the greatest losses for Black students (Figure 4). Enrollment data for UF did not show the same increase in the "race unknown" group upon the loss of affirmative action that occurred at UCLA, Berkeley, and the University of Washington. However, in 2005 there was a three-fold increase in the "race unknown" category. The reasons for this change are unknown, but potentially important if this trend continues over time. These examples demonstrate that the impact in each state/institution of losing affirmative action can be unique. Similar to UCLA and Berkeley, Black enrollment at UF has yet to return to the 12% high in 2000 despite the institution's ability to use race/ethnicity in non-admissions policies and practices (e.g., recruitment, scholarships, etc.) and the implementation of the Talented 20 percent plan used in place of race-conscious affirmative action in higher education admissions. Just as troubling is the flat enrollment share of Hispanic students despite a growing number of Hispanic students enrolling in Florida institutions of higher education, up from around 16% in 2001 to near 20% in 2005.[18]

---

[18] Authors' tabulation from IPEDS.

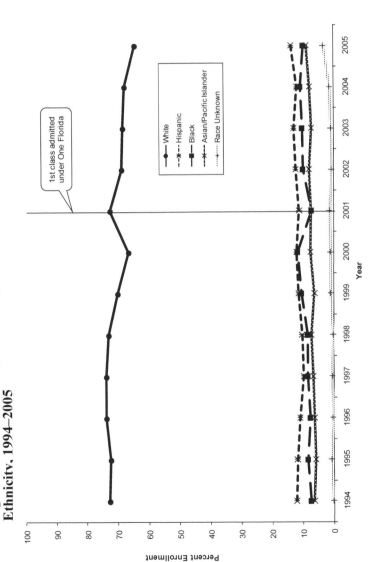

Figure 4: First-Time, Degree-Seeking Undergraduates at the University of Florida, by Race/Ethnicity, 1994–2005

1st class admitted under One Florida

White
Hispanic
Black
Asian/Pacific Islander
Race Unknown

Percent Enrollment

Year

Source: IPEDS 1994–2005.

Michigan

The next state vote on affirmative action was in Michigan. The political campaign for Proposal 2, once again spearheaded by Connerly of ACRI, was announced the day the U.S. Supreme Court issued its decisions in the University of Michigan cases. On the ballot in 2006, Proposal 2 passed with 58% of the vote. The impact it is having on Michigan's public institutions of higher education will become clearer in time as researchers observe application, admission, and enrollment rates. However, both the University of Michigan and Michigan State University reported decreased percentages in freshmen of color for fall 2007 (Baker, 2007). In addition, higher education officials in Michigan are struggling to find ways to preserve diversity in their public institutions. As Wayne State University Law School Dean Frank Wu expressed,

> What do we do if we're serious about racial integration, diversity and the competitiveness of this nation in a global economy? What Prop 2 did was eliminate one method of dealing with these issues, but it doesn't take away the urgency of the issue. (quoted in Erb, 2007, para. 5)

Although opponents of Proposal 2 brought a lawsuit challenging its constitutionality, U.S. District Court Judge David Lawson dismissed the lawsuit in March 2008 because, he argued, the plaintiffs did not make their case that the initiative intended to discriminate against people of color (Jaschik, 2008).

Ballot Initiatives in Five Targeted States

Continuing the trend of challenges to affirmative action at the state level, five states debated state ballot initiative proposals for November 2008—Arizona, Colorado, Missouri, Nebraska, and Oklahoma. Opponents of the initiative in Arizona believed that Connerly and ACRI chose Arizona because it has such a large immigrant population, and he had hoped the initiative would capitalize on related racial and ethnic divisions (Bello, 2007). For his part, Connerly maintained that racial tensions already existed in Arizona, regardless of the ballot initiative campaign (Benson, 2007). Late in August 2008, Proposition 104's supporters withdrew the initiative proposal. Many signatures on the petition to put Proposition 104 on the ballot had been declared invalid by the Arizona Secretary of State, and initiative proponents were unable to validate the signatures before the ballot deadline. Max McPhail, director of the initiative campaign, pledged to bring this issue up for a vote in 2010 (Fischer, 2008).

In Colorado, Amendment 46 was defeated by a narrow margin; 50.7% voted against and 49.2% voted for it (Denverpost.com, 2008). During the campaign, sponsors of Amendment 46 collected over 128,000 petition signatures, well over the 76,047 valid signatures needed to get the initiative on the ballot (Gandy, 2008). Like other targeted states, Colorado has relatively few students of color at its state colleges and universities, with about 72% of its 2005 first-time, degree-seeking college enrollment identifying as White.[19] This is especially true of the flagship institution, the University of Colorado at Boulder, which, in 2005 had only 1.4% African American students, 6.3% Hispanic students, and 6.5% Asian students.[20] The defeat of Amendment 46 in Colorado marked the first time such an initiative failed to pass at the state level. There are several theories as to why Coloradans voted to defeat Amendment 46 including the governor's public opposition to the measure, President Obama's strong support in Colorado, the state's large Hispanic population, the confusing language of the ballot initiative, an unprecedented grassroots effort against it, television and radio advertisements, and a state ballot that included 13 other ballot measures. However, until voter beliefs and attitudes about Amendment 46 and affirmative action in Colorado are studied, we will not be able to pinpoint the reasons definitively (Slevin, 2008). While the chilling effect of the initiative campaign itself in Colorado will be difficult to assess fully,[21] one direct result of the vote is that public institutions in Colorado can continue to have race- and sex-conscious equal opportunity programs in public education, employment, and contracting.

Missouri took an unusual approach to challenging the anti–affirmative action ballot initiative proposed there. Secretary of State Robin Carnahan and Attorney General Jay Nixon challenged the language of the proposed initiative. They argued that the language should reflect its actual purpose, which was to ban affirmative action. Had the initiative made it onto the ballot, it is likely that Missouri's ballot initiative language would have been different than the other states. Although the language suggested by Carnahan was challenged in court by the initiative's proponents and the county circuit judge struck down Carnahan's language, the language the judge put in place was still more descriptive in mentioning affirmative action than the originally proposed initiative language (Schmidt, 2007). The new ballot

---

[19] Authors' tabulation from IPEDS.

[20] Authors' tabulation from IPEDS.

[21] For example, the University of Colorado at Boulder has changed its undergraduate admissions processes to minimize the use of race and ethnicity in the decision-making process. This change is going forward even though Amendment 46 did not pass.

initiative language asked voters if the Missouri constitution should be amended to

> Ban state and local government affirmative action pro-
> grams that give preferential treatment in public contracting,
> employment or education based on race, sex, ethnicity or
> national origin, unless such programs are necessary to
> establish or maintain eligibility for federal funding or to
> comply with a court order. (Lieb, 2008, para. 13)

The issue of language is especially important because polls show that the wording of such initiatives affects how members of the public feel about them (*Inside Higher Ed*, 2008). However, we did not get the chance to assess whether the language of the Missouri initiative would have made a difference for voters in 2008. Although initiative proponents collected almost 170,000 petition signatures by the May 4 deadline—a sufficient number to make the ballot—they did not submit the signatures because it was likely that many of those signatures would not have been validated (Blank, 2008; Darnell, 2008; Franey, 2008). Despite this setback, Connerly was not dissuaded from pursuing this route in Missouri, stating, "this is a marathon not a sprint, and it's far from over" (quoted in Blank, 2008, para. 7). In fact, Connerly and others continue efforts to place similar anti–affirmative action initiatives on the ballot in Arizona and elsewhere.

In Nebraska, the anti–affirmative action initiative campaign, led by Doug Tietz, was successful in November 2008, passing with 58% of the vote (Gewertz, 2008). The Board of Regents at the state's flagship institution, University of Nebraska, had voted unanimously to oppose the initiative, citing concerns about the university's ability to increase diversity should the initiative pass (Associated Press, 2008). Proponents of affirmative action in Nebraska are worried that women and people of color will not continue to make progress in public education and hiring in the state. For example, schools and universities may need to adjust both hiring and admissions practices. Yet overall, students of color represent only 9% of the enrollment on the University of Nebraska's four campuses (Gewertz, 2008).

In Oklahoma, signature gatherers worked steadily during the fall of 2007 to get an anti–affirmative action initiative on the 2008 ballot. Oklahoma required approximately 138,970 signatures be filed with the secretary of state by December 10, 2007 (Hoberock, 2008). Initiative proponents submitted 141,184 signatures, but in February, Oklahoma's secretary of state, Susan Savage, reported the petition signatures included many duplicates. As a result, proponents withdrew the petition (Schmidt, 2008).

The Effect of Losing Affirmative Action on Student Enrollment

We now review data from several key states to examine possible challenges states may face if they are unable to use affirmative action yet wish to provide diverse experiences and environments in their selective flagship universities. Flagship universities in Texas, Michigan, and Oklahoma are important because of their different contexts. Texas was barred from using race/ethnicity under the *Hopwood* decision, moved to a "race-neutral" percent plan for admissions, and then resumed using race/ethnicity as a factor (in conjunction with the percent plan) after the *Gratz* and *Grutter* decisions in Michigan allowed its use. Michigan colleges and universities are now banned from using race/ethnicity due to the passage of Proposal 2. Finally, Oklahoma is one of those states that will likely be targeted again for future propositions. While their particular circumstances are very different from one another, these states provide a range of examples of bans or potential bans of affirmative action.

In the following analysis, we again use IPEDS data to consider student diversity at the flagship institutions and speculate on the potential impact of losing race-conscious admissions and/or other practices such as outreach and recruitment, financial aid, and other support services. This IPEDS data analysis is identical to the previous examples (California, Washington, and Florida). However, in addition, we also ***compare*** the selected states' flagship institution enrollment of first-time, degree-seeking undergraduates by race/ethnicity from 1994 to 2005 to the same category of first-time students enrolled in all public and private 2- and 4-year higher education institutions in the entire state.

We refer to this comparison group as the "state-level enrollment." While there are several limitations to this comparison group, we believe it is suitable for our purposes.[22] Those in the comparison group have demonstrated they are college-ready and have a strong enough desire to receive some level of postsecondary education that they have enrolled. This

---

[22] This methodology results in state flagship institutions being "double counted" since they are included in the overall state numbers as well as shown individually. To test the impact of this choice, we calculated the state numbers both with and without the flagship institutions and, while the numbers did change marginally, the overall story did not. In addition, there were strong substantive reasons for including the flagship institution in with the rest of the state. For instance, the state flagship institution sets the admissions tone for the rest of the state and is the most selective part of the system. If we chose to exclude the flagship from our state calculations, this could bias our picture of the state pool by excluding an important component of the overall pool—those who were attending the very institutions for whom race-conscious policies matter the most.

is an advantage over the more traditional comparison group of high school graduates in the state since many of them may not have the desire or the basic qualifications to enroll in a postsecondary institution. In addition, the public and private institutions in the state are likely to enroll both in-state and out-of-state students, which is a pool more like the one at the flagship institution than at state high schools, with only in-state residents.[23] However, by using this comparison group over the pool of high school graduates we lose the opportunity to compare the incoming freshman cohorts to the state pool as a whole (which provides potential recruitment opportunities for the flagship institution or shortcomings in preparation by the primary and secondary school systems). In effect, we are comparing the enrollments of a flagship public university in a state to the pool of students most eligible for admission to that flagship (particularly in states with less selective flagships among which are those with proposed ballot initiatives). Thus, any changes in the enrollments may be less affected by demographic or school system changes, but more by the aggregate admissions decisions of the states' institutions of higher education.

Texas

We begin by considering the University of Texas at Austin. Figure 5 shows the percent enrollment of first-time, degree-seeking undergraduates by race/ethnicity at UT Austin from 1994 to 2005. Notice that the overall share of White students at UT Austin peaked in 1997, the year the *Hopwood* decision outlawed the use of race/ethnicity in admissions, but declined steadily from that point to about 55% in 2005. Hispanic enrollments dropped nearly 2 percentage points in 1997, but increased steadily to about 18% by 2005. During this same time, Asian enrollments increased to a maximum of about 19% in 2001 and subsequently leveled out to a share equal to their Hispanic peers of about 18%. Black student enrollment dropped to an all-time low of just under 3% in 1997, but has nearly recovered to the levels seen in 1994 (about 5%).

When we compare first-time, degree-seeking undergraduate enrollment at UT to the state-level enrollment of the same population, we see that White students at UT Austin have been consistently overrepresented. During the entire period examined, Figures 5 and 6 show enrollments of about 64% and 55% for 1994 and 2005, respectively, compared to 59% and 51% for the rest

---

[23] While this may not be true of all flagship institutions—since some are likely to draw more heavily than others from out-of-state applicants—it is likely that the flagship will be the largest public draw in the state.

Figure 5: First-Time, Degree-Seeking Undergraduates at UT Austin, by Race/Ethnicity, 1994–2005

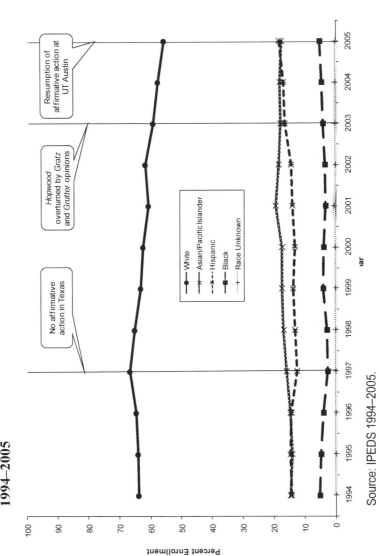

Source: IPEDS 1994–2005.

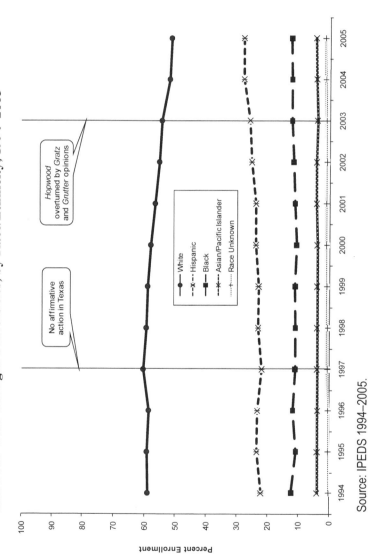

Figure 6: First-Time, Degree-Seeking Undergraduates in Texas Public and Private Two- and Four-Year Colleges/Universities, by Race/Ethnicity, 1994–2005

Source: IPEDS 1994–2005.

of the state. However, the most notable enrollment trend both overall and at UT Austin has been a pattern of a decreasing proportion of White students along with an increasing proportion of non-White students attending postsecondary institutions. Simultaneously, Hispanics and Blacks are underrepresented at UT Austin when compared to the state-level enrollment by approximately 10 and 5 percentage points, respectively (representing nearly a 30% and 50% underrepresentation), while APIs are overrepresented by about 10 percentage points (representing nearly a 200% overrepresentation). The changes in enrollment shares for Hispanic and Black students at UT Austin closely mirror the changes in state-level college enrollments. It is interesting to note that as of 2005, the proportion of Hispanic and API students at UT Austin was the same (approximately 18%) while their share in state-level college enrollment differed by over 20 percentage points (~28% and 5%, respectively).

This over- and underrepresentation does not seem to have been a result of the elimination of affirmative action since it existed during the time race-conscious policies were in place. However, the earlier trends have persisted through the extensive institutional efforts implemented by UT (see Marin & Flores, 2008) to mitigate the impact of *Hopwood*. This suggests that there may be more at work than simply the loss of race-conscious policies. One possibility may be that the University is simply achieving the outcomes it intends—the overrepresentation of White and Asian students and an underrepresentation of Black and Hispanic students. Another possibility is that as affirmative action was taken away as a tool for increasing access, UT Austin deployed all possible resources simply to maintain the status quo. Thus, by focusing attention on the issue of race, the loss of affirmative action forced UT Austin to find other ways to mitigate the potential loss of minority enrollment share.

Michigan

The University of Michigan, Ann Arbor is the state's flagship institution and is an example of an institution that has demonstrated its commitment to admitting a diverse student body through its defense of its race-conscious admissions policies. Despite this commitment, however, the University of Michigan (U-M) is facing challenging trends. Figure 7 shows that the shares of first-time, degree-seeking undergraduates for most racial/ethnic groups have been relatively stable. White students were about 65% of the student population from 1994 to 1999; there was a drop in 2000 to approximately 60%, and a slow recovery back to approximately 65% by 2005. Asian enrollment shares have been relatively stable at around 12%; Black shares

Figure 7: First-Time, Degree-Seeking Undergraduates at the University of Michigan, by Race/Ethnicity, 1994–2005

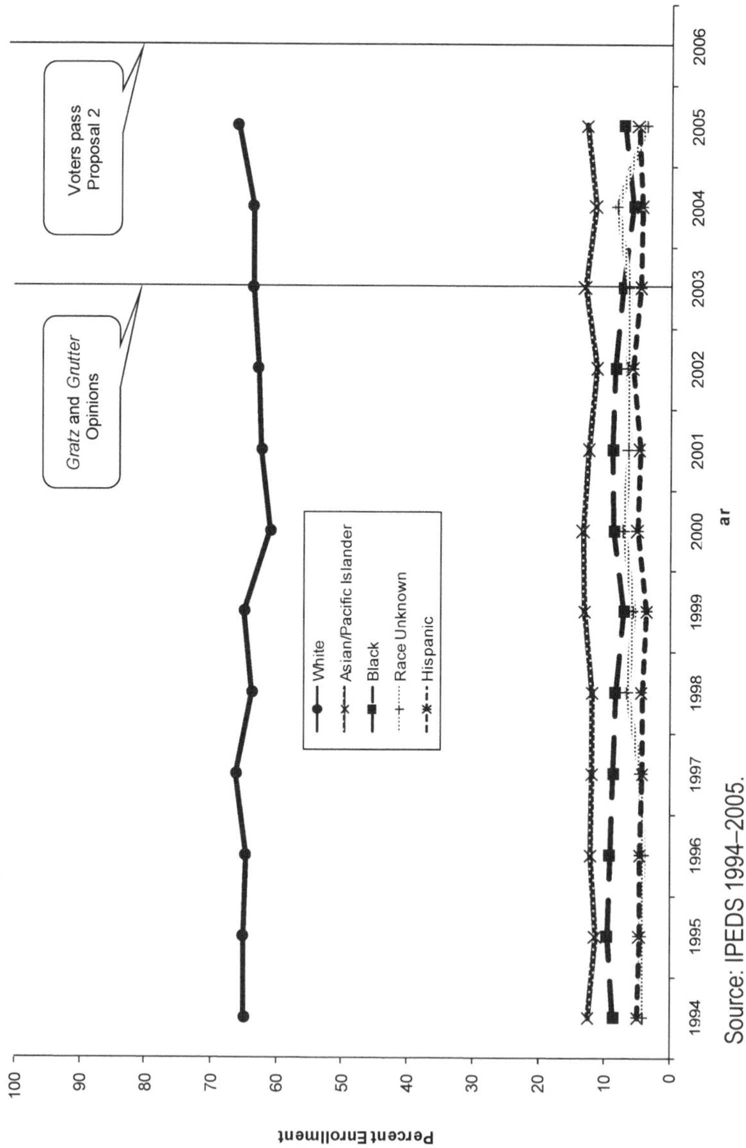

Source: IPEDS 1994–2005.

have decreased slightly during this period, from about 9% to approximately 7%; and Hispanic shares have remained stable at approximately 5%. The only other group to show a sustained trend is the "unknown" category, which has increased from approximately 4.5% pre-1998 to between 6.5% and 7% after 1998, with most of that increase happening between 1997 and 1998. Comparing its enrollment of first-time, degree-seeking undergraduates from 1994 to 2005 to state-level enrollment, White students are under-represented at U-M (Figures 7 and 8). However, while the share of White students at the state level has been steadily decreasing over time, the share of White students at U-M was stable or slightly decreasing until 2000 when it began a steady increase. This contrasting trend between the state as a whole and U-M has resulted in a substantial narrowing in the gap of under-representation for White students at U-M from about 16 percentage points in 1994 to just under 7 percentage points in 2005. Furthermore, as of 2005, APIs and Hispanics were overrepresented at U-M by 10 and 2 percentage points, respectively (over 200% for API students and 60% for Hispanic students). However, Black students were underrepresented by nearly 7 percentage points or approximately 50%. This underrepresentation is even more disturbing when examining the long-term trends for the Black enrollment share in the state as a whole. While the Black enrollment share at U-M has remained stable or slightly decreased from 1994 to 2005, the Black enrollment share in the state has steadily increased from 9% to 14%. At U-M, there was no enrollment gap for Black students in 1994, but by 2005 that gap was 7 percentage points.

What does this mean? At the very least, this analysis of Texas and Michigan suggests that institutions have the ability to alter their enrollments relative to the available pool. This ability may be influenced by several possible factors including their admissions, recruitment, and financial aid policies, as well as the composition of the state's qualified applicant pool. At U-M, this control has resulted in the consistent underrepresentation of White and Black students relative to the available pool and the overrepresentation of API and Hispanic students. This situation could be thought of as analogous to many Southern K–12 school districts that are enforcing desegregation orders and show much lower levels of school segregation when compared to the residential segregation in the district by simply redistributing available students (Reardon & Yun, 2005). Here we see that U-M is deviating from the state-level enrollment shares by disproportionately enrolling API and Hispanic students when compared to their Black and White peers. If the differing racial composition of students is the result of deliberate policy decisions, there could be many possible explanations, one of which is the "critical mass" argument, which suggests that for the benefits of diverse interactions to be realized, enough individuals of a particular group must be present to avoid tokenism and create the environment necessary for such benefits to be self-sustaining (Regents of the University of Michigan, 2003).

In the case of U-M, these data cannot give us insight into why such compositions have been consistently maintained (e.g., critical mass). However, it appears that there may well be a pool of college-ready students already seeking to attend school in-state (those represented by state-level enrollment data) who the institution could recruit and admit to achieve the diversity for which they are searching. Over the next few years we will need to track enrollment changes at U-M to better examine the impact of Proposal 2 on its student body. For example, we can see if the underrepresentation of White students continues to decline, the underrepresentation of Black students continues to increase, and/or the overrepresentation of API and Hispanic students persists.

Oklahoma

The University of Oklahoma (OU), the flagship institution in a state targeted for an anti–affirmative action ballot initiative, has experienced (with small variations) trends which are very different from the other states we have examined. For example, Figure 9 shows an increase in the share of White first-time, degree-seeking undergraduates enrolled, a decrease in the enroll-ment of Black students, and very little change in Asian and Hispanic enroll-ments. Figure 10 presents White state-level enrollment data that reveal a shift from the underrepresentation of White students at the University of Oklahoma campus (72% at OU compared to 75% in the state as of 1994) to their overrepresentation relative to the state pool (77% at OU compared to 68% in the state by 2005). This change has resulted in a 12 percentage point swing from under- to overrepresentation for White students in just 11 years.[24] Similarly, in 1994 Black students' share at OU and in the state as a whole was 9% for both (proportional). By 2005 the Black student share at OU fell to 5% and the Black share in the state increased to 11%. This shift represents more than a 50% drop in representation at OU relative to Black student enrollment in the state. These shifts are important since they suggest a change either in admissions philosophy or in the pool of available Black and White applicants to OU. Either trend should be of concern to those interested in diversity and opportunity in state flagships because it signals an important departure from previous practice that is not clearly understood.

---

[24] In 1994, White students were underrepresented at OU compared to the state by 3 percentage points; as of 2004 they were overrepresented by 9 percentage points, thus the swing of 12 percentage points from under- to overrepresentation.

Figure 8: First-Time, Degree-Seeking Undergraduates Enrolled in Michigan Public and Private Two- and Four-Year Colleges/Universities, by Race/Ethnicity, 1994–2005

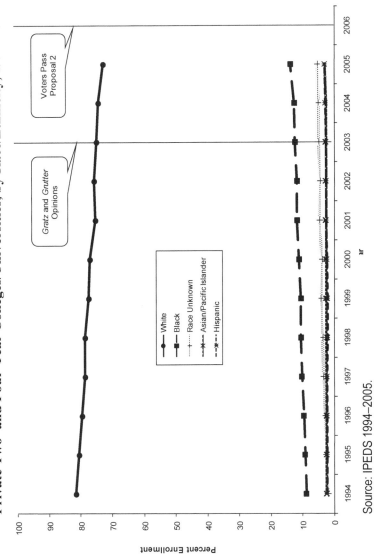

Source: IPEDS 1994–2005.

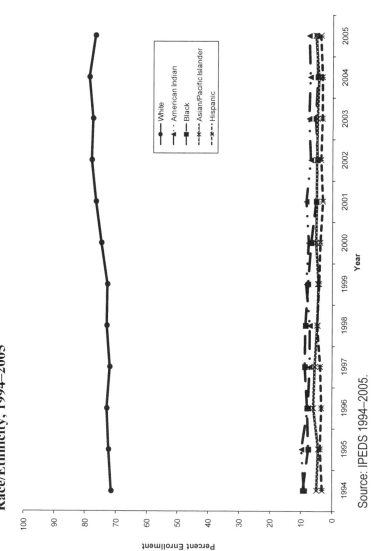

Figure 9: First-Time, Degree-Seeking Undergraduates at the University of Oklahoma, by Race/Ethnicity, 1994–2005

Source: IPEDS 1994–2005.

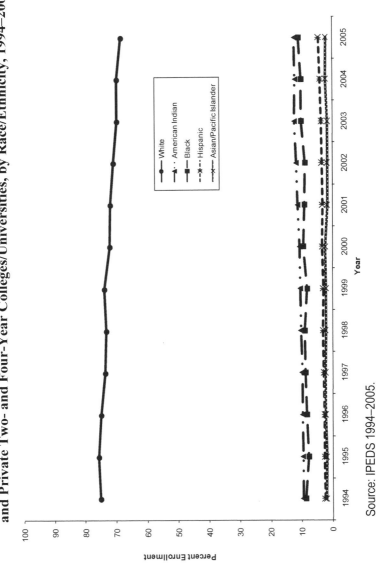

Figure 10: First-Time, Degree-Seeking Undergraduates Enrolled in Oklahoma Public and Private Two- and Four-Year Colleges/Universities, by Race/Ethnicity, 1994–2005

Source: IPEDS 1994–2005.

The story for American Indian students is similar to that of Black students. In 1994 there was almost no gap between their presence at the university and their presence in state-level enrollment (about 9% in both). However, by 2005, as the American Indian share increased about 2.5 percentage points in the overall pool, their presence at OU decreased to 7.7%, opening a gap of approximately 4 percentage points and an approximately 30% reduction compared to their presence in the state pool. Hispanic and API students are present in small numbers at OU (4% and 6%, respectively, in 2005). Hispanics are slightly underrepresented at the university relative to state-level enrollment, while API students are overrepresented by approximately 150%. With such small numbers in these groups it is difficult to say whether these differences are due to decisions being made on the campus or simply small variations in the pool or enrollment choices. In general, where differential enrollment in state flagship institutions becomes most apparent is either in the under or overrepresentation of the dominant racial minority group or in instances when the state share of a particular group is changing relatively quickly, particularly when those changes are not reflected in flagship enrollments.

It is important to note that these enrollment changes between White and Black students are occurring despite the fact that the University of Oklahoma is not a particularly selective institution. That the university is currently unable to enroll Black and American Indian students in the same proportion as they are represented in the rest of the state, even though they were able to do so just 11 years ago, suggests a more complicated story behind these numbers related to institutional decision making, state demographics, and political considerations. Regardless of the specific reasons for these changes, if the university is unable or unwilling to maintain the shares of minority students they had just a few years ago *with* race-conscious policies available to them, what impact would losing those tools have? This question is particularly critical in light of the fact that the loss of affirmative action would extend to race-conscious scholarships as well as outreach and recruitment, just a few of the practices on which the university might rely to maintain or foster a diverse student body.

In some ways, Oklahoma is a good exemplar for the situation found in the states that were targeted for (Arizona, Colorado, Missouri) or passed (Nebraska) ballot initiatives in 2008. In each of these states, White students make up the largest share of students (in Colorado, Missouri, and Nebraska, the overwhelming share), and in each of the states White students are overrepresented in their flagship institutions by varying amounts. Where the demographics of the state higher education enrollments are changing (most in Arizona and least in Nebraska), the overrepresentation of Whites and underrepresentation of the major racial group (Hispanic, Black, and/or American Indian students) at their flagship institutions is becoming exacerbated. (In general, API students in all these states remain either proportionally represented or overrepresented.)

Ultimately, given our review of the current status of affirmative action in higher education admissions and related enrollment analyses, we are skeptical that affirmative action will no longer be needed to further the goals of diversity and equality of opportunity in higher education by 2028. In our examination of how several colleges and universities have fared without affirmative action, the results are not encouraging. In particular, under-represented student access seems to be hurt by the elimination of these policies, with minority shares falling after the implementation of these bans. Because the college-eligible minority population in most states has continued to increase, even where the number of minority enrollees at state flagships recovers to pre–affirmative-action-ban levels, minorities end up even more underrepresented as a share of the eligible population than they were before the ban. Given these negative results on enrollment, the apparent effects of losing race-conscious policies are likely to impede the institution's ability to create the conditions necessary to foster the educational benefits of diversity.

Guidelines for Institutions of Higher Education

Given the large variation in institutional enrollment changes after the loss of affirmative action policies, it is difficult to predict the results of losing affirmative action on any particular institution. Further research in this area should include institutional-level case studies of universities that vary in selectivity, analyses that disaggregate racial/ethnic groups into subgroups, analyses of graduate and professional school enrollments, and the examination of the changes to the "race unknown" category. Given this uncertainty and the lack of data, it becomes necessary for institutions to seek out a variety of responses within the legal and policy frameworks both for when the use of race/ethnicity is allowable and when it is not.

Colleges and universities operating under state bans on affirmative action need to find alternative ways to recruit and admit students if they are interested in educating a diverse student body and providing greater opportunity. For example, Leonhardt (2007) noted that after UCLA witnessed large declines in its enrollment of students of color after Proposition 209, the university turned to a special program sponsored and run through a private Black alumni group, wholly separate from the university. As a result, UCLA enrolled more students of color in Fall 2007; there was a 13% increase from 2006 in applications by Black students and the rate of acceptance of Black applicants went from

11.5% to 16.2%. Such programs seem to circumvent the state bans and appear to be legal. Nevertheless, opponents of affirmative action likely will scrutinize such efforts very closely. Law professor and affirmative action critic Richard Sander has already requested UCLA's fall 2007 admissions records through the Freedom of Information Act (Leonhardt, 2007). Nevertheless, as Karabel (1999) has written, "alterations in admissions criterion [*sic*] and in process can mitigate the effects of measures such as Proposition 209, but they cannot eliminate them" (p. 112).

The Supreme Court rulings in *Gratz* and *Grutter* combined with the ongoing experiences of California, Washington, Florida, and Michigan have helped to delineate how states and institutions of higher education can craft their affirmative action policies or respond to bans on affirmative action. In response to the Seattle and Louisville decisions, the American Council on Education (ACE) pointed out that Chief Justice Roberts, writing for the majority, identified just two viable reasons for race-conscious admissions: first, in K–12 and higher education, to remedy the current effects of past institutional discrimination, and second, in higher education, to further diversity interests (Przypyszny & Tromble, 2007). Within these parameters, guiding points can be found for institutional practice from numerous sources (e.g., *Grutter*, 2003; Guess, 2007; O'Neil, 2008; Przypyszny & Tromble, 2007). Although the legal landscape surrounding affirmative action is often unpredictable, these guidelines follow current law.

Regarding institutions in the 45 states that can legally employ affirmative action programs in higher education, we know from *Gratz* and *Grutter* that institutions that choose to consider race/ethnicity in admissions decisions need to be cognizant of the following in order to comply with the high court's decisions:

- It is necessary to review student applications individually, taking into account quantitative as well as qualitative measures of student academic, social, and personal merit. Diversity may be taken into account when it is part of an institution's mission.

- Race/ethnicity can be considered as one qualification among many—that is, not as the sole or predominating factor but as a plus factor between two equally qualified applicants.

- Admissions policy cannot unreasonably constrain the rights of non-minority applicants.

- Institutions need to seriously (though not necessarily exhaustively) consider race-neutral alternatives before settling on admissions policies that take race/ethnicity into account.

- Institutions need to be careful about how they use the concept of "critical mass," making sure to connect it to the educational benefits of diversity.

- Institutions need to have a periodic process to review the policy or set up a sunset provision for the policy (*Grutter*, 2003; Joint Statement of Constitutional Law Scholars, 2003; O'Neil, 2008).

Although these guidelines will not work in states where affirmative action is banned, institutions in these states still have a number of options available for recruitment and outreach that are both legal and conscious of institutional missions regarding diversity, equality, and opportunity. In order to comply with state law, policies first need to be changed to make sure that race, ethnicity, color, sex, and national origin are not employed in admissions practices. Then institutions can focus on creative ways of reaching out to diverse students. Selective universities could benefit from less reliance on admissions metrics that are known to disadvantage minority students (such as standardized test scores) and develop more "holistic review" strategies that build on the growing social science evidence supporting the systematic consideration of noncognitive sources of academic, social, and personal merit in the admissions process (see Bowman, Chapter 8, this volume; Sedlacek, Burkum, et al., this volume; Burrus et al., this volume; powell et al. this volume).

Additional strategies for reaching out to diverse students could involve recruiting students earlier in their school careers, focusing on socioeconomic status, increasing student aid, and making sure that curricular offerings reflect diverse fields and scholarship. As already mentioned, private, external organizations such as alumni groups can work to recruit and fund diverse, underrepresented students. Although they are wary of such external programs, affirmative action opponents seem to grudgingly accept them (Guess, 2007). Finally, institutions that remain interested in increasing racial and ethnic diversity on campus even in the face of a state affirmative action ban will need to take actions to combat the negative sociopolitical climate that results when such an initiative is approved by voters. As the preceding figures illustrate, enrollment of students of color tends to decrease substantially after an anti–

affirmative action initiative passes. Students of color may find the vote to be symbolic of an unwelcoming environment for diversity.

Conclusion: Looking to the Future

Von Drehle (2007) examined what he called "the incredibly shrinking role of the Supreme Court" (p. 42) under Chief Justice John Roberts. As he reported, under Roberts's conservative leadership, the Supreme Court has heard fewer cases in a year than it has in each of the last 50 years. In addition, the editors of *The New York Times* (2008) maintained that the Supreme Court is slowly rolling back civil rights–era antidiscrimination policies related to race and sex. They wrote that "in recent years, the court's majority has been reading federal anti-discrimination laws far more narrowly than Congress intended" (*The New York Times*, 2008, para. 9). It is a bitterly divided Court, and the trend has been for the Justices to consider cases with a narrower scope than in years past. The addition of Justices Sonia Sotomayor and Elena Kagan will impact the Court as well. It was within this legal and political context that we undertook the analyses for this chapter, with the aim of making sense of the sometimes conflicting federal- and state-level affirmative action policies, especially in light of the latest state-level threats to affirmative action.

If anti–affirmative action ballot initiatives pass in increasing numbers, colleges and universities likely will face tremendous struggles to maintain or increase student diversity, as we have already seen in states that have banned affirmative action. In fact, a recent study posited that without affirmative action, the enrollment of underrepresented students of color at highly selective colleges and universities could drop by as much as 35% (Epple, Romano, & Sieg, 2008). Although state ballot initiatives may eliminate affirmative action programs in additional states, there remains a larger societal dispute about whether affirmative action is a policy that fosters diversity and equality of opportunity in the service of all Americans. In itself, the existence of state votes determining the fate of affirmative action will not go very far in deciding the larger moral and political questions surrounding whether affirmative action policy is indeed right or wrong (Moses, 2006). Further, simply allowing members of the public to vote on the issue does not mean that Americans have resolved the moral questions regarding affirmative action, nor does it mean that voters and others have learned what they need to know in order to make an informed vote. As Crenshaw (2007) notes,

the very perception that this trio of anti-affirmative
initiatives[25] constitutes a mortal wound to affirmative
action is premised on the appearance of a fair and
legitimate process by which affirmative action has been
presented, evaluated, and repudiated not only in the court
of popular opinion but in courts of law as well. (p. 124)

One thing is clear: Race-conscious affirmative action is legal in 45
states, and it is still an important tool for fostering both diversity and
opportunity in higher education. Will it still be needed in 2028? Our hope is
that widespread, meaningful equality of educational opportunity will exist
then, but our fear is that state ballot initiatives seeking to eliminate race-
conscious affirmative action programs will make it even harder to reach that
goal. Perhaps the most salient point is this: These anti–affirmative action
initiatives significantly decrease the chance for public educational
institutions to reach the ideal place about which Justice O'Connor wrote. As
our examination herein shows, higher education institutions currently are not
achieving meaningful racial/ethnic diversity and the anti–affirmative action
movement has made this more difficult. Consequently, the college and
university educational experiences of all students will suffer as equity in
higher educational opportunity remains elusive. This presents both a major
challenge and opportunity for the 21st century. Our analyses strongly
suggest that higher education leaders must take ownership of their
admissions decisions and develop more comprehensive admissions strategies
to promote diversity, equity, and opportunity.

Acknowledgments

The authors would like to note that a different version of this chapter
appeared in *Education Policy Analysis Archives*. The authors also would like
to thank Lauren Saenz for her able help with background research for the
chapter, as well as Catherine Horn and Angelo Ancheta for their insightful
feedback on earlier drafts.

References

Associated Press. (2008, January 18). NU opposes ban on affirmative action.
The Associated Press. Retrieved from http://www.kptm.com/Global/
story.asp?S=7743015&nav=menu606_2_4

---

[25] By "trio," Crenshaw is referring to the first three anti–affirmative action ballot initiatives
that had passed in California, Washington, and Michigan before her article was published.

Baker, J. (2007, November 15). Proposal 2: A year later. *The State News.* Retrieved from http://www.statenews.com/index.php/article/2007/11/proposal_2_one_year_later

Bassett, J. (2008, December 29). Connerly and Asher attempt another affirmative action ban in Missouri. *The Wilmington Journal.* Retrieved from http://www.wilmingtonjournal.com/News/article/article.asp?NewsID=93426&sID=33

Bello, M. (2007, December 27). Affirmative action may be on ballots. *USA Today.* Retrieved from http://www.usatoday.com/news/politics/2007-12-27-affirmative-action_N.htm

Benson, M. (2007, April 26). Group launches bid to ban affirmative action. *The Arizona Republic.* Retrieved from http://www.azcentral.com/news/articles/0426affirmativeaction0426-ONL.html

Blank, C. (2008, May 5). Affirmative action petition misses deadline. *St. Louis Post-Dispatch.* Retrieved from http://www.stltoday.com/stltoday/news/stories.nsf/missouristatenews/story/AB2BE2DB256DC6018625744000451E10?OpenDocument

Brown, S. K., & Hirschman, C. (2006). The end of affirmative action in Washington state and its impact on the transition from high school to college. *Sociology of Education, 79,* 106–130.

Bush, G. W. (2003, January 15). President Bush discusses Michigan affirmative action case. Retrieved from http://www.whitehouse.gov/news/releases/2003/01/

Chapa, J., & Horn, C. L. (2007). Is anything race neutral? Comparing "race-neutral" admissions policies at the University of Texas and the University of California. In G. Orfield, P. Marin, S. M. Flores, & L. M. Garces (Eds.), *Charting the future of college affirmative action: Legal victories, continuing attacks, and new research* (pp. 157–171). Los Angeles. CA: The Civil Rights Project at UCLA.

Chávez, L. (1998). *The color bind: California's battle to end affirmative action.* Berkeley: University of California Press.

Contreras, F. E. (2005). The reconstruction of merit post-Proposition 209. *Educational Policy, 19,* 371–395.

Crenshaw, K. W. (2007). Framing affirmative action. *Michigan Law Review First Impressions, 105,* 123–133.

Darnell, K. (2008, January 24). NAACP opposes petition to end discrimination-based affirmative action. *Columbia Missourian.* Retrieved from http://www.columbiamissourian.com/stories/2008/01/24/naacp-opposes-petition-end-discrimination-based-af/print-story/

Deardorff, M. D., & Jones, A. (2007). Implementing affirmative action in higher education: University responses to *Gratz* and *Grutter*. *The Social Science Journal, 44*, 525–534.

Denverpost.com. (2008, November 7). Amendment 46-Discrimination by gov results. *Denver Post*. Retrieved from http://data.denverpost.com/ election/results/amendment/2008/46-discrimination-by-gov/

Dickson, L. M. (2004). Does ending affirmative action in college admissions lower the percent of minority students applying to college? *Economics of Education Review, 25*, 109–119.

Epple, D., Romano, R., & Sieg, H. (2008). Diversity and affirmative action in higher education. *Journal of Public Economic Theory, 10*, 475–501.

Erb, R. (2007, December 10). Colleges find new ways to retain diversity. *Detroit Free Press*. Retrieved from http://www.freep.com/apps/ pbcs.dll/article?AID=/20071210/NEWS05/712100377

Firestone, D. (2001, August 28). U. of Georgia cannot use race in admission policy, court rules. *The New York Times*. Retrieved from http://aad.english.ucsb.edu/docs/firestone1.html

Fischer, H. (2008, August 30). Prop 104 backers give up. *The Arizona Daily Sun*. Retrieved from http://www.azdailysun.com/articles/2008/08/30/ news/state/20080830_arizo_180387.txt

Franey, L. (2008, April 6). Affirmative action is target of Missouri petition drive. *Kansas City Star*. Retrieved from http://www.kansascity.com/ 105/story/564203.html

Gandy, S. (2008, March 28). Foes weigh next move against anti-affirmative action initiative. 9News.com. Retrieved from http://www.9news.com/ news/local/article.aspx?storyid=88903

Gewertz, C. (2008, November 14). Effect of Nebraska's racial preference ban weighted. *Education Week*. Retrieved from http://www.edweek. org/ew/articles/2008/11/19/13electfolo.h28.html

Gill, G. R. (1980). *Meanness mania: The changed mood*. Washington, DC: Howard University Press.

Gose, B., & Schmidt, P. (2001, September 7). Ruling against affirmative action could alter legal debate and admissions practices. *The Chronicle of Higher Education*, pp. A36–A37.

Gratz v. Bollinger, 539 U.S. 244 (2003).

Greene, L. S. (2004). The constitution and racial equality after *Gratz* and *Grutter*. *Washburn Law Journal, 43*, 253–283.

Greve, M. S. (1999, March 19). The demise of race-based admissions policies. *The Chronicle of Higher Education*, pp. B6–B7.

Grutter v. Bollinger, 539 U.S. 306 (2003).

Guess, A. (2007). Race-based aid, after a statewide ban. *Inside Higher Ed.* Retrieved from http://insidehighered.com/news/2007/10/24/michigan

Healy, P. (1998, May 29). Berkeley struggles to stay diverse in post-affirmative action era. *The Chronicle of Higher Education,* pp. A31–A33.

Hoberock, B. (2008, April 7). Affirmative action ban scuttled. *Tulsa World.* Retrieved from http://www.tulsaworld.com/news/article.aspx?articleID =20080405_1_A13_hBack65184

Hopwood v. Texas, 78 F.3d 932 (5th Cir. 1996), *cert. denied*, 518 U.S. 1033 (1996).

Inside Higher Ed. (2008, January 8). Quick takes: Affirmative action ballot dispute. *Inside Higher Ed.* Retrieved from http://insidehighered.com/ news/2008/01/08/qt

Jaschik, S. (2008, March 19). Quick takes: Affirmative action ban upheld. *Inside Higher Ed.* Retrieved from http://insidehighered.com/news/ 2008/3/19/qt

Johnson v. Board of Regents of the University of Georgia, 263 F.3d 1234 (11th Cir. 2001).

Joint Statement of Constitutional Law Scholars. (2003, July). Reaffirming diversity: A legal analysis of the University of Michigan affirmative action cases. Cambridge, MA: The Civil Rights Project at Harvard University.

Kain, J. F., & O'Brien, D. M. (2001, November). Hopwood *and the top 10 percent law: How they have affected the college enrollment decisions of Texas high school graduates.* Paper presented at the National Bureau of Economic Research Meeting on Higher Education, Boston, MA.

Karabel, J. (1998). No alternative: The effects of color-blind admissions in California. In G. Orfield & E. Miller (Eds.), *Chilling Admissions* (pp. 33–50). Cambridge, MA: Harvard Education Publishing Group.

Karabel, J. (1999, Autumn). The rise and fall of affirmative action at the University of California. *The Journal of Blacks in Higher Education, 25,* 109–112.

Kever, J. (2008, April 8). White teen sues UT over admissions policy. *Houston Chronicle.* Retrieved from http://www.chron.com/disp/ story.mpl/front/5682324.html

Korrell, H. J. F. (2007). No big surprise: A review of the Seattle Schools case. *Engage, 8*(4), 11–17.

Lederman, D. (1997, October 24). Suit challenges affirmative action in admissions at U. of Michigan. *The Chronicle of Higher Education,* pp. A27–A28.

Leonhardt, D. (2007, September 30). The new affirmative action. *The New York Times Magazine*, pp. 76–80, 82.

Lieb, D. A. (2008, January 7). Judge rewrites Mo. ballot language on affirmative action. *Kansas City Star*. Retrieved from http://primebuzz. kcstar.com/?q-node/9274

Marin, P., & Flores, S. M. (2008). *Bakke* and state policy: Exercising institutional autonomy to maintain a diverse student body. In P. Marin & C. L. Horn (Eds.), *Realizing* Bakke*'s legacy: Affirmative action, equal opportunity, and access to higher education* (pp. 219–239). Sterling, VA: Stylus Publishing.

Marin, P., & Horn, C. L. (Eds.). (2008). *Realizing* Bakke*'s legacy: Affirmative action, equal opportunity, and access to higher education.* Sterling, VA: Stylus Publishing.

Marin, P., & Lee, E. K. (2003). *Appearance and reality in the sunshine state: The Talented 20 Program in Florida.* Cambridge, MA: The Civil Rights Project, Harvard University.

Meredith v. Jefferson County Board of Education, 127 S. Ct. 2738 (2007).

Moses, M. S. (2002). *Embracing race: Why we need race-conscious education policy.* New York, NY: Teachers College Press.

Moses, M. S. (2006). Why the affirmative action debate persists: The role of moral disagreement. *Educational Policy, 20*, 567–586.

The New York Times. (2008, January 30). Restoring civil rights. Retrieved from http://www.nytimes.com/2008/01/30/opinion/30wed2.html?_r=1&oref=slogin.

O'Neil, R. (2008, January–February). The Supreme Court, affirmative action, and higher education. *Academe, 94*(1), 16–20.

Parents Involved in Community Schools v. Seattle School District No. 1, 127 S. Ct. 2738 (2007).

Przypyszny, J., & Tromble, K. (2007). *Impact of* Parents Involved in Community Schools v. Seattle School District No. 1 *and* Meredith v. Jefferson County Board of Education *on affirmative action in higher education.* Washington, DC: American Council on Education.

Reardon, S. F., & Yun, J. T. (2005). Integrating neighborhoods, segregating schools: The retreat from school desegregation in the South, 1990–2000. In J. Boger & G. Orfield (Eds.), *School resegregation: Must the South turn back?* (pp. 51–69). Chapel Hill: University of North Carolina Press.

Regents of the University of California v. Bakke, 438 U.S. 265 (1978).

Regents of the University of Michigan. (2003). Why Michigan's admissions systems comply with *Bakke* and are not quotas. Retrieved from http://www.vpcomm.umich.edu/admissions/faqs/comply.html

Saenz, V. B., Oseguera, L., & Hurtado, H. (2007). Losing ground? Exploring racial/ethnic enrollment shifts in freshman access to selective institutions. In G. Orfield, P. Marin, S. M. Flores, & L. M. Garces (Eds.), *Charting the future of college affirmative action: Legal victories, continuing attacks, and new research* (pp. 79–103). Los Angeles. CA: The Civil Rights Project at UCLA.

Sandel, M. J. (1991). Morality and the liberal ideal. In J. Arthur & W. H. Shaw (Eds.), *Justice and economic distribution* (2nd ed., pp. 244–249). Englewood Cliffs, NJ: Prentice Hall.

Schevitz, T. (2001, May 16). Critics say plan fails to counter image of bias. *San Francisco Chronicle*, p. A4.

Schmidt, P. (2007, July 30). Foes of affirmative-action preferences say Missouri official's edits changed meaning of ballot measure. *The Chronicle of Higher Education*. Retrieved from http://chronicle. com/daily/2007/07/2007073005n.htm

Schmidt, P. (2008, May 6). Multistate campaign against affirmative action gets scaled back again. *The Chronicle of Higher Education*. Retrieved from http://chronicle.com/daily/2008/05/2733n.htm

Slevin, C. (2008, November 7). Colorado voters reject affirmative action ban. *Denver Post*. Retrieved from http://www.denverpost.com/ci_10926423

Smith v. University of Washington Law School, 233 F.3d 1188 (4th Cir. 2000), *cert. denied*, 532 U.S. 1051 (2001).

Sobel, L. (Ed.). (1980). *Quotas and affirmative action*. New York, NY: Facts on File.

Torres, G. (2003). *Grutter v. Bollinger/Gratz v. Bollinger*: View from a limestone ledge. *Columbia Law Review, 103*, 1596–1609.

University of Texas at Austin. (2003a, September 10). Statement on reinstatement of affirmative action in admission. Retrieved from http://www.utexas.edu/news/2003/09/10/nr_affirmative/

University of Texas at Austin. (2003b, November 24). The University of Texas at Austin proposes inclusion of race as a factor in admissions process. Retrieved from http://www.utexas.edu/news/2003/11/24/ nr_admission/

Von Drehle, D. (2007, October 22). Inside the incredibly shrinking role of the Supreme Court. And why John Roberts is O.K. with that. *Time*, pp. 42–49.

Walsh, E. (2001, August 28). Court strikes down Georgia admissions policy. *Washington Post*, p. A5.

CHAPTER 6

DIVERSITY, MERIT, AND COLLEGE CHOICE:
ROLE OF A DYNAMIC SOCIOPOLITICAL ENVIRONMENT

Rhana Natour, Angela Locks, and Phillip J. Bowman

Because of increasing global and national demand, college admissions at elite universities in the United States have become ferociously competitive as the debates over affirmative action and diversity continue to evolve in the 21st century. For example, the admissions cycle for the 2007–2008 academic year was one of the most selective in modern memory at America's elite schools (Dillon, 2007). Overall, the acceptance rate in 2001 was 71%, in 2007 it was 67%, and by 2010 it had declined to 65% (Clinedinst, Hurley, & Hawkins, 2011). In the context of national debates over affirmative action, the declining numbers of underrepresented minority students at elite flagship universities reflect two major trends. First, in contrast with the era of strong affirmative action policies, fewer minority students are admitted with borderline SAT/ACT-type test scores. Second, fewer highly qualified minority students with the most competitive SAT/ACT-type test scores choose to accept admission offers from these selective public universities. Much has been written about the first issue, but we know very little about the college choice process that results in declining yield rates among highly talented minority students who are accepted into elite flagship universities, especially those faced with strong scrutiny over race-targeted affirmative action practices.

The traditional literature points to a number of factors that go into a student's college choice including socioeconomic status (SES), parental influence, peer influence, and institutional prestige (Cabrera & La Nasa, 2000; Hossler, Braxton, & Coopersmith, 1989; Hossler & Gallagher, 1987). Hossler, Braxton, and Coopersmith (1989) conceptualize **choice among colleges** as a multistage process that results in making a decision to select "a particular college from a set of alternative colleges from which an individual student has received offerings of admission" (p. 19). Economic models of college choice have been the major focus in existing literature with emphasis on costs as a major factor in the choice of one college over a set of alternatives.

To be sure, the cost of attending elite flagship universities has grown exponentially with tuition often outpacing inflation (Arenson, 2007). Moreover, when a financial crisis affects endowment levels and revenue

111

streams of colleges and universities, it also takes a heavy toll on need-based student aid (Advisory Committee on Student Financial Assistance, 2008). If current trends persist, the pool of students who qualify for Pell grants will undoubtedly increase. For example, the U.S. Department of Education estimates that Congress will need to add billions in new funds each year or cut the size of Pell grants because of both increased applications and accumulated shortfalls from previous years (Dervarics, 2008). This financial uncertainty has had a direct effect on students' college choices. According to a report released by MeritAid.com, almost sixty percent of the 2,500 prospective college students surveyed said they are now considering a less prestigious college due to affordability (Cappex.Com, 2008; Mincer, 2008).

In addition to cost, existing literature reveals that college choice is also influenced by a range of other factors including precollege experiences, individual factors, and a range of institutional characteristics including appraisals of the quality of campus life (i.e., Hossler et al., 1989). The challenge facing college-bound students in sorting through these factors is further exacerbated by the plethora of marketing information they receive from increasingly competitive college recruitment efforts, which can make the college choice process a daunting enterprise for students. A growing number of studies also show that the college choice process of minorities, specifically Latina/o and African American students, differs from that of their White counterparts (Hossler, Braxton, & Coopersmith, 1989; Manski & Wise, 1983). However, we still know very little about the impact of affirmative action debates on the college choices of highly qualified minority students who may be repelled by the contentious sociopolitical environment and related campus climate complexities, especially within flagship universities targeted by the anti–affirmative action movement. Existing higher education literature usually focuses on the college choice process and affirmative action as two distinct policy issues despite the fact that anti–affirmative action debates may well affect college decision making among minority students with expanded college options because of high SAT/ACT scores.

Affirmative Action Debate and College Choice

To guide future research and policy-relevant practices, this chapter presents an analysis of the potential impact of affirmative action policy and related diversity commitments on college choice for students of color. Our primary focus is the college choice process of minorities[1] in general, specifically at elite public institutions.[2] This chapter first provides a framework for understanding affirmative action policy in higher education with a particular emphasis on the relationships among contentious policy debates, sociopolitical conflicts, and recruitment issues for elite flagship universities. Next, guided by college choice models, we present a second conceptual framework to better clarify how the dynamic legal and sociopolitical environment produced by the anti–affirmative action debate may affect minority students' college choice processes. Based on a review of the relevant higher education literature, our conceptual framework will link these two issues to further the policy-relevant discourse on minority access, equity, and diversity in higher education. We propose that a more thorough understanding of the ways in which affirmative action impacts a student's college choice process is imperative given the widespread opposition to race-targeted policies. A better understanding of how affirmative action debates and college choice interact can help higher education scholars and practitioners develop more proactive strategies to increase access, equity, and opportunity in elite institutions despite a contentious sociopolitical climate around race-based admission policies.

Affirmative Action Policies and Related Sociopolitical Issues

As illustrated in Figure 1, the literature suggests that a series of federal policy rulings have intensified sociopolitical conflicts, debates, and recruitment challenges in elite flagship universities. Since the 1964 Civil Rights Act, affirmative action policies to reverse historical exclusion have evolved. Overall, these policies have provided greater access to students of color, making enrollment in elite institutions a possibility despite persistent race and class barriers in K–12 school systems. However, since *Regents of the University of California v. Bakke* (1978), the anti–affirmative action movement has escalated a divisive sociopolitical debate throughout the United States with well-organized charges of pervasive racial quotas,

---

[1] For the purposes of this literature review, minorities and students of color refers specifically to African American and Latinas/os as the lack of literature addressing Native American, Asian American, and Arab American students does not allow us to identify themes or draw strong conclusions for those groups of students.

[2] See Carnegie Classification of Institutions of Higher Education, which classifies institutions by type. Regarding the banning of affirmative action, experience thus far has demonstrated that the more selective the institution, the more dramatic the decline in minority enrollments.

Figure 1. Affirmative Action Policy and Sociopolitical Issues in Elite Flagship Institutions

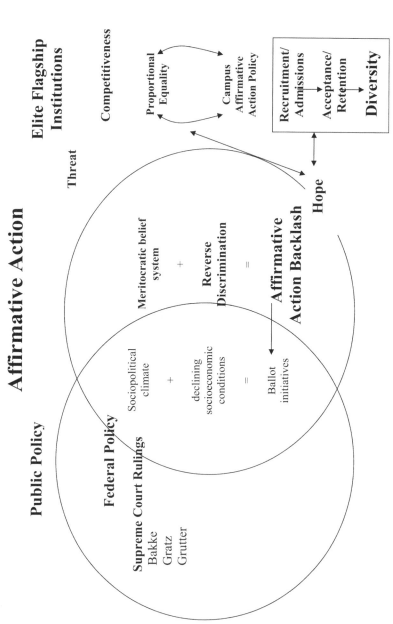

preferential treatment, reverse discrimination, and anti-meritocratic practices within selective universities. Since the 1990s, affirmative action policies within higher education have garnered ever-increasing public scrutiny as competition has intensified significantly at the nation's most selective universities with growing diversity including the number of international students.

Affirmative Action Conflicts and Sociopolitical Debates

As suggested in Figure 1, the *Bakke* Case and subsequent Supreme Court rulings have been associated with deep sociopolitical conflicts and related debates with profound implications for the campus climate and the commitment to diversity at elite flagship universities (Arriola & Cole, 2001; Bowman & Smith, 2003). These deep sociopolitical conflicts in society have resulted in proponents vs. opponents of race-targeted policies attaching very different meaning to the concept of affirmative action (Bowman & Betancur, 2010; Sears, Sidanius, & Bobo, 2000; Smith, Altbach, & Lomotey, 2002). For example, proponents often use the terms *affirmative action* and *equal opportunity* interchangeably (James, Brief, Dietz, & Cohen, 2001; Parker, Baltes, & Christiansen, 1997) with an emphasis on the proactive allocation of organizational resources to ensure people are not discriminated against on the basis of their race, ethnicity, gender, or other markers of historical exclusion (Crosby, Iyer, & Sincharoen, 2006; Harper & Reskin, 2005). In support of proponents, Bobocel and colleagues (1998) define affirmative action as "a body of policies and procedures designed to eliminate . . . discrimination against women and ethnic minorities and to redress the effects of past discrimination" (p. 653). In contrast, opponents of affirmative action policies in admissions argue that lower SAT/ACT-type scores make targeted racial/ethnic groups "less qualified" than Whites who face "reverse discrimination" (Fraser & Kick, 2000). Fraser and Kick (2000) even argue that affirmative action has been redefined in the public discourse from being an inclusive "social remedy" into being a divisive "social problem." As Arriola and Cole (2001) pointedly write, "the term 'affirmative action' has become so publicly charged that few Americans are able to separate myth from reality surrounding the purpose and procedure involved with the implementation of these public policies. Undoubtedly, this confusion has serious implications for voting and other political behavior" (p. 2480).

Federal Policy and Sociopolitical Issues
In *Regents of the University of California v. Bakke* (1978), the Supreme Court upheld the constitutionality of affirmative action but declared that a

quota system based on race was unconstitutional. Nacoste (1996) notes that this case brought into question the 14th amendment and the Equal Protection Act. In *Hopwood v. Texas* (1996), a 5th Circuit Court opinion eliminating race-based admissions became the rule for Louisiana, Mississippi, and Texas after the Supreme Court's denial of certiorari since, in the meantime, the law school being sued was no longer defending the specific admissions policy at issue (Nacoste, 1996). Some legal scholars have argued that the Hopwood decision actually flies in the face of the Supreme Court's ruling in *Bakke*, where Justice Powell's plurality opinion held that diversity may serve as a compelling justification for a race-conscious admissions scheme (Daniel & Timken, 1999, p. 391). This suggests that the success of the *Hopwood* plaintiffs was an impetus for other affirmative action opponents to directly overrule *Bakke*. They strategically used their success in the 5th Circuit Court to garner enough support and resources to push the issue back on the Supreme Court docket through the University of Michigan Cases in 2003.

Grutter v. Bollinger (2003) and *Gratz v. Bollinger* (2003) were legal challenges to the University of Michigan's law school and undergraduate admissions policies respectively. *Hopwood v. Texas* represented a legal shift from historical, corrective, and compensatory arguments based on notions of social justice (Green, 2004) to redefining access "as a benefit for all, not just for those previously excluded from higher education" (Hurtado, 2005, p. 275). *Bakke*, *Grutter*, and *Gratz* established that the racial classification necessary for affirmative action would be judged by the highest legal standard of strict scrutiny. Although the rationale behind affirmative action was upheld, it was only by a narrow margin. As Daniel and Timken (1999) note, "the Court [in *Bakke*] only managed a 5–4 decision that was neither a resounding endorsement nor a rejection of affirmative action as a general concept" (p. 392).

State Ballot Initiatives and Sociopolitical Climate

Rather than the federal government, state-level direct democracy has been the most effective challenge to affirmative action policies to date. In *Bakke*, *Grutter*, and *Gratz*, the Supreme Court upheld the constitutionality of using race and ethnicity as factors in university admissions. However, affirmative action opponents have circumvented the judicial process, court decisions, and state legislatures by sponsoring ballot initiatives. Ballot measures banning affirmative action have passed in California, Washington, Michigan, and Nebraska and have also played a large role in an executive order in Florida. In recent years, the use of ballot initiatives to shape education policies has increased dramatically in a growing number of states. Statewide initiatives placed on state ballots rose 43% from 1991 to 2000 compared to the previous decade (as cited in Bali, 2008). In the 2006 election alone there were at least thirteen ballot measures dealing specifically with education (Moses & Saenz, 2008). Not only have these education initiatives increased in frequency, they have also become more ambitious and substantive in their scope and impact on statutory and constitutional amendments. From an open-systems perspective, these ballot initiatives have also intensified sociopolitical debates at the state and local levels, which spill over into campus-level discourse, tension, and climate, especially in public flagship universities.

For all the attention to affirmative action, higher education scholars have yet to understand the determinants of electoral support for these initiatives and how these factors will affect the flagship campuses and students of color they have targeted. This is not an easy task since, as V. O. Key (1961) observes, "to speak with precision about public opinion is not unlike coming to grips with the Holy Ghost" (p. 8). Despite its elusiveness, critically evaluating public opinion is a necessary exercise as it is inextricably linked to ballot measures and plays a critical role in political action, intergroup relations, and campus climate (Bowman & Smith, 2002; Burstein, 1998; Smith et al., 2002). As illustrated in Figure 1, our conceptual framework suggests that affirmative action opponents targeted majority White institutions, specifically using the initiative process as a means of circumventing the Supreme Court's rulings in *Bakke*, *Grutter*, and *Gratz*, as well as state legislatures which were seen as being overly responsive to minority groups. However, it is an affirmative action backlash among the electorate that results in the passage of initiatives banning race-conscious admissions policies. This next section considers how the sociopolitical consequences of state ballot initiatives might be exacerbated by declining socioeconomic conditions and other determinants of electoral support for these initiatives. The possible impact of these sociopolitical consequences on institutional diversity, campus climate, and the college choice process of students of color are further discussed in the final section of this chapter.

Ballot Initiatives as Direct Democracy: Economic Insecurity and Sociopolitical Issues

In direct democracy as opposed to representative democracy, citizens or legislators place proposals on a ballot that are then directly voted on by fellow citizens. Virtually every state features some form of direct democracy; however, both the nature and extent of citizen involvement permitted within each state is widely divergent (Krislov & Katz, 2008). Direct democracy comes in three basic forms: recall, referenda, and initiative, of which we focus on the latter two. The referenda process

Readings on Equal Education

involves the legislature in the decision-making process of proposal measures,[3] while with an initiative there is no involvement by the executive branch or members of the legislature which makes this the most "direct" form of direct democracy (Krislov & Katz, 2008; Moses & Saenz, 2008). Twenty-four states provide for the initiative process as well as countless cities and towns throughout the United States. The initiative process allows citizens and economic groups outside the formal institutions of government to draft their own laws and then petition to have citizens vote directly on the proposals in statewide elections (Gerber, 1999; Magleby, 1984). Citizens do this by gathering a certain number of signatures, which varies from state to state, that qualify them to place their proposal on the ballot.

Initiatives banning affirmative action do not occur in a vacuum but are part of a national social movement that systematically results in an overall increase in racially charged ballot measures within selected states. Several empirical studies suggest that minorities consistently lose out in direct democracy initiatives, including anti-affirmative action ballot initiatives (Butler & Ranney, 1978; Ellis, 2002; Gamble, 1997; Lijphart, 1999; Tulis 2003).[4] Haidar-Markel, Querze, and Lindaman (2007) found that minority rights fare better in representative institutions than in a direct democracy, especially when a policy proposal is intended to repeal or limit minority rights.[5] Butler and Ranney (1978) suggest this is because, unlike debates in institutions such as legislatures, the intensity of preferences, opinions, and attitudes in the population ballot initiatives are difficult to gauge and facts cannot be uncovered in a systematic way. Also, with ballot measures, "actors need not compromise their preferences since the language of policy proposals is fixed and not subject to amendment during the campaign debate" (Haidar-Markel et al., 2007, p. 306). Scholars suggest that people prefer a limited role in politics but that voter cynicism towards their representation leads to embrace of ballot initiatives (Bowler, Donovan, & Karp, 2007). The initiatives targeting affirmative action and other anti-minority measures are part of a broader conservative social movement which uses race-charged propositions

---

[3] Referenda are subdivided into two parts: Popular referenda are those measures referred to the legislature by the citizenry, and legislative referenda authorize the legislature to transfer the decision directly to the citizenry (Krislov & Katz, 2008).

[4] We do not wish to imply here that direct democracy universally harms minority interests but rather that protecting against the "tyranny of the majority" is difficult (Butler & Ranney, 1978; Gamble, 1997; Gerber, 1999).

[5] Hanjal and Gerber (2004) put forward two conditions that could lead to tyranny of the (White) majority in direct democracy and thus the repeal of minority rights: First, the interests of the White and non-White voters must be opposed, and second, minority groups do not vote as a unified bloc.

to address questions of fundamental rights that go beyond simply tangential issues (Haidar-Markel, Querze, & Lindman 2007; Hanjal & Gerber, 2004; Hanjal, Gerber, & Louch 2002).

Several studies also suggest that economic factors and current economic conditions can have an impact when voting on state ballot initiatives (e.g., Bowler & Donovan, 1998; Matsusaka, 1995). Emphasizing an ideological link between economic and education issues, Bali (2008) notes, "the conservative response to the perceived education crises pushed . . . for a view of education as a competitive enterprise, subject to the forces of free markets and ruled by standards and outcomes" (p. 425). Under affirmative action, certain minority groups would be eligible for more tuition assistance and scholarships, clearly an economic issue. Accordingly, minority-issue ballots seem to occur most frequently during periods of social and economic turmoil, when policy options provided by the political parties tend to be relatively distinct (Nie, Verba, & Petrocik, 1976). For example, during the 1996 presidential elections, both parties and their respective candidates staked out opposing positions on affirmative action in their platforms (Alvarez & Bedolla, 2004; Democratic National Committee, 1997; Republican National Committee, 1996). Proposition 209 in California also came up in 1996 at a time when voters may have felt threatened economically by the state's serious economic downturn in the early 1990s and by what they perceived as minorities receiving special economic benefits (Guerrero, 1997). Several studies of voting on California propositions suggest that economic downturn appears to have increased opposition to Proposition 209 because of economic uncertainty, with voters becoming even more risk averse regarding policy change and biased toward favoring the status quo (Alvarez & Bedolla, 2004; Bowler & Donovan, 1998).

Role of Sociopolitical Ideology: Merit, Threat, and Backlash

For both theoretical and practical reasons, interdisciplinary research has explored several possible social and psychological explanations for differential attitudes toward affirmative action. For example, during the 1990s, a stigma rationale for opposition to affirmative action emerged suggesting that beneficiaries of affirmative action programs may be "stigmatized" as a result of race and gender preferences (Carter, 2001; Heilman, Battle, Keller, & Lee, 1998). However, Campbell, Wong, and Citrin (2006) found that political ideology emerged as the most important and consistent influence on voter choice in their study of race-charged initiatives in California where direct democracy is a regular part of the political landscape. Similarly, Bali (2008) found that political ideology was the most important determinant in education ballot initiatives, followed by self-interest (including race/ethnicity) and collective assessments. Campbell et al. (2006) demonstrated that racial initiatives do not necessarily trigger an automatic environmental race effect for voters and that individuals' partisan environments impact voting behavior. However, political contexts where actual or perceived threats are present have been found to induce political responses such as voter mobilization to circumvent state legislatures which have given increased access to minorities (Cain, 1992; Giles & Hertz, 1994; Key, 1949; Marcus, Neuman, & Mackuen, 2000; Radcliff & Saiz, 1995). These findings are consistent with participatory democratic theory, which suggests that the use of initiatives alters the political context in which citizens reside (Bowler & Donovan, 2004, p. 345).

Meritocratic and Reverse Discrimination Belief Systems

Studies on sociopolitical ideology have highlighted the importance of merit belief systems in opposition to race-conscious policies in university admissions and other affirmative action arenas (Bobo & Kluegel, 1993; Bowman & Smith, 2002; Kluegel & Smith, 1986; Sears et al., 2000). While studies consistently show more intense opposition against affirmative action among White Americans, there is sharp disagreement among scholars over whether this hostility rests on specific "race-neutral" objections like merit and individualism or simply masks racism (Bell, Harrison, & McLaughlin, 1997; Parker, Baltes, & Christiansen. 1997; Sears et al., 2000). Moreover, how researchers define and interpret merit is itself a cause of contention (see Bowman, Chapter 2, this volume; Miller & Clark, 1997; Tierney, 2007).[6] With an emphasis on SAT/ACT-type scores, scholars often define merit in postsecondary education as an unbiased, objective indicator of individual achievement, intelligence, and past performance. However, public under-standing of merit in the American context reveals a meritocratic belief system that encompasses a more complex and multidimensional set of values about ability, motivation, and individualism. Ozawa, Crosby, and Crosby (1996) suggest that one reason such meritocratic beliefs factor so heavily into affirmative action opposition is because "the categorical or systems oriented nature of affirmative action is likely to confuse or offend Americans because of their credo of an individualistic meritocracy" (pp. 1138–1152). However, while these affirmative action opponents argue

---

[6] There has been a debate in the literature of just how "unbiased" these intelligence measures are. The Educational Testing Service, for example, says that merit-based tests, such as the SAT, are unbiased. However, a number of higher education scholars have questioned this claim (Hendrickson, 1997) and have argued that standardized tests are not intelligence tests, but rather a measure of the quality of the individual's educational experience.

that such policies undermine the principles of merit (D'Souza, 1998; Eastland, 1996; Thernstrom & Thernstrom, 1997), many proponents argue that affirmative action makes a merit-based system more just, fair, and equitable (Moses, 2001; Winkleman & Crosby, 1994).

The role of merit debates in anti-affirmative action initiatives has also been conceptualized from a distributive and procedural justice perspective (Bobocel et al., 1998; Elkins, Bozeman, & Phillips, 2003). The distributive justice principle is based on the belief that societal rewards and resources should be allocated based on merit. Procedural justice, an associated concept, emphasizes consistency and predictability across groups. "Because the goal of affirmative action is to change a system which has been and continues to be unfair to certain groups of people, the policy necessarily generates a certain amount of flux while boundaries and expectations are being redefined" (Winkleman & Crosby, 1994, p. 324). Sensitivity to procedural inconsistency (who "gets in" and who doesn't) may explain why people generally dislike "tiebreaker" affirmative action policies, or choosing an equally qualified minority candidate over a White candidate, since merit is not violated per se.

Bobocel and colleagues (1998) investigated whether the concern for procedural and distributive justice (measured by "Belief in Consistency" and "Belief in Merit," respectively) can be a genuine determinant of attitudes towards affirmative action or whether justice-based opposition merely masks prejudice. Although they found that concern for justice is distinguishable from prejudice, they also found evidence consistent with the idea that highly prejudiced Whites use justice concerns and meritocracy to rationalize their opposition to affirmative action and equal opportunity policies. Many other studies have had similar results (e.g., Federico & Sidanius, 2002; Fraser & Kick, 2000; Sears et. al., 2000).

Perceived Threats Versus Hope

Bali (2008) and others show evidence suggesting that voting on education initiatives cannot be interpreted as racially neutral. Numerous studies have demonstrated that support for propositions ending affirmative action and other racially targeted initiatives vary significantly by race, group interests, and perceived threat (Baldassare, 2000; Branton, 2004; Hajnal, Gerber, & Louch, 2002; Tolbert & Hero, 2001). The importance of such sociopolitical issues has long been recognized in the racial threat hypothesis literature (e.g., Bobo & Hutchings, 1996; Federico & Sidanius, 2002; Kluegel & Smith, 1986; Sears et al., 2000; Tolbert & Hero, 2001).

In his seminal work *Southern Politics in State and Nation*, Key (1949) argued that high concentrations of African Americans heighten perceptions of racial threat among non-Hispanic Whites, which then produces voting decisions hostile to Black interests. However, feelings of racial threat and competitiveness from members of other racial groups share complex determinants (Bobo & Hutchings, 1996). Taking into account Latinos/as and Asians, Tolbert and Hero (2001) expand on Key's thesis by arguing that it is a convergence of high racial/ethnic diversity in addition to the frequency of direct democracy that is associated with initiatives that target minority groups. Using California as a case study, they found that White voters living in bifurcated and homogenous counties were more likely to vote for antiminority measures.[7] However, Bobo and Hutchings (1996) are careful to note that feelings of racial or competitive threat involve more than simply classic racial prejudice. They argue that perceptions of group competition tend to be based on a mix of racial alienation, prejudice, stratification beliefs, and self-interest (p. 967). They define racial alienation, a closely allied concept to racial threat, as ranging, "along a continuum from the profound sense of group enfranchisement and entitlement typical of members of the dominant racial group to a profound sense of group disenfranchisement and grievance typical of members of subordinate racial groups" (p. 956).

In contrast to perceived threat, research also suggests that affirmative action functions as a mechanism of hope not only for students of color, but also for proponents of social justice and diversity in America (Burstein, 1994; Heilman, Battle, Keller & Lee, 1998; James et al., 2001; Miller & Clark, 1997; Parker et al., 1997; Taylor-Carter, Doverspike, & Cook, 1995). For example, Moses (2001) argues that affirmative action for combating oppressive education structures, fostering more favorable social contexts of choice and, consequently, self-determination is a "crucial underpinning of an education of justice and democracy" (p. 3). Historically, court decisions consistently emphasized that affirmative action programs in both education and employment should be remedial (Kravitz & Klineberg, 2000; Nacoste, 1996). In this legal context, affirmative action required organizations to allocate resources such as time and money to ensure people were not discriminated against on the basis of their gender or their ethnicity (Crosby et al., 2006) or as a result of historical exclusions (Harper & Reskin, 2005). However, the legal context shifted significantly from a "remedial" affirmative action emphasis to a "compelling interest" diversity emphasis

---

[7] Tolbert and Hero (2001) define bifurcated social structures as "political jurisdictions with large minority and large white (non-ethnic) populations" and homogenous environments as "areas low in both racial and ethnic diversity" (p. 577).

with the 2003 University of Michigan Supreme Court decisions and subsequent state ballot initiatives. With this historic legal shift, "affirmative action strategies" have been replaced with an evolving array of "diversity strategies" especially in the recruitment and admission efforts of selective flagship institutions. However, in the absence of strong affirmative action policies, new strategies to maintain diverse and inclusive student populations continue to face challenges. Among other factors, the efficacy of these new diversity strategies in admissions is currently being challenged by high-achieving students of color who choose not to accept admission offers from selective flagship institutions.

College Choice Among Students of Color: Affirmative Action and Sociopolitical Factors

To guide future research and policy-relevant practice, we need to better understand how affirmative action debates and a contentious sociopolitical climate might affect the college choices of underrepresented students with exemplary SAT/ACT scores who choose not to attend some selective public universities when offered admission. Flagship public universities in states with bans on affirmative action have not only faced declines in the enrollment of underrepresented students but also declines in the yield rates of those admitted with especially competitive SAT/ACT scores. In addition to traditional college choice factors, the conceptual model outlined in Figure 2 suggests that the contentious sociopolitical climate surrounding anti–affirmative action debates may make some institutions less attractive if they become less numerically diverse and are perceived to be less committed to diversity and having a negative campus climate. Based on a critical review of related literature, Figure 2 represents a modified Hossler and colleagues (1989) college choice model that also considers how anti–affirmative action debates and related sociopolitical climate issues might affect the college choice process for very competitive students of color. The basic assumption is that some of these students may avoid campuses infused with a sociopolitical climate perceived as not diverse, noninclusive, or hostile despite precollege and individual characteristics conducive to admission without affirmative action considerations.

Multistage College Choice Process: Precollege, Individual, and Institutional Factors

The higher education literature on college choice has been heavily guided by econometric models, status attainment models, and multistage student choice models. As suggested in Figure 2, the multistage student choice literature has found that college choice is influenced by precollege experiences, individual factors, and several institutional characteristics (Hossler et al., 1989; Hossler & Gallagher, 1987; Hossler, Schmit, & Vesper, 1999). Hossler and Gallagher (1987) have helped to clarify a three-phase college choice model that considers a student's alternatives, stages of implementation, and objectives. Several studies also suggest that the college choice process of Hispanic and African American students differs from that of their White counterparts in a number of ways including how they perceive the quality of campus life at particular institutions (Cabrera & La Nasa, 2000; Hossler et al., 1989; 1999; Manski & Wise, 1983).

College Choice for African American and Latina/os: A Reformulation

To reformulate the Hossler and colleagues (1989) model, Figure 2 considers how the anti–affirmative action debate and related sociopolitical climate may interact with precollege, individual, and institutional factors in college choice among students of color. In recent years, a growing number of scholars have called for a specific focus on race and ethnicity in the examination of the college choice process to further clarify the distinct experiences of African American and Latina/o students (Bateman & Hossler, 1996; Pope & Fermin, 2003). Bateman and Hossler (1996) specifically call for college choice research on ethnic minority students that advances this area of research beyond the bivariate inclusion of race and ethnicity as independent variables. Comparative studies that consider race and ethnicity as moderator variables suggest that traditional factors used to explain college student choice were less predictive for African American students. Existing racial and ethnic comparisons may mask more complex patterns in the college choices of African American and Latina/o students in a changing sociopolitical environment. Qualitative studies suggest that college choice among both African American and Latina/o students may reflect their awareness of the economic, sociocultural, and sociopolitical context. For example, Freeman (1999) and others show how African American students are aware of the sociopolitical context that may constrain the translation of their degrees into economic wealth. In addition to a strong cultural affinity to stay close to family, Latina/o students also consider the implications of future earnings and expanded opportunities for earning income associated with the choice of college (Zalaquett, McHatton, & Cranston-Gringas, 2007). Latina/o students whose families are migrant farm workers ground their economic cost-benefit analyses of attending college in their desire to improve the economic and social well-being of their families.

Precollege Experiences in College Choice

Against great odds, some resilient students of color excel academically despite precollege experiences and environments characterized by restricted opportunities. Regardless of anti–affirmative action debates and sociopolitical climate, students' experiences and interactions in their precollege environments, such as their neighborhoods and high schools, shape their college choice perspectives, college options, and college destinations. As suggested in Figure 2, despite K–12 systemic barriers, resilient students of color somehow manage to take advantage of the better-resourced high schools, academic support services, rigorous curricula, and higher education pipeline programs to excel on traditional indicators of academic merit. Two themes emerged from the higher education literature as being particularly relevant to African American and Latina\o students: (a) structural resources that facilitate college readiness (advanced placement courses and dual enrollment opportunities) and (b) college pipeline and preparation programs (college counseling, tutoring, mentoring and academic skill development).

Solórzano and Ornelas (2004) found that African American and Latina/o students and their parents are aware that "schools within schools" (p. 22) exist and restrict their access to advanced placement (AP) courses, a key college-going resource. Other studies have found negative relationships between perceived educational barriers and students' career aspirations, college expectations and family support (Hill, Ramirez, & Dumka 2003). Yun and Moreno (2006) document barriers faced by African American and Latina/o students who attend high minority schools, with high concentrations of poverty and moderate to low levels of teacher certification, using the state of California as an example. These structural inequities and barriers serve to constrain choices African American and Latina/o students have when pursing higher education.

Another recurring theme in the college choice literature for African American and Latina/o students is the importance of precollege pipeline programs that facilitate learning about and exposure to college *before* the admissions process begins (Butner et al., 2001; St. John, 2000; St. John & Noell, 1989). For example, in the evaluation of one such program, Butner and colleagues (2001) found that African American students identified early contact with this program was important in their choice of college. Within a cultural capital framework, we need to better understand how counseling, mentoring and informal support networks in pipeline programs and high schools may affect high-achieving students of color in their early appraisals of the diversity commitment and campus climate—especially as they consider selective public universities engaged in sociopolitical debates over affirmative action.

Figure 2. College Choice Processes in a Dynamic Sociopolitical Environment: African American and Latina/o Students

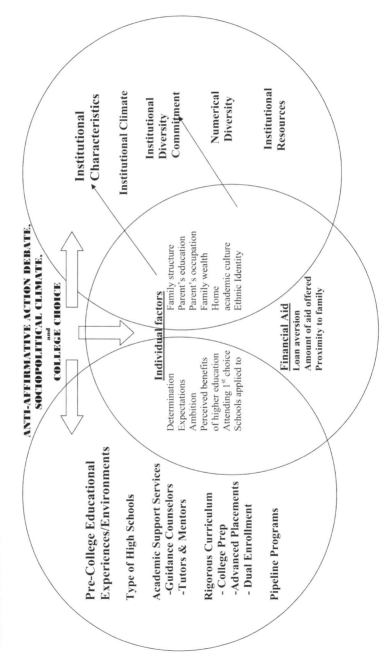

Individual Factors in College Choice

As suggested in Figure 2, a range of individual factors may also affect how high-achieving students of color make "appraisals" of institutional diversity commitment and campus climate. As with all students, the choice of which college to attend for students of color is effected by a range of individual factors such as family background, motivational orientation, and financial resources. However, family background, racial/ethnic identity, and related motivational orientations may result in some students of color choosing a minority-serving institution or a college close to home over a selective flagship institution—especially if anti–affirmative action debates erode the campus climate, diversity commitment, or numerical diversity. Moreover, such negative appraisals of institutional diversity and campus climate may also exacerbate concerns over financial aid including the amount of aid offered, loan aversion, overestimates of college costs, or the added cost of moving away from home (Perna, 2000; Post, 1990; St. John, 2000; St. John & Noell, 1989).

Future studies on sociopolitical issues in college choice among students of color can build on a growing body of related research on the role of family background, expectations, and financial resources (St. John, 2000; St. John & Noell, 1989). Family income and parental education are typically included as measures of socioeconomic status (Bean, 1980), with occupation and wealth occasionally included (see Conley, 2001). College choice studies of African Americans have highlighted the unique role of mother's education, cultural identity, and community commitment (Freeman, 1999; Freeman & Thomas, 2002; Jarmon, 1976; Pratt, 1982). For example, cultural affinity and the perceived effects of higher education on future earnings along with expected costs were found to be especially critical to college choice among African American students (Freeman, 1999; Freeman & Thomas, 2002). In addition, proximity, athletic recruitment, and the institution's academic reputation have also emerged as critical factors in the college choice process for students of color (McDonough, 1997). Kim (2002) found that financial aid was very important for African American students, but attending a college close to home had a stronger influence on college choice despite high aid offers from institutions farther away from home.

Institutional Factors in College Choice: Sociopolitical Climate and Institutional Diversity

The traditional literature on college choice has focused on the effects of a range of institutional resources and characteristics including prestige, educational expenditures, breadth of institutional offerings, size, graduate orientation, technical orientation, and rural-urban location (Hossler et al., 1989, 1999; Hossler & Gallagher, 1987). As suggested in Figure 2, anti–affirmative debate and sociopolitical climate may have the most direct effects on college choice through appraisals of institutional characteristics such as campus climate, commitment to institutional diversity, numerical diversity, and institutional resources. Future college choice research on the effects of such appraisals among high-achieving students of color should consider a range of outcomes including which colleges they apply to, first choices, selection among options, the college transition, retention, and transfer decisions (Cabrera & La Nasa, 2000; Hossler et al., 1989, 1999; S. Hurtado & Carter, 1997; Manski & Wise, 1983). Future studies should also build on related literature suggesting that such appraisals among students of color may be especially sensitive to the percentage of non-whites on campus (Cabrera & La Nasa, 2000; Freeman, 1999; Freeman & Thomas, 2002; Kim, 2002; Lopez, 2005; McDonough et al., 1997).

The higher education literature suggests that future research on students of color consider several indicators of institutional diversity commitment including the availability of retention and support services, the extent and nature of ethnic studies, and the presence of ethnic cultural centers or other multicultural spaces (Bowman & Smith, 2002; Butner et al., 2001; Nora, 2001; W. A. Smith et al., 2002). As suggested in Table 1, future research should also consider four types of *personal-institutional "diversity fit" appraisals—avoidance, attraction, curiosity,* and *indifference.* Studies should be carefully designed to investigate how each of these four types of "perceived fit" between "personal" and "institutional" diversity commit-ments might influence the college choice process among students of color. For example, under the *"institutional avoidance"* condition, highly qualified students of color with competitive SAT/ACT-type test scores and strong personal diversity commitment might decline offers from universities perceived to have low institutional diversity commitment in response to affirmative action challenges and related sociopolitical debates. In addition to the general social psychological evidence on the importance of person–environment fit, there is also a growing literature in higher education that supports the importance of diversity-related personal and institutional appraisals in college choice, campus climate and outcomes (Allen, Epps, & Haniff, 1991; Bowman & Smith, 2002; Chavez & French, 2007; Cole, 2007; Feagin, Vera, & Imani, 2002; Gurin, Dey, Hurtado, & Gurin, 2002; S. Hurtado, Milem, Clayton-Pederson, & Allen, 1998; A. W. Smith, 1991; Tierney & Chung, 2002).

Table 1. Four Types of Personal–Institutional Diversity Fit, Based on Personal Versus Institutional Diversity Commitments

		"INSTITUTIONAL" DIVERSITY COMMITMENT	
		LOW	HIGH
"PERSONAL" DIVERSITY COMMITMENT	LOW	*Institutional Indifference*	*Institutional Curiosity*
	HIGH	*Institutional Avoidance*	*Institutional Attraction*

Conclusions and Implications

This chapter provided a critical analysis of existing literature in higher education to guide future research on the college choice process among students of color within the context of a changing sociopolitical environment often characterized by contentious debate about diversity issues. Particular emphasis was placed on the importance of better understanding why fewer highly qualified minority students with competitive SAT/ACT-type test scores choose to accept admission offers from flagship public universities in the throes of legal or political debates over affirmative action. Based on our analysis of existing literature, we develop two conceptual models to better understand the potential impact of the anti–affirmative action debate, institutional climate issues, and diversity commitment on college choice for students of color. Guided by these two conceptual models, multilevel research can build on an open-systems perspective to further clarify how sociopolitical debate in the "broader society" over diversity issues such as opposition to affirmative action may spill over to affect the "institutional" climate and diversity commitment of flagship universities and, in turn, the "individual" college choices of high-achieving students of color (Cameron, 1984; Katz & Kahn, 1978; Peterson, 2007; Scott, 2003).

Future research needs to further clarify how a series of federal policy rulings and related state ballot initiatives have intensified affirmative action debates and sociopolitical conflicts over diversity in higher education and complicated recruitment strategies in elite flagship universities often faced with a highly contentious campus racial climate (Hurtado et al., 1998; W. A. Smith et al., 2002; Tierney & Chung, 2002). In addition, a reformulation of the Hossler and colleagues (1989) college choice model suggests that future studies should further examine how the anti–affirmative action debate and related sociopolitical climate may systematically interact with precollege, individual, and institutional factors to effect college choice among students of color. Our analysis of existing literature strongly suggests that future research further clarify how anti–affirmative debate and sociopolitical climate may affect students' college choice through their personal appraisals of institutional characteristics such as campus racial climate, commitment to institutional diversity, numerical diversity, and institutional resources (Bowman & Smith, 2002; Feagin et al., 2002; Freeman, 1999; Freeman & Thomas, 2002; Hurtado et al., 1998; Kim, 2002; Lopez, 2005; McDonough et al., 1997).

An especially fertile ground for future research is to better clarify how a student's appraisal of their *"personal-institutional diversity fit"* may affect their college choice, especially among students of color with exceptional academic preparation and multiple college offers. Our initial hypothesis is that high-achieving students of color with *high*-diversity commitment may *avoid* universities perceived to have a *low*-diversity commitment. Future research on the effects of students' appraisals of *diversity fit* on college choice should examine how such *institutional avoidance* appraisals may systematically differ from other diversity fit appraisals such as *institutional attraction*, *institutional curiosity*, and *institutional indifference*. Differential appraisals of *diversity fit* among high-achieving students of color may also affect which colleges they apply to, their first choices, college transition, retention, and transfer decisions (Cabrera & La Nasa, 2000; Hossler et. al., 1989, 1999; S. Hurtado & Carter, 1997; Manski & Wise, 1983).

Our reformulation of the Hossler and colleagues (1989) college choice model not only provides direction for future research but also has important practical implications for the development of proactive strategies that aim to increase access, equity, and opportunity in a diversifying nation. Overall, our analysis suggests that underrepresented students with exemplary SAT/ACT scores and strong personal diversity commitments (a) may be predisposed to avoid flagship universities with intense anti–affirmative action debates because of a sociopolitical climate perceived to be highly contested, reactionary, or hostile but (b) be more attracted to flagship universities perceived as more diverse, inclusive, and strongly committed to institutional diversity. Guided by our analysis and related literature, higher education policy makers, leaders and practitioners can respond to anti–affirmative action challenges in a more proactive manner despite bans on targeted racial and gender strategies. More specifically, in a dynamic sociopolitical context, officials in public flagship universities should consider the following proactive strategies to attract African American and Latina/o students:

1. Promote strong *institutional diversity policy statements* specifying the benefits of and campus commitment to an

inclusive student body including racial, ethnic, and class groups that face systematic barriers to higher education.
2. Collaborate with other targeted flagship universities across states and regions to *update best practices* for maintaining campus diversity and inclusion.
3. Experiment with comprehensive *admission and financial-aid* strategies that combine SAT/ACT scores with other evidence-based merit criteria to attract highly talented and diverse cohorts consistent with institutional mission.
4. Develop comprehensive *educational outreach* partnerships with K–12 schools to design pipeline interventions that reduce systemic barriers to higher education faced by African American, Latina/o, and low-income students.
5. Develop an *inclusive campus culture* to ensure a supportive, multicultural learning environment despite evolving socio-political threats and debates.

References

Advisory Committee on Student Financial Assistance. (2008, Summer). Access and Persistence. Available online at: http://www2.ed.gov/about/bdscomm/list/acsfa/apsummer08.pdf

Allen, W. R., Epps, E. G., & Haniff, N. Z. (1991). *College in black and white: African American students in predominantly White and historically Black public universities.* Albany: State University of New York Press.

Alvarez, R. M., & Bedolla, L. G. (2004). The revolution against affirmative action in California: Racism, economics and Proposition 209. *State Politics & Policy Quarterly*, *4*(1), 1–17.

Arenson, K. W. (2007, January 22). Princeton to hold the line on tuition next year, but other costs will rise. *New York Times*. Retrieved from http://www.nytimes.com/2007/01/22/education/22princeton.html?_r=1&ref=education

Arriola, K. R. J., & Cole, E. R. (2001). Framing the affirmative action debate: White identity and attitudes towards out-group members. *Journal of Applied Social Psychology*, *31*, 2462–2483.

Baldassare, M. (2000). *California in the new millennium: The changing social and political landscape.* Berkeley: University of California Press.

Bali, V. A. (2008). The passage of education citizen initiatives: Evidence from California. *Education Policy*, *22*, 422–456.

Bateman, M., & Hossler, D. (1996). Exploring the development of postsecondary education plans among African American and White students. *College & University, 72*(1), 2–9.

Bean, J. P. (1980). Dropouts and turnover: The synthesis and test of a causal model of students' attrition process. *Research in Higher Education, 12*, 155–187.

Bell, M. P., Harrison, D. A., & McLaughlin, M. E. (1997). Asian American attitudes toward affirmative action in employment: Implications for the model minority myth. *Journal of Applied Behavioral Science, 33*, 356–377.

Bobo, L., & Hutchings, V. L. (1996). Perceptions of racial group competition: Extending Blumer's Theory of Group Position to a multiracial social context. *American Sociological Review, 61*, 951–972.

Bobo, L. & Kluegel, J. R. (1993). Opposition to race-targeting: Self-interest, stratification ideology, or racial attitudes? *American Sociological Review, 58*, 443–464.

Bobocel, D. R., Son Hing, L. S., Davey, L. M., Stanley, D. J., & Zanna, M. P. (1998). Justice based opposition to social policies: Is it genuine? *Journal of Personality and Social Psychology, 75*, 653–669.

Bowler, S., & Donovan, T. (1998). *Demanding choices: Opinion, voting, and direct democracy.* Ann Arbor: University of Michigan Press.

Bowler, S., & Donovan, T. (2004). Measuring the effect of direct democracy on state policy: Not all initiatives are created equal. *State Politics & Policy Quarterly, 4*, 263–345.

Bowler, S., Donovan, T., & Karp, J. A. (2007). Enraged or engaged: Preferences for direct citizen participation in affluent democracies. *Political Research Quarterly, 60*, 351–362.

Bowman, P. J. & Betancur, J. J. (2010). Sustainable diversity and inequality: Race in the USA and beyond. In M. Janssens, M. Bechtold, G. Prarolo, & V. Stenius (Eds.), *The sustainability of cultural diversity: Nations, cities and organizations* (pp. 55–78). Cheltenham, England: Edward Elgar.

Bowman, P. J., & Smith, W. A. (2002). Racial ideology in the campus community. In W. A. Smith, P. G. Altbach, & K. Lomotey (Eds.), *The racial crisis in higher education: Continuing challenges for the 21st century* (pp. 103–120). Albany: State University of New York Press.

Branton, R. (2004). Voting in initiative elections: Does the context of racial and ethnic diversity matter? *State Politics & Policy Quarterly, 4*, 294–317.

Burstein, P. (1998). *Discrimination, jobs and politics: The struggle for equal employment.* Chicago, IL: University of Chicago Press.

Butler, D., & Ranney, A. (1978). Theory. In D. Butler & A. Ranney (Eds.), *Referendums: A comparative study of practice and theory* (pp. 23–37). Washington, DC: American Enterprise Institute.

Butner, B., Caldera, Y., Herrera, P, Kennedy, F., Frame, M., & Childers, C. (2001). The college choice process of African American and Hispanic women: Implications for college transitions. *Journal of College Orientation and Transition 9*(1), 24–32.

Cabrera, A. F., & La Nasa, S. M. (Eds.). (2000). *New Directions for Institutional Research: Vol. 107. Understanding the college choice of disadvantaged students.* San Francisco, CA: Jossey-Bass.

Cain, B. E. (1992). Voting rights and democratic theory: Toward a color-blind society? *The Brookings Review, 10*(1), 46–50.

Cameron, K. S. (1984). Organizational adaptation and higher education. *Journal of Higher Education, 55*, 122–144.

Campbell, A., Wong, C., & Citrin, J. (2006). "Racial threat," partisan climate, and direct democracy: Contextual effects in three California initiatives. *Political Behavior, 28*, 129–150.

Cappex.com. (2008). Students Sound Off on Economy in New MeritAid.com Survey. Retrieved from http://cappex.com/blog/blog/ press-release-archive/students-sound-off-on-economy-in-new-meritaid com-survey/

Carter, D. F. (2001). *A dream deferred? Examining the degree aspirations of African American and white college students*. New York, NY: Garland Publishing.

Chavez, N. R., & French, S. (2007). Ethnicity-related stressors and mental health in Latino Americans: The moderating role of parental racial socialization. *Journal of Applied Social Psychology, 37*, 1974–1998.

Clinedinst, M. E., Hurley, S. F., & Hawkins, D. A. (2011). 2011 State of college admission. Report for the National Association for College Admission Counseling. Available online at: http://www.nacacnet.org/ PublicationsResources/Research/Documents/2011SOCA.pdf

Cole, D. (2007). Do interracial interactions matter: An examination of student-faculty contact and intellectual self-concept. *Journal of Higher Education, 78*, 249–281.

Conley, D. (2001). Capital for college: Parental assets and postsecondary schooling. *Sociology of Education, 74*, 59–72.

Crosby, F. J., Iyer, A., & Sincharoen, S. (2006). Understanding affirmative action. *Annual Review of Psychology, 57*, 582–611.

Daniel, P., & Timken, K. E. (1999). The rumors of my death have been exaggerated: *Hopwood*'s error in discarding *Bakke*. *Journal of Law & Education, 283*, 391–418.

Democratic National Committee. (1997). *Affirmative action* [position paper]. Washington, DC: Author.

Dervarics, C. (2008). Pell grant deficit: The mother of all shortfalls. *Diverse Issues in Higher Education, 25*(18), 8–9.

Dillon, S. (2007, April 4). A great year for Ivy League Schools, but not so good for applicants to them. *New York Times*. Retrieved from http://www.nytimes.com/2007/04/04/education/04colleges.html

D'Souza, D. (1998). *Illiberal education: The politics of race and sex on campus*. New York: Free Press.

Eastland, T. (1996). *Ending affirmative action: The case for colorblind justice*. New York, NY: Basic Books.

Elkins, T. J., Bozeman, D. P., & Phillips, J. S. (2003). Promotion decisions in an affirmative action environment: Can social accounts change fairness perceptions? *Journal of Applied Social Psychology, 33*, 1111–1139.

Ellis, Richard J. 2002. *Democratic delusions: The initiative process in America*. Lawrence: University Press of Kansas.

Feagin, J. R., Vera, H. & Imani, N. (2002). Educational choices and a university's reputation. In W. A. Smith, P. G. Altbach, & K. Lomotey (Eds.), *The racial crisis in higher education: Continuing challenges for the 21st century* (pp. 159–186). Albany: State University of New York Press.

Federico, C. M., & Sidanius, J. (2002). Racism, ideology and affirmative action revisited: The antecedents and consequences of "principled objections" to affirmative action. *Journal of Personality and Social Psychology, 82*, 488–502.

Fraser, J., & Kick, E. (2000). The interpretive repertoires of Whites on race-targeted policies: Claims making of reverse discrimination. *Sociological Perspectives, 43*(1), 13–28.

Freeman, K. (1999). HBCs or PWIs? African American high school students' consideration of higher education institution types. *Review of Higher Education, 23*, 91–106.

Freeman, K., & Thomas, G. E. (2002). Black colleges and college choice: Characteristics of students who choose HBCUs. *Review of Higher Education, 25*, 349–358.

Gamble, B. S. (1997). Putting civil rights to a popular vote. *American Journal of Political Science, 41*, 245–269.

Gerber, E. (1999). *The populist paradox: Interest group influence and the promise of direct legislation*. Princeton, NJ: Princeton University Press.

Giles, M. W., & Hertz, K. (1994). Racial threat and partisan identification. *The American Political Science Review, 88*, 317–326.

Gratz v. Bollinger, 123 S.Ct. 2411 (2003).

Green, D. O. (2004). Justice and diversity: Michgan's response to *Gratz, Grutter* and the affirmative action debate. *Urban Education, 39*, 374–393.

Grutter v. Bollinger, 123 S.Ct. 2325 (2003).

Guerrero, J. M. (1997). Affirmative action: Race, class, gender and now. *American Behavioral Scientist, 41*, 246–255.

Gurin, P., Dey, E. L., Hurtado, S., & Gurin, G. (2002). Diversity and higher education: Theory and impact on educational outcomes. *Harvard Educational Review, 72*, 330–366.

Haidar-Markel, D. P., Querze, A., & Lindaman, K. (2007). A reexamination of direct democracy and minority rights. *Political Research Quarterly, 60*, 304–314.

Hajnal, Z. L., & Gerber, E. R. (2004). Civil rights. In S. Kernell & S. S. Smith (Eds,), *Principles and practice of American politics* (pp. 121–39). Washington, DC: Congressional Quarterly Press.

Hajnal, Z. L., Gerber, E. R., & Louch, H. (2000). Minorities and direct legislation: Evidence from California Ballot Proposition Elections. *Journal of Politics, 64*, 154–177.

Hajnal, Z. L., & Gerber, E. R., & Louch, H. (2002). Minorities and direct legislation: Evidence from California ballot proposition elections. *Journal of Politics, 64*, 154–177.

Harper, S., & Reskin, B. (2005). Affirmative action at school and on the job. *Annual Review of Sociology, 31*, 357–379.

Heilman, M. E., Battle, W. S., Keller, C. E., & Lee, A. R. (1998). Type of affirmative action policy: A determinant of reactions to sex-based preferential selection? *Journal of Applied Psychology, 83*, 190–205.

Hendrickson, R. M. (1997). The bell curve, affirmative action, and the quest for equity. In J. L. Kincheloe, S. R. Steinberg, & A. D. Gresson (Eds.), *Measured Lies* (pp. 351–366). New York, NY: St. Martin's Press.

Hill, N. E., Ramirez, C., & Dumka, L. E. (2003). Early adolescents' career aspirations: A qualitative study of perceived barriers and family support among low-income, ethnically diverse adolescents. *Journal of Family Issues, 24*, 934–959.

Hopwood v. Texas, 78 f. 3d 932 (5th cir. 1996); cert. Denied, 518 U.S. 1033 (1996).

Hossler, D., Braxton, J., & Coopersmith, G. (1989). Understanding student college choice. In J. Smart (Ed.), *Higher education: Handbook of theory and research, Vol. 5* (pp. 231–288). New York, NY: Agathon Press.

Hossler, D., & Gallagher, K. (1987). Studying student college choice: A three-phase model and implications for policymakers. *College and University, 62*, 207–221.

Hossler, D., Schmit, J., & Vesper, N. (1999). *Going to college: How social, economic and educational factors influence the decisions students make*. Baltimore, MD: John Hopkins University.

Hurtado, A. (2005). Toward a more equitable society: Moving forward in the struggle for affirmative action. *The Review of Higher Education, 28*, 273–284.

Hurtado, S., & Carter, D. F. (1997). Effects of college transition and perceptions of the campus racial climate on Latino college students' sense of belonging. *Sociology of Education, 70*, 324–345.

Hurtado, S., Milem, J. F., Clayton-Pederson, A. R., & Allen, W. R. (1998). Enhancing campus climates for racial/ethnic diversity: Educational policy and practice. *The Review of Higher Education, 21*, 279–302.

James, E. H., Brief, A. P., Dietz, J., & Cohen, R. R. (2001). Prejudice matters: Understanding the reactions of Whites to affirmative action programs targeted to benefit Blacks. *Journal of Applied Psychology, 86*, 1120–1128.

Jarmon, C. (1976). Education as a dimension of status incongruence between parents and the self-perceptions of college students. *Sociology of Education, 49*, 218–222.

Katz, D., & Kahn, R. L. (1978). *The social psychology of organizations*. New York, NY: Wiley.

Key, V. O., Jr. (1961). *Public opinion and American democracy.* New York, NY: Knopf.

Kim, M. M. (2002). Historically Black vs. White institutions: Academic development among Black students. *Review of Higher Education, 25*, 385–407.

Kluegel, J. R., & Smith, E. R. (1986). *Beliefs about inequality: Americans' views of what is and what ought to be*. New York, NY: Aldine de Gruyter.

Kravitz, D. A., & Klineberg, S. L. (2000). Reactions to two versions of affirmative action among Whites, Blacks, and Hispanics. *Journal of Applied Psychology, 85*, 597–611.

Krislov, M., & Katz, D. M. (2008). Taking state constitutions seriously. *Cornell Journal of Law and Public Policy, 17*, 295–342.

Lijphart, A. (1999). *Patterns of democracy: Government forms and performance in thirty-six countries*. New Haven, CT: Yale University Press.

Lopez, J. D. (2005). Race-related stress and sociocultural orientation among Latino students during their transition into a predominately White, highly selective institution. *Journal of Hispanic Higher Education, 4*, 354–365.

Magleby, D. B. (1984). *Direct legislation: Voting on ballot propositions in the U.S.* Baltimore, MD: Johns Hopkins University Press.

Manski, C. F., & Wise, D. A. (1983). *College choice in America.* Cambridge, MA: Harvard University Press.

Marcus, G. E., Neuman, R. W., & Mackuen, M. (2000). *Affective intelligence and political judgment.* Chicago, IL: University of Chicago Press.

Matsuska, J. (1995). Fiscal effects of the voter initiative: Evidence from the last 30 years. *Journal of Political Economy, 103,* 587–623.

McDonough, P. M., Antonio, A. L., & Trent, J. (1997). Black students, Black colleges: An African American college choice model. *Journal for a Just and Caring Education 3*(1), 9–36.

Miller, F., & Clark. M. A. (1997). Looking toward the future: Young people's attitudes about affirmative action and the American Dream. *American Behavioral Scientist, 41,* 262–271.

Mincer, J. (2008, October 17). State budget cuts push tuition higher. *Wall Street Journal.* Available online at: http://online.wsj.com/article /SB122427782919745693.html

Moses, M. S. (2001). Affirmative action and the creation of more favorable contexts of choice. *American Educational Research Journal, 38,* 3–36.

Moses, M. S., & Saenz, L. P. (2008). Hijacking education policy decisions: The case of affirmative action. *Harvard Educational Review, 78,* 289–310.

Nacoste, R. W. (1996). How affirmative action can pass constitutional and social psychological muster. *Journal of Social Issues, 52*(4), 113–144.

Nie, N., Verba, S., & Petocik, J. R. (1976). *The changing American voter.* Cambridge, MA: Harvard University Press.

Nora, A. (2001). The depiction of significant others in Tinto's "Rites of passage": A reconceptualization of the influence of family and community in the persistence process. *Journal of College Student Retention, 3*(1), 41–56.

Ozawa, K., Crosby, M., & Crosby, F. (1996). Individualism and resistance to affirmative action: A comparison of Japanese and American samples. *Journal of Applied Social Psychology, 26,* 1138–1152.

Parker, C. P., Baltes, B. B., & Christiansen, N. D. (1997). Support of affirmative action, justice perceptions, and work attitudes: A study of gender and racial-ethnic group differences. *Journal of Applied Psychology, 82,* 376–389.

Perna, L. W. (2000). Racial and ethnic group differences in college enrollment decisions. *New Directions for Institutional Research, 107,* 65–83.

Peterson, M. W. (2007). The study of colleges and universities as organizations. In P. J. Gumport (Ed.), *The sociology of higher education:*

Contributions and contexts (pp. 147–186). Baltimore, MD: Johns Hopkins University Press.

Pope, M. L., & Fermin, B. (2003). The perceptions of college students regarding the factors most influential in their decision to attend postsecondary education. *College and University, 78*(4), 19–25.

Post, D. (1990). College-going decisions by Chicanos: The politics of misinformation. *Educational Evaluation and Policy Analysis, 12,* 174–187.

Pratt, L. K. (1982, October). *An analysis of variables which discriminate between persisting and non-persisting students.* Paper presented at the Annual Conference of the Southern Association for Institutional Research, Birmingham, AL. Retrieved from the ERIC database. (ED225494)

Radcliff, B., & Saiz, M. (1995). Race, turnout and public policy in the American states. *Political Research Quarterly, 48,* 775–793.

Regents of the University of California v. Bakke. (1978) 438 U.S. 265.

Republican National Committee. (1996). *1996 Republican Party Platform.* Washington, DC.

Scott, W. R. (2003). *Organizations: Rational, natural, and open systems* (5th ed.). New York, NY: Prentice Hall.

Sears, D. O., Sidanius, J., & Bobo, L. (2000). *Racialized politics: The debate about racism in America.* Chicago, IL: University of Chicago Press.

Smith, A. W. (1991). Personal traits, institutional prestige, racial attitudes, and student academic performance in college. In W. A. Allen, E. G. Epps, & N. Z. Haniff (Eds.), *College in black and white: African American students in predominantly White and historically Black public universities* (pp. 111–141). Albany: State University of New York Press.

Smith, W. A., Altbach, P. G., & Lomotey, K. (2002). *The racial crisis in higher education: Continuing challenges for the 21st century.* Albany: State University of New York Press.

Solórzano, D. G., & Ornelas, A. (2004). A critical race analysis of Latina/o and African American advanced placement enrollment in public high schools. *The High School Journal, 87*(3), 15–26.

St. John, E. P. (2000). The impact of student aid on recruitment and retention: What the research indicates. *New Directions for Student Services, 89,* 61–75.

St. John, E. P., & Noell, J. (1989). The effects of student financial aid on access to higher education: An analysis of progress with special consideration of minority enrollment. *Research in Higher Education, 30,* 563–581.

Taylor-Carter, M. A., Doverspike, D., & Cook, K. (1995). Understanding resistance to sex and race-based affirmative action: A review of research findings. *Human Resource Management Review, 5*, 129–157.

Thernstrom, S., & Thernstrom, A. (1997). *America in Black and White: One nation, indivisible.* New York, NY: Simon & Schuster.

Tierney, W. G. (2007). Merit and affirmative action in education: Promulgating a democratic public culture. *Urban Education, 42*, 385–402.

Tierney, W. G. & Chung, J. K. (2007). Affirmative action in a post-*Hopwood* era. In W. A. Smith, P. G. Altbach, & K. Lomotey (Eds.), *The racial crisis in higher education: Continuing challenges for the 21st century* (pp. 271–283). Albany: State University of New York Press.

Tolbert, C. J., & Hero, R. E. (2001). Dealing with diversity: Racial/ethnic context and social policy change. *Political Research Quarterly, 54*, 571–604.

Tulis, J. K. (2003). The two constitutional presidencies. In M. Nelson (Ed.), *The presidency and the political system* (7th ed., pp. 79–110). Washington, DC: Congressional Quarterly Press.

Winkleman, C. S., & Crosby, F. J. (1994). Affirmative action: Setting the record straight. *Social Justice Research, 7*, 309–328.

Yun, J. T., & Moreno, J. F. (2006). College access, K–12 concentrated disadvantage, and the next 25 years of education research. *Educational Researcher, 35*, 12–19.

Zalaquett, C. P., McHatton, P. A., & Cranston-Gringas, A. (2007). Characteristics of Latina/o migrant farmworker students attending a large metropolitan university. *Journal of Hispanic Higher Education, 6*, 135–156.

CHAPTER 7

ACT'S P–16 PARTNERSHIPS:
EXPANDING OPPORTUNITY FOR ACADEMIC MERIT

Charles Ramos

The goal of this chapter is to effectively communicate the connection between focused and purposeful assessments, student testing behaviors, data-driven intervention strategies, and college and work readiness research that impact and affect access and success for all students, in particular under-represented student populations. While many students enter postsecondary education in need of remediation/developmental course work, the problem is compounded within the underrepresented student population who are more likely to come from underfunded high schools. In addition to this systemic issue—and partly due to it—many students within minority and low-income populations fail to see postsecondary education as a viable option.

Effective use and access to cognitive and noncognitive data collected through the administration of ACT assessments provides educators at all levels with the tools necessary to make useful interventions. These interventions, whether at the secondary or postsecondary level, can make a tremendous difference not only on student access but also, more importantly, on student retention, persistence, and success.

This chapter highlights current issues and obstacles for underrepresented students and provides data-based recommendations to help effect and inform effective intervention, advising, and college readiness strategies.

Assessing College Readiness

In order to understand where and how ACT assessments and solutions fit within a research and data-based educational strategy, one must first gain greater knowledge of the assessments themselves. ACT assessments are curriculum based, meaning that students taking the tests are being assessed on what they know based on the core subject areas necessary for college success (English, mathematics, reading, science) and how their levels of proficiency match with college readiness. Educators are able to use results to inform and affect intervention, curriculum, and advising strategies in the hopes of raising proficiency for all students to college-readiness levels. Since the assessments

141

test student knowledge, not student aptitude, the impact on teaching, advising, curriculum mapping, and intervention are direct and immediate.

Due to this impact at the building, district and state level, many schools and states are using ACT's assessments to inform impactful change in order to improve college readiness among all students. With the use of ACT's longitudinal system of EXPLORE (8th-/9th-grade assessment), PLAN (10th-grade assessment) and the ACT (11th-/12th-grade assessment), administrators are now able to identify deficiencies in core subject areas, inform effective intervention strategies, and monitor how those interventions are working through continued and deliberate administration of assessments during a student's secondary school career.

EXPLORE is the first in the series of assessments geared to help educators prepare all students for college and career readiness. EXPLORE's results provide educators and administrators with cognitive and noncognitive data that can help inform teaching, curriculum, and advising strategies at the early stages of high school.

Through the use of the cognitive data, educators can identify areas of strength and weakness as they compare to college and career readiness. Students can be effectively placed in courses that will assist them in gaining the needed proficiencies while there is still time to make improvements. Such information can be gathered via use of the ACT College Readiness Standards. These empirically based standards provide a narrative of student skills and proficiencies, comparing those skills to the ones needed to be college- and career-ready. This valuable information informs administrators much better than scores alone.

In addition to the cognitive data collected through EXPLORE, there is a wealth of noncognitive data that can assist administrators and educators in better serving and supporting students through their high school careers. Information on student-perceived needs (academic and other) provides insight into what types of support services should be available to assist students in their continued development. Career interests and plans inform educators about student aspirations and whether students are on track to meet their career goals and, if not, how to get them on track. Finally, the student interest inventory provides a wealth of data on whether students' interests match career aspirations and what type of career advising students may need.

PLAN provides the next step. Schools use PLAN as a mid-stage assessment to gauge whether intervention strategies are having the intended impact in ensuring that all students are on track to being college- and career-ready. As with EXPLORE, educators can use scores on PLAN to match ACT's College Readiness Standards and assess whether student proficiency in the core subject areas has increased, decreased, or remained unchanged and make any necessary adjustments while there is still time in the student's secondary career to make a significant difference.

Noncognitive data collected via PLAN also provide a wealth of information that can have a positive impact on a student's career in high school, as well as his or her potential for success in postsecondary education. Through the Needs Assessment, educators get yet another glimpse of student's perceived needs, and whether the current plan based on the EXPLORE assessment is helping to provide for those needs, both academic and non-academic. In addition, high school courses and grades are collected, providing schools with the data necessary to review course-taking patterns, achievement levels, and whether students are taking the proper courses to be ready for college and career. Such information can also identify potential issues in course rigor if students are failing to meet core course proficiencies.

The UNIACT Interest Inventory is another noncognitive component introduced with PLAN that provides students with the opportunity to explore personally relevant career options. Through UNIACT, educators can more effectively provide career guidance to students based on the student's interests, needs, and expectations.

One of the most important pieces of the PLAN Assessment is the access to postsecondary institutions it provides students. The PLAN assessment is the first opportunity for students to share their contact information with colleges and universities throughout the country via the Educational Opportunity Service (EOS). The EOS provides institutions with the opportunity to communicate with students regarding their institution and programs of study. It gives students access to information on admissions, scholarships, educational programs, postsecondary expectations, financial aid, and other information that inform families about the college selection, admission, and enrollment process. The more educated a student and family are about college admissions, the more likely they are to participate in the process. Later in this chapter we investigate research showing the direct impact student testing and release of contact information to postsecondary institutions has on access and opportunity.

The ACT, although nationally recognized as a college admissions test, is far more valuable to education than for just admissions. In secondary education, the ACT provides a final glimpse as to students' proficiency and whether students are college ready as they transition from high school to postsecondary education. It is the final piece of the longitudinal assessment system (that includes EXPLORE and PLAN) and informs educators as to whether current intervention strategies, curriculum adjustments and rigor at the building, district, and state levels are providing students with what they need to succeed following high school graduation. This is the final opportunity for intervention before students move on to postsecondary education.

As with the two previous assessments, scores received on the ACT can be matched to ACT's empirically derived College Readiness Standards to understand where a student's proficiencies lie in the core subject areas. As valuable as this information is to secondary administrators, it is also of great value to postsecondary officials as they evaluate a student's likelihood of success at their institution, what type of support services a student may need to succeed, and informs advising, placement, retention, and persistence strategies at the campus level.

ACT also provides noncognitive data that inform both secondary and postsecondary educators. Through the Student Profile Section, high schools and colleges are provided with information on each student's educational and vocational aspirations, academic and extracurricular activities, abilities, accomplishments, needs (academic and nonacademic), and future plans. This information helps inform student outreach strategies at the secondary and postsecondary levels and provides the necessary information for data-based student support services.

As with PLAN, ACT also provides students with the option of releasing their contact information to postsecondary institutions via the EOS. Through EOS, access to postsecondary education is available to all students, informing them of college admissions and expectations, and demystifying the process for students and their families. Students enter the enrollment pipeline through releasing their names/contact information and by sending official scores to institutions.

Student Test-Taking Behaviors and Postsecondary Access

Student test-taking behaviors have a direct impact on college access and opportunity. When a student chooses to take the ACT has implications; the earlier a student takes the ACT, the greater the opportunities he or she will have to access the information necessary to successfully make the move toward college. Understanding this, educators can inform students of the importance of taking their first ACT in their junior year rather than waiting until their senior year. Underrepresented student populations are most affected by these behaviors, which compound issues that currently exist regarding access for this demographic.

As discussed earlier, student participation in the EOS is vital to entering the college enrollment pipeline. Students who release contact information receive a vast amount of data, materials, and communications related to the admissions, enrollment, scholarship, and financial aid processes. All this information assists students and families in making informed decisions, meeting deadlines, and creating a more seamless process. Postsecondary institutions that use the EOS gather and collect student data in order to communicate and market their schools. Postsecondary institutions are more likely to select students who have taken the ACT earlier in the testing process, as the window for recruiting students is relatively small each year. When students first take ACT in their senior year, they limit their access to higher education. Many colleges and universities will have already finished building a "prospect pool" and are concentrating on recruiting as many students as possible from this pool. These late takers are essentially "out in the cold" without much guidance to navigate the college selection process. Table 7.1 shows the significance taking the ACT late has on access and opportunity for all students. The percentages represent the number of students in each score range for which postsecondary institutions **did not** purchase their contact information.

Table 7.1 Percentage of ACT Takers for whom Universities Did Not Purchase Contact Information by Year Test Was Taken

ACT Composite	Junior First-Time Test Takers	Senior First-Time Test Takers
1–12	37%	78%
13–15	34%	71%
16–19	15%	45%
20–23	7%	28%
24–27	4%	25%
28–32	3%	24%
33–36	3%	22%
Total	**10%**	**41%**

What we see is that in every score range, there is a significant increase in student contact information not being purchased by colleges and universities for senior first-time testers than for their junior counterparts. Even senior first-time testers who score above a 24 on the ACT are at a far greater disadvantage than if they had taken the ACT a year before. Students of all academic levels are therefore affected and are not immune to a lack of access due to their testing behaviors (Hovland, 2007).

This issue is further compounded when looking at underrepresented student populations, particularly African American and Hispanic students. These populations are more likely to take their first ACT as seniors and therefore decrease their access to higher education simply because of this test-taking behavior. Figure 7.1 shows the difference between first-time junior test takers by race/ethnicity.

African American and Hispanic juniors take the test at a rate of 40% or less. Compare this to the rate of Caucasian students (over 60% take the test as juniors) and the difference is staggering. Access and opportunity, based solely on testing behavior, are already compromised for African American and Hispanic students even without consideration of other factors that contribute to the current achievement gap in the American education system, including access to higher education.

Figure 7.1 Percentage of Students Taking the ACT in Their Junior Year, by Race

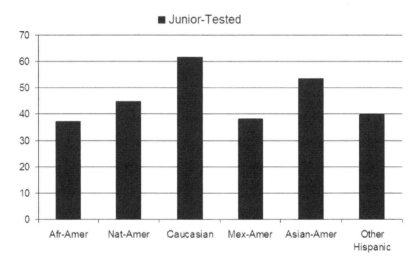

Source: Hovland, ACT, Inc., 2007

One way to provide all students with the opportunity to take the ACT as juniors is through statewide administration of the assessment. Such an administration would guarantee that all students have early access to the benefits of having the data made available to educators at both the secondary and postsecondary levels. Currently, several states have established such a program including Illinois, Colorado, Michigan, Kentucky, Tennessee, Wyoming, and North Dakota. The increased access to higher education is significant and immediate. The State of Michigan saw such an increase in access. The school year prior to statewide testing (2005–2006), 4,847 African American and 1,307 Hispanic students took the ACT as juniors. In the first year of statewide testing, the number of African American students jumped to 14,899 and Hispanics to 3,784 students (Hovland, 2007). This means there are more underrepresented students in the postsecondary pipeline, while high schools and districts gain more information to help their students become college- and career-ready.

Testing during the junior year provides educators with the opportunity to evaluate student proficiencies, identify the gaps between those proficiencies and college readiness, and establish a plan to make up for those deficiencies prior to high school graduation. Of course, the opposite is also true: First-time testing during a student's senior year gives educators little time to provide interventions a student may require to improve college- and career-readiness. If, for example, students perform below the ACT College Readiness Standards in core subject areas, instead of receiving assistance in high school, students will be forced to take developmental/remedial course work at the postsecondary level.

ACT Research Data and College Readiness

Understanding ACT's longitudinal assessments, how the cognitive and noncognitive data inform intervention and college readiness strategies, and the impact they can have on all students pertaining to access and opportunity is the first step in making postsecondary education for all a reality. The next step, and the most vital component, is understanding the research behind the assessments and best practices, and how to integrate the research, assessments and data into an effective, comprehensive, and successful college- and career-readiness and success initiative at the secondary and postsecondary levels.

ACT, Inc. has been committed to research pertaining to college and career readiness over the last several years. Through the release of policy reports[1] such as *Crisis at the Core*, *On Course for Success*, *Rigor at Risk*, *Reading Between the Lines*, *The State of College Readiness of Latino Students*, and *The Forgotten Middle*, the goal of ACT, Inc. is to improve college- and career-readiness for all students through an empirically based set of solutions geared to impact every student.

To effectively serve students and provide the necessary interventions to promote college- and career-readiness, educators need a way to identify whether students are on track to succeed, what areas need improvement, and what gaps exist between student proficiency and college- and career-readiness. In research for *Crisis at the Core* and *On Course for Success*, ACT, Inc. identified the basic courses students need to take in order to better prepare themselves for postsecondary success. At the minimum, students need: 4 years of English, 3 years of mathematics (Algebra I, Algebra II, Geometry), 3 years of social sciences, and 3 years of natural sciences (general science, Biology, Chemistry). ACT, Inc. was also able to identify empirically based College

---

[1] All ACT policy reports are available online at:
http://www.act.org/research/policymakers/reports/.

Readiness Benchmarks that, if met or exceeded, indicated at least a 50% likelihood of achieving a B or higher or at least 75% chance of achieving a C or higher in the first credit-bearing courses offered at the postsecondary level that associate with the subject tests in the ACT assessment (English, math, reading, science). The ACT College Readiness Benchmarks and their corresponding courses are shown in Table 7.2.

Table 7.2 ACT College Readiness Benchmarks

ACT Subject Test	ACT College Readiness Benchmark Score	Corresponding Credit-Bearing Courses
English	18	English Composition
Math	22	Algebra
Reading	21	Social Sciences
Science	24	Biology

Educators can use these benchmarks at the student and aggregate level to identify which students are on track for college readiness and which are not, and in what subjects. ACT research has found that most students are not college- or career-ready and, in fact, enter postsecondary education ill prepared for success in that ever-important first year.

Figure 7.2 shows how ACT testers from the 2008 national high school graduation class performed based on the College Readiness Benchmark Scores. The percentages shown for each subject area identify those students who met or exceeded the benchmark scores in the subject-specific tests. It is apparent that a great number of students are not prepared for college-level work in the core subject areas and are most likely in need of remedial/ developmental course work. Mathematics and Science are areas of great concern as is the overall readiness rate: Only 22% of all students from the 2008 high school graduating class were truly college ready as judged by meeting all four benchmark scores. It is no surprise that the number of students taking remedial courses in postsecondary education continues to rise. Such information at the aggregate and student level can inform effective intervention strategies, particularly since the College Readiness Benchmark Scores are associated with ACT's College Readiness Standards and provide a narrative of the proficiencies a student has in each core subject area.

What is even more troubling is that the state of college readiness of underrepresented populations is worse than that of the overall population. If we breakdown how many underrepresented students meet or exceed the benchmarks in each subject area, we see that there is much work still to be done to ensure that all students have true access and opportunity to succeed at the postsecondary level. Figures 7.3 through 7.6 show the percentage of students meeting or exceeding the ACT College Readiness Benchmarks by subject test and by race/ethnicity.

The disturbing trend is that underrepresented students, particularly African American and Hispanic, are less prepared for postsecondary work than are their White counterparts, especially in mathematics and science. Unfortunately, as we have discussed earlier, these students are more likely to take the ACT late in their high school career and therefore forfeit possible chances for last-minute interventions to help make up for deficiencies. Instead, these students enter postsecondary education at a distinct disadvantage or fail to proceed into higher education at all. Students should be encouraged to take the ACT earlier for intervention and access purposes, and high schools should seriously consider implementation of intervention strategies that include the use of ACT's longitudinal assessment system along with EXPLORE and PLAN.

Figure 7.2: 2008 National ACT Tested Graduates Likely to be College Ready for College-Level Work

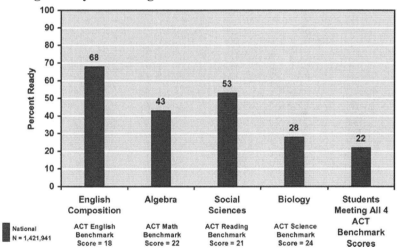

Source: ACT (2008)

The data and research highlight the need for early intervention plans and initiatives geared toward all students. Assisting with such initiatives are ACT's College Readiness Benchmarks and Standards. By tying scores to skills and identifying these skills via the College Readiness Standards, educators have a clearer understanding of student proficiencies and the lack thereof. The College Readiness Benchmarks identify where the skills for

Figure 7.3: 2008 National Readiness for Credit-Bearing College English Composition by Race/Ethnicity

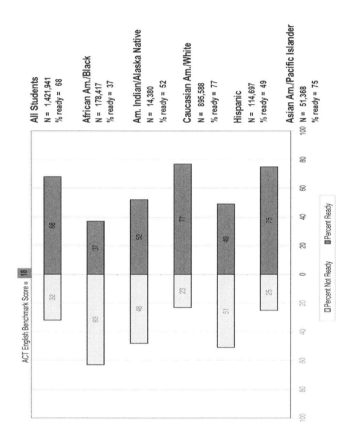

Source: ACT 2008 High School Graduating Class College Readiness Report

Figure 7.4: 2008 National Readiness for Credit-Bearing College Algebra by Race/Ethnicity

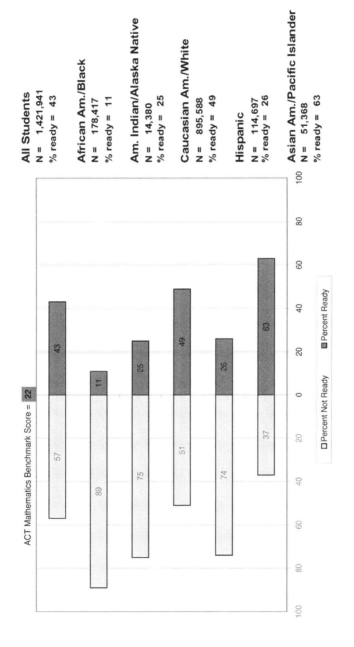

All Students
N = 1,421,941
% ready = 43

African Am./Black
N = 178,417
% ready = 11

Am. Indian/Alaska Native
N = 14,380
% ready = 25

Caucasian Am./White
N = 895,588
% ready = 49

Hispanic
N = 114,697
% ready = 26

Asian Am./Pacific Islander
N = 51,368
% ready = 63

ACT Mathematics Benchmark Score = 22

☐ Percent Not Ready   ■ Percent Ready

Source: ACT 2008 High School Graduating Class College Readiness Report

Figure 7.5: 2008 National Readiness for Credit-Bearing College Social Sciences by Race/Ethnicity

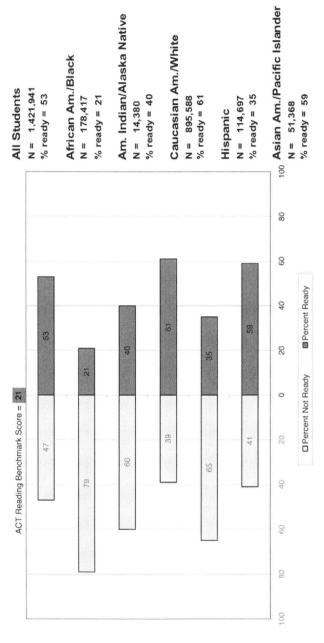

Source; ACT 2008 High School Graduating Class College Readiness Report

Figure 7.6: 2008 National Readiness for Credit-Bearing College Biology by Race/Ethnicity

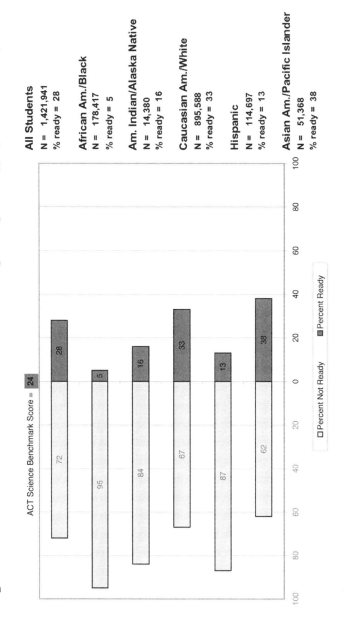

All Students
N = 1,421,941
% ready = 28

African Am./Black
N = 178,417
% ready = 5

Am. Indian/Alaska Native
N = 14,380
% ready = 16

Caucasian Am./White
N = 895,588
% ready = 33

Hispanic
N = 114,697
% ready = 13

Asian Am./Pacific Islander
N = 51,368
% ready = 38

ACT Science Benchmark Score = 24

Percent Not Ready   Percent Ready

Source: ACT 2008 High School Graduating Class College Readiness Report

college readiness fall on the ACT score range scale. This allows an easier and clearer way of implementing intervention strategies for those students who fall below the benchmarks and are at risk. In order to connect with at-risk students earlier in their high school careers, ACT, Inc. has been able to identify benchmark scores for EXPLORE and PLAN that indicate students' likelihood of meeting the ACT College Readiness Benchmarks once they take the ACT during their junior/senior year of high school (Table 7.3).

Table 7.3: EXPLORE and PLAN Scores as Predictor of ACT College Readiness Benchmarks

ACT Subject Test	EXPLORE College Readiness Benchmark Score	PLAN College Readiness Benchmark Score	Corresponding Credit-Bearing Courses
English	13	15	English Composition
Math	17	19	Algebra
Reading	15	17	Social Sciences
Science	20	21	Biology

The opportunity now exists for high school administrators and educators to provide data-based intervention plans for students throughout their high school careers, and then assess midway through high school whether or not these interventions are working and make any necessary adjustments. Without such information, schools, administrators, educators, students, and parents are "flying blind," not fully understanding whether students are on track for college- and career-readiness. Through the empirically derived ACT College Readiness Standards and College Readiness Benchmarks, it is now possible to work with students from point of entry into high school through point of entry at the postsecondary level. Only through such interventions and initiatives can the achievement gap be narrowed and true access to higher education realized and, more importantly, postsecondary access translate to postsecondary success and degree completion for all students.

Recommendations and Conclusions

Several sets of recommendations follow including an overall ACT K–16 approach as well as more specific strategies for secondary and postsecondary levels.

Overall ACT K–16 Approach

- On a national scope, encourage all students (particularly minority students) to take the ACT in their Junior Year.

- Use longitudinal assessments to inform and affect intervention and college readiness strategies.

- Ensure that students release their information for post-secondary access through the PLAN and ACT EOS programs.

- Encourage students to send official score reports to post-secondary institutions so that the cognitive and noncognitive data can be used to provide informed support services.

Specific Secondary Strategies

- Use ACT noncognitive and cognitive data to inform all intervention, guidance, course placement, and college-/career-readiness strategies at the state, district, and building levels.

- Deliberately assess students throughout their secondary school careers in order to make data-based adjustments and modifications to current intervention strategies.

- Concentrate on the skills being assessed through the use of the ACT College Readiness Standards to inform and affect interventions, guidance, and student support strategies.

Specific Postsecondary Strategies

- Take advantage of the wealth of data on score reports to personalize communications and provide information on support and other services related to student needs/wants.

- Concentrate on the skills being assessed through the use of the ACT College Readiness Standards to inform and affect student support services and admissions decisions.

- As part of a holistic admissions process, use all data and research available to make an educated decision on admissions.

- Identify outreach and recruitment efforts through the use of Official Score Report Information.

In conclusion, this chapter has highlighted ACT's P–16 Partnerships to further clarify the importance of college and work readiness research that can have an impact and can effect access and success for **all students**, but in particular underrepresented student populations. This chapter has emphasized the critical connection between focused and purposeful assessments, student testing behaviors, and data-driven intervention strategies to improve students' academic readiness. ACT focuses on the importance of *academic readiness* as one of the "Three Pillars of College Success" along with *instructional effectiveness*, and *student motivation*. The development of academic readiness remains the central focus of ACT's P–16 partnerships, although there is also a growing consideration of psychosocial and motivational factors in both the assessment of college readiness as well as related intervention strategies (see Chapter 10 in this volume).

As noted in the ACT website, The **College Readiness Standards** system highlighted in this chapter provides a comprehensive foundation for K–16 partnerships guided by EXPLORE, PLAN, and the ACT (ACT's three curriculum-based assessment programs). These programs provide a clear set of statements that enable parents, teachers, counselors, and students to

- communicate shared learning goals and educational expectations;

- relate test scores to the types of skills needed for success in high school and beyond; and

- understand the increasing complexity of skills across the score ranges in English, mathematics, reading, and science.

EXPLORE, PLAN, and the ACT measure students' progressive development of knowledge and skills in the same academic areas from Grades 8 through 12. The scores from these three programs can help educators monitor students' academic growth over time. Adopting all or part of ACT's **College Readiness System** on a statewide basis provides significant advantages for educational and career planning, assessment, instructional support, and evaluation:

- Students benefit from a longitudinal growth model that includes coordinated measurement in 8th or 9th grade (EXPLORE), 10th grade (PLAN), and 11th and 12th grade (ACT).

- The system focuses on integrated, higher-order thinking.

- An emphasis on skills students develop in grades K–12 that are important for success both during and after high school.

- Norm and criterion-referenced assessments provide meaningful data for student- and school-improvement efforts.

References

ACT. (2008). *ACT college readiness report.* Iowa City, Iowa: Author. Available online at: http://www.act.org/newsroom/releases/view.php?year=archive&p=314&lang=english

Hovland, I. (2007). Making a difference: M&E of policy research. Working Paper 281, Overseas Development Institute, London, UK. Available online at: http://www.odi.org.uk/resources/download/1751.pdf

Section III

Toward a Comprehensive Agenda for the 21st Century: Expanding Indicators of Merit for a Diversifying Population

TOWARD A STRENGTHS-BASED ASSESSMENT SYSTEM: A COMPREHENSIVE SOCIAL PSYCHOLOGICAL APPROACH

Phillip J. Bowman

There is a growing interest in strengths-based models to guide research, to develop new theories of human behavior, and to inform multilevel interventions that address a range of psychological, business, health, education, human service, and other public policy challenges (Bowman, 2006; Cameron, 2008; Rath & Conchie, 2008; Seligman, Steen, Park, & Peterson, 2005; E. J. Smith, 2006). In contrast to a traditional focus on deficits, strengths-based models signify a dramatic paradigm shift toward a focus on positive human agency, resiliency, adaptability, creativity, multiple talents, and competence development. Building on insights from psychology and a range of other fields, strengths-based models have begun to further clarify core concepts, propositions, stages, and techniques that bridge theoretical ideas with policy-relevant interventions and multilevel professional practice.

Guided by an expanding strengths-based literature, the present chapter presents a theoretical framework that provides the foundation for a *comprehensive strengths-based assessment agenda* to help broaden the conventional construct of merit in American higher education. A growing number of selective colleges and universities have begun to experiment with more systematic approaches to "holistic" review that consider SAT/ACT scores, prior grades, and a range of other "student strengths" to decide who is most qualified for admission. In addition to traditional academic skills assessment (SAT/ACT-type scores and prior grades), there is a growing consensus that a more *comprehensive assessment system* is needed to not only guide *college admissions* decisions but also related *pipeline and retention interventions*—especially for talented students with restricted opportunities (see Chapters 9, 10, 11, and 12 in this volume).

Traditional assessment systems (TASs) are too often limited to SAT/ACT-type tests as the only criteria for merit assessment in college admissions as well as related pipeline interventions to improve college readiness, retention, and career success. To be sure, similar to prior grades, TASs provide valuable information about an individual student's academic readiness for college and level of preparation for advanced academic programs. However, as the college student population continues to diversify in the 21st century, TASs are increasingly insufficient indicators of merit in both admission decisions and related interventions. A more comprehensive strengths-based approach is needed to expand the meaning of "merit" beyond a narrow focus on SAT/ACT-type scores that are strongly dependent on *past scholastic barriers and opportunities*.

For students who are underrepresented in higher education, TASs reveal systematic deficits, which are strongly associated with socioeconomic-, racial/ethnic-, or gender-related barriers that restrict equal educational opportunity. In the context of such barriers, TASs are clearly insufficient indicators of individual merit or potential for college success but very useful indicators of prior scholastic barriers and which students need and deserve additional academic intervention (see Chapters 2, 4, and 7 in this volume). For example, TASs reveal alarming multilevel achievement gaps and deficits in college readiness not only across individuals but also across schools, districts, states, and nations, gaps which are strongly associated with race, class, and gender role barriers (Darling-Hammond, 2010; Orfield & Ashkinaze, 1991). Such policy-relevant test score gaps are also associated with equally alarming dropout rates, especially in urban public school systems such as Atlanta, Chicago, Detroit, and New York City.

Beyond Deficit-Based Models: A Comprehensive Approach to Admissions and Intervention

The *theoretical and practical significance* of a more comprehensive strengths-based assessment system is enhanced because it would enable us to go beyond traditional deficit-based approaches to student success, admissions, and policy-relevant intervention program development. Focusing *narrowly* on traditional indicators of academic preparation (e.g., SAT, ACT, GRE scores, past GPA, AP courses) may obscure other student strengths that play powerful roles in successful college and career outcomes. Deficit-based approaches too narrowly focus on standardized test scores but fail to adequately consider either systemic barriers or pivotal social psychological strengths that differentiate students' academic and career success.

Over the past forty years, Sedlacek (2004) and other university-based scholars have identified a range of noncognitive strengths within students that appear to combine with traditional indicators of academic preparation to better predict college success. Both the Educational Testing Service (ETS) and American College Testing (ACT), Inc. also have very impressive research and development programs to further clarify the value of both traditional academic and nonacademic strengths to guide more comprehensive approaches to *college admissions* and related *pipeline interventions*. In addition, several governmental agencies such as the National Institutes for Health (NIH), the National Science Foundation (NSF), and the Department of Education have also begun to support related research to clarify factors that determine who benefits most from *exemplary pipeline interventions*. The emerging research supported by these agencies has placed a particular emphasis on clarifying the role of social/cognitive strengths and other factors to better understand, guide, and improve interventions to increase the number of underrepresented students who succeed in science, technology, engineering, and mathematics (STEM) fields.

As highlighted in **Table 1**, there are several conceptual approaches that help to clarify the role of students' strengths in successful college and career outcomes including a popular *eight-factor noncognitive approach, social/ cognitive models, emotional intelligence models, engagement models, stress-coping models, and a more integrative and comprehensive role strain and adaptation framework* (Astin, 1993, 1999; Bandura, 1986; Bowman, 2006; Mayer, Roberts, & Barsade, 2008; Neville, Heppner, & Wang, 1997; Sedlacek, 2004; Thomas, Kuncel, & Crede, 2007). Despite measurement issues, these various conceptual approaches guide a growing body of research that supports the importance of combining traditional indicators of academic preparation (e.g., SAT-type test scores) with systematic assess-ments of various noncognitive, psychosocial, or social psychological predictors.

Table 1: Conceptual Approaches to Students' Strengths in College and Career Success

CONCEPTUAL APPROACHES	MAJOR RESEARCHERS
Eight-Factor Noncognitive Approach	Sedlacek et. al.
Social/Cognitive Models	Bandura, Bretz, Robbins, etc.
Emotional Intelligence Models	Mayer, Roberts, Sternberg, etc.
Engagement Models	Astin, Kuh, Tinto, etc.
Stress-Coping Models	Bean, Neville, Pritchard, etc.
Role Strain & Adaptation Framework	Bowman and colleagues

In his recent book, *Beyond the Big Test: Noncognitive Assessment in Higher Education*, Sedlacek (2004) highlights the significance of **eight noncognitive factors**: Availability of a Positive Support Person, Preference for Long Term Goals, Positive Self-Concept, Knowledge Acquired in a Field, Realistic Self-Appraisal, Leadership Experience, Community Involvement, and Handling the System. It is important to note that related research and development efforts at both ACT, Inc. and ETS continue to explicate similar students' strengths that increase college readiness and related benefits from pipeline interventions that support college and career success (Kyllonen, 2008; Kyllonen, Lipnevich, Burris, & Roberts, 2009; Le, Casillas, & Robbins, 2005; Lotkowski, Robbins & Noeth, 2004; Robbins et al., 2004).

Interdisciplinary research on more comprehensive approaches to student strengths and success builds on a range of theoretical models but has especially drawn on rich insights from *social/cognitive* (Bandura, 1986; Betz, 2000; Robbins et al., 2004) and *emotional intelligence* (Kyllonen, Roberts, & Stankov, 2007; Mayer et al., 2008; Sternberg, 1996) models. In addition, studies in the higher education literature show that *engagement orientations* (Astin, 1999; Kuh, 1995, 2005; Tinto, 1993) and *stress-coping orientations* (Bean, 1985; Neville et al., 1997; Pritchard, Wilson, & Yamnitz, 2007) are also critical student strengths that need to be more systematically considered in comprehensive strategies for college admission and related pipeline interventions.

Role Strain and Adaptation Model:
Foundation for a Strengths-Based Assessment System

The growing body of evidence on the five approaches highlighted above may be a key missing component in efforts to develop a more comprehensive, fair, and impartial assessment of the likelihood of college success. However, we need a more coherent theoretical framework that systematically incorporates pivotal constructs and variables from the various approaches into a more comprehensive strengths-based approach to guide innovative admission and intervention strategies. Toward this end, there is growing support for a comprehensive *strengths-based role strain and adaptation framework* that goes beyond deficit models to incorporate key insights from the five cutting-edge strengths-based approaches—*noncognitive, social/ cognitive, emotional intelligence, engagement, and stress-coping*—to successful student and career development. The basic propositions in this multilevel role strain and adaptation approach are deeply rooted in *expectancy-value theories* in psychology (Bandura, 1986; Bargh, Gollwitzer, & Oettingen, 2009; Bowman, 1977; Feather, 1982), *blocked opportunity theories* in sociology (Goode, 1960; Merton, 1957; Pearlin, 1983), and *role-status theories* in social psychology (Allen & Vande Vliert, 1981; Barnett, Biener, & Baruch, 1987; Douvan, 1956; Kahn, Wolfe, Quinn, Snoek & Rosenthal, 1964; Ridgeway & Walker, 1995; Sarbin & Allen, 1968). In addition, this comprehensive role strain and adaptation model integrates key insights from multilevel ecological, cross-cultural and life-span development approaches to successful human development (e.g., Bowman, 1989, 2006; Kail & Cavanaugh, 2000; Triandis et al., 1980–1981).

As illustrated in **Figure 1**, the comprehensive strengths-based role strain and adaptation model integrates insights from several related approaches to explicate how **exemplary intervention** can help students overcome objective difficulties by mobilizing their strengths to enhance successful academic and career outcomes. In general, this integrative model focuses on the nature, context, moderators, and consequences of student role strain which can be exacerbated by structural inequalities (class, racial, ethnic, gender). *Student role strain* refers to *objective* role difficulty (academic preparation barriers) and related *cognitive* appraisals (role discouragement, conflict, overload, ambiguity) that increase risky coping and impede successful student or career development outcomes. *Student role adaptation* is the related process through which *resilient students* faced with objective role difficulty benefit more from interventions by mobilizing *multilevel strengths* (social psychological, familial, institutional) that enable more adaptive coping, achievement-related behaviors, and successful outcomes.

As highlighted in Figure 1, this *strengths-based approach* specifies *pivotal social psychological mechanisms* that can *impede* or *enhance* the *efficacy of exemplary interventions* designed to support successful student and career development outcomes (Bowman, 1977, 1984, 1989, 1990, 1996, 2006; Bowman & Howard, 1985; Bowman & Sanders, 1998). A better understanding of such theory-driven mechanisms can *guide innovation* in exemplary interventions. For example, theory-driven innovation in intervention settings could further improve successful outcomes by *strategically mobilizing multilevel strengths* to support adaptive modes of coping with role strain processes. Among under-represented students in exemplary interventions, there are hypothesized pathways between inequality, role strain, adaptive strengths, coping processes, and successful program outcomes. Within this model, the deleterious impact of student role strain on successful outcomes can be *exacerbated* by multilevel risks but can be *mitigated* by multilevel strengths. In general, there are *two basic propositions*. First, structured inequalities systematically combine with chronic role strain, multilevel risks, and risky coping strategies to impede successful intervention outcomes. Second, despite role strain, multilevel support and related strengths can promote personal resiliency, more achievement-related coping strategies, and successful intervention outcomes.

Figure 1. A Strengths-Based Model of Role Strain and Adaptation: Toward a Comprehensive Approach to Successful Student and Career Development

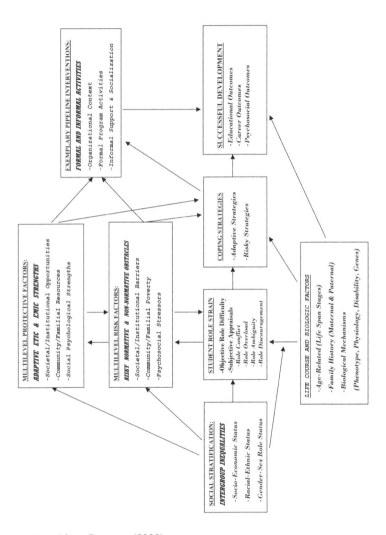

Source: Adapted from Bowman (2006).

Strengths-based Assessment and Intervention Efficacy: A Social Psychological Approach

The strengths-based role strain and adaptation model has both important theoretical and practical implications. At a *practical level*, this integrative framework can guide the development of a *strengths-based assessment system* (SAS) to further inform both college admissions and related pipeline interventions, especially for talented students from under-represented backgrounds with restricted opportunities. As outlined in **Table 2**, such an SAS should specify key sets of variables to systematically investigate how the efficacy of *exemplary interventions* on *student development outcomes* may be impeded or enhanced by pivotal social psychological mechanisms. This SAS could provide the basis for a better understanding of how both *formal and informal* intervention strategies combine with *student role strain* and *adaptive social psychological strengths* to differentiate successful outcomes.

As suggested in Table 2, a viable SAS needs to be grounded in the development of more reliable and valid measures of specific role strain and adaptation variables (Bernhard, 1996; Bowman, 1977; 2006; Ebreo, 1998; Feldman, 1999; McAdams, Reynolds, Lewis, Patten, & Bowman, 2001; McNeil, 1999; Orellana & Bowman, 2003; Reyes, 2002; Rowley & Bowman, 2009; Sanders, 1997; Shiraishi, 2000). Sedlacek (2004) illustrates how a related assessment system based on his eight noncognitive predictors has been translated into innovative strategies for selecting, advising, counseling, and retaining talented nontraditional students and by promoting their success within a wide range of educational programs. Similarly, a viable **SAS** with high-quality measures of student role strain and social psychological strengths could further inform admission decisions and help in the design of innovative strategies within pipeline interventions.

Bowman (2006) suggests that a viable SAS also needs to pay closer attention to critical life-span development and cross-cultural issues. For example, with respect to life-span issues an SAS can be adapted to be developmentally appropriate for exemplary pipeline interventions designed to promote successful outcomes during critical transition periods (i.e., middle school to high school, high school to college, undergraduate to graduate school, and college to successful career).A better understanding of how SAS indicators may operate in unique ways at different stages of the life course has both theoretical and practical implications (e.g., Bowman, 1989; Kail & Cavanaugh, 2000). Related research could help to better tailor

Table 2. Major Concepts in the Role Strain–Adaptation Model:
Foundations for a Comprehensive Strengths-Based Assessment System

ROLE STRAIN & ADAPTATION MODEL

I. **STUDENT DEVELOPMENT OUTCOMES**
    A. Academic Performance
    B. Educational Plans/Outcomes
    C. Career Plans/Outcomes
    D. Psychosocial Development Outcomes

II. **EXEMPLARY PIPELINE INTERVENTIONS**
    A. Intervention Context and Participation
    B. Formal Intervention Activities
    C. Formal Role of Mentors
    D. Formal Role of Staff

III. **STUDENT ROLE STRAIN & ADAPTATION VARIABLES**
    A. Student Role Strain
        1. *Objective Role Strain:* Risky Systemic Barriers
            -   Education Barriers: Academic Preparation
            -   Economic Barriers: Financial Need
            -   Racial/Ethnic-Related Barriers
            -   Gender-Related Barriers
        2. *Subjective Role Strain:* Risky Cognitive Appraisals
            -   Role Conflict
            -   Role Ambiguity
            -   Role Overload
            -   Role Discouragement
    B. ADAPTIVE SOCIAL PSYCHOLOGICAL STRENGTHS
        1. Perceived Informal Support (*A Strong Support Person*)
            -   Intervention Mentor Support
            -   Intervention Staff Support
            -   Peer Support
            -   Extended Family Support
        2. Social-Cognitive Motivational Orientations
            -   Path-Goal Beliefs (Long-Term Goals)
            -   Academic Self-Efficacy (Positive Self-Concept)
            -   Career-Related Efficacy (Knowledge in a Field)
            -   Resilient Problem-Solving Efficacy (Realistic Self-Appraisal)
        3. Multilevel Engagement Orientations
            -   Leadership Commitment (Leadership Experience)
            -   Service Commitment (Community Involvement)
            -   Diversity Commitment (Handling the System)

the design of innovative strategies to enhance intervention efficacy through more developmentally specific informal support strategies to mobilize strengths, promote resiliency, guide achievement-related coping, and improve successful outcomes.

With respect to cross-cultural considerations, a growing literature also supports the particular utility of innovative strengths-based assessment and related intervention strategies for students from ethnic groups that face both class and racial barriers such as African Americans and Latina/os (i.e., Banks, 2004; Gonzalez, Moll, & Amantqi, 2005; Gutiérrez, 2006; Hill, 1998; Lee, 2003). Cross-cultural considerations both across and within groups may also become increasingly important in innovative strengths-based assessment and related intervention strategies to build on the unique strengths of the growing numbers of women, new immigrants, and international students in American colleges and universities (e.g., Brislin, 1993; Chapter 2, this volume). An SAS that systematically addresses such cross-cultural issues can help higher education go beyond the traditional focus on academic deficits and remediation to a more comprehensive approach to student merit, potential, and talent development. Therefore, an SAS can provide the basis to design innovative strategies to assess, reinforce, and mobilize social psychological assets among all students; in turn, such innovative strategies can help empower students with diverse backgrounds, role strains, and strengths to successfully strive toward successful outcomes.

Exemplary Intervention Efficacy:
Formal Activities, Informal Support, and Outcomes

University-based, ETS, and ACT scholars have shown a growing interest in the assessment of social psychological strengths to not only guide more comprehensive review of merit in college admissions, but also to inform pipeline interventions to promote college readiness, retention, advanced studies and career success (see Chapters 9, 10, and 11 in this volume). In addition, there is growing external support for related research on innovative assessment systems to further ***understand and improve the efficacy of pipeline interventions*** for talented students from underrepresented backgrounds with restricted educational opportunities. Governmental agencies such as the NIH, the NSF, and the Department of Education along with private foundations currently support a range of ***pipeline interventions*** to increase the number of underrepresented students who excel in college, pursue advanced degrees, and succeed in competitive careers.

More systematic evaluation has begun to identify *exemplary* pipeline interventions that show especially strong efficacy and benefits for participants. However, there is a growing interest in better understanding why some participants benefit from formal intervention activities more than do others. The most *rigorous outcome evaluation* studies show clear *average benefits* for pipeline intervention participants over control groups—but *do not* adequately explain *differential benefits* among participants within intervention groups. A unique collaboration among NIH, NSF, and other scientific agencies has begun to provide additional insight into factors associated with pipeline intervention efficacy and differential benefits (Chubin, DePass, & Blockus, 2009; DePass & Chubin, 2008; Olson & Fagen, 2007). This unique collaboration also identifies exemplary pipeline interventions with especially strong efficacy in increasing the number of underrepresented students who pursue advanced studies and careers in the biomedical/behavioral sciences and other scientific fields.

As highlighted in Table 2, *exemplary pipeline interventions* provide participants not only with *access* to appropriate facilities but also with a range of *formal activities* that often include *expert mentors* and *program staff* to supervise structured activities. For example, NIH-National Institute for General Medicine has developed a bold new initiative to study *exemplary pipeline interventions to promote research careers* among talented participants from underrepresented groups based on *two core assumptions* regarding program success: (a) When participants are provided the opportunity to engage in state-of-the-art research with faculty mentorship, appropriate facilities, and structured activities, their motivation is strengthened for achieving advanced graduate studies to enter research careers, and (b) once focused, participants will subsequently show improved academic performance and other career-related competencies needed to successfully pursue scientific research careers.

Guided by a comprehensive role strain and adaptation model, the SAS variables outlined in Table 2 can help to further clarify both intervention efficacy and differential intervention benefits for participants. An SAS with high-quality measures of these variables can provide new insight into pivotal social psychological factors that *impede* or *enhance* the *efficacy of exemplary research opportunity interventions.* More specifically, SAS measures can help clarify (a) how *role strain and related risk processes* may operate to *impede* exemplary intervention efficacy and reduce intervention benefits among participants and (b) how *social psychological strengths and related protective processes* may *improve* intervention efficacy and enhance benefits among intervention participants.

Assessment of Student Role Strain:
Objective Difficulty and Risky Cognitive Appraisals

A viable SAS should provide high-quality measures of both role strain and related risk factors to better clarify how they might operate to impede exemplary intervention efficacy and reduce intervention benefits among participants. As outlined in Table 2, the *objective* aspects of student role strain can be assessed with established indicators of *prior* barriers to academic preparation as reflected in test scores, course rigor, and curricular quality. However, the reliable and valid assessment of risky *subjective* appraisals (e.g., role conflict, overload, ambiguity, and discouragement) will require additional refinement of existing measures (Bernhard, 1999; Coverman, 1989; Kahn & Byosiere, 1992; Kahn, et al., 1964; Kelloway & Barling, 1990; King & King, 1990; Tracy & Johnson, 1981). Chronic role strain may be especially challenging for low-income, African American, Latina/o or other students who not only face *normative challenges* (i.e., competitive academic demands) like all students, but also *nonnormative* college and career obstacles associated with class, race, ethnic, and/or gender inequalities (e.g., Bowman, 2006; Kahlenberg, 2010; Lopez, 2005; Neville, 1997; Orellana & Bowman, 2003; Takagi, 1992). Therefore, benefits from exemplary interventions may be systematically constrained by nonnormative student role strain (academic barriers, family poverty, multi-level psychosocial stressors, etc.) but facilitated by adaptive strengths (support, motivation, engagement orientations, etc.) that promote achievement-related coping.

In a viable SAS, the assessment of *objective aspects* of student role strain can utilize established indicators of academic (e.g., low SAT/ACT scores, curricula tracking), socioeconomic (e.g., family poverty, financial need), and status-related (e.g., race, gender) barriers. However, we also propose to explore how *risky but modifiable subjective role appraisals* such as *role conflict, overload, ambiguity, and discouragement* might further impede successful program outcomes, especially among underrepresented students. To investigate such subjective aspects of role strain, Bernhard (1998) refined an existing scale and found there were no gender differences in *student role overload,* but males experienced greater levels of both *role ambiguity* and *role conflict*. Regardless of gender, *role ambiguity* emerged as the most powerful risk factor for both psychological distress and unsuccessful academic outcomes. However, *role overload* was associated with higher grades for females, but lower grades and the expression of anger for male students. Moreover, Feldman (1999) found that a useful measure of *student role discouragement* during the freshman year had negative short-term and long-term psychosocial consequences.

Assessment of Social Psychological Strengths: Support, Motivation, and Engagement

A comprehensive SAS with measures of ***adaptive social psychological strengths*** could not only help to expand merit considerations in college admission decisions but also guide research to help explain why some students derive greater benefits from exemplary pipeline interventions than others. As suggested in Table 2, a basic proposition is that ***formal intervention activities*** combine with pivotal ***social psychological strengths***—*informal support*, *social-cognitive motivation*, and ***multilevel engagement orientations***—to improve successful program outcomes. For example, two studies of a research opportunity intervention suggest that informal support and socialization that reinforce such student strengths may help to explain why some students benefit more than do others from program participation (Berkes, 2007; Lopatto, 2007). These positive benefits may operate through supportive mentor–mentee socialization where faculty mentors help student mentees manage higher levels of academic and social integration into the intervention program—and to acquire the necessary research skills, knowledge, competencies, confidence, and identity for future educational and career success.

Assessment of Informal Support Orientations. As indicated in Table 2, the proposed SAS can draw on a substantial literature to refine existing measures of informal social support orientations to better clarify how students perceive and mobilize ***informal support*** from program **mentors, staff, peers,** and/or **extended family** members to further enhance successful intervention efficacy (e.g., Baron & Kenny, 1986; Ebreo, 1998; Reyes, 2002). This literature identifies excellent measures for an SAS and clarifies powerful mechanisms through which informal support orientations might promote successful outcomes among under-represented students. For example, strong informal support from *various intervention sources* may *offer* students *material assistance* or *relevant advice, guidance, or information* to ***directly*** promote successful education or career outcomes. Moreover, informal support may also offer *socio-emotional encouragement* from multiple sources (mentor, staff, friends, extended family) to ***buffer*** the deleterious effects of role strain often faced by underrepresented students to further enhance successful intervention outcomes (e.g., Baron & Kenny, 1986).

Two dissertation studies employed useful measures of *informal support orientations* to investigate: (a) cross-ethnic *similarities (etics)* and *differences (emics)* in perceived support during the stressful college transition and (b) the function of support as a source of protection in the face of student role strain (Ebreo, 1998; Reyes, 2002). Ebreo (1998) found that a useful measure of **perceived support** from both **family** and **friends** helped to clarify adaptive coping, resilience, and academic success. Hierarchical regressions revealed that support from *family* significantly predicted *resilient psychosocial adjustment* for all students only during the first year of college, while support from *friends* predicted *resilient outcomes* for ethnic minority students during both the first and third years. Surprisingly, support from both *friends and family members* was significantly related to *successful academic outcomes* for White students, but not ethnic minority students.

An innovative dissertation study of college students by Reyes (2002) employed a unique **extended family support measure** to assess support from specific family members **within three subsystems: nuclear family**, **intergeneration-kin**, and **para-kin**. Perceived support from each extended family member was measured along three dimensions: *perceived closeness*, *helpfulness*, and *frequency of contact*. African Americans perceived *lower support* from their fathers relative to all ethnic groups, but the *greatest support* from intergeneration or blood kin. Similar to African Americans, Latina/o students also perceived greater support from intergeneration-kin beyond the nuclear family than did European American and Asian American students. However, only European Americans appeared to perceive greater support from their grandparents than from other intergeneration-kin such as aunts, uncles, or cousins. Finally, some evidence was found for a buffering model where the relationship between role strain and psychological distress was reduced at high levels of extended family support.

Assessment of Social-Cognitive Motivation. A viable SAS can also build on a growing **social-cognitive motivation literature** to further refine measures and investigate the benefits of **path-goal beliefs** (Bowman, 1977; Covington, 2000; Eccles & Wigfield, 2002) and **various self-efficacy beliefs** (Bandura, 1986) including **academic self-efficacy** (Feldman, 1999; Gore, 2006; Le, Casillas, & Robbins, 2005), **career-related efficacy** (Betz, 2007; Gainor, 2006; Hatchett & Lent, 1992), and **problem-solving efficacy** (Heppner, Witty, & Dixon, 2007; Shiraishi, 1999; Weiner, 1986) in successful academic and career outcomes.

Assessment of Path-Goal Beliefs. Building on the rich social cognitive theoretical foundation, a growing number of studies demonstrate the powerful effects of path-goal beliefs and related expectancy-value beliefs—outcome, performance-outcome, future goal, or instrumentality beliefs—on motivation and achievement outcomes in a broad range of contexts (Bandura, 1986; Bowman, 1977; Covington, 2000; Le et. al, 2005; Eccles & Wigfield, 2002; Husman & Lens, 1999; Simons, Dewitte, & Lens, 2004). In general, various measures of such **path-goal beliefs** focus on the extent to which a student believes that successful academic or career performance is the best pathway to achieve their highly valued goals. In an especially useful review of related literature, Eccles and Wigfield (2002) show how such **path-goal beliefs** can combine with **personal values** and **academic beliefs** to better explain a range of motivation and achievement outcomes. However, Bowman (1977) also shows how the explanatory power of such path-goal expectancy beliefs may be systematically moderated by role barriers, opportunities, and personal strengths, especially among underrepresented students.

Assessment of Self-Efficacy Beliefs. Guided by Bandura's (1986) social-cognitive theory, a growing number of studies show how *various measures of self-efficacy* tap especially *important student strengths* that enhance motivation and achievement outcomes. Self-efficacy is defined as one's belief in her or his own ability to engage successfully in a specific performance domain (e.g., academic, career, problem solving).

A cross-ethnic dissertation study by Feldman (1999) examined the link between a measure of *academic self-efficacy* and successful student development outcomes. In support of social-cognitive theory, a longitudinal analysis revealed that high initial academic self-efficacy was related to both short-term and long-term academic and psychosocial outcomes. However, among African Americans higher academic self-efficacy during the freshman year was inversely related to self-esteem in their junior year. Moreover, a high level of academic self-efficacy did not buffer a deleterious relationship between student role discouragement in the freshman year and adverse short- and long-term psychosocial consequences. A substantial literature on *career-related efficacy* also consistently shows significant positive relationships to career interests, choices, plans, and outcomes (Betz, 2000, 2007; Gainor, 2006; Hatchett & Lent, 1992). However, Byars and Hackett (1998) suggest that future research on women of color and other underrepresented students must better clarify how effects of career-related efficacy may be moderated by a range of role barriers, sociocultural strengths, and intervention opportunities.

For over ten years, policy-relevant debate about merit in university admissions has emphasized the need to systematically reward *"highly motivated"* students, especially *"resilient strivers"* who are able to overcome past educational disadvantages and discouraging life problems to excel academically against the odds (Carnevale, 1999; Goggin, 1999;

Kahlenberg, 2004, 2010; St. John, Simmons, & Musoba, 2002; Zwick, 2002). Despite lower SAT/ACT scores, there is growing respect for such *"resilient strivers"* who somehow excel academically despite discouraging educational, economic, and systemic barriers. However, there is much less agreement on assessment procedures to systematically identify such strivers or how to utilize their unique strengths in more comprehensive admission, retention, and pipeline strategies.

To help clarify strengths among resilient strivers, a viable SAS should build on the social cognitive tradition to develop a new measure of *resilient problem-solving efficacy—a person's belief in her or his ability to solve and overcome stressful life problems that threaten successful striving.* In addition to the stress-coping literature, the development of a viable measure of resilient problem-solving efficacy can build on insights from studies on *problem-solving and attribution orientations* (Heppner & Peterson, 1982; Heppner, Witt, & Dixon, 2004; Sternberg, 2004; Weiner, 1986). For example, Heppner et al. (2004) review over 20 years of research on a *Problem Solving Inventory* which assesses "perceptions of one's problem-solving ability as well as behaviors and attitudes associated with problem-solving style" (p. 352).

There is also a substantial literature suggesting that *attribution orientations,* or how people tend to perceive the causes of their role performance problems, may be a critical component of resilient problem-solving efficacy (Cokley, 2003; Shiraishi, 1999; Weiner, 1986). For example, Shiraishi (1999) conducted a cross-ethnic study of *attribution orientation* to explore the hypothesis that adaptive student outcomes are *impeded* by *ability attribution (internal and stable)* but *facilitated* by *effort attribution (internal and unstable)* as the perceived cause for academic problems. This study investigated the relationship between both *attribution style (generalized tendencies)* and *attribution response (situation specific)* and both achievement-related outcomes (e.g., academic performance and motivation) and psychosocial outcomes (e.g., self-esteem and depression). As hypothesized, analyses of variance found that both "ability" attribution *style* and *response* were related to lower psychosocial outcomes regardless of ethnicity or acculturation (Peterson & Seligman, 1984; Weiner, 1986). However, in contrast to Weiner's (1986) hypothesis, *effort attribution responses to* academic difficulty were often *negatively* related to achievement-related outcomes. There were also some distinct findings for particular ethnic groups which support the importance of further clarifying cross-cultural similarities (etics) and differences (emics).

Assessment of Multilevel Engagement Orientations. As noted in Table 2, a growing literature suggests that a viable SAS should include measures of ***multilevel engagement orientations*** for a more systematic assessment of ***leadership orientation*** (Good et al., 2000; Logue et al., 2005; McAdams et al., 2001), ***service orientation*** (Jones & Hill, 2003; Taylor & Pancer, 2007), and ***diversity orientation*** (Bowman & Howard, 1985; Bowman & Smith, 2002; Gurin et. al, 2002; Jayakumar, 2007). Within an ecological framework, each of these engagement orientations could operate at multiple levels—proximal campus, community, or more macro national or global levels—to help explain successful student development outcomes. One approach for systematic assessment of multilevel engagement orientations would be to build on expectancy-value and social/cognitive theories to go beyond behaviors to focus on ***leadership, service,*** and ***diversity commitments.*** In this context, ***a strong commitment*** is based on both a person's (a) ***path-goal beliefs*** that each mode of engagement is necessary to achieve cherished goals, values or needs and (b) ***efficacy beliefs*** in her or his ability to engage successfully in each mode of engagement.

Several multi-ethnic dissertation studies support the importance of *leadership, service, and diversity orientations* among underrepresented students (Ebreo, 1998; McNeil, 1999; Sanders, 1997; D. G. Smith, 1989). Utilizing a Non-Cognitive Questionnaire (NCQ), Sedlacek (2004) and others have found particular measures of leadership, service, and diversity orientations to be associated with successful student outcomes. For example, Sanders (1997) used NCQ measures to assess leadership involvement, community service, and interracial efficacy, and each emerged as independent factors in a diverse sample of African American, Asian American, Latina/o, and White students. Furthermore, related multiple regression analyses supported the relative predictive power of admission test scores and gender for academic success, but the engagement orientation measures were stronger predictors of psychosocial adjustment outcomes (e.g., self-esteem). Ebreo (1998) noted the important distinction between prior diversity experiences and diversity preferences based on a factor analysis of a unique multidimensional measure of student's diversity orientation within a multi-ethnic sample. White students had the least prior engagement with other racial/ethnic groups while African Americans were the most segregated from Whites followed by Latina/o and Asian American students. Regardless of prior experience, an increasing body of research shows a growing awareness of the benefits of diversity engagement for college students from all racial/ethnic groups (e.g., Graham, Baker, & Wapner, 1985; Gurin et. al, 2002; Harper & Quaye, 2009; Jayakumar, 2008; Page, 2007; D. G. Smith, 1989, 2009).

Conclusions and Implications

This chapter highlights the theoretical and practical implications of a strengths-based role strain and adaptation approach to successful student and career development. This strengths-based approach provides a comprehensive and multilevel social psychological framework to systematically address complex diversity, merit, and opportunity issues in higher education. Particular emphasis has been placed on the practical implications of this multilevel framework for developing a **strengths-based assessment system (SAS)** to inform more comprehensive strategies for holistic review in college admissions and innovation in exemplary pipeline interventions. This integrative conceptual framework and related SAS go beyond conventional deficit approaches to systematically incorporate insights from cutting-edge noncognitive, emotional intelligence, social-cognitive, engagement, and stress-coping models to further clarify the importance of students' strengths in successful college and career outcomes.

Future efforts to further develop a viable SAS should be guided by exchanges among university-based, ETS and ACT, Inc. experts engaged in interrelated programs of research on the importance of both *academic* and *nonacademic* strengths in successful student outcomes across the K–20 pipeline and beyond (see Chapters 9, 10, 11, and 12 in this volume). In addition, SAS translational research and development activities could also benefit from related exchanges, collaboration, and even partnerships to bridge new findings with comprehensive admissions and innovative intervention strategies. Collaborative research on an SAS can also make significant contributions to ongoing efforts by NIH, NSF, U.S. Department of Education, and other stakeholders to better understand and improve exemplary pipeline interventions to increase the number of talented students from underrepresented groups who succeed in college, pursue advanced degrees, and excel in competitive careers.

Finally, a viable SAS can help to systematically expand the very meaning of "merit" beyond a narrow focus on SAT/ACT-type scores by clarifying how a range of student strengths differentiate successful academic and career outcomes. This SAS can help to develop a more rigorous empirical foundation for a comprehensive role strain and adaptation model as well as an evidence base for strategic multilevel interventions within a rapidly diversifying student population in the 21st century. Such multilevel interventions, in turn, can more systematically combine high-stakes SAT/ACT-type testing with strengths-based strategies to mobilize both social psychological strengths and *systemic resources* within educational settings, families, communities, and other major societal institutions.

References

Allen, V., & Vande Vliert, E. (1981). *Role transitions.* New York, NY: Plenum.

Astin, A. W. (1993). *What matters in college? Four critical years revisited.* San Francisco, CA: Jossey-Bass.

Astin, A. W. (1999). Student involvement: A developmental theory for higher education. *Journal of College Student Development, 40,* 518–529.

Bandura, A. (1986). *Social foundations of thought and action: A social cognitive theory.* Englewood Cliffs, NJ: Prentice Hall.

Banks, J. A. (2004). *Handbook of research on multicultural education* (2nd ed.). San Francisco, CA: Jossey-Bass.

Bargh, J.A., Gollwitzer, P.M., & Oettingen, G. (2009). Motivation. In S. T. Fiske, D. T. Gilbert, & G. Lindzey (Eds.), *Handbook of social psychology* (5th ed., pp. 268–316.). New York, NY: Wiley.

Barnett, R.C., Biener, L., & Baruch, G.K. (1987). *Gender and stress.* New York, NY: Free Press.

Baron, R. M., & Kenny, D. A. (1986). The moderator-mediator variable distinction in social psychological research: Conceptual, strategic, and statistical considerations. *Journal of Personality and Social Psychology, 51,* 1173–1182.

Bean, J. P. (1985). Interaction effects based on class level in and explanatory model of college student dropout syndrome. *American Educational Research Journal, 22,* 35–64.

Berkes, E. (2007). Practicing biology: Undergraduate laboratory research, persistence in science, and the impact of self-efficacy beliefs. *Dissertation Abstracts International Section A: Humanities and Social Sciences, 68*(6-A), 2388.

Bernhard, E. (1997). *Gender differences in role stress: Role ambiguity, conflict and overload during the college transition* (Unpublished doctoral dissertation). Northwestern University, Evanston, IL.

Betz, N. E. (2000). Self-efficacy theory as a basis for career assessment. *Journal of Career Assessment, 8,* 205–222.

Betz, N. E. (2007). Career self-efficacy: exemplary recent research and emerging directions. *Journal of Career Assessment, 15,* 403–422.

Bowman, P. J. (1977). *Motivational dynamics and achievement among urban community college students: A situationally-oriented path goal expectancy approach* (Unpublished doctoral dissertation). University of Michigan: Ann Arbor, Michigan.

Bowman, P. J. (1984). A discouragement-centered approach to studying unemployment among Black youth: Hopelessness, attributions and psychological distress. *International Journal of Mental Health*, *13*, 68–91.

Bowman, P. J. (1989). Research perspectives on Black men: Role strain and adaptation across the adult life cycle. In R. L. Jones (Ed.), *Black adult development and aging* (pp. 117–150). Berkeley, CA: Cobbs & Henry.

Bowman, P. J. (1990). The adolescent to adult transition: Discouragement among jobless Black youth (pp. 87–105). In V. C. McLoyd & C. Flanagan (Eds.), *New directions in child development* (pp. 87–105). San Francisco: Jossey-Bass.

Bowman, P. J. (1996). Naturally occurring psychological expectancies: Theory and measurement among African Americans. In R. L. Jones (Ed.), *Handbook of tests and measurements for Black populations* (pp. 553–578). Berkeley, CA: Cobbs & Henry.

Bowman, P. J. (2006). Role strain and adaptation issues in the strength-based model: Diversity, multilevel, and life-span considerations. *Counseling Psychologist*, *34*, 118–133.

Bowman, P. J., & Howard, C. S. (1985). Race-related socialization, motivation and academic achievement: A study of Black youth in three-generation families. *Journal of the American Academy of Child Psychiatry*, *24*, 134–141.

Bowman, P. J., & Sanders, R. (1998). Unmarried African American fathers: A comparative life span analysis. *Journal of Comparative Family Studies*, *29*, 39–56.

Bowman, P. J., & Smith, W. A. (2002). Racial ideology in the campus community (pp. 103–120). In W. A. Smith, P. G. Altbach, & K. Lomotey (Eds.), *The racial crisis in higher education: Continuing challenges for the 21st century* (pp. 103–120). Albany: State University of New York Press.

Brislin, R. (1993). *Understanding culture's influence on behavior*. New York, NY: Harcourt Brace Jovanovich.

Byars, A. G., & Hatchett, G. (1998). Applications of social cognitive theory to the career development of women of color. *Applied and Preventive Psychology*, *7*, 255–267.

Cameron, K. S. (2008). *Positive leadership*. San Francisco, CA: Berrett Koehler.

Carnevale, A. P. (1999, October). Wanted: Strong thinkers. *Scientific American*, 89.

Chubin, D. E., DePass, A. L. & Blockus, L. (2009). *Understanding interventions that broaden participation in research careers:*

Embracing the breadth of purpose (Vol. 3). New York, NY: American Association for the Advancement of Science.

Cokley, K. O. (2003). What do we know about the motivation of African American students? Challenging the "anti-intellectual" myth. *Harvard Education Review, 73*, 524–558.

Coverman, S. (1989). Role overload, role conflict, and stress: Addressing consequences of multiple role demands. *Social Forces, 67*, 965–982.

Covington, M. V. (2000). Goal theory, motivation, and school achievement: An integrative review. *Annual Review of Psychology*, 51, 117–200

Darling-Hammond, L. (2010). Structured for failure: Race, resources, and student achievement. In H. R. Markus and P. M. L. Moya (Eds.), *Doing race: 21 essays for the 21st century* (pp. 295–321). New York, NY: W. W. Norton.

DePass, A. L., & Chubin, D. E. (2008). *Understanding interventions that encourage minorities to pursue research careers: Building a community of research and practice (Vol II)*. Bethesda, MD: American Society of Cell Biology.

Douvan, E., & Walker, A. (1956). Sense of effectiveness in public affairs. *Psychological Monographs, 70*, 1–19.

Ebreo, A. C. (1998). *Subjective culture, perceived social support, and adaptive coping*: *A multi-ethnic study of the transition to college* (Unpublished doctoral dissertation). University of Illinois, Urbana–Champaign.

Eccles, J. S., & Wigfield, A. (2002). Motivational beliefs, values, and goals. *Annual Review of Psychology, 53*, 109–132.

Feather, N. T. (1982). *Expectations and actions: Expectancy-value models in psychology*. Hilldale, NJ: Erlbaum.

Feldman, G. S. (1999). *Self efficacy and outcome expectations in successful student development: A multi-ethnic study of the college transition* (Unpublished doctoral dissertation). Northwestern University, Evanston, IL.

Gainor, K. A. (2006). Twenty-five years of self-efficacy in career assessment and practice. *Journal of Career Assessment*, 14, 161–178.

Goggin, W. J. (1999, May). A "merit-aware" model for college admissions and affirmative action. *Postsecondary Education Opportunity Newsletter,* pp. 6–12.

Gonzalez, N., Moll, L., & Amantqi, C. (2005). *Funds of knowledge: Theorizing practices in households, communities, and classrooms.* Mahwah, NJ: Erlbaum.

Good, J. M, Halpin, G., & Halpin, G. (2000). A promising prospect for minority retention: Students becoming peer mentors. *Journal of Negro Education*, 69, 375–383.

Goode, W. J. (1960). A theory of role strain. *American Sociological Review*, *11*, 483–496.

Gore, P. A. (2006). Academic self-efficacy as a predictor of college outcomes: Two incremental validity studies. *Journal of Career Assessment*, *14*, 92–115.

Graham, C., Baker, & Wapner, S. (1985). Prior interracial experience and Black student transition into predominantly White colleges. *Journal of Personality and Social Psychology*, *47*, 1146–1154.

Gurin, P., Dey, E. L., Hurtado, S., & Gurin, G. (2002). Diversity and higher education: Theory and impact on educational outcomes. *Harvard Educational Review*, *72*, 330–366.

Gutiérrez, K. (2006) *Culture matters: Rethinking educational equity*. New York, NY: Carnegie Foundation.

Hatchett, G., & Lent, R. W. (1992). Theoretical advances and current inquiry in career psychology. In S. D. Brown & R. W. Lent (Eds.), *Handbook of counseling psychology* (pp. 419–451). Oxford, England: Wiley.

Harper, S. R., & Quaye, S. J. (2009). *Student engagement in higher education: Theoretical perspectives and practical approaches for diverse populations*. New York, NY: Routledge.

Heppner, P. P., & Peterson, C. (1982). The development and implications of a personal problem-solving inventory. *Journal of Counseling Psychology*, *29*, 66–75.

Heppner, P. P, Witty, T. E., & Dixon, W. A. (2004). Problem-solving appraisal and human adjustment: A review of 20 years of research using the Problem Solving Inventory. *The Counseling Psychologist*, *32*, 344–428.

Hill, R. B. (1998). *Strengths of African American families: 25 years later*. New York, NY: R&B Press.

Husman, J., & Lens, W. (1999). The role of future in student motivation. *Educational Psychology*, *34*, 113–125.

Jayakumar, U. (2008). Can higher education meet the needs of an increasingly diverse global society? Campus diversity and cross-cultural workforce competencies. *Harvard Educational Review*, *78*, 615–649.

Jones, S. R., & Hill, K. E. (2003). Understanding patterns of commitment: Student motivation for community service involvement. *Journal of Higher Education*, *74*, 516–539.

Kahlenberg, R. D. (2004). *America's untapped resource: Low income students in higher education*. New York, NY: Century Foundation Press.

Kahlenberg, R. D. (2010). *Rewarding strivers: Helping low-income students succeed in college*. New York, NY: Century Foundation Press.

Kahn, R. L., & Boysiere, P. (1992). Stress in organizations. In M. D. Dunnette & L. M. Hough (Eds.), *Handbook of industrial and organizational psychology* (Vol. 2, pp. 571–650). Palo Alto, CA: Consulting Psychologists Press.

Kahn, R. L., Wolfe, D. M., Quinn, R., Snoek, J. D., & Rosenthal, R. A. (1964). *Organizational stress*. New York, NY: Wiley.

Kail, R. V. & Cavanaugh, J. C. (2000). *Human development: A life span view*. Belmont, CA: Wadsworth.

Kelloway, E. K., & Barling, J. (1990). Item content versus item wording: Disentangling role conflict and role ambiguity. *Journal of Applied Psychology, 75*, 738–742.

King, L. A., & King, D. W. (1990). Role conflict and ambiguity: A critical assessment of construct validity. *Psychological Bulletin*, 107, 48–64.

Kuh, G. D. (1995). The other curriculum: Out-of-class experiences associated with student learning and personal development. *Journal of Higher Education, 66*, 123–155.

Kuh, G. D. (2005). Student engagement in the first year of college. In L. M. Upcraft, J. N. Gardner, & B. O. Barefoot (Eds.), *Challenging and supporting the first-year student: A handbook for improving the first year of college* (pp. 86–107). San Francisco, CA: Jossey-Bass.

Kyllonen, P. C. (2008). *The research behind the ETS Personal Potential Index.* Princeton, NJ: Educational Testing Service. Retrieved from http://www.ets.org./Media/Products/PPI/10411_PPI_bkgrd_report_RD4.pdf.

Kyllonen, P. C., Lipnevich, A. A., Burris, J. & Roberts, R. D. (2009). *Personality, motivation, and college readiness: A prospectus for assessment and development* (Educational Testing Service Research Report No: RR-09-xx). Princeton, NJ: Educational Testing Service.

Kyllonen, P. C., Roberts, R. D., & Stankov, L. (2007). *Extending intelligence: Enhancement and new constructs*. New York, NY: Erlbaum.

Le, H., Casillas, A., & Robbins, S. B. (2005). Motivational and skills, social, and self-management predictors of college outcomes: Constructing the student readiness inventory. *Educational and Psychological Measurement*, 65(3), 482–508.

Lee, C. (2003). Guest Editor. Reconceptualizing race and ethnicity in educational research. *Educational Researcher*, 32 (5), 3–5.

Lopatto, D. (2007). Undergraduate research experiences support science career decisions and active learning. *CBE Life Science Education, 6*, 297–306.

Lopez, J. D. (2005). Race-related stress and sociocultural orientation among Latino students during their transition into a predominantly White, highly selective institution. *Journal of Higher Education*, 4, 354–365.

Lotkowski, V. A., Robbins, S. B., & Noeth, R. J. (2004). *The role of academic and non-academic factors in improving college retention* (ACT policy report). Available from www.act.org/research/policy/index.html

Louge, C. T., Hutchens, T. A., & Hector, M. A. (2005). Student leadership: A phenomenological exploration of postsecondary experiences. *Journal of College Student Development*, *46*, 393–408.

Mayer, J., Roberts, R. D., & Barsade, S. G. (2008). Human abilities: Emotional intelligence. *Annual Review of Psychology*, *59*, 507–536.

McAdams, D. P., Reynolds, J., Lewis, M. Patten, A., & Bowman, P J. (2001). When bad things turn good and good things turn bad: Sequences of redemption and contamination in life narrative and their relations to psychosocial adaptation in midlife adults and students. *Personality and Social Psychology Bulletin*, *27*, 486–496.

McNeil, J. D. (1998). *Racial and ethnic socialization among college students: A multi-ethnic family ecology approach* (Unpublished doctoral dissertation). Northwestern University, Evanston, IL.

Merton, R. (1968). *Social theory and social structure.* New York, NY: Free Press.

Neville, H. A., Heppner, P. P., & Wang, L. F. (1997). Relations among racial identity attitudes, perceived stressors, and coping styles in African American college students. *Journal of Counseling and Development*, *75*, 303–311.

Olson, S., & Fagen, A. P. (2007). *Understanding interventions that encourage minorities to pursue research careers: Summary of a workshop* (Vol. 1). Washington, DC: National Academies Press.

Orellana, M. F., & Bowman, P. (2003). Cultural diversity research on learning and development: Conceptual, methodological, and strategic considerations. *Educational Researcher*, *32*, 26–32.

Orfield, G. & Ashkinaze, C. (1991). *The closing door: Conservative policy and Black opportunity.* Chicago, IL: University of Chicago Press.

Page, S. (2007). *The difference: How the power of diversity creates better groups, firms, schools, and societies.* Princeton, NJ, and Oxford, England: Princeton University Press.

Pearlin, L. I. (1983). Role strains and personal stress. In H. B. Kaplan (Ed.), *Psychosocial stress: Trends in theory and research* (pp. 3–32). New York, NY: Academic Press.

Peterson, C., & Seligman, M. E. P. (1984). Causal explanations as a risk factor for depression: Theory and evidence. *Psychological Review*, *91*, 347–374.

Pritchard, M. E., Wilson, G. S., & Yamnitz, B. (2007). What predicts adjustment among college students: A longitudinal panel study. *Journal of American College Health, 56*, 15–21.

Rath, T. & Conchie, B. (2008). *Strengths and leadership: Great leaders, teams, and why people follow*. New York, NY: Gallup Press.

Reyes, E. A. (2002). *Extended family support as a protective factor among college students: An exploratory multi-ethnic study* (Unpublished doctoral dissertation). Northwestern University, Evanston, IL.

Ridgeway, C.L., & Walker, H. (1995). Status structure. In K. Cook, G. Fine, & J. House (Eds.), *Sociological perspectives in social psychology* (pp. 281–310). New York, NY: Allyn & Bacon.

Robbins, S. B., Lauver, K., Le, H., Davis, D., Langley, R., & Carlstrom, A. (2004). Do psychosocial and study skill factors predict college outcomes? A meta-analysis. *Psychological Bulletin, 130*, 261–288.

Rowley, L., & Bowman, P .J. (2009). Risk, protection, and achievement disparities among African American males: Cross-generation theory, research and comprehensive intervention. *Journal of Negro Education, 78*, 305–320.

Sanders, R. T. (1997). *Intellectual and psychosocial predictors of success in the college transition: A multi-ethnic study of freshmen students on a predominantly white campus* (Unpublished doctoral dissertation). University of Illinois at Urbana-Champaign.

Sarbin, T. R., & Allen, V. L. (1968). Role theory. In G. Lindzey & E. Aronson (Eds.), *Handbook of Social Psychology* (pp. 488–568). Reading, MA: Addison-Wesley.

Sedlacek, W. E. (2004). *Beyond the big test: Noncognitive assessment in higher education*. San Francisco, CA: Jossey-Bass.

Seligman, M. E. P., Sten, T., Park, N., & Peterson, C. (2005). Positive psychology progress: Empirical validation of interventions. *American Psychologist, 60*, 410–421.

Shiraishi, Y. (2000). *Attributional patterns and adjustment in the college transition: A cross-cultural study* (Unpublished doctoral dissertation). Northwestern University, Evanston, IL.

Simons, J., Dewitte, S., & Lens, W. (2004). The role of different types of instrumentality in motivation, study strategies, and performance: Know why you learn, so you'll know what to learn. *British Journal of Educational Psychology, 74*, 343–360.

Smith, D. G. (1989). *The challenge of diversity: Involvement or alienation in the academy*. Washington, DC: George Washington University.

Smith, D. G. (2009). *Diversity's promise for higher education: Making it work*. Baltimore, MD: John Hopkins University Press.

Smith, E. J. (2006). The strength-based counseling model. *The Counseling Psychologist, 34*, 13–79.

St. John, E. P., Simmons, A. B., & Musoba, G. D. (2002). Merit-aware admissions in public universities: Increasing diversity. *Thought & Action, 17*(2), 35–46.

Sternberg, R. J. (1996). *Successful Intelligence.* New York, NY: Plume.

Sternberg, R. J. (2004). What is wisdom and how can we develop it? *The Annals of the American Academy of Political and Social Science, 591*, 164–174.

Takagi, D. Y. (1992). *The retreat from race: Asian Americans admissions and racial politics.* New Brunswick, NJ: Rutgers University Press.

Taylor, T. P., & Pancer, S. M. (2007). Community service experience and commitment to volunteering. *Journal of Applied Social Psychology, 37*, 320–345.

Tinto, V. (1993). *Leaving college: Rethinking the causes and cures of student attrition.* Chicago, IL: University of Chicago Press.

Thomas, L. L., Kuncel, N. R., & Crede, M. (2007). Noncognitive variables in college admissions: The case of the Non-Cognitive Questionnaire. *Educational and Psychological Measurement, 67*, 635–657.

Tracy, L., & Johnson, T. (1981). What do the role conflict and role ambiguity scales measure? *Journal of Applied Psychology, 66*, 464–469.

Triandis, H. C., Lambert, W., Berry, J., Lonner, W., Hernon, A., Brislin, R., & Draguns, J. (Eds.). (1980–1981). *Handbook of cross-cultural psychology, 1–6.* Boston, MA: Allyn & Bacon.

Weiner, B. (1986). Attribution theory of motivation and emotion. New York, NY: Springer-Verlag.

Zwick, R. (2002). *Fair game?* New York, NY: RouteledgeFalmer.

CHAPTER 9

USING NONCOGNITIVE VARIABLES IN ASSESSING READINESS FOR HIGHER EDUCATION

William E. Sedlacek

Introduction

There has been a recent focus on "college readiness" in educational literature. This is an important shift in emphasis from viewing admissions in higher education as a function separate from the wide range of attributes a student will need once enrolled (Conley, 2005). While readiness for college includes taking the appropriate courses, getting good grades, and scoring well on admissions tests, there is evidence that many other attributes determine whether most students will succeed in higher education.

Courses

While students continue to need courses in math, English, foreign languages, etc., there has been a tendency among educators and college admissions staff to feel that more is better. The logic goes that if we would just require more math courses, students would be better prepared. However, the law of diminishing marginal utility becomes relevant at some point. For example, Sawyer (2008) in a study of 245,175 students from 9,507 high schools who took the EXPLORE (8th grade), PLAN (10th grade), and ACT (12th grade) tests concluded that taking additional standard college prepara-tory courses in high school, taking advanced/honors courses, and earning higher grades would, by themselves, only modestly increase the percentage of students who leave high school adequately prepared to take credit-bearing courses in the first year of college. Sawyer also concluded that taking additional courses and earning higher grades mostly benefit students who by grade eight are already well "on-target" in preparing themselves for higher education and that psychosocial variables such as motivation, self-discipline, and social connectedness were important developmental variables that also need to be considered.

In summary, up to a point, more math and other courses are useful in preparing students for higher education; beyond that point, other variables become more important for student success. Some ideas for what these variables might be are discussed in the following sections.

187

Grades

Recent literature has shown that grades are becoming increasingly less useful as indicators of student achievement or as predictors of future student success. This is largely due to the statistical artifact that students at all levels of education are being assigned higher grades. Are current students just smarter and/or more accomplished than their predecessors? This seems unlikely, but even if true it does not help us prepare students for higher education, since grades no longer appear as useful in differentiating student academic achievement as they once were.

Grades have become more of a constant because of "grade inflation." For example, Woodruff and Ziomek, (2004) found that the mean grade point average (GPA) of high school students taking the ACT assessment had increased from 1991 to 2003 a total of .20 to .26 points on a four-point system, depending on the subject area. Rojstaczer (2009) showed that the GPA in higher education nationally had risen from 2.94 in 1991–1992 to 3.11 in 2006–2007, on a four-point system. Additionally, many K–12 schools are not assigning grades to students and are using extramural and portfolio assessments instead (Washor, Arnold & Mojkowski, 2008).

Tests

Admission tests were created initially to help select as well as advise students. They were intended to be useful to educators making decisions about students. While they were always considered useful in evaluating candidates, tests were also considered to be more equitable than using prior grades because of the variation in quality among preparatory schools. The College Board has long felt that the SAT was limited in what it measured and should not be relied upon as the only tool to judge applicants (Angoff, 1971).

In 1993, the verbal and mathematical reasoning sections of the SAT were lengthened and the multiple-choice Test of Standard Written English was dropped. The name was changed from Scholastic Aptitude Test to Scholastic Assessment Tests, while retaining the SAT initials. Currently it is just called the SAT-I. In 2003, the College Board announced that an essay would be added and that the analogies item type removed as of 2005. Despite various changes and versions over the years, the SAT in essence still measures what it did in 1926, verbal and math ability; it is basically still considered a general intelligence test (Sedlacek, 2003, 2004b).

We seem to have come to a point where the "Big Test" has become the primary object of attention in many schools (Lemann, 2000). It has become the standard by which we judge ourselves and others. Many assume that if an individual has high ACT, SAT, or Graduate Record Examination (GRE) scores, or if a school has high mean scores on such tests, the students must be learning something, and the school must be good. To cite that common metaphor, the tail is wagging the dog.

Standardized tests remain controversial in general, particularly their fairness for people of color (Helms, 2009). Much of the debate centers on statistical artifacts, measurement problems, and poor research methodology, including biased samples and inappropriate statistical analyses and interpretations (Sackett, Borneman, & Connelly, 2009). While this discussion and controversy are useful and interesting to academics, we may have lost track of why tests were developed to begin with and how they can be used. Test results should be useful to educators, student service workers, and administrators by providing the basis to help students learn better and to analyze their needs. As currently designed, tests do not accomplish these objectives. Many teachers tend to teach to get the highest test scores for their students, student service workers may ignore the tests, and too many administrators are satisfied if the average test score rises in their schools. We need something from our tests that currently we are not getting. We need measures that are fair to all and provide a good assessment of the developmental and learning needs of students, while being useful in selecting outstanding applicants. Our current tests don't do that.

Keeping Up With Change

The world is much different than it was when the SAT and other tests were developed in the last century. International students, women, people of color, gays, lesbians and bisexuals, and people with disabilities among others are participating in higher education in more extensive and varied ways (Knapp, Kelly, Whitmore, Wu, & Gallego, 2002). Commonly employed tests have not kept up with these changes (Sedlacek, 2004a).

We need a new approach. It is not good enough to feel constrained by the limitations of our current ways of conceiving tests. Instead of asking, "How can we make the SAT and other such tests better?" we need to ask, "What kinds of measures will meet our needs now and in the future?" The purpose of this chapter is to present the underlying logic and research supporting a method that yields such measures. We do not need to ignore our current tests, we need to add some new measures that expand the potential we can derive from assessment.

Noncognitive Variables

Noncognitive is used here to refer to variables relating to adjustment, motivation, and student perceptions, rather than the traditional verbal and quantitative areas (often called cognitive) typically measured by standardized tests (Sedlacek, 1998a, 1998b, 2004a). While noncognitive variables are useful for all students, they also provide viable alternatives in fairly assessing the abilities of people of color, women, international students, older students, students with disabilities, or others with experiences that are different than those of young, White, heterosexual, able-bodied, Eurocentric males in the United States (traditional students). Standardized tests and prior grades provide only a limited view of one's potential. Below is a discussion of the eight variables recommended for inclusion in college readiness assessment systems (see Appendix 1). For a more detailed discussion of each of these dimensions and the research supporting their use, see Sedlacek (2004a).

1. Positive Self-Concept

Successful students possess confidence, strong "self" feeling, and strength of character, determination, and independence. A strong self-concept seems important for students of color and women at all educational levels at which it has been investigated. The student who feels confident of "making it" through school is more likely to survive and graduate. For example, although many students of color have had to overcome incredible obstacles and setbacks even to reach the point of applying for college, they need even greater determination to continue. Determination is needed precisely because students may come from a different cultural background or have had different gender-related experiences than the students and faculty members they will encounter in college.

Seeing oneself as part of the system and feeling good about it is an important component of how self-concept is used here. Feeling a part of the system is generally easier for traditional students since so much of the system is designed for them. In summary, a positive self-concept is predictive of success in higher education for students of color and other nontraditional students. While having a good self-concept is important for any student, it becomes even more important for those with nontraditional experiences because of the added complexity of dealing with a system that was not designed for them.

2. Realistic Self-Appraisal

Realistic self-appraisal is the ability to assess one's strengths and weaknesses, allowing for self-development. Realism in self-appraisal by nontraditional persons does not connote cultural, racial, or gender deficiency or inferiority. For example, White students do well pursuing their own interests (internal control) in a society designed to meet their needs, while students of color need to be aware of the external control that negotiating the racism in the system requires. In summary, students of color and women of all races who are able to make realistic assessments of their abilities, despite obstacles to making those assessments, do better in school than do those less able to make those judgments. Realistic self-appraisal is also a predictor of success for students with more traditional experiences.

3. Understands and Knows How to Handle Racism: Navigating the System

The successful nontraditional student is a realist based on personal experience with discrimination; is committed to fighting to improve the existing system; is not submissive to existing wrongs, nor hateful of society, nor ready to "cop out"; is able to handle a racist system; and asserts that the school has a role or duty to fight racism. Institutional racism is defined as the negative consequences that accrue to a member of a given group, regardless of any other attributes of the individual, because of the way a system or subsystem operates in society (e.g., college admissions). Racism can take many forms and is used here to cover all types of "isms" (e.g., sexism, ageism, "disabilityism"). While racism can be individual rather than institutional, the primary concern here is for dealing with the policies, procedures, and barriers, intentional or not, that interfere with the development of people.

For traditional students, this variable takes the form of handling the system without the addition of racism. How we learn to handle the circumstances with which we are confronted tells us much about our ability and potential. Learning to make the systems of society work for them is important for all students, but the overlay of racism upon those systems makes it more difficult to understand and negotiate for students of color and women. Hence, it is critical to their success in school.

4. Long-Range Goals

Having long-range goals predicts success in college for students. Since role models often are more difficult to find and the reinforcement system has been relatively random for them, many nontraditional students have difficulty understanding the relationship between current efforts and the ultimate practice of their professions. In other words, since students of color tend to face a greater culture shock than do White students in adjusting to a White-student-oriented campus culture, students of color are not as predictable in their academic performance in their first year as are traditional students; by their second year, students of color are about as predictable as others. Hence, students who show evidence of having long-range goals do better in college than those without such goals.

5. Strong Support Person

Students who have done well in school tend to have a person who has a strong influence on them who provides advice, particularly in times of crisis. This individual may be in the education system or in the immediate family, but for nontraditional students it is often a relative or a community worker. Many students of color do not have the "props" or support to fall back on that traditional students typically have. Therefore, students of color, women, gays, lesbians and bisexuals, and others for whom the educational system was not designed do better in college if they have a history of developing supportive relationships than those who have not had this experience.

6. Leadership

Nontraditional students who are most successful in higher education have shown an ability to organize and influence others. The key here is nontraditional evidence of leadership among students. Application forms and interviews typically are slanted in directions likely to yield less useful information about the backgrounds of nontraditional students. Many White applicants know how to "play the game" and will have "taken up," and then be sure to list, a wide variety of offices held in traditional school organizations. Many students of color will not have had the time or the inclination for such activities.

The most promising students, however, may have shown their leadership in less typical ways, such as working in their communities, through religious organizations, or even as street gang leaders. It is important to pursue the culture- and gender-relevant activities of the applicants rather than to treat them as if they come from a homogenous environment.

7. Community

Having a community with which students of color and women can identify and from which they can receive support is critical to their academic success. The community often is based on racial, cultural, or gender issues, but it may not be for all students. Students of color, women, and other persons with nontraditional experiences who are active in a community learn how to handle the system, exhibit leadership, and develop their self-concepts in such groups. Therefore, those who have been involved in a community, often based on race and/or gender, are more successful in college than are those not so involved.

8. Nontraditional Knowledge Acquired

Persons of color are more apt to learn and develop using methods that are less traditional and are outside the education system. The methods may be culture- or gender-related, and the field itself may be nontraditional. Assessing what a student learns outside school should be an important part of an evaluation program for any student. Those who have experienced discrimination within the education system may be more likely to show evidence of their ability through nontraditional learning prior to college than students with a more traditional experience.

Measuring Noncognitive Variables

The Noncognitive Questionnaire (NCQ) was designed to assess the eight noncognitive variables discussed above and shown in Appendix 1 (Sedlacek, 1996). Several forms of the NCQ have been developed and employed in different contexts. Test-retest reliability estimates on NCQ scores for various samples range from .74 to .94, with a median of .85 (Sedlacek, 2004b). Inter-rater reliability on scores from the three open-ended NCQ items ranged from .73 to 1.00.

The variables shown in Appendix 1 have been successfully assessed in ways other than the NCQ. In the Gates Millennium Scholars program funded by the Bill & Melinda Gates Foundation, a review of an entire application is scored on the noncognitive variables and makes up about 80% of the weight used in selection. The application includes short-answer questions based on each of the noncognitive variables shown in Appendix 1, a personal statement by the applicant, letters of recommendation by the nominator and another person, and demographic, background, and activity questions. Raters were trained to identify and consider all this information in scoring each of the eight noncognitive variables. The raters were educators of color, familiar with multicultural issues in education and working with the kinds of students that were applying. Inter-judge reliability was estimated at .83 for a sample of raters in the first year (Sedlacek & Sheu, 2004, 2008). More than 11,000 Gates Scholars have attended more than 1,450 different colleges and universities with a 97% first-year retention rate, an 87% 5-year retention rate and a 78% 5-year graduation rate. More than 60% are majoring in STEM (science, technology, engineering, mathematics) fields. Their Realistic Self Appraisal score has a significant relationship with their first-year college GPA, and their Leadership score has a significant relationship with engaging in academic activities while in college.

The Bill & Melinda Gates Foundation (2009) has initiated a program focusing on college readiness. This program has the major goal of ensuring that 80% of students graduating from high school are prepared for college, with a focus on low-income and minority students reaching this target. The Foundation recognizes that preparing for higher education involves more than coursework. Having elementary and secondary teachers work with students on behaviors beyond the typical classroom activities is critical to the success of this initiative (Bill & Melinda Gates Foundation, 2009). The noncognitive variables shown in Appendix 1 provide a method for achieving those program goals. Sedlacek (2004a) provides extensive information on the behaviors that students might demonstrate that would positively or negatively affect each noncognitive variable. Teachers can work with students to encourage the positive behaviors and reduce the negative ones (see Appendix 2). Administrators can also evaluate students' school environments to determine how the school supports or hinders student development on each of the variables.

Oregon State University (OSU) has developed a student evaluation system based on the noncognitive variables shown in Appendix 1. The OSU admissions application contains six short-answer questions that cover the eight noncognitive variables. Responses are limited to 100 words and are scored independently from other application materials. Raters from many parts of the campus are trained to score the six questions. Interrater agreement was estimated at .85. OSU uses its system in selection, academic advising, student services, on- and off-campus referrals, financial aid, and teaching. OSU noncognitive scores correlate with retention, and since employing noncognitive variables the OSU retention rate is higher, there is more diversity in the applicant pool and first-year class, campus offices are working better together, applicant GPA is up, referrals are better, and new courses and student services have begun based on the noncognitive information.

Alternative high schools have begun to employ the noncognitive variables in a variety of creative ways. The Big Picture, Inc. does not own schools or manage school charters but employs the noncognitive variables in helping set school goals, designing teacher training, and securing funding from public and private sources. They have a primary goal of helping students make the transition to higher education. The student population of schools using Big Picture is predominantly low-income, urban, and non-White, and many students speak a first language other than English (Washor et al., 2008). Big Picture schools are employing a number of methods to assess the noncognitive variables including the basic NCQ questionnaire (Sedlacek, 2004a), behavioral checklists, advisor rating forms, and interview techniques. Utilizing different approaches and creating new forms that fit the particular needs of schools or programs is encouraged and increases the probability that noncognitive variables can be used to benefit students in a variety of contexts.

Uses of Noncognitive Variables

The noncognitive variables can be used along with any other variables, models, or techniques employed in whatever role or type of mentoring, advising, or teaching is involved. Teachers, advisors, or counselors who use the system can expect to obtain better student outcomes in terms of grades, retention, and satisfaction, as well as greater satisfaction themselves as a result of employing something systematic with demonstrated utility in an area that often produces confusion and anxiety. Major benefits include:

First, attributes of students can be assessed that correlate well with their eventual success at an institution of higher education. While a school could select a class that would do well academically solely based on grades and test scores, those predictions could be improved by adding noncognitive variables which would give a more complete picture of applicant abilities.

Second, the diversity of an entering class can be increased. Students of color and those with less traditional backgrounds than typical students can be identified and admitted with a high probability of success. This would help discourage future challenges to the lack of diversity at a school.

Third, noncognitive variables can be employed in teaching, advising, and student services on campus. This would be beneficial for all students, traditional and nontraditional alike in, for example, designing and implementing retention programs. Aside from their value for nontraditional students, noncognitive variables would be helpful in identifying how traditional students, admitted with high grades and test scores, who are having difficulty on some of the noncognitive dimensions can be helped.

Fourth, noncognitive variables can provide an important link between K–12 education and college. Too often, each system works independently at the expense of student development. If precollege counselors and university admissions officers, student service personnel, faculty, and administrators were to all work within the same system, students could be assisted in their development and transition throughout the educational process. For example, Roper and Sedlacek (1988) discussed and evaluated a course on racism and how to help students develop on noncognitive dimensions, and Lechuga, Clerc, and Howell (2009) presented an experience-based system of learning activities focused on promoting social justice.

Fifth, noncognitive variables can be successfully employed in graduate and professional education thus extending the benefits of the system throughout an institution (Sedlacek, 2004b). Sedlacek, Benjamin, Schlosser, and Sheu (2007) also provided examples and case studies of how noncognitive variables can be used in postmatriculation programs in higher education.

All programs should be evaluated as to their success. Statistical analyses and models should be employed in program evaluation where possible. However, simpler methods such as noting the increase in students graduating or going on to higher education after initiating the use of noncognitive variables are also helpful.

References

Angoff, W. H. (1971). *The College Board admissions testing program*. New York, NY: College Entrance Examination Board.

Bill & Melinda Gates Foundation (2009). *College ready*. Seattle, WA: Bill & Melinda Gates Foundation.

Conley, D. (2005). *College knowledge: What it really takes for students to succeed and what it takes to get them ready*. San Francisco, CA: Jossey-Bass.

Helms, J. E. (2009). Defense of tests prevents prevents objective considerationsof validity and fairness. *American Psychologist, 64*, 283–284.

Knapp, L G., Kelly, J E., Whitmore, R W., Wu, S, & Gallego, L M. (2002). *Enrollment in postsecondary institutions, fall 2000 and financial statistics, fiscal year 2000* (NCES 2002–212). Washington DC: National Center for Education Statistics.

Lechuga, V. M., Clerc, L. N., & Howell, A. K. (2009). Power, privilege, and learning: Facilitating encountered situations to promote social justice. *Journal of College Student Development, 50*, 229–244.

Lemann, N. (2000). *The big test: The secret history of the American meritocracy*. New York, NY: Farrar, Straus and Giroux.

Rojstaczer, S. (2009). *College grade inflation*. Retrieved from http://www .gradeinflation.com/

Roper, L., & Sedlacek, W. E. (1988). Student affairs professionals in academic roles: A course on racism. *National Association of Student Personnel Administrators Journal, 26*(1), 27–32.

Sawyer, R. (2008). *Benefits of additional coursework and improved course performance in preparing students for college* (ACT Research Report 2008–1). Iowa City, IA: ACT, Inc.

Sackett, P. R., Borneman, M. J., & Connelly, B. S. (2009). Responses to issues raised about validity, bias, and fairness in high-stakes testing. *American Psychologist, 64*, 285–287.

Sedlacek, W. E. (1996). An empirical method of determining nontraditional group status. *Measurement and Evaluation in Counseling and Development*, *28*, 200–210.

Sedlacek, W. E. (1998a). Admissions in higher education: Measuring cognitive and noncognitive variables. In D. J. Wilds & R. Wilson (Eds.), *Minorities in higher education 1997–98: Sixteenth annual status report* (pp. 47–71). Washington, DC: American Council on Education.

Sedlacek, W. E. (1998b). Multiple choices for standardized tests. *Priorities*, *10*, 1–16.

Sedlacek, W. E. (2003). Alternative measures in admissions and scholarship selection. *Measurement and Evaluation in Counseling and Development*, *35*, 263–272.

Sedlacek, W. E. (2004a). *Beyond the big test: Noncognitive assessment in higher education*. San Francisco, CA: Jossey-Bass.

Sedlacek, W. E. (2004b). Why we should use noncognitive variables with graduate and professional students. *The Advisor: The Journal of the National Association of Advisors for the Health Professions*, *24*(2), 32–39.

Sedlacek, W. E., Benjamin, E., Schlosser, L. Z., & Sheu, H. B. (2007). Mentoring in academia: Considerations for diverse populations. In T. D. Allen & L. T. Eby (Eds.), *The Blackwell handbook of mentoring: A multiple perspectives approach* (pp. 259–280). Malden, MA: Blackwell.

Sedlacek, W. E., & Sheu, H. B. (2004). Academic success of Gates Millennium Scholars. In E. P. St. John (Ed.), *Readings on Equal Education: Vol. 20. Improving access and college success for diverse students: Studies of the Gates Millennium Scholars Program* (pp. 181–197). New York, NY: AMS Press.

Sedlacek, W. E. & Sheu, H. B. (2008). The academic progress of undergraduate and graduate Gates Millennium Scholars and non-scholars by race and gender. In W. T. Trent & E. P. St. John (Eds.), *Readings on Equal Education: Vol. 23. Resources, assets, and strengths among successful diverse students: Understanding the contributions of the Gates Millennium Scholars Program* (pp. 143–177). New York, NY: AMS Press.

Washor, E., Arnold, K., & Mojkowski, C. (2008). *Taking the long view on student success*. Providence, RI: Big Picture.

Woodruff, D. J., & Ziomek, R. L. (2004). *High school grade inflation from 1991 to 2003* (ACT Research Report 2004–04). Iowa City, IA: ACT, Inc.

Appendix 1

Description of Noncognitive Variables

Variable #	Variable Name
1	*Positive Self-Concept* Demonstrates confidence, strength of character, determination, and independence.
2	*Realistic Self-Appraisal* Recognizes and accepts strengths and deficiencies, especially academic, and works hard at self-development. Recognizes need to broaden his/her individuality.
3	*Understands and Knows How to Handle Racism; Navigate the System* Exhibits a realistic view of the system based upon personal experience of racism. Committed to improving the existing system. Takes an assertive approach to dealing with existing wrongs, but is not hostile to society nor is a "cop-out." Able to handle racist system and make the system work for him/her.
4	*Long-Range Goals* Able to respond to deferred gratification, plans ahead, and sets goals.
5	*Strong Support Person* Seeks and takes advantage of a strong support network or has someone to turn to in a crisis or for encouragement.
6	*Leadership* Demonstrates strong leadership in any area of his/her background (e.g., church, sports, noneducational groups, gang leader, etc.).
7	*Community* Participates and is involved in his/her community.
8	*Nontraditional Knowledge Acquired* Acquires knowledge outside the education system in sustained and/or culturally related ways.

Appendix 2

Positive and Negative Noncognitive Behaviors

VARIABLES 1 THROUGH 8

In the following, you will find the definition of the variable and a list of questions to guide you in the assessment of each variable

---

Variable Item #1: POSITIVE SELF CONCEPT

This variable assesses the student's confidence, self-esteem, independence, and determination, all vital components of future achievement and success.

Positive Evidence	Negative Evidence
Does the student feel confident of making it through graduation?	Does the student express any reason he/she might not complete school or succeed and attain his/her goals?
Does the student make positive statements about him/herself?	Does the student express concerns that other students are better than he/she is?
Does the student expect to achieve his/her goals and perform well in academic and nonacademic areas?	Does the student expect to have marginal grades?
Does the student provide evidence of how he/she will attain his/her goals?	Does the student have trouble balancing his/her personal and academic life?
Does the student link his/her interests and experiences with his/her goals?	Does the student appear to be avoiding new challenges or situations?
Does the student assume he/she can handle new situations or challenges?	

Variable #2: REALISTIC SELF APPRAISAL

This variable assesses the student's ability to recognize and accept his/her strengths and deficiencies, especially in academics, and that the student works hard at self-development to broaden his/her individuality.

Positive Evidence		Negative Evidence
Is the student aware of his/her strengths and weaknesses?		Is the student unaware of how evaluations are done in school?
Does the student know what it takes to pursue a given career?		Is the student not sure about his/her own abilities?
Is the student realistic about his/her abilities?		Is the student uncertain about how his/her peers or superiors rate his/her performances?
Does the student show an awareness of how his/her service, leadership, extracurricular activities, or school-work has caused him/her to change over time?		Does the student overreact to positive or negative reinforcement rather than seeing it in a larger context?
Has the student learned something from these structured or unstructured activities?		Is the student unaware of how he/she is doing in classes until grades are out?
Does the student appreciate and understand both positive and negative feedback?		Is the student unaware of positive and negative consequences of his/her grades, actions, or skills?
Does the student provide evidence of overcoming anger, shyness, and lack of discipline?		
Does the student face a problem, like a bad grade, with determination to do better?		

Variable #3: UNDERSTANDS HOW TO HANDLE RACISM; NAVIGATE THE SYSTEM

This variable assesses the student's ability to understand the role of the "system" in life and to develop a method of assessing the cultural/racial demands of the system and responding accordingly/assertively.

Positive Evidence		Negative Evidence
Is the student able to overcome challenges or obstacles he/she is confronted with as a result of racism in a positive and effective way?		Is the student unaware of how the "system" works?
Does the student understand the role of the "system" in his/her life and how it treats nontraditional persons?		Is the student preoccupied with racism or does not feel racism exists?
Does the student reveal ways that he/she has learned to "deal" with the "system" accordingly?		Does the student blame others for his/her problems?
		Does the student react with the same intensity to large or small issues concerned with race?
		Is the student's method for successfully handling racism that does not interfere with personal and academic development nonexistent?

Variable #4: LONG-RANGE GOALS

This variable assesses the student's persistence, patience, long-term planning, and willingness to defer gratification and success in college.

Positive Evidence	Negative Evidence
Does the student reveal experience setting both academic and personal long-term goals?	Does the student lack evidence of setting and accomplishing goals?
Does the student provide evidence that he/she is planning for the future?	Is the student likely to proceed without clear direction?
Has the student determined a course of study and anticipated the type of career or path he/she might or could pursue?	Does the student rely on others to determine outcomes?
Is the student aware of realistic and intermediate steps necessary to achieve goals?	Does the student focus too much attention on the present?
Has the student participated in activities (volunteer work, employment, extra courses, community work) related to his/her anticipated career goal?	Is the student's plan for approaching a course, school in general, an activity, etc. nonexistent?
	If the student states his/her goals, are the goals vague or unrealistic?

Variable #5: STRONG SUPPORT PERSON

This variable assesses the availability for the student of a strong support network, help, and encouragement and the degree to which he/she relies solely on her/his own resources.

Positive Evidence		Negative Evidence
Does the student have a strong support system? (This can be a personal, professional, or academic support as long as it is someone the student can turn to for advice, consultation, assistance, encourage-ment, etc.)		Does the student avoid turning to a support person, mentor, or close advisor for help?
Is the student willing to admit that he/she needs help and able to rely on other resources, other than him/herself, to solve problems?		Does the student keep his/her problems to him/herself?
		Does the student state that he/she can handle things on his/her own?
		Does the student state that access to a previous support person may have been reduced or eliminated?
		Is the student unaware of the importance of a support person?

Variable #6: LEADERSHIP

This variable assesses the student's skills developed or influence exercised from his/her formal and informal leadership roles.

Positive Evidence	Negative Evidence
Has the student taken leadership initiative, for example by founding clubs/organizations? What other evidence is there?	Is the student unable to turn to others for advice or direction?
Does the student describe the skills s/he has developed as a leader, skills such as assertiveness, effectiveness, organization, and time management?	Does the student lack confidence or leadership skills?
Has the student shown evidence of influencing others and being a good role model?	Is the student passive or does he/she lack initiative?
Is the student comfortable providing advice and direction to others?	Is the student overly cautious?
Does the student describe a commitment to being a role model for siblings, community members, or schoolmates?	Does the student avoid controversy?
Does the student show sustained commitment to one or two types of organizations through increased involvement, skill development, and responsibility?	
Does the student take action and initiative?	

Variables #7: COMMUNITY

This variable assesses the student's identification with a cultural, geographic, or racial group and his/her demonstrated activity within that community grouping.

Positive Evidence	Negative Evidence
Does the student show sustained commitment to a service site or issue area?	Does the student lack involvement in cultural, racial, or geographical group or community?
Does the student demonstrate a specific or long-term commitment or relationships within a community?	Is the student involved in his/her community in name only?
Has the student accomplished specific goals in a community setting?	Does the student engage more in solitary rather than group activities (academic or nonacademic)?
Does the student's community service relate to career or personal goals?	

Variable #8: NONTRADITIONAL KNOWLEDGE ACQUIRED

This variable assesses the student's experiences gained in a field through study and experiences beyond the classroom. This variable pays particular attention to the ways the student gains nontraditional, perhaps culturally or racially based views of the field.

Positive Evidence		Negative Evidence
Does the student use his/her knowledge to teach others about the topic?		Does the student lack evidence of learning from the community or nonacademic activities?
Is the student working independently in his/her field? (Be sensitive to variations between academic fields and the experiences that can be gained. For example, if in the sciences, by doing independent research, or if in the arts or crafts, by participating in competitions or compositions.)		Is the student traditional in his/her approach to learning?
		Is the student unaware of his/her possibilities in a field of interest?

CHAPTER 10

ADMISSIONS, ACADEMIC READINESS, AND STUDENT SUCCESS: IMPLICATIONS FOR GROWING A DIVERSE EDUCATION PIPELINE

Kurt Burkum, Steve Robbins, and Richard Phelps

A postsecondary credential has become the entry ticket to myriad social, civic, and, in particular, personal economic opportunities. As educational attainment levels required for higher paying and higher employment-security jobs have risen, the demand for *unskilled* jobs has declined. Concomitantly, wage differentials have widened between college graduates and others. While the U.S. labor market signals a need for more college graduates, however, the U.S. higher education system finds it difficult to get some of its students into and many of its students through college. This is particularly true for disadvantaged and minority students (Ryu, 2008). As the United States' population diversifies, gaps persist in the number of disadvantaged and minority students admitted to and succeeding in postsecondary institutions (U.S. Department of Education, 2008). Since at least 1972, college enrollment rates have differed by race/ethnicity, with minority student enrollment and graduation rates lagging behind those of Whites (Figure 1).

Four features of college enrollment rates over the past 30 years are apparent. First, enrollment rates for White, Black, and Hispanic 18- to 24-year-old high school graduates have all increased over time. Since 1976, the college enrollment rate for Black high school graduates has increased by 8.6 percentage points and for Whites by 13.7 percentage points. The enrollment rate trend for Hispanic high school graduates fluctuated widely, making trends more difficult to discern, but there has been an increase over the period depicted in Figure 1.

Second, despite the increases in enrollment rates for all groups, racial/ethnic gaps in U.S. higher education persist. Since 1979, White high school graduates have enrolled in college at noticeably higher rates than have their Black and Hispanic peers.

Third, race/ethnicity enrollment gaps have widened. For example, the White–Black gap increased from 1.9 to 4.5 percentage points between 1979 and 2006; the gap between White and Hispanic high school graduates increased from 1.1 to 11.0 percentage points.

Figure 1. College Enrollment Rates of 18- to 24-Year-Old High School Completers by Race/Ethnicity, 1972–2006

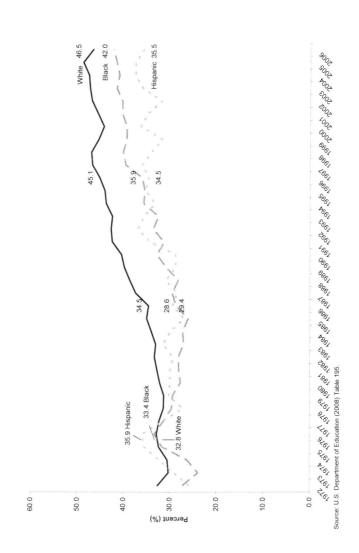

Source: U.S. Department of Education (2008) Table 195.

Fourth, these gaps exist even among students who should be on a level playing field academically—high school graduates.

In response to the persistence of these college enrollment gaps, school-based efforts have been implemented. In the wake of the 2003 *Grutter v. Bollinger* and *Gratz v. Bollinger* Supreme Court decisions, however, some have called for revising college admissions criteria as the most effective policy solution for mitigating race-/ethnicity-based college enrollment gaps—changes that may have the unintended consequence of lowering the academic expectations of college enrollees (e.g., Commission on the Use of Standardized Tests in Undergraduate Admission, 2008). The argument proffered supporting these and similar efforts suggests that current admissions criteria (e.g., SAT or ACT scores) negatively affect minority student enrollment. Advocates note that minority students often do less well on these measures than do their White peers, are more apt to demonstrate academic achievement in other ways, or have other qualities (academic or other) that are more germane to college success. In their view, then, current admissions requirements that emphasize traditional academic performance measures necessarily and artificially limit college access. Consequently, other admissions criteria are needed to ensure a more equitable selection process and more balanced enrollments.

This posture, however, misinterprets two important aspects of the college admissions process and the goals of the higher education enterprise. First, it presents a straw-man argument. Since the beginning of higher education in the colonies in 1636, colleges and universities have always voluntarily used multiple admissions criteria, including some unrelated to academic performance. It is the colleges and universities that determine the admission criteria and the array of measures they use to make admissions decisions. Indeed, between 1995 and 2005, higher education institutions have employed an increasingly varied set of admissions criteria (Hawkins & Clinedinst, 2006). In annual surveys, more than half of colleges and universities report seven different admissions criteria as being of considerable or moderate importance.

Second, and more consequential, a strategy that seeks to increase minority college enrollments by lessening the importance of academic readiness presents a false choice, as college enrollment is only part of the story. Most of the benefits of college are realized only upon completion of college; to that end, enrollment is a necessary but insufficient condition. Matriculation to degree completion is almost exclusively based on college academic achievement; a student earns a degree by fulfilling specific academic requirements. Colleges and universities seem to understand this reality: Since at least 1979, the three most important admissions criteria, *as indicated by college and university admissions officers*, are measures of academic readiness for college (Breland, Maxey, Gernand, & Trapani, 2002; Hawkins & Clinedinst, 2006).

Unfortunately, while the United States boasts one of the higher rates of entry into postsecondary education in the world, we also claim one of the lowest rates of postsecondary completion (Organisation of Economic Co-operation and Development [OECD], 2008, p. 68). The ratio of 4-year college graduates to college entrants was only 56% in the United States in 2005.

Students from underserved racial/ethnic groups enroll in college at lower rates, yet even from this abbreviated number they are less likely to persist and eventually complete college (U.S. Department of Education, 2009). For example, for the cohort of first-year students seeking a bachelor's degree who attended a 4-year institution in 2000, 60% of White students completed a degree within 6 years. This degree completion rate was 18 percentage points higher than that of their Black peers (42% graduation rate) and 11 percentage points higher than that of their Hispanic peers (49% graduation rate). When comparing college enrollment and degree completion, larger race/ethnicity gaps are found with degree completion than with enrollment (Figure 2).

Policies designed to close enrollment gaps by lowering or minimizing the importance of academic readiness admission criteria assume more racial/ethnic minority students will enroll in college as a result. However, a lack of academic readiness can be found among all demographic groups. Indeed, *most* students are not academically ready for college (ACT, 2008a). Unfortunately, the lack of academic readiness is more acute for African American and Hispanic high school graduates than for White graduates (ACT, 2008a). Arguably, low levels of college readiness are the chief culprit behind low U.S. college entrance and completion rates. While decreasing the enrollment gap is possible as a result of an admission criteria policy change, the unintended consequence could be even fewer students completing a degree, maintaining or even exacerbating the current race-/ethnicity-based degree completion gap.

Racial/ethnic gaps in various college outcome measures are preceded by others. In reverse chronological order, a gap in college completion is pre-ceded by one in college academic achievement, which is preceded by gaps in college enrollment, readiness, high school course taking, and college aspira-tions. Each gap widens the preceding one. High school students who do not aspire to college are less likely to seek advice and plan for it (ACT, 2005a, 2008b; Smeeding, 2009). Those who do not take a core curriculum and challenge themselves with rigorous courses are less likely to become college ready (ACT, 2004, 2005b, 2007). Those who do not become college ready are

Figure 2. 2000 Recent High School Graduate College Enrollment Rates and 2006 6-Year Bachelor's Degree Completion Rates[1]

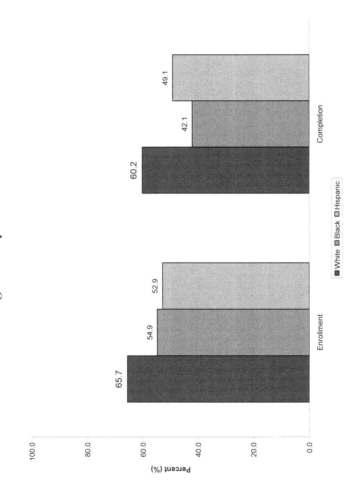

less likely to enroll in college (Noble & Radunzel, 2007). And, obviously, those who do not enroll in college cannot complete a college degree.

Meanwhile, the racial/ethnic composition of the U.S. college student population is changing. The number of Hispanic and Asian American public high school graduates should increase by more than 62% and 51%, respectively, between 2010 and 2022 (King, 2008; Western Interstate Commission for Higher Education [WICHE], 2008). The number of African American graduates should decline by less than 10% during this period, while non-Hispanic White public high school graduates are projected to decline by over 14%. If current trends hold, sometime between 2020 and 2030 non-Hispanic Whites will become a minority of U.S. high school graduates, and historically underserved racial/ethnic groups will compose the majority (King, 2008; WICHE, 2008). In order for U.S. colleges to graduate more students, the completion rates of some previously underserved demographic groups will need to rise substantially. Consequently, the persistence of race-/ethnicity-based college enrollment and completion gaps has substantial national policy and personal implications due to the centrality of postsecondary success in the economic and social well-being of the United States and its citizens.

Overview of the Chapter

From our perspective, too many students, especially racial/ethnic minority students, are lost in the transition from high school to college, and even greater percentages are lost in college. We believe the most important challenges and opportunities for closing the race-/ethnicity-based college enrollment *and degree completion* gaps will come from growing the pipeline of students academically ready for postsecondary success and from postsecondary and secondary education systems targeting factors associated with college success. The essential goal is to ensure that students are not only enrolling but also persisting in college to completion by helping students become more academically ready.

To meet these challenges, we should understand the key determinants of academic achievement and persistence and adopt effective practices that promote academic success, retention, and degree attainment. What factors are most associated with college success? What can postsecondary institutions do to promote student success?

In this chapter, we report on three different research programs to answer these questions. The first is a national longitudinal study of entering 2- and 4-year college students where a profile of traditional demographic, academic achievement, psychosocial, career, and institutional factors was completed. By tracking these students, now in Year 7, we can answer important questions about college academic success, persistence, and degree attainment.

The second program tests a model of institutional interventions mediated by student individual differences to predict academic mastery and retention. Using integrated meta-analytic path analyses we test, first, the efficacy of academic, social, and self-management interventions on student motivation, social engagement, and self-regulation, and, second, how these student factors mediate interventions to promote (or not) academic success and retention.

The third research program looks at developmental education by examining the degree to which cognitive and psychosocial risk factors predict developmental English and mathematics course outcomes, and the role student in-class behavior has on academic and dropout behaviors. We also highlight the partnership between ACT and Wilbur Wright Community College (Chicago) in improving classroom instructional effectiveness and student risk assessment. By examining the factors associated with success in developmental or remediation mathematics and English classes, we can better understand how to help our underprepared students who are placed into remedial classes, whether ultimately entering 2- or 4-year postsecondary institutions. The inability to successfully accelerate academic readiness for general education courses is an underlying cause of drop out and affects disadvantaged students disproportionately as they are at the greatest risk of entering postsecondary institutions without being ready to master college algebra and college-level English.

From these longitudinal and meta-analytic findings, we identify policy implications for postsecondary and secondary systems. The analysis indicates that much of the solution to low postsecondary success rates can be found at the secondary level of education and below.

A National Longitudinal Study: Why College Students Stay

In this section, we identify key factors associated with student persistence, which we believe essential to postsecondary success. We sampled a large cross section of students entering both two- and four-year postsecondary institutions and have been following their progress for seven years (see Robbins, Allen, Casillas, Peterson, & Le, 2006, and Allen, Robbins, Casillas, & Oh, 2008, for reports on the longitudinal research project and its findings). The 4-year colleges and universities vary in selectivity, whereas the 2-year community colleges typically offer open enrollment.

In order to develop a broad profile of cognitive, curricular, extracurricular, career, and family related information for each student, we chose institutions that maintained ACT or COMPASS score records in such a way that we could match them to other components of students' records.[1] We requested that participating institutions have matriculating students complete the Student Readiness Inventory (SRI) during summer/fall orientation. The SRI is an inventory of key student attributes organized within motivational, self-management, and social engagement domains. It was built using a rational-empirical approach to capture the key determinants of college academic success and retention. Participating postsecondary institutions also were asked to annually update the academic status of students in the cohort.

Finally, we incorporated records from the National Student Clearing-house, whose mission is to monitor the enrollment status of students and ex-students both in and out of U.S. postsecondary institutions (they claim a 92% institutional participation rate). Their records are of critical importance for tracking students not only within institutions but also across and outside institutions. With Clearinghouse data, we can identify students who have transferred, dropped out, or stopped out and reenrolled.

We separated our models depending on whether students enrolled in 2- or 4-year institutions. This is important because community college outcomes are much more complex, requiring multinomial options including complete versus dropout, complete and transfer versus dropout, transfer versus dropout, and dropout but reenroll versus dropout.

Findings: Community College-Bound Students

Table 1 presents longitudinal data ranging over 5 years on our partici-pants. As one can see, precollegiate academic preparation—a combination of high school grade point average and standardized achievement test score—is the strongest predictor of outcomes. Student motivation, in particular the willingness to do homework, attend classes, and ask questions, distinguishes retained and graduating students from transfers and dropouts. Further, social connection, or the sense of fitting in or belonging, is predictive of 2-year college students who continue their postsecondary education by transferring to 4-year institutions upon graduation. Finally, we see an effect for socioeconomic status (SES), in which those students with higher SES are more likely to transfer than to drop out.

Findings: 4-year College Students

With 4-year students, first-year collegiate GPA is the strongest predictor of retention and transfer (Table 2). Motivation and precollegiate academic preparation indirectly affect retention via first-year GPA. Social connection

---

[1] The ACT is a college admission test and COMPASS is a postsecondary place-ment examination, both developed by ACT, Inc.

directly affects retention, with the more socially connected students more likely to persist than to drop out. As with 2-year students, SES predicts transfer behavior. Ironically, African American students reveal high levels of commitment to college completion but, due to weaker academic preparation, perform substantially lower academically and drop out more often.

Summary

As can be seen in Table 3, academic preparation and first-year academic performance are the key predictors of college retention and eventual success. Simply put, students who master their school work are likely to persist. This does not mean that other factors, such as motivation, academic discipline, and social connection, are not important; they work both directly and indirectly to influence academic performance and retention.

Table 1. Why College Students Stay: 2-Year Colleges

1.	**Precollegiate academic preparation** is the strongest predictor of all outcomes
2.	**Motivation** (Academic Discipline) distinguishes retained and graduating students from transfers and drop outs
3.	**Social connection** affects only those students who transfer to 4-year institutions
4.	**Socioeconomic status** distinguishes all groups from drop outs: higher SES students are more likely to transfer and low-SES students more likely to drop out

Source: Robbins et al. (2006).

Table 2. Why College Students Stay: 4-Year Colleges

1.	**First-year GPA** strongly affects the likelihood of retention or transfer
2.	**Motivation** (Academic Discipline) **and precollegiate academic preparation** indirectly affect retention and transfer via first-year GPA
3.	**Social connection** directly affects retention
4.	**SES** predicts transfer behavior: Higher SES students transfer while poorer students dropout
5.	**African American students** reveal a high commitment but their academic performance is weaker and drop out likelihood higher

Sources: Robbins et al. (2006); Allen et al. (2008).

Table 3. Common Findings Across 2- and 4-Year Studies

1.	Academic preparation, socioeconomic status (SES), and academic discipline are all critical.
2.	Four-year college students with higher first-year GPAs are more likely to stay in college.
3.	Socially connected students are more likely to transfer upon 2-year graduation or stay (4-year).

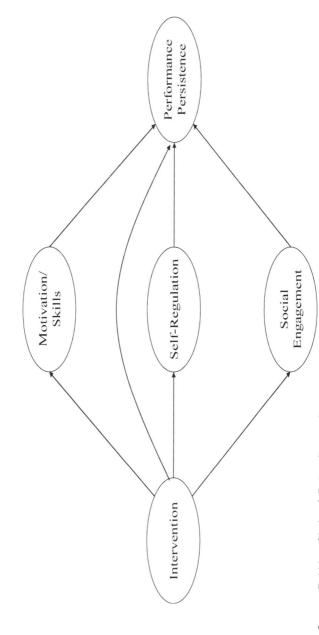

Figure 3. Testing Integrated Meta-Analytic Path Analysis: The Effects of College Interventions on College Outcomes as Mediated by Psychosocial Factors (PSFs)

Source: Robbins, Oh, Le, & Button (in press).

What Works to Promote Student Success

Myriad institutional resources and practices are geared toward helping college students stay in college (e.g., Habley & McClanahan, 2004; Lotkowsky, Robbins, & Noeth, 2004). Their selection, however, can be based on historical legacy or anecdotal evidence as much as performance or data-driven findings. For whatever reasons, many postsecondary educators assume the following factors drive student success: institutional climate and social engagement, peer group and faculty interaction, financial aid availability and tuition costs, quality of academic support, and advising and career center support. Yet, we have found limited empirical evidence to support these notions. Perhaps more importantly, we have not well understood how intervention strategies work through student factors to affect academic performance and retention.

Robbins, Oh, Le, and Button (2009) propose a model of institutional intervention for student success diagrammed in Figure 3. It incorporates self-regulation and self-management theories to target individual student differences as mediators of institutional interventions. It suggests that academic performance and persistence primarily drive student retention, so improving performance and persistence through psychosocially oriented interventions will raise retention rates. The three psychosocial factors (PSFs) placed in the center of Figure 3—Motivation, Self-Regulation, and Social Engagement—are those that positively influence college academic performance and persistence, according to our and others' research.

Using integrated meta-analytic path analyses, Robbins and colleagues (2009) tested the mediation effects of student individual differences on a range of academic interventions. Table 4 summarizes three broad mediator groups that influence academic performance, while Table 5 lists popular intervention strategies.

The categorization of institutional intervention strategies is somewhat dependent on available research studies (i.e., studies with specified treatments that rely on either a comparison/control group or pre–post design). As can be seen in Table 5, commonly studied strategies range from First-Year Experience (FYE) and Orientation to Academic Skills and Self-Management. Coded interventions found within research studies vary in intensity and length. In Table 5, we report the average durations across multiple studies within any intervention category.

Findings

Table 6 reports the mean effect sizes on college persistence/retention and GPA found in research studies on five different popular types of interventions. Academic interventions moderately affect GPA and weakly affect persistence. Surprisingly, self-management interventions moderately affect both outcomes while socialization and freshman year experience (FYE) interventions reveal only small to negligible effects.

Turning to the effects of interventions on individual student mediating factors as highlighted in Table 7, we see that academic and hybrid interventions affect both motivation and self-regulatory management, while hybrid interventions strongly affect self-regulatory processes. FYE has a

Table 4. Categorizing Psychosocial Factors (PSFs)

Three Categories of Psychosocial Factors

Motivation

Academic Discipline	The amount of effort a student puts into schoolwork and the degree to which students see themselves as hardworking and conscientious.
Commitment to College	A student's commitment to stay in college and get a degree.

Self-Regulation

Steadiness	A student's responses to strong feelings and how they manage those feelings.
Academic Self-confidence	The extent to which students believe they can perform well in school.

Social Engagement

Social Connection	A student's feelings of connection and involvement with the college/school community.
Social Activity	How comfortable students feel meeting and interacting with other people.

Sources: Robbins et al. (2006); Robbins, Lauver, Le, Langley, Davis, & Carlstrom (2004).

Table 5. Categorizing College Interventions

1.	**Orientation** (21 hours)—summer, early fall, time-limited
2.	**Freshman Year Experience** (45 hours)
3.	**Academic** (8 hours) Study skills Learning strategies Note taking
4.	**Self-Management** (6 hours) Stress management Self-control Anxiety management
5.	**Hybrid of Academic and Self-Management** (12 hours)

small effect on social engagement. Several paths could not be calculated due to limitations in the research literature.

Finally, as highlighted in Table 8 (Robbins et al., 2004), we see that all three psychosocial mediators have moderate effects on both performance and persistence outcomes.

We can use these mean effect size tables to build integrated meta-analytic path analyses, and test our hypotheses about how various institutional intervention strategies are mediated (see Robbins, Oh, et al., 2009, for full description). In Figure 4 we diagram an academic intervention's significant direct effect on academic performance as measured by college GPA (path coefficient of .13) and the indirect effect of academic intervention (path coefficient of .11) on academic performance mediated through the psychosocial factors of motivation and self-regulation. Self-management interventions also demonstrate both strong direct and indirect effects (.10 and .11, respectively), whereas hybrid interventions show an extraordinarily strong direct effect (.70) but a negative indirect effect (–.13).[2]

Interestingly, as depicted in Figure 5, we find both strong direct and weaker indirect effects for self-management strategies on persistence (path coefficients of .21 and .06, respectively), but negligible effects for FYE interventions (coefficients of .00 and .05).

The results are compelling: Interventions that directly or indirectly target academic skills and achievement are essential to student academic performance and persistence in college. In contrast, the negligible effect of First-Year Experience (FYE) programs is surprising, given their popularity, and further reinforces the importance of specifically targeting academic skills and behaviors.

Table 6. Effects of Intervention on Outcomes

	Outcomes	
Intervention	**Persistence / Retention**	**GPA**
Academic	.15	.23
Self-management	.29	.21
Hybrid	NC	.57
Socialization	.11	NC
Freshman-Year Experience.	.11	.03

Note: NC = not calculated due to absence of studies; 0 = no effect, .1–.2 = small effect, .2–.4 = moderate effect, .4+ = strong effect.

[2] Please note that when calculating the direct effects via path analysis the results are not necessarily the same as the binary effect sizes found in Tables 6 through 8.

Table 7. Effects of Interventions on Psychosocial Factors

Intervention	Psychosocial Mediators		
	Motivation	Self-Regulation	Social Engagement
Academic	.27	.34	NC
Self-management	NC	.37	.10
Hybrid	.65	.36	NC
Socialization	NC	NC	.22
Freshman-Year Experience	.21	.09	.08

Note: NC = not calculated due to absence of studies; 0 = no effect, .1–.2 = small effect, .2–.4 = moderate effect, .4+ = strong effect.

Table 8. Effect Sizes of Psychosocial Factors on College Outcomes

Psychosocial Factors	Outcomes	
	Persistence/Retention	GPA
Motivation	.29	.24
Self-regulation	.22	.29
Social engagement	.32	.16

Note: 0 = no effect, .1–.2 = small effect, .2–.4 = moderate effect, .4+ = strong effect.
Source: Robbins et al. (2004).

Figure 4. Testing Integrated Meta-Analytic Path Analysis

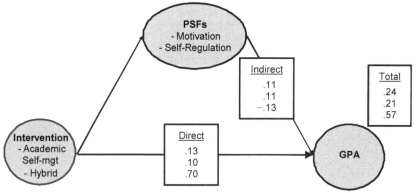

Figure 5. Testing Integrated Meta-Analytic Path Analysis

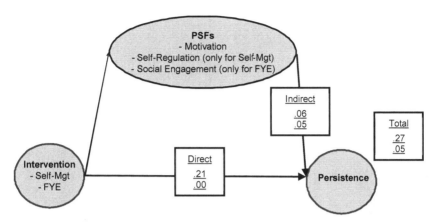

Figure 6. COMPASS/SRI Assessment and Intervention Strategy

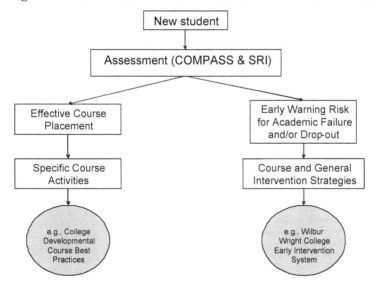

Figure 7. College Developmental Course Best Practices

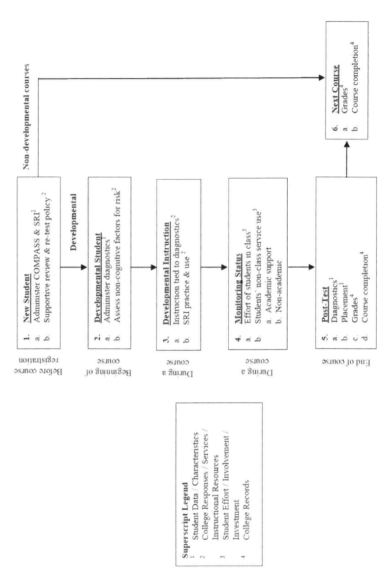

Promoting Effective Developmental Education

The need for remediation for entering postsecondary students is endemic, particularly among disadvantaged students. As we have now highlighted, however, the ability to succeed academically is central to student success. Accordingly, improving the academic aspect of developmental education—its effectiveness in raising student achievement—should be considered essential to the success of disadvantaged students.

To address this issue, we built and are testing the models displayed in Figures 6 and 7. In the first, we propose that effective risk assessment combines both cognitive assessment of academic readiness within specific curricular areas and psychosocial assessment of motivation and compliance behavior. Institutions must determine how best to identify at-risk students and accommodate their needs (see Robbins, Allen, et al., 2009, for an example of one institution-wide effort).

After identification, a second key step is designing interventions for at-risk students that include both academic and psychosocial components so students can be more effectively placed in the most appropriate courses; this process is illustrated in Figure 7. Effective diagnostic assessment pinpoints exactly where students are having problems. These difficulties must be addressed using effective instructional techniques targeting specific areas of weakness.

At the same time, we have seen in our previous research that motivation and self-management are essential to mediating academic skill interventions and to directly affecting academic and persistence behaviors. We recommend using the Student Readiness Inventory (ACT, 2008d; Le et al., 2005; Robbins et al., 2006) to determine the degree to which students demonstrate the effective motivational and management skills required to succeed within the classroom. For those students at risk, the institution can determine what to do to promote improved student attitudes and skills. Instructors and support service staff must work together to identify and intervene with students who do not seem academically engaged in the classroom.

Currently, ACT is collaborating with Wilbur Wright Community College in Chicago to implement the model identified in Figures 6 and 7 (see Robbins & Lewis, 2009, for a full description). As a first step, we observed the relationship between students at-risk academically and/or psychosocially and their college outcomes—post-test achievement scores and persistence in both English (Table 9a) and mathematics (Table 9b) courses. Students at risk either academically or psychosocially are most likely to drop out and improve less academically. Perhaps most importantly, students who demonstrate higher motivation levels will do better than those who do not, pointing to the importance of coupling motivation and instructional effectiveness strategies.

Conclusions and Recommendations

We have attempted to highlight key factors essential to promoting student success. We do not believe loosening or broadening our admission criteria represents the best policy solution; we must face the fact that too many of our students are not academically prepared for college. Middle schools, high schools, and postsecondary institutions all need to better identify and intervene with students academically and/or psychosocially at risk. The "Three Pillars of College Success" are student motivation, instructional effectiveness, and academic readiness (Figure 8). All three are essential to improving postsecondary retention and academic success.

Despite the inclusion of psychosocial factors in retention and intervention strategies in this chapter, it is important to remember that *academic* factors remain more important in most respects (Figure 9). All else held equal, a student who is strong academically but weak psychosocially is more likely to complete college than her reciprocal twin who is strong psychosocially but weak academically.

Table 9a. Completion of Developmental Courses Dependent on Academic and Psychosocial Risk Success Rates in English Composition, by Academic and Psychosocial (SRI) Risk Levels

		SRI Risk Level		
		High	Medium	Low
Academic Risk Level	High	23%	40%	44%
	Medium	32%	47%	58%
	Low	53%	68%	78%

Table 9b. Completion Rates in Elementary Algebra, by Academic and Psychosocial (SRI) Risk Levels

		SRI Risk Level		
		High	Medium	Low
Academic Risk Level	High	15%	28%	27%
	Medium	32%	41%	52%
	Low	50%	67%	69%

Figure 8. The Three Pillars of College Success

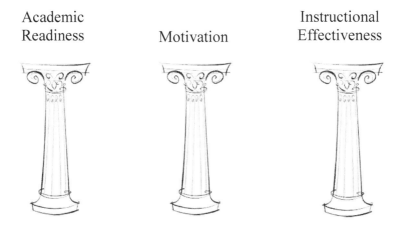

Figure 9. Psychosocial Factors Supplement but Do Not Replace Academic Factors

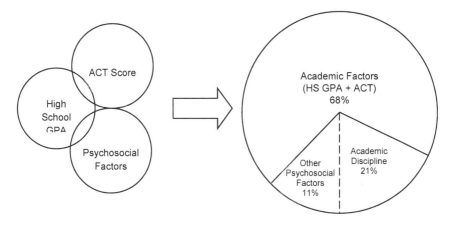

Race-/ethnicity-based gaps in college enrollment and success begin as gaps in college readiness; their antecedents appear long before college, and they widen over time. Reverse engineering this process requires us to narrow each in a succession of ever-widening gaps from college back toward their origin, before high school. As such, our recommendations for narrowing each of the successive race-/ethnicity-based gaps initially and primarily target the development of academic readiness.

Table 10a. Mean COMPASS Posttest Scores for Elementary (precredit) Math, by COMPASS Pretest and Behavior Rating Levels

		Behavior Rating Level		
		High	Medium	Low
COMPASS Pretest Scores	High	57.4	48.8	45.9
	Medium	43.5	38.3	34.1
	Low	39.8	33.9	32.6

Table 10b. Mean COMPASS Gain Scores for Elementary (precredit) Math, by COMPASS Pretest and Behavior Rating Levels

		Behavior Rating Level		
		High	Medium	Low
COMPASS Pretest Scores	High	19.5	8.9	8.7
	Medium	15.7	11.4	6.2
	Low	19.7	14.0	12.0

Table 10c. Completion Rates in Elementary (precredit Math, by COMPASS Pretest and Behavior Rating Levels)

		Behavior Rating Level		
		High	Medium	Low
COMPASS Pretest Scores	High	92%	77%	59%
	Medium	91%	62%	17%
	Low	69%	44%	6%

To increase college enrollment and completion rates, we recommend improvements in student academic preparation for college through policy and practice avenues at the K–12 level and additional practices implemented by postsecondary education institutions.

Close the Gap Between Student Aspirations and High School Course Plans

We need to ensure that all students, especially those from under-represented racial/ethnic and income groups, are offered guidance to eliminate the disparities between their educational aspirations and the high school course work they plan to complete to be prepared to meet these aspirations. Directing middle or high school students toward easier courses can handicap their futures.

First, we need to raise the expectations of all students. The message of high expectations can begin early and should be repeated often. Elementary school students expecting to graduate from college are more likely to take appropriate academic-preparatory high school courses, graduate from high school, and apply to, enroll in, and graduate from college (Cabrera & La Nasa, 2001).

Second, we need to make sure that all students take a core preparatory curriculum, regardless of whether they aspire to college or career after high school. Core preparatory work can be academically or career focused, but should be based on the same college-career readiness standards. ACT research suggests that the math and reading skills needed to be ready for success in workforce training programs are comparable to those needed for success in the first year of college (ACT, 2006).

Close the Gap in the Quality of High School Courses

K–12 course titles can be deceiving; courses with the same title can vary widely in quality and intensity across schools (ACT, 2004; Dougherty, Mellor, & Jian, 2006). The more students learn in their K–12 careers, the better prepared they are for college, and they learn more in rigorous courses, irrespective of course title (ACT, 2007; ACT & Education Trust, 2005; Adelman, 1999, 2006; National Commission on the High School Senior Year, 2001). For example, vocational courses have too often been used as a repository for low-achieving students, with disastrous results for their careers (Rasinski & Pedlow, 1998). All students, even those planning to enter workforce training immediately after high school, need to master a "college preparatory" core curriculum (ACT, 2006).

We must ensure that all students, including those from under-represented racial/ethnic and lower income groups, have access to high-quality high school courses taught by teachers who are qualified to provide sufficient depth and breadth to adequately prepare students for college and career and that students are provided supplemental instruction as needed to succeed in those courses. Students who arrive from middle school already behind academically must get the extra help they need. If they can get this help before and during their freshman year, they may still be able to fully benefit from a rigorous high school curriculum.

Close the Gap in the Alignment of High School Courses With College and Career Readiness Standards

Not all academic standards are the same. High-quality, empirically derived college and career readiness standards lead students and educators in the right direction because they are anchored by known postsecondary academic and workplace requirements. Moreover, the most important content and performance standards—embedded in the core curriculum—are common to both college and career readiness. They may be taught in different contexts and use different source material (e.g., in "college track" and "tech prep" courses) but, to a large degree, they comprise the same essential knowledge and skills (ACT, 2006).

Close the Gap in Student Academic Behaviors That Enhance College and Career Readiness

While academic achievement is foundational to college readiness, certain academic behaviors play a supplemental role in helping students become college ready. Developing these behaviors (e.g., academic discipline) can help any student become college ready and improve their academic achievement (ACT, 2008c).

Implementing monitoring and intervention strategies as early as middle school (e.g., sixth grade) offers educators ample time to identify and intervene with student academic behaviors in need of additional support. Waiting until the end of high school to determine if a student has developed habits that will support college readiness is too late for effective intervention (Noeth & Wimberly, 2002; Wimberly & Noeth, 2005). Programs such as Gaining Early Awareness and Readiness for Undergraduate Programs (GEAR UP) are aligned with this approach, as they provide supplemental services to students for improving their academic behaviors beginning no later than the seventh grade (ACT & National Council for Community and Educational Partnerships, 2007).

This is a societal agenda. An individual postsecondary institution has no direct control over K–12 policies; postsecondary educators can lobby for more favorable K–12 public policies, but cannot directly determine them. Individual postsecondary institutions or systems of institutions can influence K–12 behavior only indirectly, through means such as admission policies and articulation agreements.

Among available practices that postsecondary institutions can directly control, however, we suggest the following activities.

Designate a visible individual to coordinate a campuswide retention planning team. Recent studies of postsecondary practices indicate that just over half (51.7%) of all postsecondary institutions designate a specific campus individual to coordinate retention activities at the institution (Habley & McClanahan, 2004). Higher education institutions rhetorically state that all campus personnel are responsible for retaining students. If, in fact, this is true, and many campus-based units (e.g., individual academic departments, student life departments) implement independent retention efforts, these efforts may not be as cost-effective as campuswide coordination.

Conduct systematic analyses of students. While most higher education institutions collect a lot of data on their students, many lack a systematic institutional research approach focused on understanding the differences between students who persist to degree completion and those who do not (Habley & McClanahan, 2004). Developing an understanding of these differences overall and for student subgroups requires the systematic collection of data about student demographics, academic performance, academic plans, self-reported needs, student attitudes, and the psychosocial and other non-academic student variables identified in this chapter.

Implement an early-alert assessment and monitoring system. Once profiles of typical students who persist to degree completion are completed, an early monitoring system comparing the profiles with data about new students can identify those students most at risk of not persisting. This system can also be used to inform the development of appropriate inter-vention strategies to increase the likelihood of student degree attainment. Over time, these systems can also provide the data needed to assess the efficacy of intervention programs and suggest program modifications or the need for additional programs.

Develop customizable intervention programs tailored to different combinations of academic and psychosocial needs. An array of policies and programs can be designed for different types of students based on their respective academic and psychosocial needs. Implementing programs and policies using such a strategic, tailored approach may prove to be a more effective and efficient approach than indiscriminately implementing a single intervention or two. Students who do not demonstrate strong academic needs but have psychosocial needs, for example, are more likely to benefit from intervention programs that primarily develop psychosocial skills. Institutions can more optimally allocate institutional resources to retention and college degree completion programs when the programs themselves are designed and coordinated to meet the specific needs of individual students.

In general, postsecondary institutions would do well to be clear in their goals when formulating intervention and retention policies and strategic in their use of limited resources. They should also be unafraid of nudging their students, to be more intrusive in student advising. Many, and perhaps most, at-risk students will not themselves initiate an intervention until it is too late, either because they do not know how, do not know that they can, or do not appreciate the depth of their problem.

College enrollment is the precursor but not the final outcome needed for all students, regardless of race or ethnicity, to achieve the social, civic, and, in particular, personal economic benefits associated with college degree attainment. The debate, then, should not be focused on how to alter admissions criteria per se, but rather on how to expand the college-ready pipeline by strengthening students' academic readiness for entry into and success in college.

References

ACT. (2004). *Crisis at the core: Preparing all students for college and work.* Iowa City, IA: Author.

ACT. (2005a). *Career planning: Students need help starting early and staying focused.* Iowa City, IA: Author.

ACT. (2005b). *Courses count: Preparing students for postsecondary success.* Iowa City, IA: Author.

ACT. (2006). *Ready to succeed: All students prepared for college and work.* Iowa City, IA: Author.

ACT. (2007). *Rigor at risk: Reaffirming quality in the high school core curriculum.* Iowa City, IA: Author.

ACT. (2008a). *ACT high school profile report: The graduating class of 2008*: National. Iowa City, IA: Author.

ACT. (2008b). *The economic benefits of academic and career preparation.* Iowa City, IA: Author.

ACT. (2008c). *The forgotten middle.* Iowa City, IA: Author.

ACT. (2008d). *SRI user's guide.* Iowa City, IA: Author.

ACT & Education Trust, The. (2005). *On course for success: A close look at selected high school courses that prepare all students for college.* Iowa City, IA: Authors.

ACT & National Council for Community and Educational Partnerships, The. (2007). *Using EXPLORE® and PLAN® data to evaluate GEAR UP programs.* Iowa City, IA: Authors.

Adelman, C. (1999). *Answers in the tool box: Academic intensity, attendance patterns, and bachelor's degree attainment.* Washington, DC: U.S. Department of Education.

Adelman, C. (2006). *The toolbox revisited: Paths to degree completion from high school through college.* Washington, DC: U.S. Department of Education.

Allen, J., Robbins, S., Casillas, A., & Oh, I. (2008). Third-year college retention and transfer: effects of academic performance, motivation, and social connectedness. *Research in Higher Education, 49*, 647–664.

Breland, H., Maxey, J., Gernand, T., & Trapani, C. (2002). *Trends in college admission: A report of a national survey of undergraduate admission policies, practices, and procedures*: *Summary Report*. Alexandria, VA: National Association for College Admission Counseling, ACT, Inc., the Association for Institutional Research, the College Board, & Educational Testing Service.

Cabrera, A., & La Nasa, S. (2001). On the path to college: Three critical tasks facing America's disadvantaged students. *Research in Higher Education, 42*, 119–150.

Commission on the Use of Standardized Tests in Undergraduate Admission. (2008). *Report of the commission on the use of standardized tests in undergraduate admission*. Arlington, VA: National Association for College Admissions Counseling.

Dougherty, C., Mellor, L., & Jian, S. (2006). *Orange juice or orange drink? Ensuring that "advanced courses" live up to their labels* (NCEA Policy Brief No. 1). Austin, TX: National Center for Educational Accountability.

Gratz v. Bollinger, 539 U.S. 244 (2003).

Grutter v. Bollinger, 539 U.S. 306 (2003).

Habley, W.R., & McClanahan, R. (2004). *What works in student retention?—All survey colleges*. Iowa City, IA: ACT, Inc.

Hawkins, D. A., & Clinedinst, M. (2006). *State of college admission 2006*. Alexandria, VA: National Association for College Admission Counseling.

King, J. E. (2008). *Student demographic trends: Findings from three new studies*. Washington, DC: American Council for Education, Center for Policy Analysis.

Le, H., Casillas, A., Robbins, S., & Langley, R. (2005). Motivational and skills, social, and self-management predictors of college outcomes: Constructing the Student Readiness Inventory. *Educational and Psychological Measurement, 65*, 482–508.

Lotkowsky, V.A., Robbins, S.B., & Noeth, R.J. (2004). *The role of academic and non-academic factors in improving college retention*. Iowa City, IA: ACT, Inc. Retrieved from ERIC database. (ED485476)

National Commission on the High School Senior Year. (2001). *Raising our sights: No high school senior left behind*. Washington, DC: U.S. Department of Education.

Noble, J., & Radunzel, J. (2007, June). *College readiness = college success beyond the first year*. Paper presented at the Annual Forum of the Association for Institutional Research, Kansas City, MO.

Noeth, R. J., & Wimberly, G. L. (2002). *Creating seamless educational transitions for urban African American and Hispanic students*. Iowa City, IA: ACT, Inc.

Organisation for Economic Co-operation and Development. (2008). *Education at a glance: OECD indicators 2008.* Paris, France: Author.

Rasinski, K. A., & Pedlow, S. (1998). The effect of high school vocational education on academic achievement gain and high school persistence: Evidence from NELS:88. In A. Gamoran (Ed.), *The quality of vocational education: Background papers from the 1994 National Assessment of Vocational Education.* Washington, DC: U.S. Department of Education. Available online at: http://www2.ed.gov/pubs/VoEd/Chapter5/index.html

Robbins, S., Allen, J., Casillas, A., Akamigbo, A., Saltonstall, M., Cole, R., . . . Gore, P. (2009). Associations of resource and service utilization, risk level, and college outcomes. *Research in Higher Education, 50,* 101–118.

Robbins, S., Allen, J., Casillas, A., Peterson, C., & Le, H. (2006). Unraveling the differential effects of motivational and skills, social, and self-management measures from traditional predictors of college outcomes. *Journal of Educational Psychology, 98,* 598–616.

Robbins, S., Lauver, K., Le, H., Langley, R., Davis, D., & Carlstrom, A. (2004). Do psychosocial and study skill factors predict college outcomes? A meta-analysis. *Psychological Bulletin, 130,* 261–288.

Robbins, S. & Lewis, S., (2009, March). *Course placement strategies and motivational skill tools to promote effective enrollment management.* Invited presentation at the Innovations Conference 2009, Reno, NV.

Robbins, S., Oh, I., Le, H., & Button, C. (2009). Intervention effects on college performance and retention, mediated by motivational, emotional, and social control factors: integrated meta-analytic path analyses. *Journal of Applied Psychology, 94*(5), 1163–1184.

Ryu, M. (2008). *Minorities in higher education 2008: Twenty-third status report.* Washington, DC: American Council on Education.

Smeeding, T. (2009, Spring). Differences in higher education: Investments, costs, and outcomes. *LaFollette Policy Report, 18*(2), 1–4.

U.S. Department of Education. (2008). *Digest of education statistics 2007.* Washington, DC: Author.

U.S. Department of Education. (2009). *Condition of education 2009.* Washington, DC: Author.

Western Interstate Commission for Higher Education. (2008). *Knocking at the college door: Projections of high school graduates by state and race/ethnicity 1992–2022.* Boulder, CO: Author.

Wimberly, G. L., & Noeth, R. J. (2005). *College readiness begins in middle school.* Iowa City, IA: ACT, Inc.

CHAPTER 11

NONCOGNITIVE CONSTRUCTS IN K–16: ASSESSMENTS, INTERVENTIONS, EDUCATIONAL AND POLICY IMPLICATIONS

Jeremy Burrus,[1] Carolyn MacCann,[2] Patrick C. Kyllonen,[1] and Richard D. Roberts[1]

Introduction

Noncognitive (also referred to as psychosocial) factors are important in education, from prekindergarten right on through to graduate school. Numerous studies have shown that noncognitive factors are correlated with academic achievement and associated outcomes. For example, as early as preschool the personality factor of Conscientiousness predicts school achievement (Abe, 2005), and there is evidence that emotional understanding is a better predictor of social and academic outcomes for students at risk than most educational factors (Izard et al., 2001). In middle school, noncognitive factors (including self-efficacy, self-concept, self-discipline, and confidence) predict reading, science, and math achievement after controlling for IQ, demographics, school attendance, and home educational materials (Campbell, Voelkl, & Donahue, 1997; Connell, Spencer, & Aber, 1994; Duckworth & Seligman, 2005; J. Lee, Goodman, Bauer, & Redman, 2007).

In college, several meta-analyses have shown that noncognitive factors add both to grades and test scores in predicting achievement, retention, and other valued educational outcomes (e.g., engagement). Noncognitive factors that predict college achievement are listed first, followed by factors that predict retention.

Noncognitive factors shown to predict college achievement (GPA)
- Academic motivation (Robbins et al., 2004)
- Conscientiousness (e.g., Poropat, 2009)
- Neuroticism (anxiety and impulsiveness facets) (Kuncel et al., 2005)
- Self-efficacy (Robbins et al., 2004)
- Study habits (e.g., Crede & Kuncel, 2007)
- Study skills (e.g., Crede & Kuncel, 2007)

[1] Center for New Constructs, R&D, Educational Testing Service; [2] School of Psychology, University of Sydney

- Study motivation (e.g., Crede & Kuncel, 2007)

Noncognitive factors shown to predict college retention
- Academic goals (Robbins et al., 2004)
- Study skills (e.g., Crede & Kuncel, 2007)
- Self-efficacy (Robbins et al., 2004)

Indeed, the positive outcomes associated with psychosocial skills do not end in school and college, but continue through the transition into the workforce. The primary noncognitive skills to predict job performance and labor economic outcomes (e.g., wages, employment, incarceration rates) are Conscientiousness and Ethics (integrity) (e.g., Borghans, Duckworth, Heckman, & ter Weel, 2008; Heckman, Malofeeva, Pinto, & Savelyev, 2007; Heckman & Rubinstein, 2001; Schmidt & Hunter, 1998). In short, these noncognitive factors appear related to important human endeavors across the life span.

The purpose of this chapter is to describe recent research on some key noncognitive constructs in the educationa sector currently designated K–16 (i.e., from kindergarten to postsecondary school). The constructs we focus on are by no means exhaustive; we tend to place emphasis on noncognitive skills emerging as especially important in policy documents such as *Are They Really Ready to Work?* (Casner-Lotto & Barrington, 2006) and/or those noncognitive skills that we contend can be improved with training programs and other intervention strategies (including policy implementation). This review aims nonetheless to cover diverse literatures and methods attesting to the importance of noncognitive factors across K–16. By the chapter's end, we hope to have made the case that (a) noncognitive factors are important for a variety of educational outcomes, (b) we know how to measure these noncognitive factors, and (c) we can improve educational outcomes, particularly for underserved students, by doing so. To fulfill these goals, the chapter is organized into three main sections, each structured around a series of focused questions:

1. Noncognitive Constructs: Assessment and Relations to Educational Outcomes: What are some of the key noncognitive factors (e.g., emotional intelligence, work ethic, teamwork, health attitudes) that are currently defined in the literature? What empirical evidence is there that these factors relate to educational outcomes across K–16? What is the empirical evidence for the relationship between the different noncognitive factors and academic outcomes such as school grades, standardized test scores, and staying in school?

2. Enhancing Noncognitive Constructs: Can noncognitive factors be improved? If so, is there any evidence that improving these psychosocial factors will result in improvements in educational outcomes? Are there some approaches that appear more promising than others for enhancing these noncognitive constructs?

3. Summary and Recommendations for Future Research: Is it conceivable that a comprehensive, academic non-cognitive assessment system for K–16 could be developed? How could it be used (e.g., high-stakes admissions, policy monitoring, outcomes evaluations, self-help)? Finally, how can assessments guide under-standing of how these noncognitive skills can be improved?

Noncognitive Constructs:
Assessment and Relations to Educational Outcomes

There are several noncognitive constructs that relate to valued educational outcomes, including academic achievement, college readiness, and student retention/attrition. Compared to their cognitive counterparts, these noncognitive constructs appear to offer reduced adverse impact in their potential uses in selection, counseling and guidance, training and development, and/or evaluating institutional outcomes. A selection of these constructs, coming from our own particular program of research, is described in the following sections.

Emotional Intelligence and Related Constructs

An increased emphasis on social and emotional learning has led to a greater interest among researchers and practitioners on the role of emotional intelligence (EI), social intelligence, and other emotion-related capacities in predicting school achievement and student well-being (e.g., Zins, Bloodworth, Weissberg, & Walberg, 2004). The primary tool used to measure EI is the Mayer-Salovey-Caruso Emotional Intelligence Test (MSCEIT; Mayer, Salovey, Caruso, & Sitarenios, 2003). In general, EI is defined by four related emotional capacities (Mayer & Salovey, 1997; R. D. Roberts, Schulze, & MacCann, 2008) measured by the MSCEIT:

a. *Emotion Perception and Expression.* This factor includes the recognition of emotional content in facial expressions, tone of voice, and other stimuli, and the accurate expression of one's own feelings.

  b. *Emotion Facilitation of Thought*. This construct combines the knowledge of which types of mood states are helpful or debilitating for the performance of different kinds of tasks with the ability to generate and successfully recognize such mood-states in oneself.

  c. *Emotional Understanding*. This represents the knowledge of how emotions change over time and how feelings are related to different situations.

  d. *Emotion Management*. This is an ability to evaluate the effectiveness of different courses of action in managing complicated emotional situations so as to achieve the desired emotional and task outcomes (see, e.g., Mayer, Roberts, & Barsade, 2008). This involves complex real-world judgments using emotional information (e.g., evaluating the best response to a colleague's confidential admission that he fears his depression might worsen if the current level of school or workplace stress continues).

  There are two broad approaches to measuring emotional intelligence: (a) using maximum-performance ability scales, where the test taker must process emotional information in order to infer a correct answer (e.g., "Does this tone of voice express anger?"), and (b) using typical-performing rating-scales (e.g., "By looking at facial expressions, I recognize the emotions people are experiencing?"; Schutte et al., 1998). These two approaches are often referred to as *ability EI* and *trait EI*, respectively, and there is evidence that trait and ability EI in fact represent different constructs (Mayer et al., 2008). Ability EI more closely maps on to the four competencies described earlier, whereas trait EI represents an individual's perception or self-assessment of his or her own ability.

  One of the arguments for the importance of EI in academic achievement is that achievement in school depends on social and contextual factors as well as the three Rs (Zeidner, Matthews, & Roberts, 2009). For example, the ability to arouse sympathy rather than irritation in a college professor when requesting an extension for an assignment might be quite influential in determining one's final college GPA. At a simpler level, the ability to accurately express friendliness and warmth to other kindergarten students might result in better access to learning materials, since the other kindergartners might then be more likely to share their crayons, toys, and books. The expression of warmth and friendliness leading to social connections may also lead to success at the college level. The formation of friendships, study groups, and informal social and academic support networks are crucial to student retention, and may be particularly important for students who do not already have access to university-educated family or friends for advice and support.

Research demonstrates that EI does in fact predict students' GPA, even after accounting for students' cognitive ability (Mayer et al., 2008). The social mechanisms or causal pathways for EI's role in school achievement seem reasonable and intuitive, but there are also nonsocial pathways by which EI might affect learning, such as coping with stress and maintaining positive feelings about school. Our research group has examined both of these factors in school achievement.

Emotional Intelligence, Coping, and School Achievement. EI may influence students' school grades through high emotion management skills leading to the choice of more appropriate coping strategies for dealing with stress. Recently, we examined this issue in both middle school and community college students, finding support for the idea that coping mediates the relationship between EI and achievement. MacCann, Fogarty, Zeidner, and Roberts (in press) examined whether three strategies for coping (i.e., emotion-focused, problem-focused, and avoidant coping) would act as mediators in the relationship between emotion management and grades in a sample of 159 community college students. Emotion management was measured using the MSCEIT. MacCann et al. found that the indirect pathway for predicting grades was significant: Emotion management predicts grades through its effect of on coping.

Among eighth graders, high EI related to both problem-focused coping and school grades (Fogarty, Games, MacCann, & Roberts, 2010). In this study, 383 eighth graders completed a situational judgment test of emotion management—a downward extension of the Situational Test of Emotion Management (STEM; MacCann & Roberts, 2008). An example item from the STEM-Youth is "You start a new school in a new neighborhood where you don't know anyone. So far, the other students haven't been very friendly. What would you do in this situation? (a) Make an effort to talk to people and be friendly, (b) Continue to have fun with your old friends after school and on weekends, (c) Concentrate on doing your work well at the new school, or (d) Join a school club or become involved in a sport?" Students also completed a coping inventory that assessed the frequency with which they used problem-focused, emotion-focused, and avoidant-based coping in school-based stressors (e.g., studying for a test). Results indicated that EI predicted school performance (student's grades) but that most of this contribution was mediated by problem-focused coping. That is, the mechanism by which EI predicted school performance was through high EI students' greater use of problem-focused coping.

Maintaining Positive Emotions and School Achievement. An explicit mechanism under the EI framework is to "manage emotion in oneself and others by moderating negative emotions and enhancing pleasant ones" (Mayer & Salovey, 1997, p. 11). Such a statement contains the implicit assumption that positive emotions will, in general, lead to better outcomes than negative emotions. Broadly speaking, the positive psychology movement has a similar basis, in that happiness is a goal valued in and of itself, as well as for its effects on other outcomes (e.g., Seligman, 2002). Our research group examined this proposition in terms of school achievement, examining whether experiencing more positive and fewer negative emotions lead to better grades and greater life satisfaction. Across four studies of high school students, positive feelings toward school situations showed positive (albeit relatively small) associations with students' grades, whereas negative feelings toward school situations showed a small to moderate negative association with grades. Both positive and negative feelings also related to students' life satisfaction in the expected direction, with positive affect generally showing a stronger degree of relationship than negative affect (Lipnevich, MacCann, Bertling, & Roberts, 2009).

Observer Effects in Reporting Emotion Management Behaviors. Emotion management, the highest branch of EI, is frequently assessed through situational judgment assessments, where test takers are presented with an emotional situation and several possible alternatives for managing such a situation (Freudenthaler & Neubauer, 2007; MacCann & Roberts, 2008; Mayer et al., 2003). In the MSCEIT, test takers are requested to rate the effectiveness of each response, whereas both the Freudenthaler and Neubauer (2007) and MacCann and Roberts (2008) assessments may be answered in terms of *what the test-taker would actually do in that situation.* When the test assesses potential behavior (i.e., what the test taker would do) rather than knowledge (as in the MSCEIT), judgments from external observers might be used as a replacement or supplement to the test takers' own judgments of what they would do.

Our research group has examined the extent to which parent-judgments of emotion management differ from self-judgments in a sample of eighth-grade students (MacCann, Wang, Matthews, & Roberts, 2010). Both parental judgments and self-judgments of emotion management were associated with school achievement ($r \approx .30$) and student life satisfaction($r \approx .20$). However, parental judgments of emotion management were substantially different from self-judgments ($r = .19$), relating more strongly to Extroversion ($r = .38$ vs. .06) and less strongly to Agreeableness ($r = .14$ vs. .44). Taken together, results indicate that self- and parental reports may be equally accurate representations of emotion management tendencies, but may index the frequency of different types of strategies for emotion management. Both Extroversion and Agreeableness have been linked with coping strategies such as positive reappraisal and planning, suggesting that consideration of either trait might feasibly lead to an accurate assessment of emotion management behavior (Watson & Hubbard, 1996). However, parental judgments might relate to observable emotion management strategies such as interaction with others (e.g., seeking social support, talking through the issues), whereas self-judgments might relate to internal strategies such as positive reappraisal. These results highlight that the source of information used to assess emotional competence may in fact affect the particular processes that are uncovered. As such, assessment and training programs or institutional reviews of social and emotional climates might benefit from considering multiple sources of information.

Personality Superfactors and Components

Behavioral tendencies or patterns of typical thoughts, emotions, and behaviors can generally be conceptualized under the five-factor model of personality (FFM; Costa & McCrae, 1992) or variants such as Eysenck's (1990) three-factor Psychoticism-Extroversion-Neuroticism model, or the six-factor Honesty-Emotionality-eXtroversion-Agreeableness-Conscientiousness-Openness (HEXACO) model (K. Lee & Ashton, 2004). Using Costa and McCrae's (1992) five-factor conceptualization of personality, individuals high and low on each of the five factors might be described as follows.

I. *Extroversion (E).* Extroverted people are likely to be talkative, highly energetic, and sensation seeking, and to look for and enjoy social interactions. In contrast, introverted people are quieter, more easily over-stimulated, with lower needs for social interaction. Example item: "I feel comfortable around people."

II. *Agreeableness (A).* Agreeable people tend to trust others, and be kind, helpful, and humble. Persons low on Agreeableness tend to be more cynical, distrustful, ruthless, and scheming. Example item: "I believe that others have good intentions."

III. *Conscientiousness (C).* Conscientious people tend to be orderly, self-disciplined, detail focused, and achievement striving. In contrast, people who are low in Conscientiousness tend to be unconcerned with

achievement and use few resources on striving to achieve. Example item: "I pay attention to details."
IV. *Neuroticism (N)*. People high on Neuroticism tend to experience emotions strongly and often. They may quickly become nervous, unhappy, irritable, or stressed. At the opposite pole, emotionally stable people tend to be calm and tranquil, experiencing few strong emotions. Example item: "I have frequent mood swings."
V. *Openness to Experience (O)*. People high on Openness are accepting of new values, opinions and activities, and tend to be interested in intellectual, imaginative and artistic activities. By contrast, people low on Openness may be uncomfortable with novel or unfamiliar ideas, activities, or values. Example item: "I have a vivid imagination."

As alluded to in the introductory passages, meta-analyses and comprehensive studies demonstrate that one factor in particular—Conscientiousness—relates to educational achievement, attainment, and outcomes at primary, secondary, and tertiary levels (Noftle & Robins, 2007; O'Connor & Paunonen, 2007; Poropat, 2009; Trapmann, Hell, Hirn, & Schuler, 2007). In fact, Conscientiousness correlates from .23 to .27 with college grades, and .21 with academic achievement at high school, with these relationships holding after accounting for general cognitive ability (Noftle & Robbins, 2007; O'Connor & Paunonen, 2007; Poropat, 2009). Two large-scale meta-analyses have demonstrated that no significant Black/White differences are found for Conscientiousness (Foldes, Duehr, & Ones, 2008; Tate & McDaniel, 2008): Tate and McDaniel found a nonsignificant effect size difference of .02 ($k = 81$, $N = 193,455$), and Folder and colleagues found a nonsignificant effect size difference of .07 ($k = 67$, $N = 180,476$), with average scores lower for Whites in both cases.

Conscientiousness. Given that Conscientiousness promises no adverse impact and appears to play a key role in educational achievement, our group examined which particular facets or components of Conscientiousness are the key drivers of school achievement and related behaviors. MacCann, Duckworth, and Roberts (2009) uncovered eight underlying components of Conscientiousness in factorial analyses of personality items from 12 different theoretical models of personality. The eight components are (1) *Industriousness*: a good work ethic, tendency to work hard (example item: "I accomplish a lot of work."); (2) *Perfectionism*: tendency toward achievement drive and competitive instincts (example item: "I detect mistakes"); (3) *Tidiness*: organization of one's possessions or workspace (example item: "I like to organize things"); (4) *Proactivity:* tendency to start tasks without delay (example item: "I get to work at once"; (5) *Control*: tendency to control rash impulses, to show restraint (example item: "I do unexpected things" [reverse coded]); (6) *Cautiousness*: deliberativeness and carefulness (example item: "I avoid mistakes"); (7) *Task Planning*: organization of one's time, priorities, and tasks, and tendency to engage in time management practices (example item: "I am a goal-oriented person"); and (8) *Perseverance*: persevering at difficult or challenging tasks rather than giving up (example item: "I am easily discouraged" [reverse coded]).

Findings from MacCann, Duckworth, and Roberts (2009) and MacCann, Minsky, Ventura, and Roberts (in press) demonstrated that the Industriousness or work-ethic component of Conscientiousness was the most important for educational outcomes. MacCann, Duckworth, and Roberts (2009) found that students with unauthorized absences scored nearly a full standard deviation lower on Industriousness than did students with perfect attendance at high school ($d = .92$). After controlling for cognitive ability, MacCann, Minsky, et al. (in press) found that self-reported Industriousness explained an additional 9% of the variation in students' grades, whereas parent-reported Industriousness explained an additional 19% of the variation in students' grades. In contrast, the weakest predictor of both absenteeism and scholastic achievement was Tidiness. Such results demonstrate that continued effort may be far more important for achievement than the organization of learning materials or outward displays of organization (Blackwell, Trzesniewski, & Dweck, 2007).

Time Management. Time use, planning, and attitudes to time are all significant predictors of students' grades in college, suggesting that time management plays an important role in student achievement (Britton & Tesser, 1991; Kelly, 2002). Recently, we have shown this relationship holds across both 2-year and 4-year college samples (MacCann, Fogarty, & Roberts, in press; R. D. Roberts, Schulze, & MacCann, 2007; R. D. Roberts, Schulze, & Minsky, 2006). Liu, Rijmen, MacCann, and Roberts (2009) have also demonstrated that time management tendencies predict grades in middle school students ($r = .21$ to .42) and that time management was unrelated to cognitive ability, suggesting that the prediction of grades from time management was due to the processes of time management, rather than a situation where the more-able students showed more skill in time management. Time management was assessed with the *Abbreviated Time Management Index (ATMI)* (R. D. Roberts, Krause, & Suk-Lee, 2001). Based on theoretical, applied, and empirical approaches to time management, the ATMI assesses six facets of time management behaviors and attitudes. Each item was answered on a scale from 1 (*Never or Rarely*) to 4 (*Usually or Always*).

1. *Having a Workspace (6 items):* measures a person's preference for being organized and keeping their workspace neat and tidy; several items pertain to the degree to which a person views messiness or disorganization as counterproductive. Example: "I keep my desk uncluttered."

2. *Meeting Deadlines (6 items):* the extent to which people perceive themselves to be in control of time and to use their time wisely and efficiently. Example: "I leave things to the last minute" (reverse coded).

3. *Organizing Time and Tasks (6 items):* assesses actions, strategies, and preferred ways of behaving associated with successful TM practices. Example: "I write a daily to-do-list."

4. *Planning Ahead (6 items):* reflects an individual's preference for structure and routine over flexibility, unpredictability, and lack of constraint. Example: "I like to leave things to chance" (reverse coded).

5. *Setting Goals (6 items):* an individual's sense of purpose, level of focus, and goal-setting capacity. Example: "I am driven to achieve my goals."

6. *Staying Focused (6 items):* Reflects an individual's potential to cope with change and their ability to adapt when change occurs. Example: "I can't cope with change" (reverse coded).

MacCann and Roberts (2009a) demonstrated that the organization components of time management show substantial relationships with Conscientiousness. Clearly, a student's desire and ability to master course material can only come into play once the student has actually arrived at the lecture theater in time for the beginning of a seminar. The relationship between time management and Conscientiousness suggests that time management may be at least one of the behavioral mechanisms explaining how a component of personality, Conscientiousness, translates into achievement-enhancing behavior (better management of time) to result in increased achievement (higher grades) (see also MacCann, Fogarty, Zeidner, et al., in press).

Teamwork. Given that students' learning and achievement may relate to social demands in the classroom, cognitive demands of mastering academic material, and teachers stressing collaborative approaches to learning, teamwork skills are clearly important components of academic success (Ahles & Bosworth, 2004). Teamwork can be measured in several ways, including Situational Judgment Test (SJT) items such as the following: *You are part of a study group that has been assigned a large presentation for class. As you are all dividing up the workload, it becomes clear that both you and another member of the group are interested in researching the same aspect of the topic. Your colleague already has a great deal of experience in this area, but you have been extremely excited about working on this part of the project for several months. Which of the following is the best approach to dealing with this situation?*

A) *Flip a coin to determine who gets to work on that particular aspect of the project.*

B) *Insist that, for the good of the group, you should work on that aspect of the project because your interest in the area means you will do a particularly good job.*

C) *Compromise your preferences for the good of the group and allow the other person to work on that aspect of the project.*

D) *Choose a different group member to work on that aspect of the project so that no one person is privileged over another.*

Wang, MacCann, Zhuang, Liu, and Roberts (2009) found that a multi-method measure of teamwork related to students' high school grades. The relationship between teamwork and grades was particularly pronounced in subject areas where collaboration and group work formed part of the subject area, with music grades showing the strongest relationship to teamwork. Playing pieces as a group is an essential part of the subject, with the negotiation of piece selection, solos, and group practice times playing a role in final performance and grade. Such a focus on team performance is not essential for many other subjects, although it is certainly relevant to the performing arts, debating, or team sports (although note that the importance of teamwork might differ depending on pedagogical approach to learning, for example, with the "mathlete" competitive teams for mathematics). No significant gender or ethnic differences were found for any component of the teamwork assessment system, indicating that use of such measures should not result in adverse impact.

Noncognitive Constructs and Mathematics Achievement

Students' attitudes, confidence, and self-concept regarding mathematics have shown significant relationships with their mathematics achievement across multiple age groups and in multiple cultures. Marsh, Hau, Artelt, Baumert, and Peschar (2006) found a cross-culturally invariant relationship of mathematics self-concept to mathematics achievement of .33 across 25 countries. Meta-analyses estimate the relationship between math anxiety and math performance to be between –.27 to –.34 in K–12 students and –.31 in college students (Hembree, 1990; Ma, 1999). In an analysis of data from 25 countries, J. Lee (2009) showed that self-concept, self-efficacy, and math anxiety were distinct rather than overlapping constructs, and that each of these related to mathematics achievement, with average values of .23 for math self-concept, .43 for math self-efficacy, and –.39 for math anxiety. Clearly, students' conceptualizations of mathematics and of themselves as mathematicians shape the ways in which they approach the discipline of mathematics as well as the success they achieve.

Attitudes Toward Mathematics. Our research group has reexamined attitudes toward mathematics using the Theory of Planned Behavior (TpB; Azjen, 1991) to construct assessments and interventions for math attitudes. The advantage of using the TpB over alternative ways of conceptualizing students' thoughts and feelings toward mathematics lies in its strong theoretical links to intervention via attitude change. The TpB delineates four basic attitudinal dimensions that determine behavior:

1. *Attitudes*: the overall positive or negative evaluation of the behavior. In general, the more favorable the attitude toward the behavior, the stronger the individual's intention is to perform it.

2. *Subjective Norms*: the social pressures to perform (or in some cases not to perform) a particular behavior. That is, if an individual perceives that significant others endorse (or disapprove of) the behavior, they are more (or less) likely to intend to perform it.

3. *Perceived Behavioral Control*: acts as a co-determinant of behavior, the factor thought to affect both intention and behavior. Perceived behavioral control "provides information about the potential constraints on action as perceived by the actor, and is held to explain why intentions do not always predict behavior" (Armitage & Conner, 2001, p. 472).

4. *Intentions*: The TpB is an intentional or volitional theory of behavior in that the proximate cause of a behavior is thought to stem from the individual's intention or willingness to perform the behavior. The intentions component is thus the final link to behavior.

The TpB attitudinal dimensions are based on the earlier theory of reasoned action (Ajzen & Fishbein, 1973), which proposes that behavior is determined by intentions, which are in turn determined by attitudes and social norms. For example, if a person forms a negative view of smoking (attitude) and believes that their friends and family want them to quit (subjective norms), then they will intend to quit (intention) and therefore stop smoking (behavior). The TpB additionally considers the effect of perceived control on behavior, such that a person may have strong intentions but low control (e.g., the physical addiction to nicotine may override attitudes, norms, and intentions to predict smoking behavior). The theoretical model for the TpB is shown in Figure 1.

Meta-analyses support the general principles of the TpB model, showing that the TpB accounts for 27% and 39% of the variance in behavior and intention, respectively, with perceived behavioral control independently accounting for an additional 6% of the variation in intention (Armitage & Conner, 2001; Sheeran, 2002). Different TpB components show different magnitudes of relation to intentions, although this differs across various behaviors and situations (Ajzen, 1991). Armitage and Conner's (2001) meta-analysis suggests that intention is most strongly predicted by attitudes (ρ = .49), is also strongly predicted by control (ρ = .43), and shows the weakest

Figure 1. Theory of Planned Behavior (TpB)

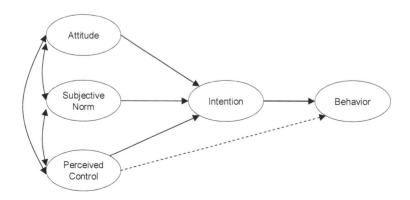

relationship with subjective norms ($\rho = .34$). However, Armitage and Conner suggest that weak relationships between subjective norms and intention may be due to the problematic development of many subjective norm scales.

In examining the relationship of TpB mathematics attitudes to mathematics achievement, Lipnevich, McCann, Bertling, and Roberts (2011) demonstrated that the TpB structural model held in samples of middle school students from Belarus ($n = 339$) and the United States ($n = 382$), although attitudes and intentions were quite strongly related in both groups ($r = .73$ and .72). For both groups, the TpB explained a sizeable proportion of the variation in students' mathematics grades: 24.5% for the U.S. sample and 31.5% for the Belarusian sample. Such results highlight the importance of attitudinal factors in predicting scholastic achievement. It would appear worth exploring whether the TpB model extends to other domains (e.g., reading) and to older, college-aged populations.

Health, Health Attitudes, and Achievement

Obesity and Academic Outcomes. Claims from multiple sources indicate an "obesity epidemic" among children and adolescents of Organisation of Economic Co-operation and Development (OECD) nations over the last decade (Pyle et al., 2006). Worldwide, 1 in 10 children aged 5 to 17 is classified as overweight or obese, with the rate increasing by half a percent per year (Lobstein, Baur, & Uauy, 2004). This figure rises to one in five for Europe, and one in three for the Americas (Lobstein et al., 2004). Aside from the obvious negative health consequences, the obesity epidemic may also have important consequences for academic achievement. Research demonstrates that obese students obtain lower grades and test scores than do healthy-weight students, with some longitudinal designs in the early school grades suggesting a causal relationship (Datar & Sturm, 2002; Datar, Sturm, & Magnabosco, 2004; Kaestner & Grossman, 2007; Sigfúsdúttir, Kristjánsson, & Allegrante, 2007; Sabia, 2007). In fact, research from our group has demonstrated that an obese/nonobese achievement gap is of similar size to the Black/White achievement gap: Obese middle school students achieve a GPA 0.83 standard deviations lower than do healthy-weight students, and obese college students achieve lower grades at both high school (.46 of a standard deviation) and college (.36 of a standard deviation) (MacCann, 2009); the Black–White achievement gap for math and reading in the National Assessment of Educational Progress ranges from about .40 to .60 (Rampey, Dion, & Donahue, 2009). Since obesity rates in the United States differ by race, sex, and socioeconomic status (SES), it is worth considering the role ethnic differences in obesity might play in the various documented achievement gaps (Ogden et al.,

2006). Statistically speaking, the relationship between race and achievement is certainly mediated by obesity, though this causal relationship is entangled with socioeconomic status, sex, and other demographic characteristics. Nevertheless, there is compelling evidence for plausible causal pathways that link obesity directly with lower school achievement without SES as a mediating pathway. For example, experiencing sleep apnea, a common chronic condition associated with obesity, can result in difficulty on memory and learning tasks (Rhodes et al., 1995). In addition, obesity can cause school absences due to related medical problems, thus lowering grades through absenteeism (Taras & Potts-Datema, 2005).

The two simple reasons an individual becomes obese without genetic etiology—increased calories and decreased physical activity—have a complex myriad of dynamically changing causes. These include the availability and expense of nonprocessed versus processed food, increased use of motorized transport, increasing replacement of water with carbonated drinks on school campuses and elsewhere, increased portion sizes, and rising levels of promotion and marketing of high-calorie foods (Lobstein et al., 2004). Individuals from ethnic minority groups or those with low socioeconomic status are particularly at risk for becoming obese (Lobstein et al., 2004; Ogden, Flegal, Carroll, & Johnson, 2002; Parsons, Power, Logan, & Summerbell, 1999). Within the constraints of these situational factors, an individual's behavior, determined from his or her attitudes and knowledge of nutrition and exercise, also constitutes an important causal framework for obesity and health.

Attitudes Toward Nutrition and Exercise. Research from our group has examined the relationship of attitudes and knowledge to health behaviors, obesity, and academic outcomes, using the Knowledge-Attitude-Behavior (K-A-B) model. In the K-A-B model, knowledge affects attitudes, which affect behaviors (see Baranowski, Cullen, Nicklas, Thompson, & Baranowski, 2003). For example, if people are informed about the health consequences of tobacco use (knowledge), they will form a negative view of smoking (attitude) and quit (behavior). Knowledge may additionally act as an enabler of behavior (e.g., knowledge about nicotine patches or other methods for quitting may be used to stop smoking). In examining nutrition and exercise under the K-A-B model, attitudes are conceptualized according to the TpB. Although the TpB has been frequently used to study health behavior, relatively little of this research has, to date, been conducted on student populations or with ethnically diverse samples (Baranowski et al., 2003).

Our group examined the role of attitudes in determining food consumption and exercise behaviors in a sample of 1036 tertiary education students (64% female) from universities ($n = 574$) and community colleges ($n = 462$) in the United States (MacCann, 2009). Nutrition and exercise attitude assessments were developed, as shown in the examples in Figure 2. Students' knowledge of vitamins, minerals, and the abstract facts of nutrition showed no relationship to junk-food consumption and a negative relationship to health-food consumption, whereas students' applied knowledge of nutrition (i.e., food choices and meal preparation) were significantly related to more consumption of nutritious foods and less consumption of unhealthy food. Such a result suggests that interventions using knowledge acquisition should use contextualized, applied, procedural types of information rather than decontextualized facts about vitamins, fat content, and the chemical or biological bases for nutrition. Structural models of the attitude–behavior link showed that the TpB explained 31% of the variation in students' healthy-eating behaviors (e.g., consumption of green vegetables, fresh fruits, nuts, or legumes), 26% of the variation in "junk-food" consumption (e.g., soda or pop, fried foods, or desserts), and 34% of the variation in exercise behaviors (e.g., frequency of walking, playing sports, doing cardiovascular activities). In addition, exercise and nutrition attitudes differed in obese and normal-weight students, with stronger differences for exercise ($d = .44$) than for nutrition ($d = .22$). Similar results were found for middle school students ($n = 383$), with the TpB explaining 34% of the variation in exercise, 21% of the variation in healthy eating, and 9% of the variation in junk-food consumption (MacCann & Roberts, 2009b). Given the importance of health for student well-being, as well as the known links between obesity and academic achievement, attitudes to health and well-being might constitute an important new avenue for exploring the noncognitive causes of student success.

Enhancing Noncognitive Constructs

There is evidence from a wide range of promotion, prevention, and treatment interventions that noncognitive constructs of the type discussed in the previous section can be improved (see Kyllonen, Lipnevich, Burrus, & Roberts, 2010). Below we discuss the evidence suggesting whether EI, personality superfactors and components, and math and health attitudes can be improved. We include a discussion of some emerging methods for creating interventions designed to improve these noncognitive constructs. Again our review is not exhaustive, though we do provide coverage of almost all of the constructs reviewed in the preceding passages.

Figure 2. Prototypical Items Associated With Health Attitudes

Prototypical Examples of Nutrition Attitudes Items

1. *Attitudes to Nutrition: overall evaluation of whether eating nutritiously is important/enjoyable*—e.g., "Healthy food tastes boring" (reverse coded).

2. *Subjective Norms About Nutrition: perceived social pressure to eat nutritiously*—e.g., "My parents would be disappointed if I ate a lot of unhealthy food."

3. *Perceptions of Control of Nutrition: estimate of one's capacity to follow a nutritious diet*—e.g., "Whether I eat a healthy diet is up to me."

4. *Intentions to Eat Nutritiously: resolute determination to follow a nutritious diet*—e.g., "I will avoid eating junk food."

Prototypical Examples of Exercise Attitudes Items

1. *Attitudes to Exercise: overall evaluation of whether exercising is enjoyable/important*—e.g., "I like to be active."

2. *Subjective Norms about Exercise: perceived social pressure to exercise*—e.g., "My friends expect me to join in when playing sports."

3. *Perceived Control over Exercise: estimate of one's capacity to engage in regular exercise*—e.g., "I am too busy to exercise every day" (reverse coded).

4. *Intentions to Exercise: the determination to exercise regularly*—e.g., "My plans for the week involve regular exercise."

Emotional Intelligence Interventions

Several social and emotional learning (SEL) programs exist in schools across the United States that are designed to improve students' emotional capabilities (e.g., Cohen, Freeman, & Thompson, 1998; Zeidner et al., 2009; Zins, Bloodworth, Weissberg, & Walberg, 2004). Such programs aim to help students recognize emotions in themselves and others, regulate their own emotions, develop a sense of empathy, improve their communication skills, and improve their decision making (Zins, Payton, Weissberg, & O'Brien, 2007). These programs go by several different names, including, "life skills training," "conflict resolution training," and "social awareness training" (Zeidner et al., 2009). Importantly, several SEL programs have been found to be effective in groups of ethnically and racially diverse students, and thus hold promise as a useful tool in reducing the achievement gap (Payton et al., 2008). Some of the largest SEL programs are summarized in Zeidner et al. (2009; pp. 236–238), and three are briefly described in the following sections.

Improving Social Awareness Social Problem-Solving Project (Elias & Clabby, 1992). In this program, K–12 students are taught skills related to emotional intelligence such as anger and stress management, coping, and perspective taking. Students achieve these skills by learning to recognize emotions in pictures and by developing the ability to associate emotions and facial expressions. Research on this program has demonstrated that it can be effective in reducing student responses to stressful situations and increasing student prosocial behavior and self-efficacy (Elias & Clabby, 1992).

Promoting Alternate Thinking Strategies (PATHS) (Greenberg, Kusche, & Riggs, 2004). The PATHS program aims to improve K–12 students' ability to express and understand emotions, take others' perspectives, and solve social problems. Specifically, students are taught how to express and handle their negative emotions, how to control impulses, and how to have empathy for others. The PATHS program has been shown to improve second- and third-grade students' emotional fluency and emotional vocabulary.

Resolving Conflicts Creatively Program (Aber, Jones, Brown, Chaudry, & Samples, 1998). Goals of the program include reducing youth violence by helping students control their anger and diffuse conflict. Students are taught emotional intelligence skills such as the ability to identify their own negative feelings, controlling their anger, and taking perspective. One study of this program indicated that 87% of participating teachers said the program was having a positive impact on their students and that 92% of participating students felt "good about themselves" (Patti & Lentieri, 1999).

The results of a meta-analysis of SEL programs suggest these programs have several benefits for students (Durlak & Weissberg, 2007). For example, students who participate in SEL programs tend to

      a. have higher achievement scores and GPAs;
      b. have better attendance records; and
      c. like school more.

Furthermore, the meta-analysis compared four different contexts for SEL-based interventions: the school, the family, the community, and the family and school relationship (Durlak & Weissberg, 2007). Results revealed that school-based interventions had the largest effect on student outcomes. One should be cautious, however, in interpreting the effects of many SEL programs and indeed the previously discussed meta-analysis since questions about the validity and reliability of many social and emotional outcome measures remain (Zeidner et al., 2009).

Personality Superfactors and Component Interventions
     Up to the mid-1990s, the predominant perspective of personality psychologists was that personality stabilizes in early adulthood and does not change as one gets older (McCrae & Costa, 1994, 1999). If personality were indeed fixed, then interventions designed to change personality would be futile. However, the perspective now, based on numerous longitudinal studies, is that personality traits do in fact change across the life span (Haan, Millsap, & Hartka, 1986; Helson & Moane, 1987; Helson & Wink, 1992; B. W. Roberts, Caspi, & Moffitt, 2001; Robins, Fraley, Roberts, & Trzesniewski, 2001). For example, a meta-analysis by B. W. Roberts, Walton, and Viechtbaur (2006) revealed that personality traits changed more often in young adulthood than any other period of the life course, including adolescence. Furthermore, mostly in young adulthood, people tend to become more socially dominant, conscientious, and emotionally stable. Also, up to about age 20, individuals tend to increase in Social Vitality and Openness to Experience. Collectively, these results suggest that interventions designed to change personality can be especially effective for college-age people. In the following, we discuss possibilities for interventions for each of the five factors of personality.
     Extroversion. One possible way to influence students' level of Extroversion is through training in leadership. Leadership is highly represented in items that measure Extroversion, including items such as, "I try to lead others" and "I can talk others into doing things." Students' leadership ability can be improved through programs geared specifically toward leadership development. A longitudinal study of the effectiveness of leadership education programs found that such programs had an impact on educational and personal development (Cress, Astin, Zimmerman-Oster, & Burkhardt, 2001), with participants showing a growth in civic responsibility, leadership skills, multicultural awareness, understanding leadership theories, and personal and societal values. Programs that give students the opportunity to volunteer, to participate in internships and to participate in group projects seem to be the most successful in promoting leadership and, by extension, Extroversion (Cress et al., 2001).
     Agreeableness. Interventions that influence Extroversion can also have the effect of influencing many of the facets of Agreeableness. Specifically, leadership programs can have an impact on aspects of Agreeableness such as

trust, morality, altruism, cooperation, and sympathy. Indeed, Agreeableness items include "I trust what people say" and "I anticipate the needs of others." As such, any intervention that influences leadership should also influence Agreeableness because leadership involves issues such as taking advantage of others, anticipating the needs of others, and trusting others.

Conscientiousness. One way Conscientiousness can be improved is by focusing on students' study skills. In a meta-analysis of 109 studies, Robbins et al. (2004) concluded that there were "moderate relationships" between study skills and success in college as indexed by cumulative grade point average and persistence. Study skills interventions have been used to improve several aspects of Conscientiousness including one's level of achievement striving, orderliness, self-discipline, and self-efficacy. Providing students with extensive feedback and helping them to gain initial levels of competence in a certain domain tend to lead to increased self-efficacy and achievement in future tasks (Bandura, 1997; S. Lee & Klein, 2002; Linnenbrink & Pintrich, 2003; Schunk, 1990, 1995).

Study skills intervention programs that take into account the interaction of behavior, cognition and personal and environmental factors tend to be the most successful in influencing students' academic performance and motivation (Dignath, Buettner, & Langfeldt, 2008). The most effective training programs provide students with feedback about their strategic learning. One study found that college freshmen placed on academic probation showed significant improvements in grade point average and academic hours attempted and earned when they were enrolled in a study skills course; this trend persisted over two years and boosted the probability of students' staying in college (Lipsky & Ender, 1990). In summary, study skills intervention programs have been shown to successfully influence students' Conscientiousness and thus enhance their academic achievement.

Neuroticism. Interventions designed to decrease student Neuroticism may involve techniques to help improve one's self-esteem, coping skills, and level of anxiety (e.g., test or math). Zeidner (1998) has indicated that interventions can be effective if an individual

a. has at least some level of skill (i.e., problem solving and test taking),
b. has at least a moderate interest and motivation to participate; and
c. is given the opportunity to practice the skills taught in the intervention process, apply them to real-world situations, and evaluate them realistically.

Smith, Arnkoff, and Wright (1990) have stated that a multidimensional approach to intervention (e.g., focused on cognitive, emotional, academic, and social skills) is more effective than any approach with a singular focus.

Interventions designed to improve one's coping ability often teach individuals how to manage the cognitive and behavioral aspects perceived as controllable by an individual (Compas et al., 2001). This typically includes techniques such as positive reappraisal, problem solving, and stress avoidance that help the individual deal with and handle stress (see Ayers, Sandler, West, & Roosa, 1996; Compas, 1998; Ebata & Moos, 1991; Lengua & Long, 2002; Rudolph, Dennig, & Weisz, 1995).

Openness to Experience. One important aspect of Openness to Experience is the ability to think critically; there has recently been an increased demand for interventions that enhance these skills. Researchers have stated that critical thinking skills training should involve instruction, demonstration, and practice in order to most effectively help individuals identify and handle different types of information (Cohen, Freeman, & Thompson, 1998). Overall, research in this area has demonstrated that critical thinking skills are successfully enhanced when a variety of skills and domains are addressed throughout the teaching period.

Programs shown to increase critical thinking skills tend to focus on teaching elementary logic, inference, and transfer (applying something learned in one setting to another setting), creative thinking, and philosophical thinking (Cotton, 1991). Although these studies tend not to treat Openness to Experience as an outcome variable, they do suggest that Openness to Experience may be modified through interventions.

Time Management. Time management interventions and training courses have been in existence for several decades, with McCay (1959) developing one of the first. Critical elements of this course include helping people gain insight into time-consuming activities, changing their time expenditures, and increasing their workday efficiency by teaching them how to make a daily plan, prioritize tasks, and handle unexpected tasks. Since then, several time management interventions have been created. However, a recent review of the time management literature came to the conclusion that evidence varies as to whether time management training has a positive impact on one's ability to manage their time (Claessens, van Eerde, & Rutte, 2007).

Teamwork. There are several interventions and training courses designed to improve student teamwork skills. In fact, a recent internet search on "teamwork skills" revealed about 3,860,000 links. These links emphasize building skills such as communication, conflict resolution, vision, consensus building, and helping. Despite the fact that education and the workforce both emphasize the importance of building teamwork skills (e.g., Casner-Lotto & Barrington, 2006), very little, if any, research exists on the effectiveness of programs that attempt to improve these skills. One aspect of teamwork is leadership and, as described previously, some research has been conducted on influencing student leadership (e.g., Cress et al., 2001). However, leadership is only one part of teamwork. Indeed, a team with too many leaders and not enough "team players" will not function well.

Development of a Noncognitive Intervention System

Partly due to the inconclusive nature of previous work, our research team has recently developed a system of creating interventions designed to improve time management and teamwork skills (among other constructs). Students are first given individualized feedback concerning their relative level of each construct compared to the average student. Next, they are given a set of suggestions (action plans) generated by experts in the field for improving their skills in that construct. Experts typically include experienced teachers, faculty advisors, and guidance counselors. Students' parents and/or teachers have access to student feedback and are also given a set of action plans designed to help students improve.

The basic process for developing feedback and action plans for these noncognitive constructs:

1. A review of the literature is conducted to identify constructs related to important outcomes and likely to be amenable to intervention.
2. Assessments of the identified constructs are developed.
3. Assessments are pilot tested on a large and diverse sample of students and their psychometric characteristics (reliability, structural validity) are evaluated and refined.
4. Based on the distribution of scores from the pilot studies, cut scores are created to determine whether a student is "high," "medium," or "low" on the construct. Currently, the distribution is "cut" such that students are considered "high" in a construct if they are more than one standard deviation higher than the mean score for that construct and "low" if they are more than one standard deviation lower than the cut score.
5. Expert panel interviews are held to develop and refine action plans and suggestions for improvement. Expert panelists provide and critique concrete action plans for

the development and improvement of these noncognitive constructs. Separate action plans are developed for distribution to students, teachers, parents, and institutions.

6. Suggestions are assessed for sensitivity and fairness by a diverse group of experts trained in this process.

It is important to note that we are currently evaluating the efficacy of this approach for developing interventions designed to improve noncognitive constructs. Currently, quasi-experimental studies are being conducted on high school and community college samples. Plans are underway to study the efficacy of the feedback and action plans on inner city low SES and high school dropout samples in conjunction with a literacy program. This system has several advantages. First, the feedback and action plans are individualized for the student (i.e., each student receives a different set of feedback and action plans that are tailored to their individual score profile). This should cause students to become more engaged with the intervention than they would be with a more generic feedback system, which should, in turn, lead to more motivation to work on the plan. Furthermore, it should make students' efforts to improve their noncognitive characteristics more efficient, as they will have the advantage of being able to focus on improving their weaknesses rather than spending time working on characteristics that are already strengths. Second, the action plans are provided at different levels to students, teachers, and school administrators so everyone has a common language and common set of goals to work toward. Administrators can use feedback to guide policy decisions. For example, they may be informed that the student body is generally weak on time management, but strong on teamwork. In this instance, financing a study skills program might be much more effective than introducing a peer-support program aimed at increasing social cohesion. Similarly, if classroom teachers are aware of the strengths and weaknesses of their classes, they may be able to adapt their pedagogy to best meet the needs of a particular class.

The theoretical argument for the efficacy of this system is depicted in Figure 3; examples of feedback and action plans created for time management are depicted in Figure 4. As a supplement to the feedback and action plans, students are given a series of exercises designed to assist them in improving their time management skills (see "helpful tools" column in Figure 4). In the following sections, three example exercises are described.

Figure 3. Theoretical Argument for Feedback and Action Plans

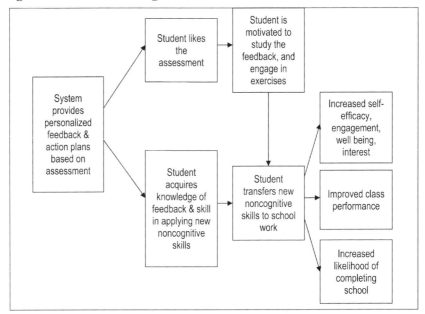

Note: Based on the noncognitive assessment, the system provides feedback and action plans. The results of that intervention are shown on the other boxes in the diagram. First, students are expected to have a positive reaction to the assessment, which motivates them to study the feedback and to carry out the action plans. Students are also expected to learn about their noncognitive skills and from the feedback about how to improve them. Both the motivation to improve and the increased knowledge of noncognitive skills are expected to transfer to the classroom. The outcomes are increased engagement, improved academic performance, and greater retention in school.

Figure 4a. Time Management Feedback and Action Plans Examples

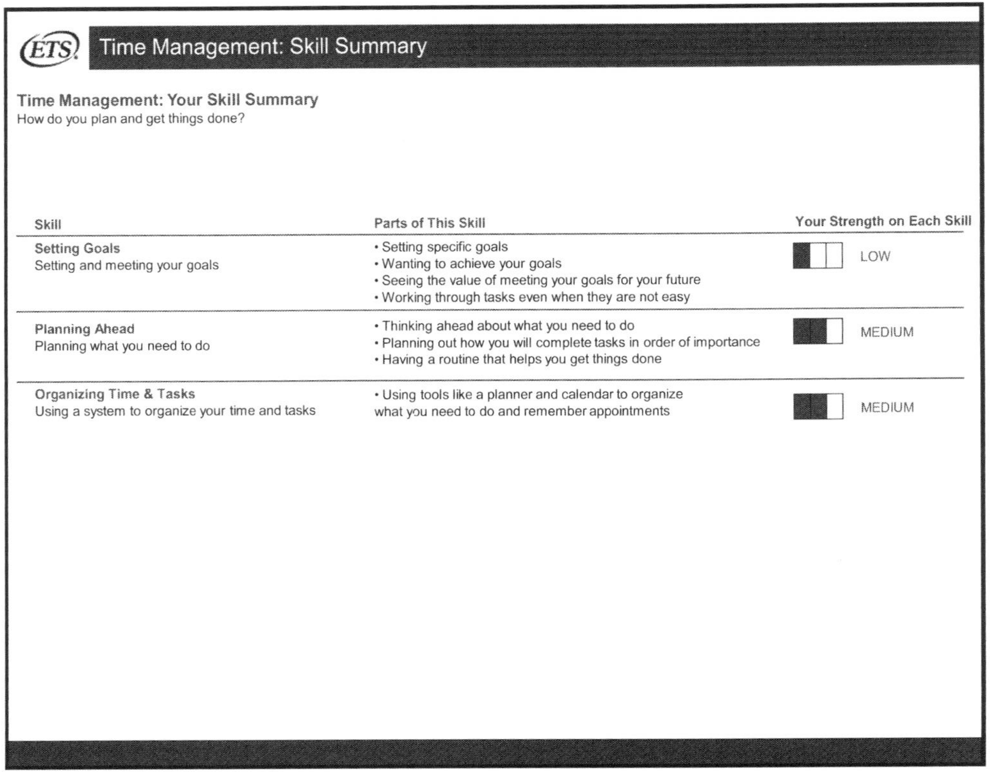

(ETS) Time Management: Skill Summary

Time Management: Your Skill Summary
How do you plan and get things done?

Skill	Parts of This Skill	Your Strength on Each Skill
Setting Goals Setting and meeting your goals	• Setting specific goals • Wanting to achieve your goals • Seeing the value of meeting your goals for your future • Working through tasks even when they are not easy	LOW
Planning Ahead Planning what you need to do	• Thinking ahead about what you need to do • Planning out how you will complete tasks in order of importance • Having a routine that helps you get things done	MEDIUM
Organizing Time & Tasks Using a system to organize your time and tasks	• Using tools like a planner and calendar to organize what you need to do and remember appointments	MEDIUM

Figure 4b. Time Management Feedback and Action Plans Examples

(ETS) Time Management: Action Plan: Setting Goals

Time Management: Action Plan
How can you better plan and get things done?

Skill	Ways to Improve This Skill	Helpful Tools
Setting Goals Setting and meeting your goals	o Having goals helps you take action toward something that you want to achieve. Consider what your educational and career goals are. If you need help defining your goals, your academic advisor or guidance counselor has tools and strategies to help you.	Goal-Setting Worksheet
	o Write down your goals. Start with one long-term educational and/or career goal then break it down into smaller goals that you will complete over time. For example, your long-term goal might be "Graduate high school with good grades so I can attend college." Use the Goal-Setting Worksheet to describe your goal and the steps you will take to meet it.	
	o Having goals helps you decide how to spend your time. Ask yourself, "What do I need to do this week to work toward my goals? What do I need to do today?"	
	o Remind yourself regularly of your goals. If you find yourself spending too much time on activities that distract you from your goals, bring your focus back to your priorities for that day.	
	o Get the support you need from your family, friends, housemaster, and academic advisor. Discuss what you might have to give up to make time for your school work. For example, you may have less free time and may not be able to enjoy leisure activities as frequently.	
	o Reward yourself, but not until *after* you finish the task you set out to do. For example, watch a show, go out for coffee, or catch up with a friend *after* you have read those chapters and reviewed your class notes.	

Time Management Exercises

Goal-Setting Worksheet. Students complete worksheets where they set academic, extracurricular, and interpersonal goals. These worksheets require students to choose a goal they hope to complete within the next year. Next, they are instructed to write down everything they can think of that will help them complete their goal. Then they select what they think are the three most important things from their list. Finally, they create a chart that includes the steps they will take to reach their goal and when they plan to do this. This visual representation helps students "unpack" a seemingly difficult goal into smaller, more manageable steps, which is important in goal attainment. Many individuals do not reach their goals because they have underestimated the time it will take to complete them. This phenomenon, called the *Planning Fallacy*, frequently keeps people from reaching their goals (e.g., Kruger & Evans, 2004). If students are instructed to think about each step they need to take to reach their goals, they may be able to set more realistic time estimates, which in turn will help them meet their goals.

This worksheet asks students to specify the exact dates they will begin to work on each of these tasks. This is referred to as creating "implementation intentions" for students. Research has demonstrated that having students do this tends to lead to greater goal achievement and less procrastination (Gollwitzer, 1990). It is theorized this works because creating an implementation intention takes task completion out of the hands of the students and into the hands of the situation.

Day Reconstruction Method. Students are given day reconstruction worksheets to complete (e.g., Kahneman, Krueger, Schkade, Schwarz, & Stone, 2004). This five-part exercise requires students to (a) think about how satisfied they are with their lives in and out of school; (b) provide an hourly view of what they did yesterday, who they did it with, and how they felt while participating in a particular activity; (c) record information about their overall mood yesterday; (d) record how they believe others perceived them; and (e) reflect on the number of hours they spent doing each activity, who they spent time with, and how they felt. Students are prompted to note anything that surprises them as they look for trends in their information.

We hypothesize that the exercise of writing down daily tasks in detail will increase student awareness of how they really spend their time. This is analogous to the practice of dieters using a food diary to keep track of how much they eat; in the process, dieters often report they are surprised at the amount of unhealthy food they are eating. In the same way, we predict that the Day Reconstruction Method should increase students' awareness of how they spend their time.

Planner Use: Students are also given information about how to choose the right planner for them (e.g., paper and pencil vs. digital). They are given a paper planner and asked to complete it (for practice purposes—even if digital is their preferred planner). Plant, Ericsson, Hill, and Asberg (2005) noted that, in their sample of college students, an organized and systematic approach to planning was associated with higher GPAs.

Changing Health and Academic Attitudes

It is beyond the scope of this chapter to provide a detailed review of this literature; however, it is important to note that there has been a great deal of research on interventions that influence health attitudes. The Theory of Planned Behavior has been used as a guide to influence health-related attitudes (e.g., Ajzen & Manstead, 2007) as has goal framing (Cesario, Grant, & Higgins, 2004). Since parents' health attitudes have been found to be indicative of their children's health attitudes, interventions that encourage parents to model healthy behaviors should be effective (Tinsley, 1992).

On the other hand, little to no empirical research has been conducted on interventions for math attitudes. We propose that interventions can be created; however, to influence math attitudes, interventions need to be developed based on theory and research in social psychology.

Ajzen (2006) states that people may hold false attitudinal beliefs that influence their behavior. For instance, an assessment of student math attitudes might reveal a negative attitude toward math based on the fact that the student incorrectly overestimates the time it takes to learn math. In this case, an intervention can be created that influences the strength of this belief by showing the student that it does not take as long to learn math as they thought it would. The researcher might instead discover the student overestimates the painfulness of the experience of studying math, feeling they will be bored while studying. In this case, an intervention can be created that shows the student that studying math can be enjoyable, such as by turning it into a game. In sum, these false beliefs can be corrected by targeting the strength of the attitude (e.g., the student overestimates the time it takes to study) and/or the valence of the attitude (e.g., the student incorrectly estimates the boredom experienced when studying math) (Ajzen, 2006).

In addition to correcting beliefs, interventions can be created that introduce new beliefs. In the example of the student who thinks studying math will take too much time, he/she believes the time would be better spent working at a part-time job and that the benefits of earning a part-time wage outweigh the benefits of studying math. The researcher could construct an intervention focused on introducing a new belief. Specifically, this student might not be aware of the increase in salary he or she may attain by completing a high school or college education or, more specifically, by working in an industry that is highly math-oriented, and that this increase in salary will greatly exceed the amount of money that can be earned at a part-time job. An introduction of this new knowledge, or belief system, would potentially improve the student's attitudes toward studying math.

Several other principles of social psychology could also be used to influence math attitudes. For example, interventions can influence attitudes by appealing to students' needs for affiliation, accuracy, and positive self-concept (Cialdini & Goldstein, 2004); basic principles of conditioning (e.g., classical, evaluative, operant) can be used when designing attitude interventions (Clore & Schnall, 2005; Pavlov, 1927; Skinner, 1953); and attitudes can be altered through social learning (e.g., Bandura, 1997) such as encouraging parents and teachers to model positive attitudes for students.

Summary and Recommendations for Future Research

In the preceding review, we have concentrated on research conducted with a specific construct (e.g., time management), most generally for a specific population. This approach was used largely because of page constraints but also a desire to concentrate on studies we have published, since we have analogous data for most of the constructs for middle school, high school, community college, four-year colleges, graduate school, and workforce populations. Future reviews may be more comprehensive, especially since some of these studies are longitudinal in nature (see MacCann, Minsky, et al., in press) and bridge the high school to post-secondary school to workforce pipelines.

The knowledgeable reader might claim our coverage of noncognitive constructs misses a number of factors. Among those we have reviewed in various other outlets are character strengths, critical thinking, grit, psychological mindedness, self-concept, self-esteem, self-regulation, self-control, social intelligence, test anxiety, virtues; indeed the list is voluminous (see, e.g., Kyllonen et al., 2010; Kyllonen & Roberts, 2008; Kyllonen, Walters, & Kaufman, 2005; MacCann & Roberts, 2009a; R. D. Roberts et al., 2007; R. D. Roberts, Stankov, Schulze, & Kyllonen, 2008; Zeidner et al., 2009). However, the Kyllonen et al. (2010) review shows that many of these constructs are redundant and most can be subsumed under a combination of the Big Five personality traits and motivational constructs. Another limitation we acknowledge is our sparse treatment of the academic spectrum from preK to Grade 5, something we hope to remedy after gathering some compelling empirical evidence for the efficacy of interventions on this population. This type of research may need to adopt different assessments; for example, self-reports may not capture noncognitive constructs below middle school, especially for those students who most need interventions.

Although we have focused on reviewing either assessments or interventions that might go hand in hand to form an assessment-intervention system, it is undoubtedly the case that assessments of the noncognitive constructs described throughout this chapter could be used in other ways, including the following.

High Stakes. In education, high stakes assessments of noncognitive factors have not been implemented in any large-scale sense, other than letters of recommendation. Recently, Sedlacek (in press) proposed that eight noncognitive factors should be considered when admissions decisions are made: positive self-concept, recognition of strengths and deficiencies, ability to handle racism, ability to defer gratification, availability of a strong social network, leadership experience, community service experience, and knowledge about a field. These factors are typically assessed with self-reports such as the Noncognitive Questionnaire (NCQ) (Sedlacek, 1996). However, one barrier to using self-report assessments such as the NCQ is that they tend to be fairly easily faked and coached (Ziegler, MacCann, & Roberts, 2010). However, ratings by others are less susceptible to this validity threat. With the growing appreciation of the importance of noncognitive factors in education, it is not surprising that a large-scale, high-stakes noncognitive assessment, based on faculty ratings, has been implemented recently for graduate school admissions (Kyllonen, 2008). If successful, it is reasonable to expect that a similar application for college could follow. A benefit of noncognitive high-stakes assessments is that they signal to the student the importance of noncognitive factors.

Developmental Scales. One can imagine developmental scales based on annual noncognitive assessments made available to students and institutions to assist in monitoring student progress from middle school to high school graduation. Developmental scales with norms could be presented for each of the core psychosocial factors and perhaps additional factors. This would enable comparisons among schools, districts, even states, and enable trend comparisons.

It would be important to present these constructs and facets to education users (teachers, schools, districts, and state administrative personnel) in order to find language that would be most useful for score reporting. For example, terms like Neuroticism might not be readily accepted within the context of the public school system. New terminology could be developed in focus groups and telephone surveys.

A useful supplement to developmental scales would be proficiency standards (e.g., basic, proficient, advanced) for different target groups. These standards could be established based on contrasts with populations from various workforce sectors (e.g., health care, personal services, retail, manufacturing, professional), 2-year and 4-year college populations, or with other methodologies commonly used in standard setting (see Kyllonen et al., 2010).

Policy Decisions. The benefit of developmental scales or proficiency reports to the institution and the school is primarily to provide information on where the institution or student stands with respect to the most important psychosocial factors. As with any large-scale assessment, such as the Programme for International Student Assessments or the National Assessment of Educational Progress, reliable, high-quality data on these factors provides the background from which policies and interventions carried out at the school, district, state, or even national level can be tried out, and their effects evaluated using assessment scores as the basis for the evaluation.

To provide one illustrative example of how the assessment of noncognitive variables can influence policy decisions, we recently conducted an extensive assessment of students for a local high school. Results revealed that students' stress, anxiety, and depression levels were peaking during their junior year of high school, and in fact, a substantial percentage of students were reaching extreme levels; these peaks coincided with SAT/ACT preparations. After hearing this result, the school made several policy decisions intended to decrease the amount of stress students felt as they prepared for the SAT/ACT.

Summary. We believe noncognitive factors represent a neglected area of research and that they have an important place in policy and in the way scientific knowledge can fuel educational practice. Indeed, there appears a burgeoning zeitgeist both within and outside education, championed in particular by psychology and economics, which demands these psychosocial skills be given greater consideration by educators. In this review, we have focused in particular on an assessment-intervention system, but it is likely these constructs could (and will) play major roles in high-stakes selection, developmental models and score reports, as well as large-scale national and international assessments and the policy decisions that might accompany their successful implementation.

Acknowledgments

The project represents an ongoing collaboration between staff of the Center for New Constructs at the Educational Testing Service (ETS), Princeton, New Jersey, United States, and the School of Psychology at the University of Sydney, Sydney, Australia. We are grateful to a number of individuals from both organizations that helped to shape this paper. We would also like to acknowledge the helpful suggestions of the editors and a number of reviewers at ETS. Portions of this paper were supported in part by U.S. Army Research Institute (ARI) Contract W91WAW-07-C-0025 to the Educational Testing Service (ETS). The views expressed represent the views of the authors and not of the Educational Testing Service.

References

Abe, J. A. A. (2005). The predictive value of the Five-Factor Model of personality with preschool age children: A nine-year follow-up study, *Journal of Research in Personality*, *39*, 423–442.

Aber, J. L., Jones, S. M., Brown, J. L., Chaudry, N., & Samples, F. (1998). Responding to conflict creatively: Evaluating the developmental effects of a school-based violence prevention program in neighborhood and classroom context. *Development and Psychopathology*, *10*, 187–213.

Ahles, C. B., & Bosworth, C. C. (2004). The perception and reality of student and workplace teams. *Journalism & Mass Communication Educator*, *Spring*, 42–59.

Ajzen, I. (1991). The theory of planned behavior. *Organizational Behavior and Human Decision Processes*, *50*, 179–211.

Ajzen, I. (2006). Behavioral interventions based on the Theory of Planned Behavior. Retrieved from http://www.unix.oit.umass.edu/~aizen/pdf/tpb.measurement.pdf

Ajzen, I., & Fishbein, M. (1973). Attitudinal and normative variables as predictors of specific behavior. *Journal of Personality and Social Psychology*, *27*, 41–57.

Ajzen, I., & Manstead, A. S. R. (2007). Changing health-related behaviors: An approach based on the theory of planned behavior. In K. van den Bos, M. Hewstone, J. de Wit, H. Schut, & M. Stroebe (Eds.), *The scope of social psychology: Theory and applications* (pp. 43–63). New York, NY: Psychology Press.

Armitage, C., & Conner, M. (2001). Efficacy of the theory of planned behaviour: A meta-analytic review. *British Journal of Social Psychology, 40*, 471–499.

Ayers, T. S., Sandler, I. N., West, S. G., & Roosa, M. W. (1996). A dispositional and situational assessment of children's coping: testing alternative models of coping. *Journal of Personality, 64,* 923–958.

Bandura, A. (1997). *Self-efficacy: The exercise of control.* New York, NY: Freeman.

Baranowski, T., Cullen, K. W., Nicklas, T., Thompson, D., & Baranowski, J. (2003). Are current health behavioural change models helpful in guiding prevention of weight gain efforts? *Obesity Research, 11S,* 23S–43S.

Blackwell, L. S., Trzesniewski, K. H., & Dweck, C. S. (2007). Implicit theories of intelligence predict achievement across an adolescent transition: A longitudinal study and an intervention. *Child Development, 78,* 246–263.

Borghans, L., Duckworth, A. L., Heckman, J., & ter Weel, B. (2008). The economics and psychology of personality traits. *Journal of Human Resources, 43,* 972–1059.

Britton, B. K., & Tessor, A. (1991). Effects of time-management practices on college grades. *Journal of Educational Psychology, 83,* 405–410.

Campbell, J. R., Voelkl, K. E., & Donahue, P. L. (1997). *NAEP 1996 trends in academic progress* (NCES Publication No. 97985r). Washington, DC: U.S. Department of Education.

Casner-Lotto, J., & Barrington, L. (2006). *Are they really ready to work? Employers' perspectives on the basic knowledge and applied skills of new entrants to the 21st century U.S. workforce.* New York, NY: The Conference Board. Retrieved from http://www.conference-board.org/pdf_free/BED-06-Workforce.pdf

Cesario, J., Grant, H., & Higgins, E. T. (2004). Regulatory fit and persuasion: Transfer from "feeling right." *Journal of Personality and Social Psychology, 86,* 388–404.

Cialdini, R. B., & Goldstein, N. J. (2004). Social influence: Compliance and conformity. *Annual Review of Psychology, 55,* 591–621.

Claessens, B. J. C., van Eerde, W., & Rutte, C. G. (2007). A review of the time management literature. *Personnel Review, 36,* 255–274

Clore, G. L., & Schnall, S. (2005). The influences of affect on attitude. In D. Albarracín, B. T. Johnson, & M. P. Zanna (Eds.), *Handbook of attitudes* (pp. 437–489). Mahwah, NJ: Erlbaum.

Cohen, M. S., Freeman, J. T., & Thompson, B. (1998). Critical thinking skills in tactical decision making: A model and a training strategy. In J. A. Cannon-Bowers, A. Janis, & E. Salas (Eds.), *Making decisions under stress: Implications for individual and team training* (pp. 155–189). Washington, DC: American Psychological Association.

Compas, B. E. (1998). An agenda for coping research and theory: Basic and applied developmental issues. *International Journal of Behavioral Development, 22*, 231–237.

Compas, B. E., Connor-Smith, J. K., Saltzman, H., Harding Thomsen, A., & Wadsworth, M. E. (2001). Coping with stress during childhood and adolescence: Problems, progress, and potential in theory and research. *Psychological Bulletin, 127*, 87–127.

Connell, J. P., Spencer, M. B., & Aber, J. L. (1994). Educational risk and resilience in African-American youth: Context, self, action, and outcomes in school. *Child Development, 65*, 493–506.

Costa, P. T., & McCrae, R. R. (1992). Four ways five factors are basic. *Personality and Individual Differences, 13*, 653–665.

Cotton, K. (1991). Close-up #11: Teaching thinking skills. Retrieved from Northwest Regional Educational Laboratory's School Improvement Research Series website: http://www.nwrel.org/scpd/sirs/6/cu11.html

Crede, M., & Kuncel, N. R. (2008). Study habits, skills, and attitudes: The third pillar supporting collegiate academic performance. *Perspectives on Psychological Science, 3,* 425–453.

Cress, C. M., Astin, H. S., Zimmerman-Oster, K., & Burkhardt, J. C. (2001). Developmental outcomes of college students' involvement in leadership activities. *Journal of College Student Development, 42*, 15–27.

Datar, A., & Sturm, R. (2006). Childhood overweight and elementary school outcomes. *International Journal of Obesity, 30*, 1449–1460.

Datar, A., Sturm, R., & Magnabosco, J. L. (2004). Childhood overweight and academic performance: national study of kindergartners and first-graders. *Obesity Research, 12*, 58–68.

Dignath, C., Buettner, G., & Langfeldt, H. P. (2008). How can primary school students learn self-regulated learning strategies most effectively? A meta-analysis on self-regulation training programs. *Educational Research Review, 3*, 101–129.

Duckworth, A. L., & Seligman, M. E. P. (2005). Self-discipline outdoes IQ predicting academic performance in adolescents. *Psychological Science, 16*, 939–944.

Durlak, J. A., & Weissberg, R. P. (2007). *The impact of after-school programs that promote personal and social skills.* Chicago, IL: Collaborative for Academic, Social, and Emotional Learning.

Ebata, A., & Moos, R. (1991). Coping and adjustment in distressed and healthy adolescents. *Journal of Applied Developmental Psychology, 12*, 33–54.

Elias, M. J., & Clabby, J. (1992). *Building social problem solving skills: Guidelines from a school-based program.* San Francisco, CA: Jossey-Bass.

Eysenck, H. J. (1990). Biological dimensions of personality. In L. A. Pervin (Ed.), *Handbook of personality: Theory and research* (pp. 244–276). New York, NY: Guilford.

Fogarty, G. J., Games, N., MacCann, C., & Roberts, R. D. (2010). Emotional intelligence, coping and school performance. In R. Hicks (Ed.) *Personality and individual differences: Current directions.* Brisbane, Australia: Australian Academic Press.

Foldes, H. J., Duehr, E. E., & Ones, D. S. (2008). Group differences in personality: Meta-analysis comparing five U.S. racial groups. *Personnel Psychology, 61,* 579–616.

Freudenthaler, H. H., & Neubauer, A. C. (2007). Measuring emotional management abilities: Further evidence of the importance to distinguish between typical and maximum performance. *Personality and Individual Differences, 42,* 1561–1572.

Gollwitzer, P. M. (1999). Implementation intentions: Strong effects of simple plans. *American Psychologist, 54,* 493–503.

Greenberg, M. T., Kusche, C. A., & Riggs, N. (2004). The PATHS curriculum: Theory and research on neurocognitive development and school success. In J. E. Zins, M. R. Bloodworth, & H. J. Walberg (Eds.), *Building academic success on social and emotional learning: What does the research say?* (pp. 170–188). New York, NY: Teachers College Press.

Haan, N., Millsap, R., & Hartka, E. (1986). As time goes by: Change and stability in personality over fifty years. *Psychology and Aging, 1,* 220–232.

Heckman, J. J., Malofeeva, L., Pinto, R. R., & Savelyev, P. (2007). *The effect of the Perry Preschool program on the cognitive and noncognitive skills of its participants.* Unpublished manuscript, University of Chicago, Department of Economics.

Heckman, J. J., & Rubinstein, Y. (2001). The importance of noncognitive skills: Lessons from the GED Testing Program. *American Economic Review, 91,* 145–149.

Helson, R., & Moane, G. (1987). Personality change in women from college to midlife. *Journal of Personality and Social Psychology, 53,* 176–186.

Helson, R., & Wink, P. (1992). Personality change in women from the early 40s to the early 50s. *Psychology and Aging, 7,* 46–55.

Hembree, R. (1990). The nature, effects, and relief of mathematics anxiety. *Journal for Research in Mathematics Education, 21,* 33–46.

Izard, C. E., Fine, S. E., Schultz, D., Mostow, A. J., Ackerman, B. P., & Youngstrom, E. A. (2001). Emotion knowledge as a predictor of social behavior and academic competence in children at risk. *Psychological Science, 12*, 18–23.

Kaestner, R., & Grossman, M. (2008). Effects of weight on children's educational achievement. *Economics of Education Review, 28*(6), 651–661.

Kahneman, D., Krueger, A. B., Schkade, D., Schwarz, N., & Stone, A. A. (2004). A survey method for characterizing daily life experience: The Day Reconstruction Method (DRM). *Science, 306*, 1776–1780.

Kelly, W. E. (2002). Harnessing the river of time: A theoretical framework of time use efficiency with suggestions for counselors. *Journal of Employment Counseling, 39*, 12–21.

Kruger, J., & Evans, M. (2004). If you don't want to be late, enumerate: Unpacking reduces the planning fallacy. *Journal of Experimental Social Psychology, 40*, 586–594.

Kuncel, N., Hezlett, S.A., Ones, D. S., Crede, M., Vannelli, J. R., Thomas, L. L., . . . Jackson, H. L. (2005, April. *A Meta-Analysis of Personality Determinants of College Student Performance.* Presented at the 20th annual meeting of the Society of Industrial-Organizational Psychology, Los Angeles, CA.

Kyllonen, P. C. (2008). *The research behind the ETS Personal Potential Index.* Princeton, NJ: Educational Testing Service. Retrieved from http://www.ets.org/Media/Products/PPI/10411_PPI_bkgrd_report_RD4.pdf5

Kyllonen, P. C., Lipnevich, A. A., Burrus, J., & Roberts, R. D. (2010). *Personality, motivation, and college readiness: A prospectus for assessment and development.* Princeton, NJ: Educational Testing Service.

Kyllonen, P. C., & Roberts, R. D. (2008). Developing noncognitive assessments. *Resource Materials for NCME Invited Workshop.* New York: Crowne Plaza.

Kyllonen, P. C., Walters, A. M., & Kaufman, J. C. (2005). Noncognitive constructs and their assessment in graduate education: A review. *Educational Assessment, 10*, 153-84

Lee, J. (2009). Universals and specifics of math self-concept, math self-efficacy, and math anxiety across 41 PISA 2003 participating countries. *Learning and Individual Differences,* v19 n3 p355-365 Sep 2009.

Lee, J., Goodman, M., Bauer, M., & Redman, M. (2007). *Enhance: Noncognitive assessments for K–12.* Paper prepared for the annual conference of the National Council of Measurement in Education, Chicago, IL.

Lee, K., & Ashton, M. C. (2004). Psychometric properties of the HEXACO Personality Inventory. *Multivariate Behavioral Research, 39*, 329–358.

Lee, S., & Klein, H. J. (2002). Relationships between conscientiousness, self-efficacy, self-deception, and learning over time. *Journal of Applied Psychology, 87*, 1175–1182.

Lengua, L. J., & Long, A. C. (2002). The role of emotionality and self-regulation in the appraisal-coping process: Tests of direct and moderating effects. *Applied Developmental Psychology, 23*, 471–493.

Linnenbrinck, E. A., & Pintrich, P. R. (2003).The role of self-efficacy beliefs in student engagement and learning in the classroom. *Reading and Writing Quarterly, 19*, 119–137.

Lipnevich, A. A., McCann, C., Bertling, J, & Roberts, R. D. (2009). Emotional reactions to school in high school, middle school, and college students: Relationships to academic outcomes. In R. D. Roberts (Chair), Symposium on assessment of affect in educational settings, APA 117th national convention, Toronto, Ontario, Canada, August 6–9, 2009.

Lipnevich, A. A., MacCann, C., Krumm, S., Burrus, J., & Roberts, R. D. (2011). Mathematics attitudes and mathematics outcomes of U.S. and Belarusian middle school students. *Journal of Educational Psychology, 103*(1), 105–118.

Lipsky, S. A., & Ender, S. C. I. (1990). Impact of a study skills course on probationary students' academic performance. *Journal of the Freshman Year Experience, 2*, 7–15.

Liu, O. L., Rijmen, F., MacCann, C., & Roberts, R. D. (2009). Measuring time management abilities for middle school students. *Personality and Individual Differences, 47*, 174–179.

Lobstein, T., Baur, L., & Uauy, R. (2004). Obesity in children and young people: A crisis in public health. *Obesity Reviews, 5S*, 4–85.

Ma, X. (1999). A meta-analysis of the relationship between anxiety toward mathematics and achievement in mathematics. *Journal for Research in Mathematics Education, 30*, 520–540.

MacCann, C. (2009). Obesity in secondary school and beyond: Academic consequences and relationship to health knowledge and attitudes. Presentation at the School of Psychology, University of New South Wales, Sydney, NSW, Australia.

MacCann, C., Duckworth, A. L., & Roberts, R. D. (2009) Empirical identification of the major facets of Conscientiousness. *Learning and Individual Differences, 19*, 451–458.

MacCann, C., Fogarty, G., & Roberts, R. D. (in press). Strategies for success in vocational education: The role of time management. *Learning and Individual Differences*.

MacCann, C., Fogarty, G., Zeidner, M., & Roberts, R. D. (in press). How emotional intelligence and coping affect academic success. *Contemporary Educational Psychology*.

MacCann, C., Minsky, J., Ventura, M., & Roberts, R. D. (in press). Comparing self- and parent-reported personality in predicting academic achievement: Mother knows best. *Personality and Social Psychology Bulletin*.

MacCann, C., & Roberts, R. D. (2008). New paradigms for assessing emotional intelligence: Theory and data. *Emotion*, *8*, 540–551.

MacCann, C., & Roberts, R. D. (2009a). Do time management, grit, and self-control relate to academic achievement independently of conscientiousness? In R. Hicks (Ed.), *Personality and individual differences: Current directions*. Brisbane, Australia: Australian Academic Press.

MacCann, C., & Roberts, R. D. (2009b). *Development of a student health assessment system: Health knowledge, attitudes, and behaviors in middle-schoolers* (ETS Research Report RR-10-04). Princeton, NJ: Educational Testing Service.

MacCann, C., Wang, L., Matthews, G., & Roberts, R. D. (2010). Emotional intelligence and the eye of the beholder: Comparing self- and parent-rated situational judgments in adolescents. *Journal of Research in Personality*,

Marsh, H. W., Hau, K. T., Artelt, C., Baumert, J., & Peschar, J. L. (2006). OECD's brief self-report measure of educational psychology's most useful affective constructs: Cross-cultural, psychometric comparisons across 25 countries. *International Journal of Testing*, *6*, 311–360.

Mayer, J. D., Roberts, R. D., & Barsade, S. G. (2008). Human abilities: Emotional intelligence. *Annual Review of Psychology*, *59*, 507–536.

Mayer, J. D., & Salovey, P. (1997). What is emotional intelligence? In P. Salovey & D. Sluyter (Eds.), *Emotional development and emotional intelligence: Educational implications* (pp. 3–31). New York, NY: Basic Books.

Mayer, J. D., Salovey, P., Caruso, D. R., & Sitarenios, G. (2003). Measuring emotional intelligence with the MSCEIT V2.0. *Emotion*, *3*, 97–105

McCay, J. T. (1959). *The management of time*. New York, NY: Simon & Schuster.

McCrae, R. R., & Costa, P. T., Jr. (1994). The stability of personality: Observation and evaluations. *Current Directions in Psychological Science, 3*, 173–175.

McCrae, R. R., & Costa, P. T., Jr. (1999). A five-factor theory of personality. In L. A. Pervin & O. P. John (Eds.), *Handbook of personality theory and research* (Vol. 2, pp. 139–153). New York, NY: Guilford Press.

Noftle, E. E., & Robins, R. W. (2007). Personality predictors of academic outcomes: Big Five correlates of GPA and SAT scores. *Journal of Personality and Social Psychology, 93*, 116–130.

O'Connor, M., & Paunonen, S. V. (2007). Big Five personality predictors of post-secondary academic performance. *Personality and Individual Differences, 43*, 971–990.

Ogden, C. L., Carroll, M. D., Curtin, L. R., McDowell, M. A., Tabak, C. J., & Flegal, K. M. (2006). Prevalence of overweight and obesity in the United States, 1999–2004. *Journal of the American Medical Association, 295*, 1549–1555.

Ogden, C. L., Flegal, K. M., Carroll, M. D., & Johnson, C. L. (2002). Prevalence and trends in overweight among US children and adolescents, 1999–2000. *JAMA, 288*, 1728–1732.

Parsons, T. J., Power, C., Logan, S., & Summerbell, C. D. (1999). Childhood predictors of adult obesity: A systematic review. *International Journal of Obesity and Related Metabolic Disorders, 23S*, 1–107.

Patti, J., & Lantieri, L. (1999). Waging peace in our schools: Social and emotional learning through conflict resolution. In J. Cohen (Ed.), *Educating minds and hearts: Social emotional learning and the passage into adolescence* (pp. 126–136). New York, NY: Columbia University Press.

Pavlov, I. P. (1927). *Conditioned reflexes.* London, England: Oxford University Press.

Payton, J., Weissberg, R.P., Durlak, J.A., Dymnicki, A.B., Taylor, R.D., Schellinger, K.B., & Pachan, M. (2008). *The positive impact of social and emotional learning for kindergarten to eighth-grade students: Findings from three scientific reviews.* Chicago, IL: Collaborative for Academic, Social, and Emotional Learning.

Plant, E. A., Ericsson, K. A., Hill, L., & Asberg, K. (2005). Why study time does not predict grade point average across college students: Implications of deliberate practice for academic performance. *Contemporary Educational Psychology, 30*, 96–116.

Poropat, A. E. (2009). A meta-analysis of the five-factor model of personality and academic performance. *Psychological Bulletin*, *135*, 322–338.

Pyle, S. A., Sharkey, J., Yetter, G., Felix, E., Furlong, M. J., & Poston, W. S. C. (2006). Fighting an epidemic: The role of schools in reducing childhood obesity. *Psychology in the Schools*, *43*, 361–376.

Rampey, B. D., Dion, G. S., & Donahue, P. L. (2009). *NAEP 2008 Trends in Academic Progress* (NCES 2009–479). Washington, DC: National Center for Education Statistics, Institute of Education Sciences, U.S. Department of Education.

Rhodes, S. K., Shimoda, K. L., Weid, L. R., Mahlen, P., Oexmann, M. J., Collop, N. A., & Will, S. M. (1995). Neurocognitive deficits in morbidly obese children with obstructive sleep apnea. *Journal of Pediatrics*, *127*, 741–744.

Robbins, S. B., Lauver, K., Le, H., Davis, D., Langley, R., & Carlstrom, A. (2004). Do psychosocial and study skills factors predict college outcomes? A meta-analysis. *Psychological Bulletin*, *130*, 261–288.

Roberts, B. W., Caspi, A., & Moffitt, T. (2001). The kids are alright: Growth and stability in personality development from adolescence to adulthood. *Journal of Personality and Social Psychology*, *81*, 670–683.

Roberts, B. W., Walton, K., & Viechtbauer, W. (2006). Patterns of mean-level change in personality traits across the life course: A meta-analysis of longitudinal studies. *Psychological Bulletin*, *132*, 1–25.

Roberts, R. D., Krause, H., & Suk-Lee, L. (2001). Australian time organization and management scales. Unpublished Inventory: University of Sydney.

Roberts, R. D., Schulze, R., & MacCann, C. (2007, April). *Student 360^{TM}: A valid medium for noncognitive assessment?* Paper presented at the 2007 National Council on Measurement in Education, Chicago, IL.

Roberts, R. D., Schulze, R., & MacCann, C. (2008). The measurement of emotional intelligence: A decade of progress? In G. Boyle, G. Matthews, & D. Saklofske (Eds.), *The SAGE handbook of personality theory and assessment* (pp. 461–482). Thousand Oaks, CA: Sage.

Roberts, R. D., Schulze, R., & Minsky, J. (2006, April). *The relation of time management dimensions to scholastic outcomes.* Paper presented at 2006 annual meeting of the American Educational Research Association, San Francisco, CA.

Roberts, R. D., Stankov, L., Schulze, R., & Kyllonen, P. C. (2007). Extending intelligence: Conclusions and future directions. In P. C. Kyllonen, R. D. Roberts, & L. Stankov (Eds.), *Extending intelligence:*

Enhancement and new constructs. (pp. 433–452). New York, NY: Erlbaum.

Robins, R. W., Fraley, R. C., Roberts, B. W., & Trzesniewski, K. (2001). A longitudinal study of personality change in young adulthood. *Journal of Personality, 69,* 617–640.

Rudolph, K. D., Dennig, M. D., & Weisz, J. R. (1995). Determinants and consequences of children's coping in the medical setting: Conceptualization, review, and critique. *Psychological Bulletin, 118,* 328–357.

Sabia, J. (2007). The effect of body weight on adolescent academic performance. *Southern Economic Journal, 73,* 871–900.

Schmidt, F. L., & Hunter, J. E. (1998). The validity and utility of selection methods in personnel psychology. *Psychological Bulletin, 124,* 262–274.

Schunk, D. H. (1990). Goal setting and self-efficacy during self-regulated learning. *Educational Psychologist, 25,* 71–86.

Schunk, D. H. (1995). Self-efficacy and education and instruction. In J. E. Maddux (Ed.), *Self-efficacy, adaptation, and adjustment: Theory, research, and application* (pp. 281–303). New York, NY: Plenum Press.

Schutte, N. S., Malouff, J. M., Hall, L. E., Haggerty, D. J., Cooper, J. T., Golden, C. J., & Dornheim, L. (1998). Development and validation of a measure of emotional intelligence. *Personality and Individual Differences, 25,* 167–177.

Sedlacek, W. E. (1996). An empirical method of determining nontraditional group status. *Measurement and Evaluation in Counseling and Development, 28,* 200–210.

Sedlacek, W. E. (in press). Noncognitive measures for higher education admissions. In B. McGaw, E. Baker, & P. L. Peterson (Eds.), *International Encyclopedia of Education, Third Edition.* Amsterdam, the Netherlands: Elsevier.

Seligman, M. E. P. (2002). *Authentic happiness: Using the new positive psychology to realize your potential for lasting fulfillment.* New York, NY: Simon & Schuster.

Sheeran, P. (2002). Intention-behavior relations: A conceptual and empirical review. *European Review of Social Psychology, 12,* 1–36.

Sigfúsdúttir, I. D., Kristjánsson, A. L., & Allegrante, J. P. (2007). Health behaviour and academic achievement in Icelandic school children. *Health Education Research, 22,* 70–80.

Skinner, B. F. (1953). *Science and human behavior.* New York, NY: Macmillan.

Smith, R. J., Arnkoff, D. B., & Wright, T. L. (1990). Test anxiety and academic competence: A comparison of alternative models. *Journal of Counseling Psychology, 37*, 313–321.

Taras H, & Potts-Datema W. (2005). Obesity and student performance at school. *Journal of School Health, 75,* 291–295.

Tate, B., & McDaniel, M. A. (2008, August). *Race differences in personality: An evaluation of moderators and publication bias.* Paper presented at the 2008 Academy of Management Annual Meeting, Anaheim, CA.

Tinsley, B. J. (1992). Multiple influences on the acquisition and socialization of children's health attitudes and behavior: An integrated review. *Child Development, 63*, 1043–1069.

Trapmann, S., Hell, B., Hirn, J.W., & Schuler, H. (2007). Meta-analysis of the relationship between the big five and academic success at university, *Journal of Psychology, 215*, 132–151.

Wang, L., MacCann, C., Zhuang, X., Liu, O. L., & Roberts, R. D. (2009). Assessing teamwork skills: A multi-method approach. *Canadian Journal of School Psychology, 24*, 108–124.

Watson, D., & Hubbard, B. (1996). Adaptational style and dispositional structure: Coping in the context of the five-factor model. *Journal of Personality, 64*, 737–774.

Zeidner, M. (1998). *Test anxiety: The state of the art.* New York, NY: Plenum.

Zeidner, M., Matthews, G., & Roberts, R. D. (2009). *What we know about emotional intelligence: How it affects learning, work, relationships, and mental health.* Cambridge, MA: MIT Press.

Ziegler, M., MacCann, C., & Roberts, R. D. (Eds.). (2010). *New perspectives on faking in personality assessment.* New York, NY: Oxford University Press.

Zins, J. E., Bloodworth, M. R., Weissberg, R. P., & Walberg, H. (2004). The scientific base linking social and emotional learning to school success. In J. Zins, R. P. Weissberg, M. Wang, & H. J. Walberg, (Eds.), *Building academic success on social and emotional learning: What the research says* (pp. 3–22). New York, NY: Teachers College Press.

Zins, J. E., Payton, J. W., Weissberg, R. P., & O'Brien, M. U. (2007). Social and emotional learning for successful school performance. In G. Matthews, M. Zeidner, & R. D. Roberts (Eds.), *Emotional intelligence: Knows and unknowns.* New York, NY: Oxford University Press.

CHAPTER 12

A DEMOCRATIC MERIT AGENDA: AN ALTERNATIVE APPROACH

john a. powell and Becky Reno[1]

If we are to move higher education into the 21st century, we must recognize the increasing national pluralism and globalization. The approach used in higher education aimed at achieving diversity needs to be radically altered. Universities and colleges need to ensure they are educating a student body that hails from diverse and unevenly situated communities. This has a number of implications on the individual level, as other authors in this volume illustrate, but it also calls into question larger institutional practices as well as the needs of communities. By and large, the competitive, individualist, meritocratic approach our nation's colleges and universities subscribe to is rooted in tradition and remains largely unexamined. This construction of the individual is not only in conflict with our democratic aspirations; it also neglects the reality that individuals exist within a larger society composed of structures that may either advance or inhibit life opportunities. Instead of an isolated perspective where individual advancement occurs in spite of the community, we wish to explore the perspective of Ruth Benedict who advanced the notion of "high synergy" societies in which individual good is linked to the advancement of the community (Maslow & Honigmann, 1970).

Our current meritocratic approach to higher education is not only limited, it is historically incorrect. Democratic principles constitute the very foundation of our public higher education system, and the Supreme Court has upheld the social responsibility colleges and universities have to the greater public good. In 1979, for example, the Supreme Court in *Ambach v. Norwick* (1979) identified an objective of public education to be "the inculcation of fundamental values necessary for the maintenance of a democratic political system." Moreover, in 2002 the Supreme Court in *Grutter* acknowledged the importance of higher education in preparing students for citizenship. The legitimacy and sustainability of our nation depends on reestablishing and reinforcing this link between education and our democratic principles.

There are a number of ways we can realign the public mission of higher education through admissions practices, some of which are already in place

---

[1] Special thanks to Cheryl Staats for all her hard work and diligent research.

275

across the country. We examine a number of these practices, advocating for a broader institutional transformation that reconnects admission practices to schools' missions, a reshaping of the meaning of identity to recognize our inherent connection to community, and the development of a collective national movement into a more democratic space.

The Alignment of Schools and Our Values

An appropriate analysis of the state of the current U.S. educational system, from preK to college, requires reflection, a willingness to address challenging questions regarding the forces driving this system, and an acknowledgment of the resulting outcomes of our current educational practices. Any efforts to reform education should begin with the question: What educational outcomes are schools trying to achieve? Given the current emphasis on standardized testing as well as controversies surrounding whether teachers do/should "teach to the test," it would seem our priorities have shifted from fostering inquisitive minds and equipping students with critical thinking skills to rote memorization and regurgitation of factoids. This ongoing, national shift provokes a crucial question: For what are we preparing students?

- Are we simply preparing them to pass a test?

- Are we preparing them to graduate from high school?

- Are they being equipped with the skills necessary to enter the workforce?

- Are they receiving the preparations necessary to gain admission, enroll in, and ultimately graduate from college?

- And, is a lifelong love of learning being fostered in them?

Some schools may be able to answer these questions affirmatively; however, most cannot claim to be truly preparing students to participate in our democratic society. As previously noted, many of the most important court cases dealing with education have affirmed the significant relationship between education and the health of our democracy. Accordingly, we should not just prepare students to be workers, but also to be citizens. Thus, our reflections on education should also embrace these themes:

- Are schools equipping students with the knowledge and sensitivity to operate in a multiracial and multicultural society?

- Are schools providing the foundation for students to be culturally fluent in our increasingly global society?

It is questions such as these—difficult questions by any measure—that are worthy of reflection and discussion and should be at the center of any education reform.

Many of the discussions around education reform focus on a narrowly constructed conception of equity. We are mired in the details of teacher quality, school funding, curriculum at the K–12 level, and numerical representation in higher education. Certainly these issues are critical and deserve attention and remediation, but without a macro-analysis and broader dialogue on the purpose and function of education, these approaches will ultimately amount to merely tinkering within the system. Instead, we call for an approach that places a deliberate emphasis on creating an inclusive, effective system of education that aligns our educational policies and practices with overarching democratic missions. At the center of this approach is an examination of the subtle, underlying texts which run throughout our educational practices, the notion of merit and how it is defined and operationalized. Amartya Sen (1999) defines merit as an incentive system to reward those actions valued by a society. This approach illuminates the connection between institutional values and behaviors. Following this logic, prior to defining merit, it is necessary to recognize what ideals we adhere to and what we are seeking to accomplish for the greater good. Accordingly, merit is not an acontextual "good" that belongs to an individual; instead, it is a way for us to collectively express the values we, as a society, adhere to. This conceptualization calls us to collectively posit two critical questions:

- What constitutes merit in our system of education?

- Are our educational practices aligned with what we claim to value?

An overview of the academic subjects emphasized in most school systems is a concrete means of examining what values we seek to uphold. Standardized tests, grade point averages, and other forms of testing often focus on measuring skills such as reading, science, and math. Conversely, a similar emphasis is typically not placed on social studies, civic education, and other topics related to understanding and perpetuating democratic principles. If we claim to value diversity and democracy, then why are civics courses rarely taught and state and national standards of these subjects less rigorously assessed? When political participation and community engagement are denied the same focus as other academic disciplines, this makes a statement about where our values lie. Accordingly, regardless of how goals of education are conceptualized, our assessments generally fail to capture notions of "good citizenship" or "giving back to the community."

Of course, a variety of conceptualizations of citizenship exist. One view is that democracy is the practice of aggregating the private preferences of isolated egotistical individuals. This is not the form of democracy being advanced in this chapter. Instead, we refer to a model of democracy that is both constitutive and deliberative. Democracy as a political community confers membership, extending rights and privileges unavailable to those who are not members. However, members and nonmembers alike do not exist in isolation; instead, their identity is in part constituted by their inclusion or exclusion. In a democracy, membership is in part predicated on education. Our historical legacy of differentiated access to opportunity (including education) based upon race puts minorities at a disadvantage in a society in which individualism and personal success appear to be more highly valued than the common good. This national adoption of the promotion of self-interest has infiltrated and shaped all of our institutions, failing to recognize the shared fate between the collective and the nation itself. For the legitimacy of our democracy and the strength and cohesiveness of our nation moving forward, higher education needs to redefine merit in a way that reconnects the individual with the community, creating a more inclusive arrangement by broadening membership to those who have historically been excluded (powell & Menenedian, 2008).

Beyond a discussion of democracy, identity, merit, and societal values, it is necessary to address how we perceive higher education. The academy is often viewed as a scarce resource into which only those who are deemed particularly deserving are admitted. The degree of an institution's selectivity is often related to its perceived prestige. For example, Harvard, Yale, Stanford, and MIT are highly renowned universities with exceptionally low admission rates, including historic or near-record low rates of 7%, 7.5%, 7.6%, and

10.2%, respectively, for the class of 2013.[2] With such selectivity, the quality of the applicants is clearly emphasized. This focus on applicants and their achievements may even be construed as more valued than are the graduates of these institutions. The value placed on the potential an applicant has for having a positive impact on society in the long term may be undermined by standardized test results, admissions essays, and other measures of an applicant's "worthiness" to attend a given academic institution; this focus on inputs rather than on potential outputs in selection criteria is troublesome and shortsighted.

Institutions of higher education increasingly operate as businesses as they face constant pressure to fare well in national and global rankings (Bok, 2003). In order to attract research dollars and to ultimately remain sustainable, colleges and universities must be able to continually attract "high-quality" students.[3] Although most schools, if not all, have *some* comprehensive evaluation of applicants, the reality is standardized scores, including the SAT and GPA, are typically given far more weight than any other criteria in a student's application package. SAT scores are assumed to be predictive of a student's college performance, with the belief that the higher the score, the greater the odds of success. In reality, there is likely a threshold score above which any student could thrive. Success in college and beyond is not only dependent on a student's ability to succeed on a standardized exam; it is also dependent on a number of additional factors such as motivation, learning strategies, personal and professional networks, and institutional support. Furthermore, success is all too often narrowly defined through such measures as students' grades, completion rates, and earnings later in life. While important to the individual, attention must be paid to identifying characteristics of students who are more likely to give back to their university, community, and society, in order to reconnect the schools to their democratic foundations. This more robust type of assessment would redefine what constitutes a "high-quality" student and has ramifications for admission. Exploring alternative admissions criteria would move higher education institutions closer to the fulfillment of their democratic missions.

---

[2] All data are from spring 2008 freshman admissions (class of 2013) (Dey, 2009; *Harvard University Gazette Online,* 2009; Shtrakhman, 2009; Sridharan, 2009).
[3] Of course, the definition of 'quality' is continually evolving and rising with each new class of students.

Questioning Individualistic Conceptualizations of Merit in Higher Education

Our current system of higher education typically embraces a concept of merit that focuses on individuals as isolated from their communities and history. In this model, merit is considered a static attribute that a person inherently possesses, independent of family background, class, race, neighborhood, or the opportunity structures that may (or may not) be present. This regard for merit as a possession ignores the possibility of merit being manifested in different forms and obscures the reality: Merit is currently ascribed through our inequitable, racialized social institutions, including (but certainly not limited to) K–12 education.

This individualistic outlook on merit regards achievements and accolades as the product of individual effort and the result of biological determinism. From this perspective, successes are borne out of the actions and abilities of individuals without regard to any circumstances that may have smoothed their pathway to success. To illustrate, a student who scores higher than another student on a standardized test such as the ACT or the SAT may be deemed more meritorious even if the former enjoyed considerable advantages such as a high-quality high school, test preparation classes, and extensive tutoring.[4]

One significant concern related to individualized measures of merit based on standardized tests is confusion and contention regarding their precise purpose. Some argue these tests are intended to measure mastery of materials taught in academic coursework, particularly the curricula covered in late middle school and high school. In contrast, others view standardized tests as aptitude tests, meaning their intent is to assess reasoning abilities or even innate intelligence. Regardless of the perceived objective, the underlying reality is that standardized tests often remain heavily weighted in admissions decisions and are strongly influenced by class and race. Given that higher education is a scarce resource, admissions officers are typically overwhelmed by the number of applicants, with fewer available slots than qualified students to fill them. Admissions officers often rely heavily on that which is quantifiable and can be held steady in the comparison of students. Over time, this has reified the validity of the test and has distorted the original purpose of the SAT, which, ironically, was to identify students from

---

[4] Notably, research indicates that test preparation activities tend to yield an increase of 20 to 30 points on the SAT (National Association for College Admission Counseling, 2008; see also Tully, 2008).

lower quality secondary schools who would otherwise not be considered college material.

Standardized tests are flawed. Despite a stated commitment to fairness, biases and other imbalances still exist. Notable score differences have been documented between different gender, ethnic, and socioeconomic groups (Zwick, 2010). Furthermore, standardized tests have drawn criticism for their ability (or inability) to accurately predict future academic performance. A 2004 College Board research report by Bridgeman, Pollack, and Burton analyzed a sample of 41 colleges to explore "how many students at different levels of SAT score reach different criteria of success in college, after controlling on the selectivity of the college, the academic intensity of the students' high school curriculum, and the students' high school grades" (p. 1). Using a definition of success as a 2.5 or 3.5 college GPA, researchers concluded there were considerable differences in the percentage of students who succeeded at the conclusion of 1 year or 4 years in college by SAT-score level, even when accounting for the intensity of high school curriculum and high school grades (Zwick & Sklar, 2005). Conversely, other studies have contested the effectiveness of standardized tests as predictors, noting that high school GPA is a stronger predictor than is SAT score.

One of the concerns associated with overreliance on standardized tests and other "objective" measures of merit is the quantitative nature of these assessments. If the goal, first and foremost, is to create an inclusive democratic environment and experience, consideration must be given to the background and attributes of students who constitute the very fabric of the institution. Quantitative measures properly conceived have their strengths, but they should not be stressed at the expense of the qualitative attributes an applicant may bring to the college or university. Qualities such as leadership skills, conflict-resolution abilities, a community-centered orientation, and fine arts talents will not register on standardized tests, yet may make vital contributions both within and beyond the boundaries of the campus. It may be argued that some of these attributes would become apparent in other portions of a prospective student's application, such as his or her teacher recommendations, application essay, or portfolio submission. However, research indicates that SAT scores are given excessive weight in admissions decisions in order to bolster schools' rankings (Alon & Tienda, 2007; Horn, & Yun, 2008).

The emphasis on the isolated individual within conceptualizations of merit is also troubling (powell, 2005). Within an individual-based analysis, the systemic contributors or impediments to success are obscured. This reifies the logic behind the pervasive American "bootstraps" mentality, reinforcing the myth of the "American dream." It legitimizes claims that success is solely the product of hard work and that failure results from personal inadequacies without a consideration of context. With the historic election of Barack Obama as this nation's first Black president, this narrative is becoming both more pervasive and accepted. Former secretary of education Bill Bennett spoke for many when he declared, "I'll tell you one thing [Obama's win] means . . . you don't take any excuses anymore from anybody who says, 'The deck is stacked. I can't do anything. There's so much in-built this and that'" (Grant-Thomas, 2009).

This widespread belief that hard work is the dominate ingredient in success is problematic across multiple dimensions. It fails to recognize that in reality all of us live, work, and otherwise exist within a system and network of social institutions and structures that confer or deny opportunity (Gladwell, 2008). Despite what may be an apparent neutrality, these institutions operate along race and class-based lines, barring or severely limiting many people of color and other marginalized populations from the types of opportunities and experiences necessary to be productive, thriving members of society.[5] This is something we are all keenly aware of despite the notable absence of the public discourse surrounding this topic. We can all differentiate the high opportunity and low opportunity neighborhoods in urban areas. Typically, an examination of student demographics alone can illuminate which schools are more likely to be high performing, with a large proportion of their student body attending college, and which schools will have high dropout rates, a declining physical infrastructure, and pervasive disciplinary issues. Geography should not define opportunity, and the reality that it does is perhaps the most compelling evidence against the erroneous belief in the myth of meritocracy.

Nontraditional Measures of Merit

In spite of the typically stringent focus on individual merit within college and university admissions, some nontraditional measures of merit are gaining traction. For example, some admissions processes pay particular attention to "strivers," students who do better than anticipated while overcoming challenges, such as attending a disadvantaged secondary school. Strivers consistently exceed normative expectations based on their demographics. They are often identified by their performance on standardized test scores. In essence, there is an approximate score that each

---

[5] For more information on this topic, please see the Kirwan Institute's work on Opportunity Communities at http://www.kirwaninstitute.org/research/opportunity-communitieshousing/index.php.

student is reasonably expected to attain given his or her socioeconomic status and the quality of his or her high school. These anticipated scores are based on the performance of peers at their school or in similar schools. Strivers are those who exceed expectations; consequently, strivers are students who may perform better in college than might be anticipated based on their academic record. Being a striver should be considered a positive factor in the college and university admissions process, as these students have demonstrated their ability to overcome challenging circumstances and would likely carry this determination with them into subsequent academic pursuits.

Another nontraditional measure of merit involves assessing an applicant's "diversity capital." This refers to the student's unique interests, life experiences, and/or family background that would enrich the academic atmosphere. Diversity capital places value on such things as attending a diverse school and rewarding parents who send students to diverse schools, sometimes by providing incentives. Information regarding whether a student possesses diversity capital can be deduced through a variety of means. Basic documents such as résumés, lists of activities/extracurriculars, and personal statements may provide insights into the diversity of experiences that students possess. Other possible areas of inquiry include languages spoken or important life experiences (Bingham, McCutcheon, Morrison & Foerster, and Heller Ehrman White & McAuliffe, 2004). Admitting students who possess diversity capital allows the student body to be exposed to a broad range of perspectives and experiences, thus contributing to a dynamic learning environment both within and beyond the classroom.

The creation of an "institution-specific, non-standardized assessment tool that measures academic preparation and potential, cultural competence, and other competencies that are essential to success in college and meaningful participation in democracy"[6] is another possibility. These tests would be designed to be free of cultural and gender bias. Rather than relying on narrow, one-dimensional definitions of "quality" or potential, they would inclusively and comprehensively assess the potential of a student. This assessment could begin with schools elucidating their vision for the type of institution they would like to become. They could then identify characteristics of students who would best fulfill this vision and develop assessments and measurements that assign value to those factors. This type of nontraditional, comprehensive assessment ensures that schools are deliberately and mindfully constructing their student body and, in doing so, their entire institution.

---

[6] Interim Progress Report for The Democratic Merit Project, the Kirwan Institute.

Democratic Merit

While these non-traditional measures of merit are superior to solely individualistic approaches, they remain distinct from democratic merit. With a transformative agenda in mind, democratic merit would transition higher education admissions away from a system that rewards past achievements to an investment-based system that endows the democratic potential applicants bring to the broader society.

While the idea of considering what students may accomplish for society in the long term may seem somewhat unusual, it is far from radical. In fact, democratic merit principles are well situated within our broader educational tradition. The land-grant movement, GI Bill, and the perspectives of Thomas Jefferson and American philosopher John Dewey all lay the foundation for a robust discussion of democratic merit within American education.

One of the premises underlying democratic merit is the idea that higher education institutions have not only a relationship with but also an obligation to the larger community. Dating back to when land-grant institutions were founded following the Justin Smith Morrill Acts of 1862 and 1890, many colleges and universities receive both public money and public land. Land-grant institutions were founded with the goal of providing education in the areas of "agriculture, home economics, mechanical arts, and other practical professions" (U.S. Department of Agriculture, 2000). In 1887, 25 years after the passage of the Act, Senator Morrill reinforced the aim of his Act when speaking at the Massachusetts Agricultural College. He declared,

> *The land-grant colleges were founded on the idea that a higher and broader education should be placed in every State within the reach of those whose destiny assigns them to, or who may have the courage to choose industrial locations where the wealth of nations is produced; where advanced civilization unfolds its comforts, and where a much larger number of the people need wider educational advantages, and impatiently await their possession . . .*
> ("About the Land-Grant System," n.d., "The Purpose,"
> para. 2)

Senator Morrill reiterated his aim when addressing the Vermont legislature in 1888:

The fundamental idea was to offer an opportunity in every State for a liberal and larger education to larger numbers, not merely to those destined to sedentary professions, but to those much needing higher instruction for the world's business, for the industrial pursuits and professions of life. . . . ("About the Land-Grant System," n.d., "The Purpose," para. 6)

This close relationship between educational institutions and the larger community founded in the Morrill Acts reinforces schools' responsibility to promote civic engagement and public service.

Similarly, the Servicemen's Readjustment Act of 1944, more commonly known as the GI Bill, united education and democratic principles. Signed by President Franklin Delano Roosevelt on June 22, 1944, the GI Bill opened the door for millions of World War II veterans to enter college and achieve homeownership, two objectives that would otherwise have been unattainable for many veterans. At its peak in 1947, veterans comprised 49% of college admissions (U.S. Department of Veterans Affairs, n.d.). The opportunities provided in the GI Bill were seized by millions. From 1944 to 1952, the Veterans Administration backed approximately 2.4 million home loans for WWII veterans while putting 7.8 million veterans in education or training programs by July 1952 when the original bill expired. The GI Bill was updated in 1984 (the Montgomery GI Bill). It was also updated in 2008 for those in active duty following September 11, 2001. The premise of the GI Bill in its various manifestations clearly connects educational opportunities with democratic principles, as it brings those who have served our nation as soldiers into full participation on a civilian level.

Two great American thinkers also influenced the American educational system. Philosopher John Dewey (1859–1952) believed that "school should rather be viewed as an extension of civil society and continuous with it, and the student encouraged to operate as a member of a community, actively pursuing interests in cooperation with others" (Field, 2007, "Ethical and Social Theory," para. 7). In his view, education should guide children towards becoming responsible members of the democratic community in which they live. Similarly, Thomas Jefferson stressed the importance of education and saw it as a key to the democratic future of a then-young nation (National Park Service, 1992). Jefferson viewed enlightenment as the key to the existence of a democracy, noting that, "If a nation expects to be ignorant and free, in a state of civilization, it expects what never was and never will be" (Jewitt, 1996).

Building off these sentiments, many universities already have mission statements that claim to embrace democratic ideals. The University of Texas–Austin declares that its "core purpose" is "to transform lives for the benefit of society" (http://www.utexas.edu/about-ut/mission-core-purpose-honor-code/). Similarly, the University of California, Berkeley freshman selection process seeks students who are able "to contribute meaningfully and uniquely to intellectual and social interchanges with faculty and fellow students, both inside and outside the classroom; and to make a special contribution to our society and culture" (UC Berkeley Office of Undergraduate Admissions, n.d., "Evaluation," para. 11). Given that some schools' missions and vision statements already allude to this orientation, the implementation of democratic merit principles should not seem altogether radical or unforeseen. Admissions officers should consider how applicants might contribute to the larger society after graduation.

In addition to the relationship and obligation that higher education institutions have to society, these entities also share a similar obligation to the larger democracy, as noted by Jefferson and Dewey. One of education's primary objectives is preparing people to be citizens in an increasingly diverse country. The U.S. Census Bureau (2008) projects the nation will be "majority minority" by 2050, and that more than half of all children will be minorities by 2023. We need to prepare students to be citizens and productive members of a society that will be radically diverse in a very short period.

Another benefit of taking this broader perspective on merit is that it provides an opportunity for students who may not have excelled under traditional academic measures the opportunity to capitalize on their strengths. Democratic merit stimulates critical discussions on how merit is conceptualized and the implications of that definition. As emphasized by Steven T. Syverson, Vice President for Enrollment and Dean of Admissions and Financial Aid at Lawrence University in Appleton, Wisconsin, "Success isn't a grade-point average. I've got lots of students who get C's but who have a fabulous college experience. They develop social skills and leadership skills. Being a good citizen is a successful outcome" (Hoover, 2008).

Democratic merit maintains a group-level focus; it functions as a mechanism to improve the greater society. Marginalized groups do not benefit from only uplifting individuals; instead, we need to seek interventions that strengthen the group collectively. The focus within democratic merit is on uplifting those who are likely to positively affect society, thus improving the circumstances of the collective through the contributions an individual is likely to make in the future.

In short, a democratic perspective seeks to link people. Education should help communities rather than simply serving as a pathway out of them. Under an individual approach, education, especially for people of color, is seen as an escape from communities that are underresourced and struggling. Education is, in essence, a ticket out. While this can be seen as positive for the individual receiving this opportunity, we should also consider what that does to the community. If we take the best and brightest and remove them from the community, the community as a whole, which desperately needs their knowledge and skills, is not improved. A democratic merit perspective transitions from an individual-based mindset and instead considers what would benefit the broader community.

Current Initiatives

Several programs currently exist that embrace democratic merit ideals. These initiatives include both pipeline programs that link K–12 education with higher education and university–community partnerships.

Texas Ten Percent Program

One of the more recognizable of these initiatives is the Texas Ten Percent Program (TTP). The Texas Ten Percent Law (House Bill 588) was passed in 1997 as a reaction to the 1996 *Hopwood v. Texas* decision in which the use of race was prohibited in college admissions and financial aid decisions (Kain, O'Brien, & Jargowsky, 2005). The Top Ten Percent plan guarantees admission to any Texas public college or university to students in the top 10% of each high school's graduating class. Because students are drawn from all types of communities in the state, these students bring diversity of race, class, and geography to the academic environment. Prior to the realization of the Texas Ten Percent plan, approximately 10% of the state's high schools (mostly White, suburban high schools) provided anywhere from 50% to 75% of the incoming freshman class at UT-Austin (Guinier, 2003); now, many high schools send students to the state's flagships.

Some feared that students admitted under the TTP rather than traditional admissions policies would not do as well in college; instead, these students often outperform those students admitted primarily on the basis of traditional admissions procedures. As Harvard Law School Professor Lani Guinier (2003) notes, "TTP students have actually earned higher freshman-year grades than students with higher SAT scores who were admitted under a more discretionary set of criteria" (p. 166). In short, it was not that TTP students were in need of remedial assistance; what they were really lacking was the information and resources necessary to pursue an education and achieve success.

The Texas Ten Percent Plan has been increasingly scrutinized recently due to the proportion of University of Texas students admitted under the plan. Of the first-year students enrolling at the University of Texas-Austin in the 2008–2009 academic year, 81% were admitted under the TTP; projections forecast this percentage will reach 86% in 2009–2010 (Haurwitz, 2009). Critics claim that the saturation of TTP enrollees would ultimately lead to admissions limitations in the future, including the rejection of all Texas high school graduates who are not in the top 10% of their high school class by 2013, and the elimination of admissions for students from other states or countries by 2015. As of this writing, legislation seeking to limit the number of TTP students to 75% of UT-Austin's admissions has passed in both the Texas House and Senate, with Texas Governor Rick Perry expected to sign this measure (Mangan, 2009).

The Texas Ten Percent plan is not without its critics. Some believe students who graduate from competitive high schools are at a disadvantage because it can be challenging even for especially bright students to rank in the top decile of their class in high-quality high schools (Schmidt, 2008). Conversely, many have praised the TTP for its larger achievements, such as its ability to reconnect K–12 with higher education. The TTP has also been commended for reconnecting higher education to its public mission because of the transparency in the admissions process (Guinier, 2003). Guinier (2003) reflected on how the Texas Ten Percent Plan links education with the production of democratically minded and civically engaged citizens:

> *Although it was enacted in response to a court decision, the TTP was animated by the belief that distributing access to educational opportunity broadly is consistent with the educational mission of higher education, necessary to economic viability in the global economy, important for training a representative group of citizens who will contribute to the public good, central to reconnecting the university to the K-12 educational system, and indicative of greater legitimacy within higher education.*

Indiana 21st Century Scholars Program

The Indiana 21st Century Scholars program is a statewide initiative that began in 1990. The program, funded by the state of Indiana and a federal GEAR UP grant, seeks to raise the educational goals of students from low- and moderate-income families by ensuring them a college education will be affordable. As seventh or eighth graders, students have the opportunity to sign a pledge indicating their resolve for good citizenship, specifically to graduate from high school with at least a cumulative 2.0 GPA on a 4.0 scale; not use illegal drugs, alcohol, or commit a crime; apply for admission to an Indiana college on time; and meet state and federal deadlines for financial aid. "Upon completion of the Scholar's Pledge, the cost of four years of college tuition is provided at any participating public college or university in Indiana. If the student attends a private institution, the state will award an amount comparable to that of a public institution" (http://www.indstate.edu/sasc/programs/century_scholars/). Once a student is enrolled in the program, subsequent changes to the family income do not affect the student's eligibility (21st Century Scholar Program, n.d.). The 21st Century Scholars must enroll as full-time students in their higher educational institution of choice. The scholarship can be applied to eight semesters toward an undergraduate degree, and students have up to 2 years following high school graduation to begin using their scholarship. This program exhibits the principles of democratic merit, as it awards students, in part, for being good citizens.

Clark University—Geographic Merit

Geographic merit at Clark University in Worchester, Massachusetts, is another innovative model that seeks to more closely align university practices with their specific democratic responsibility. At Clark, administrators deliberately focused on investing in the declining infrastructure of the diverse and poor community in which the school is located instead of relocating to a higher opportunity area. Clark worked to revitalize and uplift the surrounding community and its members by partnering with the community to build a small public school for Grades 7 through 12 that opened in 1997. The University Park Campus School (UPCS) admitted local students, many of whom had fallen considerably below grade-level expectations, based on a geographic lottery. The students flourished in their new environment with the support of the university. When the first class graduated in 2003, graduates went on to attend prestigious universities such as Brown, Georgetown, and Holy Cross. "For the last five years, UPCS has ranked first among urban schools serving low-income students on state-mandated English and math graduation exams and in the top quartile of all high schools in the state . . . Over 95% of graduates from its first four graduating classes have gone on to college," nearly all of whom are first-generation college students (Clark University, n.d., para. 2). Clark was successful in looking beyond the future of the university to have an impact on the surrounding neighborhood, thus transforming both the lives of individual students and the entire area. By measuring the school's value in terms of what it enables its graduates to do not just by whom its applicants are, the University Park Campus School reinforces the relationship between democratic merit and democratic mission.

The Posse Program

Democratic merit is not only about broadening admissions criteria but also transforming the institution itself to ensure it is functionally diverse. This has implications for practices throughout the university including retention and support strategies. The Posse Foundation accomplishes this through a comprehensive program that supports the student through his or her tenure. The Foundation gathers diverse public high school students from disadvantaged backgrounds who might be overlooked by traditional college admissions processes. These highly motivated students who possess exceptional leadership potential are united into multicultural posses—groups of 10 students who support one another in their pursuit of academic excellence—and sent to college as a collective group. The 33 university partners that currently work with the Posse Foundation award Posse scholars four-year, full-tuition leadership scholarships (The Posse Foundation, n.d.-a). With the support of their posse behind them, 90% of Posse scholars graduate from college, a rate significantly higher than the national average.

A national initiative founded in 1989, Posse has since sent over 2,600 students to top-tier schools in 17 states (The Posse Foundation, n.d.-b). Vanderbilt was Posse's first university partner, and it has since been joined by a variety of institutions nationwide, including the recent addition of the University of California, Berkeley. Posse's Class of 2013, which began matriculation in autumn 2009, consists of 419 scholars selected from a pool of 9,000 nominees.

Posse participants are selected using a Dynamic Assessment Process that extends beyond traditional measures of academic potential to recognize the talents and leadership potential that prospective students exhibit (The Posse Foundation, n.d.-c). Students who receive Posse scholarships participate in an eight-month training program prior to starting college. This series of workshops builds rapport among Posse students and trains them to be successful college students and leaders. The posses unite to serve as an academic and social support system for each other while serving as "agents of change" on campus.

One of the unique aspects about the Posse program is its conceptualization of what it means to be a leader. Posse's understanding of leadership extends beyond traditional definitions, such as being student council president or a team captain. Instead, Posse acknowledges a range of leadership activities, such as holding a job to support the family, caring for siblings, or serving as a tutor. Many students who complete the Posse program serve as leaders in the workforce.

Diversity is another term that Posse recognizes beyond typical conceptualizations. In the eyes of Posse, diversity includes not only racial, ethnic, gender, and cultural diversity, but also "economic, academic, religious, political and geographic diversity." Diversity "encompasses all ways that people are different from each other, and all the different ways they can learn from each other" (The Posse Foundation, n.d.-c, para.).

Consistent with democratic merit, the Posse program encourages universities to rethink how they make admissions decisions. As noted by Denison University president, Dr. Dale T. Knobel, "Posse in particular has been an asset to Denison, because it seeks out exactly the kind of student that we think makes Denison a special place . . . [who] we might never find without the assistance of the Posse program" (The Posse Foundation, 2006, p. 29). In lieu of some traditional measures of merit, Posse scholars bring unique attributes such as leadership skills to the university community. Posse students are interested in building a diverse community, and they seek to positively affect their campus and community. The presidents at Posse university partner schools also acknowledge the impact Posse students make extends beyond the boundaries of their campuses and into the larger community and workforce. Dr. Jehuda Reinharz, President of Brandeis University, reflected, "For nearly a decade, Posse students have enlivened and enriched our campus and gone on to make outstanding contributions in the workplace and in society. The Posse Foundation is a positive investment in all of our futures" (The Posse Foundation, 2006, p. 10).

Implementing Democratic Merit

Having introduced the concept of democratic merit, we turn our focus now to implementation. This is not necessarily a call for the complete banishment of standardized tests and other measures of individual merit; instead, we advocate that admissions officers and universities more broadly recognize attributes students may possess that, when nurtured in a higher education institution, may yield active, engaged citizens who are committed to upholding and promoting democratic principles.

How, then, is democratic merit applied to admissions? Adopting a democratic merit perspective requires a focus first on the end goals of the institution. University administrators should reflect on the qualities they hope to nurture within their graduates and the skills they seek to cultivate. This reflection should include input from the larger community regarding its needs.[7] Is this institution committed to producing graduates who are actively engaged in their communities? Inclined to civic participation? Willing to commit to leadership roles? Once the end goals are clearly defined, attention should turn toward how the educational institution can work backwards to achieve these goals. Administrators should ask themselves what type of students are likely to support these goals, and in turn, how this new goal-oriented perspective will affect how they view and judge applicants. In short, the implementation of democratic merit principles involves embracing outcomes and working backwards to achieve them.

As recognized in the discussion of the goals of higher education, the idea of democratic merit is not drastically different or new; many colleges and universities already possess mission statements that claim to embrace democratic ideals. The professed interest these schools place on transformative agendas such as the betterment of society should have implications for admissions policies and practices. Our focus, then, needs to be on aligning missions and admissions so that universities are reconnected with their public obligations.

Implementing the principles of democratic merit would clearly transform educational institutions. As the presidents of schools involved in the Posse program indicated, the presence of students who may not fit traditional measures of merit enriched their campus cultures significantly. They noted how Posse scholars continued to be positive social forces in their workplaces and communities once they graduated from college and left the Posse program. These students transformed not only their college campuses, but continued to reflect the ideals of democratic merit beyond commencement, thus benefiting all of society.

Incorporating democratic merit considerations into admissions practices requires forward-thinking goals. Success needs to be defined by measures that extend beyond simply retaining students and seeing them through to graduation. Instead, our views of success should have a long-term perspective. What are students doing 20 or 30 years after college graduation? How have they had a positive impact on society? In what ways are the ideals imparted into students by colleges and universities manifesting themselves for the betterment of our world? This extended vision of success will foster recognition of the importance of democratic merit and its consideration in the admissions process.

---

[7] In *Justice and the Politics of Difference*, Iris Marion Young (2000) asserts that public goods such as education are not distributed in ways that are neutral. The values of the larger community give these goods social and political meaning.

Implementing the principles of democratic merit is not simply an add-on to current university practices or something that only happens in the admissions process; achieving democratic merit and true integration has implications that reverberate throughout the institution.[8] Democratic merit calls us to also look at the representation of people of color throughout the college or university in faculty and staff positions. However, while numerical representation is a necessary start, it is just that. By and large, our approach to education, even diversity, has centered on how to prepare an individual for the university. A more radical approach calls for allowing the space for the university to transform in response to the inclusion of diverse populations. Our social structures and institutions have been constructed in culturally biased ways, with White, middle-class norms at the center. Taking seriously the goal of creating a more democratic system of higher education requires the social and political space to incorporate the voices and experiences of those who have historically been relegated to the margins. Only by accomplishing this will we truly achieve a representative, diverse, integrated, and functionally democratic system of higher education.

Finally, although colleges and universities are in many ways a cornerstone of our society, they cannot single-handedly bring about the transformation needed to achieve a more just, equitable, and sustainable society. The reason students of color and low-income students are historically underrepresented in higher education is that they experience crippling institutional failures across their entire life span. Democratic merit is an example of one transformative change that can realign education with our nation's democratic ideals. In reality, this type of institutional transformation is needed across the board in order to truly level the playing field and ensure that every student has equal opportunity. We must continue to re-imagine society at every opportunity, within every institution. We must allow the space for those historically excluded to have a voice in this transformation; to do this we must ensure they are lifted up through higher education.

References

21st Century Scholars Program. (n.d.). Frequently asked questions about the 21st Century Scholars Program Retrieved from http://www.indiana .edu/~iub21cs/iub21cs_FAQ.html

About the land-grant system. (n.d.). Retrieved from http://www.ext.wvu.edu/ about_extension/land_grant_system

---

[8] For a more in-depth discussion about the distinction between desegregation and true integration see powell, 2005.

Alon, S., & Tienda, M. (2007) Diversity, opportunity, and the shifting meritocracy in higher education. *American Sociological Review, 72,* 487–511.

Ambach v. Norwich, 441 U.S. 68 (1979).

Bingham McCutcheon, Morrison & Foerster, and Heller Ehrman White & McAuliffe. (2004). *Preserving diversity in higher education: A manual on admissions policies and procedures after the University of Michigan decisions.* Retrieved from the Equal Justice Society website: http://www.equaljusticesociety.org/compliancemanual

Bok, D. (2003). *Universities in the marketplace: The commercialization of higher education.* Princeton, NJ: Princeton University Press.

Bridgeman, B., Pollack, J., & Burton, N. (2004). *Understanding what SAT Reasoning Test Scores™ add to high school grades: A straightforward approach* (College Board Research Report No. 2004-4). New York, NY: College Entrance Examination Board. Retrieved from https://professionals.collegeboard.com/profdownload/pdf/041434RDCBR04-4dc.pdf

Clark University (Worcester, MA), Jacob Hiatt Center for Urban Education. (n.d.). The school with a promise. Retrieved from http://www.clarku.edu/departments/education/upcs/index.cfm

Dey, A. (2009, March 17). Number of applicants increases; Acceptance rate is record 10.2%. *The Tech.* Retrieved from http://tech.mit.edu/V129/N13/admissions.html

Field, R. (2007). John Dewey (1859–1952). In *The Internet Encyclopedia of Philosophy.* Retrieved from http://www.utm.edu/research/iep/d/dewey.htm#H4

Gladwell, M. (2008) *Outliers: The story of success.* New York, NY: Little, Brown.

Grant-Thomas, A. (2009). *A referendum on race. Colorlines* web exclusive. http://colorlines.com/archives/2009/01/a_referendum_on_race.html

Guinier, L. (2003). Admissions rituals as political acts: Guardians at the gates of our democratic ideals. *Harvard Law Review, 117,* 113–224.

Harvard University Gazette Online. (2009). Financial aid program draws record number of applications. Retrieved from http://www.news.harvard.edu/gazette/ 2009/04.02/99-admissions.html.

Haurwitz, R. K. M. (2009, March 5). UT President Warns of Consequences to Automatic-Admission Law. *American-Statesman.* Retrieved from http://www.statesman.com/news/content/news/stories/local/03/05/0305topten.html

Hopwood v. Texas, 78 F.3d 932 (5th Cir. 1996).

Hoover, E. (2008, September 22). Admissions group urges colleges to "assume control" of debate on testing. *The Chronicle of Higher*

Education. Retrieved from http://chronicle.com/daily/2008/09/4685n. htm?utm_source=at&utm_medium=en

Horn, C. L. & Yun, J. (2008). Is 1500 the new 1280? The SAT and admissions since *Bakke.* In P. Marin & C. L. Horn (Eds.) *Realizing Bakke's legacy: Affirmative action, equal opportunity, and access to higher education* (pp. 145–169). Sterling, VA: Stylus Publishing.

Jewett, T. (1996). Jefferson, education and the franchise. *Early America Review, 1*(3). Retrieved from http://www.earlyamerica.com/review/ winter96/jefferson.html

Kain, J. F., O'Brien, D. M., & Jargowsky, P. A. (2005). Hopwood *and the Top 10 Percent law: How they have affected the college enrollment decisions of Texas high school graduates* (A report to the Andrew W. Mellon Foundation). Dallas: University of Texas. Retrieved from http://www.utdallas.edu/research/tsp-erc/pdf/wp_kain_2005_hopwood _top_10_percent.pdf.pdf

Mangan, K. (2009, June 1). Legislature gives U. of Texas at Austin More Leeway on Top-10% Admissions. *The Chronicle of Higher Education.* Retrieved from http://chronicle.com/daily/2009/06/19119n.htm?utm _source=at&utm_medium=en

Maslow, A. H. and Honigmann, J. J. (1970). Synergy: Some notes of Ruth Benedict. *American Anthropologist, 72,* 320–333.

National Association for College Admission Counseling. (2008). *Report of the Commission on the Use of Standardized Tests in Undergraduate Admission.* Arlington, VA: Author.

National Park Service (1992). Education as the keystone to the new democracy. Retrieved from http://www.nps.gov/history/NR/twhp/ wwwlps/lessons/92uva/92facts1.htm

The Posse Foundation. (2006). *Presidents & their posses: The Posse Foundation 2006 annual report.* New York, NY: Author. Retrieved from http://www.possefoundation.org/m/posse-annual-report-06.pdf

The Posse Foundation. (n.d.-a). About Posse. Retrieved from http://www .possefoundation.org/about-posse/

The Posse Foundation. (n.d.-b). Our history and mission. Retrieved from http://www.possefoundation.org/about-posse/our-history-mission/

The Posse Foundation. (n.d.-c). Quick facts. Retrieved from http://www. possefoundation.org/quick-facts/

powell, j. a. (2005). Dreaming of a self beyond Whiteness and isolation. *Washington University Journal of Law and Policy, 18,* 13–46.

powell, j. & Menenedian, S. (2008). Little Rock and the legacy of *Dred Scott.* 52 St. Louis U. L.J. 1153.

Schmidt, P. (2008, June 6). New twists mark the debate over Texas' Top 10-Percent Plan. *The Chronicle of Higher Education*. Retrieved from http://chronicle.com/weekly/v54/i39/39a02001.htm

Sen, A. (1999). *Development as freedom.* New York, NY: Anchor Press.

Shtrakhman, D. (2009, April 2). Admit rates decrease at most Ivies. *The Daily Pennsylvanian.* http://media.www.dailypennsylvanian.com/media/storage/paper882/news/2009/04/02/News/Admit.Rates.Decrease.At.Most.Ivies.Interactive.Graph-3693289.shtml

Sridharan, V. (2009, April 1). Stanford admission rate at record low. *San Francisco Business Times*. Retrieved from http://www.bizjournals.com/sanfrancisco/stories/2009/03/30/daily48.html

Tully, S. (2008, August 15). Interpreting test scores: More complicated than you think. [Interview with Daniel Koretz, author of *Measuring Up: What Educational Testing Really Tells Us*]. *The Chronicle of Higher Education.* Retrieved from http://chronicle.com/weekly/v54/i49/49a02301.htm?utm_source=at&utm_medium=en

University of California, Berkeley Office of Undergraduate Admission. (n.d.). UC Berkeley freshmen selection process. Retrieved from http://students.berkeley.edu/admissions/freshmen.asp?id=56&navid=N

U.S. Department of Agriculture. (2000). About Us. Cooperative State Research, Education, and Extension Service. Retrieved from http://www.csrees.usda.gov/qlinks/extension.html

U.S. Census Bureau. (2008, August 14). An older and more diverse nation by midcentury [Press Release]. Retrieved from http://www.census.gov/newsroom/releases/archives/population/cb08-123.html

U.S. Department of Veterans Affairs. (n.d.). The GI Bill's history. Retrieved from http://www.gibill.va.gov/benefits/history_timeline/index.html

Young, I. M. (2000). *Inclusion and democracy* Oxford, England: Oxford University Press.

Zwick, R. (2010). *College admission testing.* Arlington, VA: National Association for College Admission Counseling. Available online at: https://webportal.nacacnet.org/Purchase/ProductDetail.aspx?Product_code=5640e46b-0c55-de11-980c-001c23c77e56

Zwick, R., & Sklar, J. G. (2005). Predicting college grades and degree completion using high school grades and SAT scores: The role of student ethnicity and first language. *American Educational Research Journal, 42*, 439–464.

Section IV

Bridging Scholarship with Comprehensive Intervention

CHAPTER 13

DIVERSITY AND COMPREHENSIVE STRATEGIES IN HIGHER EDUCATION

Angela Ebreo, Gloryvee Fonseca-Bolorin, and Phillip J. Bowman

At a time when racial and ethnic minorities represent an increasing proportion of the United States population, it becomes imperative that selective colleges and universities develop more comprehensive strategies to identify the most meritorious students in precollege pipeline, admissions, and retention interventions. However, selective public institutions are increasingly confronted with a challenge—how to develop a comprehensive merit approach that combines SAT/ACT-type assessments with evidence-based strategies that promote opportunity, diversity and inclusiveness. This challenge is especially contentious in efforts to promote college success among talented students of color who are faced with restricted opportunities in K–12 public schools that systematically depress SAT/ACT scores, impede college readiness, and widen higher education "achievement gaps" (Bowman, Chapter 2, this volume; Rowley & Bowman, 2009). This challenge is further exacerbated by anti-affirmative action policies that result in proportionately fewer African American, Latino/a, and American Indian students applying to and enrolling in flagship public universities.

This chapter provides an extensive *review of existing literature* on comprehensive merit-based strategies in higher education followed by related *highlights from personal interviews* with university-based admini-strators on the role of noncognitive factors in college admissions, precollege pipeline, and college retention efforts. First, a systematic review of existing evidence supports the growing importance of comprehensive merit-based approaches in higher education and beyond. Next, a critical review of more specific literature on comprehensive approaches in college admissions, precollege pipeline, and college retention efforts reveal several gaps. Finally, to help to fill gaps in existing literature, we provide highlights from interviews with university-based leaders actually engaged in admissions, pipeline, and retention programs on the role of noncognitive factors in more comprehensive strategies to provide clearer direction for future research, practice, and policy.

Comprehensive Merit-based Approach:
Noncognitive Factors in Admissions and Beyond

Critics, particularly those who are concerned about admission to selective educational institutions, have attacked comprehensive strategies, stating that the use of nonacademic criteria is just another means of reinstating race-conscious criteria into decisions. Other critics argue that attention to noncognitive factors in more comprehensive approaches devalues the importance of academic merit in decisions about students' qualifications to attend selective institutions of higher education. Still other critics have suggested that nonacademic criteria such as noncognitive factors have no relevance to academic success. Moreover, as the number of applicants to selective universities has increased, some institutions have made admissions decisions based on formulas that simply increase the weight of traditional academic criteria rather than applying multiple criteria with unique value to the university. Such arguments against comprehensive reviews hinge upon a narrow definition and measurement of merit or talent—prior evidence of academic achievement and opportunity.

In contrast to such critics, more comprehensive (also called "holistic") review and assessment procedures add a range of nonacademic consider-ations along with traditional academic criteria. A variety of nonacademic criteria have been used by universities, and a few authors have begun to arrange them into substantively, conceptually, theoretically, and empirically meaningful categories (e.g., Bowman 2006; Kyllonen, Lipnevich, Burris, & Roberts, 2009; Robbins et al., 2004; Sedlacek, 2004). A widely used self-report system of eight noncognitive variables (i.e., *preference for long-term goals, positive self-concept, knowledge acquired in a field, realistic self-appraisal, availability of a strong support person, leadership experience, community involvement*, and *successfully handling the system*) has proved to be a useful adjunct to standardized test scores as a predictor of student success in college (Bowman, Chapter 8, this volume; Sedlacek, 2004, Chapter 9, this volume).

A large body of work has already shown that, generally speaking, noncognitive factors are positively related to various student academic outcomes. For instance, several studies of the noncognitive factors named in Sedlacek's typology show the power of these factors in predicting academic persistence and performance. *Perceived social support* has been found to be positively related to academic persistence (Gloria, Robinson-Kurpius Hamilton, & Willson, 1999; Nicpon et al., 2006–2007) and academic and social integration into college (Milem & Berger, 1997) but negatively related to intentions to drop out of college (Pritchard & Wilson, 2003). Other studies have shown that being *self-efficacious* is positively related to academic persistence (Brown et al., 2008; Rayle, Kurpuis, & Arredondo, 2006) and performance (Close & Solberg, 2007), and negatively related to withdrawal from courses (Devonport & Lane, 2006). Additional research findings show that students who make *realistic self-appraisals, engage in successful leadership experiences,* or *are involved in community service activities* tend to perform better academically (Adebayo, 2008; Ting, 2000). Other researchers have found that *preference for long-term goals* predicts student retention from their first to their second year of college (Arbona & Novy, 1990) as well as academic performance (Ting & Robinson, 1998). Some authors (Arbona & Novy, 1990; Sedlacek & Sheu, 1994) have found that *being able to handle the system/handling racism* predicts persistence. *Knowledge acquired in a field* is predictive of college success (Fuertes, Sedlacek, & Liu, 1994) and noncognitive factors such as academic goals, academic motivation, and social engagement have been shown to predict both college retention and academic performance (Robbins et al., 2004).

In addition to admissions, a growing number of colleges and universities have begun to combine SAT/ACT-type testing with noncognitive assessments in more comprehensive merit-based approaches to financial aid, precollege pipeline, retention, and other student support service interventions (Sedlacek, 2004). Financial aid offices have long reviewed application materials for merit-based scholarships and made awards based on a range of noncognitive factors and assets. Increasingly, university outreach and precollege programs use comprehensive assessments of both academic readiness and a range of noncognitive strengths, talents, and assets. Similarly, student affairs units increasingly seek more comprehensive assessment strategies to better identify and respond to students who need additional support services to promote retention and success during the stressful college transition.

Comprehensive College Admissions Strategies

The majority of the existing literature about the importance of comprehensive merit-based approaches focuses on the systematic use of noncognitive factors in university admissions rather than on precollege and retention interventions (Gilbert, 2008; Harris & Owen, 2007; Hedlund, Wilt, Nebel, Ashford, & Sternberg, 2006; Hojat et al., 1993; Kulatunga-Moruzi & Norman 2002b; Sedlacek, 2004; Stolte, Scheer, & Robinson, 2003; Strefflyer, Altmaier, Kuperman, & Patrick, 2005; Urlings-Strop, Stijnen, Themmen, & Splinte, 2009). Surprisingly, however, most studies relating to the benefits of noncognitive factors do not focus on undergraduate admissions, but rather on graduate or professional program admissions and the validity of noncognitive factors in predicting academic and career success. Of the eight noncognitive factors described by Sedlacek (2004), *specialized knowledge in a chosen field* or the direct, successful experience in the areas in which applicants desire to obtain further training, is a powerful predictor of student success in professional schools.

Sternberg and his colleagues (Sternberg, 2004; Hedlund et al., 2006) examined the long-term predictive validity of noncognitive factors among business school students and found that measures of practical business skills accounted for students' performance in and out of the classroom and added to the amount of variance in performance that was predicted by the students' GMAT scores and college GPAs. Similarly, Gibson and her colleagues (2007) found that mid-career professionals in a master of public administration program who had waived admissions test scores had slightly higher grade point averages than did their nonwaiver colleagues. This finding shows that the quality of enrollees does not necessarily decline if specialized talents, skills, or work experience replace test scores for admission purposes. Moreover, in a study of distance educated, nontraditional doctor of pharmacy students, Stolte and colleagues (2003) found that noncognitive admissions criteria were significantly related to the students' composite portfolio scores, didactic GPAs, and overall GPAs.

Comprehensive merit-based approaches that systematically utilize noncognitive factors have been especially prevalent in medical school admissions including assessments of the comparative effectiveness of different admissions criteria in selecting candidates who will be high achieving once admitted. For example, in a study of medical school applicants, Hojat and colleagues (1993) found that psychosocial factors such as locus of control and self-esteem predicted variance in applicants' post-admission academic performance above variance that could be predicted by their MCAT scores and GPAs. In an interesting prospective study, Urlings-Strop and colleagues (2009) conducted a controlled investigation to examine whether students selected using both noncognitive and traditional admissions criteria would perform better in their subclinical medical school curricula than would students who had been selected randomly via a lottery. Their findings showed that the selection-criteria group of students dropped out at a lower rate than did the lottery group of students.

Several medical school studies also suggest that academic factors and noncognitive factors predict different types of outcomes and suggest that comprehensive merit strategies should include both predictive factors and consider multiple criteria of success (Kulatunga-Moruzi & Norman, 2002a; Strefflyer et al., 2005). For instance, Kulatunga-Moruzi and Norman (2002a) found that information from personal medical school interviews solidly predicted communication skills, but undergraduate GPA was the strongest predictor of academic and clinical performance. Strefflyer and colleagues (2005) found that the conventional admissions predictors (i.e., GPA and MCAT scores) predicted subsequent performance on written tests taken during medical school, while noncognitive factors predicted peer evaluations and medical facilitator ratings of skills needed by practicing physicians.

Enhancement of the perceived favorableness of selection procedures was noted in the literature as another benefit of including noncognitive factors in comprehensive strategies (Harris & Owen, 2007; Hofmeister, Lockyer, & Crutcher, 2008). Applicants appear to view selection decisions more positively when admissions committees include criteria such as characteristics or personal qualities associated with professional success as being valued in persons who practice a specific profession. Harris and Owen (2007), for example, examined what happened when one medical school elicited a set of noncognitive variables from its faculty that were subsequently used in mini-interviews of applicants. This method of selection proved to be both efficient for faculty and satisfactory for the interviewees. Similar findings have been found in studies of mini-interviews for selecting medical residents (Hofmeister et al., 2008).

While most studies focus on noncognitive factors as positive predictors of successful student outcomes, there is also evidence that noncognitive factors may also operate as indicators of risk in some situations (Bowman, 2006; Neville, Heppner, & Wang, 1997; Robbins et al., 2004). For example, in a retrospective study of matriculated medical students, Elam and her colleagues (1999) delineated the academic and noncognitive factors related to successful performance during the first two years of medical school. Although this study was conducted on matriculants from only one medical school, the findings suggest that active engagement in community service, one of Sedlacek's noncognitive factors, may sometimes be associated with more "modest" MCAT scores.

Beyond Self-Report Measurement of Noncognitive Factors in Admissions: At the present time, existing literature (primarily related to professional and graduate admissions) offers some answers related to the modalities beyond self-reported measures through which information about noncognitive factors can be gathered. As noted earlier, the assessment of noncognitive factors by admissions personnel is usually subjective and obtained by methods that are difficult to standardize, although there have been attempts at standardization. For example, Ziv and colleagues (2008) developed a simulation-based assessment center approach for evaluating four qualities (interpersonal communication, ability to handle stress, initiative and responsibility, and self-awareness) of medical school applicants and demonstrated that these simulations convey the importance of noncognitive factors in the medical profession to both students and faculty. In addition, applicants perceived the procedures as fair.

Other authors have described or evaluated the use of mini-interviews as an alternative to the more traditional style of interviews conducted with medical school applicants (Bownell, Lockyer, Collin, & Lemay, 2007; Lemay, Lockyer, Collin, & Brownell, 2007). Mini-interviews, which allow a larger number of applicants to be screened, were developed to obtain information on applicants' noncognitive characteristics such as empathy, compassion, and integrity. Research on this method indicates that performance on mini-interviews prior to medical school acceptance predicts relevant practice skills assessed at a later point in time (Reiter et al., 2007) and that mini-interviews have greater reliability and validity than the more conventional type of admissions interviews (Lemay et al., 2007). Interviews are not without their disadvantages, one of which is bias on the part of the interviewers. Research by Kulatunga-Moruzi and Norman (2002b), for example, indicates that interviewers tend to attribute interviewees' performance to stable personality characteristics while discounting the influence of situational factors that might enhance or detract from performance on that specific interview.

Fewer studies have examined the reliability and validity of letters of recommendation. Although some recent attempts have been made to standardize information from letters (Lui, Minsky, Ling, & Kyllonen, 2009), some researchers (Mavis, Shafer, & Magallanes, 2006) argue that reference letters may not contain sufficient information about noncognitive variables and therefore may not be reliable indicators for assessment purposes.

Comprehensive Precollege Pipeline Strategies

As selective public universities face greater restrictions on race-targeted admissions, they have expanded precollege outreach and pipeline interventions to help improve the college readiness of students in K–12 public school systems with restricted opportunities. However, the authors of this chapter found no studies in which the benefits of using noncognitive factors to select students into college readiness programs were compared with the benefits of solely using traditional academic factors. To date, the majority of published works consist of descriptions of precollege outreach and pipeline initiatives or evaluations of specific programs. Moreover, most existing program evaluations have serious methodological limitations and do not systematically compare the efficacy of comprehensive precollege readiness strategies to the traditional pre-college focus on the assessment of severe academic preparation deficits among underrepresented students in at-risk public schools. However, comprehensive precollege programs in addition to expanding K–12 opportunities for academic readiness included goals to promote underrepresented students' motivation for college and realistic appraisals of resiliency, leadership, civic engagement, and diversity values.

Precollege pipeline interventions consist of both a growing array of early K–12 outreach programs and intensive summer-bridge programs prior to the first semester of college. For example, Watt, Huerta, and Lozano (2007) compared students participating in two K–12 college readiness programs—Advancement Via Individual Determination (AVID) and the federally funded GEAR UP—with a control group of students attending the same institution. The authors examined the influence of students' educational aspirations, expectations, knowledge of college entrance requirements and financial aid on the academic achievement of the students. AVID focuses on preparing students for college through exposure to rigorous course work and teaching academic survival skills, while GEAR UP programs provide a more comprehensive set of services and strategies including parental involvement services, counseling, mentoring, and outreach. Watt, Huerta, and Lozano found that the level of educational aspirations across the groups was not significantly different. However, AVID students were significantly more involved in pre–Advanced Placement courses than were students in GEAR UP and the control group, but they did not differ from the other groups in their level of college knowledge or math performance. The authors attribute the modest evidence of intervention program efficacy to the small number of students in the study. Future research should clarify if interventions such as AVID and GEAR UP tend to emphasize either academic or noncognitive factors rather than a more comprehensive focus on both.

In a longitudinal study of a summer-bridge program, Walpole and colleagues (2008) found that students' educational aspirations remained high at the end of their third year of college. However, students adjusted the length of time they believed it would take for them to earn a bachelor's degree, possibly because they developed more *realistic self-appraisals*. This study's findings also suggest these summer-bridge program students had an opportunity to better learn *how to handle the system*, as indicated by their increased use of campus services such as tutoring, career planning, counseling and financial aid. Similarly, Zhang and Richards (1999) found that summer bridge programs help students make *realistic appraisals* of the demands of college and solidify specific social psychological strengths such as the *preference for long-term goals* (operationalized as delayed gratification).

Comprehensive College Retention Strategies

In addition to admissions and pipeline strategies, there is also a growing literature on the importance of comprehensive merit-based approaches to a successful college transition and college retention (Noble, Flynn, Lee, & Hilton, 2007; Sedlacek, 2004). Most well represented in this literature are studies that link noncognitive factors to college retention and persistence (Lotkowski, Robbins, & Noeth, 2004; Robbins et al., 2004; Tracey & Sedlacek, 1984). An early study by Tracey and Sedlacek (1984) supported the importance of noncognitive and psychosocial factors such as self-efficacy, self-esteem, and perceived social support as predictors of college persistence. In addition to counseling strategies to promote such personal empowerment, Kennett and Reed (2009) demonstrated the importance of comprehensive curricular interventions in a study of students attending a postsecondary success course; college retention improved when the course emphasized resourcefulness, self-efficacy, a positive explanatory style, and strategic coping skills in addition to the acquisition of basic academic skills. While retention studies have focused on the importance of various types of social support, Campbell and Campbell (1997) affirmed the particular importance of mentors in a study clearly showing that students with mentors had a lower dropout rate.

Existing literature suggests that both quantitative and qualitative studies of retention programs can help further clarify the importance of more comprehensive merit strategies that include a consideration of noncognitive factors in successful college transition and retention (Keenan & Gabovitch, 1995; Pike, Schroeder, & Berry, 1997; Reyes, 2007). For example, a quantitative study of first year students by Pike and colleagues (1997) found that formal residential learning communities indirectly affected *social support* in the form of faculty–student interactions and that faculty–student interactions, in turn, affected persistence. Similarly, a quantitative study by Keenan and Gabovitch (1995) found that students in a first-year seminar gained in their sense of *self-efficacy* (operationalized as confidence in learning skills) and increased their *knowledge of how to handle the system* (as measured by familiarity with college policies and procedures). Despite their importance, quantitative studies of retention and support programs may not always reveal the significant impacts on noncognitive processes which may sometimes be more specific, nuanced, and subtle. For example, Fortson (1997) found that participation in a course designed to increase career planning, cultural awareness and academic responsibility had no effect on African American students' *academic self-concept*. However, a qualitative study by Reyes (2007) helps to clarify the complex processes through which retention interventions may operate to enhance a students' sense of self-empowerment in college settings. This qualitative study found that participation in a college assistance intervention designed to promote retention changed migrant students' *self-concepts* through various program activities helping participants gain a more positive sense of themselves as capable college students.

Interviews With University Administrators

As suggested previously, there are several gaps in existing literature on noncognitive factors in higher education that tend to focus disproportionately on medical or professional school admissions. Therefore, we still know very little about the operation of noncognitive factors in undergraduate admissions despite the growing popularity of more "comprehensive" or "holistic" reviews. There is even less literature on comprehensive merit based approaches in higher education precollege pipeline and college retention programs. To help fill these current gaps in existing literature, we conducted interviews with several university-based administrators with extensive experience in undergraduate admissions, pipeline, and retention programs on the role of noncognitive factors in more comprehensive strategies.

Comprehensive Merit-Based Approaches: Administrators' Perspectives and Themes

To build on our review of existing literature, intensive interviews were conducted with five university administrators employed by a public flagship university located in the midwestern United States. Three administrators had extensive experience in undergraduate admissions—general, engineering, and business—and two with extensive experience in both precollege pipeline and college retention programs. Similar to other flagship universities, this highly selective institution has responded in strategic ways to anti–affirmative action policies prohibiting the consideration of race/ethnicity and gender in admissions, precollege outreach, retention programming, and related diversity policies. A major component of this university's response has been a move toward more comprehensive merit-based strategies—including holistic review of college admission and scholarship applications and the inclusion of diverse groups in programs originally targeted for racial/ethnic minorities and/or females. This university was selected for examination due to its long-standing reputation as an institution committed to the diversification of its student body.

The five administrators interviewed were selected based on their professional expertise, length of employment at the university and their respective levels of responsibility in units related to undergraduate admissions, precollege outreach, or college retention. The interviews were semistructured and contained questions focusing on whether or not noncognitive factors were perceived as being an important component within these comprehensive strategies and how noncognitive factors are incorporated into these strategies as they are implemented. The interviewees' perspective on comprehensive merit-based strategies is presented in this section with an emphasis on the three dominant themes that emerged from these intensive interviews about noncognitive strategies— their *importance*, their *utilization*, and their *development*.

Importance of Noncognitive Strategies

All administrators were asked if they believed that noncognitive factors are an *important* part of comprehensive strategies. A quote from an administrator from the school of engineering who had worked in both undergraduate recruitment and admissions illustrates a common theme that comprehensive reviews which include noncognitive considerations are perceived as providing a more total picture of students' potential:

> I think it gives a more realistic picture of a student that can be successful, a student that has the skill set to persevere and be successful.

This notion of a "realistic picture" of college applicants is echoed in a comment from a business school administrator. This administrator's remarks show that noncognitive factors provide additional information about students beyond grade point averages and standardized test scores. More importantly, the quote illustrates the skills represented by noncognitive factors are valuable assets for the students' future careers:

> The noncognitive things help us fill out the picture of who each applicant is. We really don't want the 4.0, 1600 SAT student who doesn't have any social skills or no ability to work with anyone else, because that's not going to work in the business world. We don't want someone who has absolutely no experience in the community, because we want to know that people know how to work with one another . . .

While the prior two quotes were from undergraduate administrators in the university's professional schools, the administrator working with undergraduate admissions at the liberal arts college also emphasized community involvement and leadership experiences. The administrator stressed that combining traditional academic measures with noncognitive factors as assessed through college essays results in a more informed admission selection. However, the administrator also admitted that grade point averages and standardized test scores remain an essential part of the college admission process, but believed that noncognitive factors play a distinct role in referring students to programs that can facilitate their transition to college. For instance, noncognitive factors facilitate discussions regarding students who meet the criteria for assistance from student support programs:

> It certainly is something that we consider and it does help us in some cases to make decisions about students that we want to give special opportunities to, whether it's through bridge or *a retention program*[1] or advising them to go someplace else and come to *this institution* at some later point.

Administrators employed in undergraduate admissions were not the only ones who believed noncognitive factors provide information complementary to the traditional indicators of prior academic achievement. Such factors are indicative of personal strengths students use to navigate environments that have presented barriers to their academic trajectory. An administrator who has worked with precollege pipeline, transition, and retention programs argues that noncognitive factors predict student development within challenging environments:

> [T]he noncognitive factors provide us with information about how a student behaves, reacts, and will develop within a context. And that context is the whole socio-personal context of higher education or, even prior to that pipeline, how that student is going to get through middle and secondary school.

The same administrator gave an example of how an accurate awareness of one's capabilities can be as crucial to the success of students from more

---

[1] Italics indicate a change in the original interview dialogue. The name of the program was changed in order to keep the institution's identity confidential.

privileged socioeconomic backgrounds as they are to the success of students who have been underrepresented on university campuses:

> I've seen lots of people come to college with just excellent test scores and grades but they don't make it. The socio-economic status of the family may be one of the things that contributed to their high test score. But maybe the parents also kept saying "you're great, Johnny" when Johnny isn't so great and Johnny now doesn't have a realistic self-appraisal of himself in comparison to other students. So he comes to a place like *this institution* and although he had a good up-bringing and good family and good test scores, went to a good school, got good grades, he doesn't have the realistic self-appraisal about how much it takes and he doesn't have the resiliency to deal with negative feedback.

The ability to be "resilient and adaptable" in new and changing situations is a major predictor of college retention and is one of several noncognitive factors that interviewees mentioned. A second administrator who works with precollege pipeline and retention programs states that being successful in college requires that a student not only be academically capable but also have the ability to adjust to and navigate the campus environment. In addition, he argues that having a strong sense of self influences a student's overall success.

Another major reason mentioned by the administrators for why comprehensive strategies are necessary was to promote diversity in the university's student body. Such interest in comprehensive strategies to promote diversity have been especially salient in flagship universities with a decrease in enrollment of underrepresented students because of statewide anti–affirmative action bans prohibiting the use of gender and racial/ethnic background as criteria for college admissions or access to services and programs. Primary reliance on standardized test scores for college admission increases the possibility of a homogenous student population that scores well on tests yet neglects other indicators of talent and future career success. One administrator who works in the area of precollege readiness and retention expressed deep frustration with the fact that our society defines meritocracy in a way that rewards individuals from privileged backgrounds who are more likely to have higher standardized test scores while not recognizing that students with less privileged backgrounds can show talent and academic promise on other indicators of merit.

The value of diversity in the student body was also a focal point of discussion for the business school administrator. More specifically, the administrator argued that there would be "no depth" to the admission process if academic factors were the only measures for selecting students. From this administrator's perspective, consideration of noncognitive factors contributes to an admission process that results in an entering class of committed students to the field of business who at the same time represent a diversity of backgrounds that creates a stimulating environment:

> One of the things that we look for in the application essays is trying to get away from students who look exactly alike, who sound exactly like, who articulate the same concerns and reasons for being here. So when somebody stands out in their application essay because they lived for two years in the Middle East after high school, that's a great experience that would be wonderful to have represented here at the business school.

The same administrator further explained that the diversity of admitted students has helped create a unique learning environment that is beneficial to both students and faculty:

> I think, on the whole, the dean's office, our administrators, our faculty are very pleased with the types of students that are here. ... I think it has created a competitive yet collaborative environment. It has created a very stimulating environment for the students. It has helped to make undergraduate classes interesting for the faculty to teach. So, I think those are some ways in which it's been a success using this [comprehensive strategy that includes noncognitive factors].

Overall, findings from the interviews illustrate that the five administrators agreed it is ***important*** to include noncognitive factors as a component of comprehensive strategies. Notably, three major underlying reasons for the importance of including noncognitive factors emerged from the interviews: (a) noncognitive factors more accurately measure "student potential"; (b) noncognitive factors "predict college success" beyond academic factors alone; and (c) noncognitive factors "increase the diversity" of the student body.

Utilization of Noncognitive Strategies

Administrators were also asked how university units **utilize or incorporate** noncognitive factors into their comprehensive strategies. Administrators who directed units focusing on admissions clearly had more to say about how noncognitive factors have been included in their strategies. The majority of administrators noted that the application process for either admission to the university or to pre collegiate programs associated with the university utilized the students' application materials to gain information about various noncognitive factors. For example, the administrators from the business school and the college of engineering stated that students' essays specifically raised questions related to noncognitive factors to gain insight into whether a student has overcome challenging experiences. Specifically, one administrator comments that

> The application components include several different aspects of noncognitive factors. For example, essay questions include demonstration of interest in Engineering. Also, students are asked to speak about any obstacles they have overcome, which is a way of examining whether students have persevered against challenges. There is also a committee during the Admission process that reviews applicants who may have had extenuating circumstances that could have impacted their academic performance or standardized test scores.

Administrators from undergraduate liberal arts and business admissions units both stated their admissions selection procedures had departed from the assignment of numeric values to specific criteria towards a holistic review where factors such as leadership potential, civic and cultural awareness, motivation, and intellectual curiosity are highlighted. All components of students' applications (i.e., application form, responses to short questions, essay, college transcripts, test scores, letters of recommendation) are reviewed to gain information about applicants and rate their potential contributions to the university.

The administrator from undergraduate liberal arts admissions spoke more specifically about holistic reviews providing more than just a checklist of the characteristics of an ideal entering student at the university. Generally, in reviewing applicants, a holistic review is conducted using the students' essays and letters of recommendation from counselors and teachers and taking into account the context in which students have exhibited specific noncognitive assets:

[A]ny student that is confident, and we can ascertain that, in their writings or their comments from counselors. . . . We consider all of these, but in the context of that student's file, and in the context of how well those students look within, how well they compared to other students from their high school that are also applying to the *university* . . . the kinds of write-ups and ratings that the counselors and teachers give us . . . say the students are extremely motivated in class or not so motivated in class. We ask them to talk about character. Sometimes they rate these students with excellent character, other times they don't. So there are all of those things we look at, but not any one of them would be a factor that we would necessarily say, "this is the reason to admit" or "this is the reason not to admit."

In other words, noncognitive factors are not considered the sole criteria for the evaluation of admissions applications, but these factors are likely to be considered in combination with traditional academic and intellectual factors. Beyond saying that their processes take noncognitive factors into account, the interviewees did not offer details, particularly in terms of how noncognitive factors are weighted relative to academic factors. One administrator working with undergraduate admissions mentioned that the admissions process is complex and can be viewed as being "more art than science." This person also noted there are no clear guidelines for weighting the relative importance of noncognitive factors in relation to academic factors. The administrator from the business school describes how her unit continues to struggle with this issue each year:

How much weight is going to be put on test scores and the academic assessment versus these other factors, that sort of shifts a little bit from year to year. Our approach, at least in the business school right now, we want to know that the students can do the work. There is sort of a certain minimum level of academic performance that has to be there. But beyond that, we are looking at all those things [noncognitive factors] we have been talking about."

In a different example, the administrator from the engineering school expressed appreciation for the fact that the school's admissions process takes into account students' extenuating circumstances. Using an applicant's short answer responses, essays, letters of recommendation, and socioeconomic background measures, a reviewer can often determine whether a student demonstrates academic promise and has been resilient despite extreme economic or social circumstances. Similarly, the business school administrator noted that assessing leadership skills and potential growth was important for evaluating students' potential and professional growth, especially decisions regarding high school seniors. Students are asked to consider a situation in which they are starting their own community organization, define their goals and approach, and then discuss how their approach might be different after completing their undergraduate degree:

> We're getting at a lot of those noncognitive factors there. Particularly their ability to imagine a process, to think what they are going to get out of their education, how their approach will differ from "when I'm 18 compared to when I'm 22."

The Development of Noncognitive Strengths: Precollege and Retention Strategies

Admissions units use information about noncognitive factors as input for decisions in which the goal is to select the students who are most likely to enroll, succeed, and excel at the university. In contrast, precollege outreach units, whose goals are preparing students for college or retention programs to retain students after they have arrived on campus, collect information about noncognitive factors as the outcomes of student development. The assumption is that the programs and activities offered by these units assist students in developing, maintaining, and improving these non-academic strengths. However, this assumption is implicit rather than explicit in the interviewees' comments.

For instance, one administrator with extensive experience as a retention program director noted that the program was designed to provide an environment where students can thrive and where the advisors support students' development of noncognitive factors:

> The advising challenge is largely one of identifying and reinforcing a wide variety of noncognitive factors as a way to enable college success. I don't think you'll find much of the advising focusing specifically on cognitive kinds of things. It's not a large part of what they do.

Similar to admissions officers, understanding the context in which students have developed their intellectual and noncognitive capabilities appears to be valued by administrators who oversee precollegiate and college retention programs. One administrator with extensive experience with retention programs remarked on how qualitative information from essays, recommendations, and interviews provides insight into why students experience challenges and barriers, and that such insights are a crucial part of understanding how to intervene and assist students in navigating the college transition:

> Similar kinds of things, essays, recommendations, not very often interviews and just personal contacts. When I was in *program* I know that part of what would take place with interactions between an advisor and the student, where here you get a lot of information because students are now sharing with you their circumstances, why they're having challenges. And what I mean by that is adjustment challenges in the institution. Some of those adjustments might be academic, some of them might be personal, some of them might be social.

Generally speaking, administrators were unwilling to make any general statements about the relative importance of specific noncognitive factors in making decisions, but pipeline and retention administrators were able to articulate the noncognitive factors they thought were important to consider in terms of student development. In particular, *leadership, navigating the system*, and *self-concept* emerged as key noncognitive factors that university pre-college and retention programs either reinforced or integrated into their respective programs. For example, one administrator who works with retention programs stated that unit staff reinforced leadership qualities as they saw their students developing:

> [W]e certainly applaud the leadership skills as we see them. Students are working in small groups so you see some of that develop and come out. And I think that you just in many ways acknowledge and encourage when you see the characteristics, and I say that because with many of the summer programs you got them here for four to six weeks. You really are able to observe and see those characteristics as they come out, as they display themselves.

In terms of retention of college students, another administrator noted that advising has always incorporated several noncognitive elements into the unit's work with students. In particular, advising includes discussions of the student's academic plan and how this plan can be used in facilitating discussions around students' *self-confidence, managing the university system*, and, most importantly, helping students make *realistic self-appraisals* so that they can create appropriate goals.

Overall, the administrators agreed that they wanted to understand how noncognitive factors influence student outcomes. Although several administrators either have reviewed students' material looking for specific noncognitive factors or have incorporated these factors into their programs, in practice, they have not conducted systematic assessments of the impact of these factors. These administrators were very open to assistance with future assessment and evaluation of the impact of such factors. The administrator from engineering felt that evaluation was a necessary next step and wanted to see research conducted on the impact of noncognitive factors after matriculation to the university:

> I think if they [noncognitive factors] are more broadly used and if there would be a way that we could truly assess them, a way to do a good job of assessing them . . . to be able to show how they play out once students are here. So let's move it from the point of admissions and pipeline, but once students are here if we really could in some way measure how a particular noncognitive variable really ends up having this type of characteristic that plays out in the classroom, that plays out in performance, that would be great.

The same administrator also stressed the importance of going beyond merely identifying/assessing student strengths to teach students how to put their strengths to good use:

> identifying what works based on noncognitive factors, helping students to incorporate it, use what they have, or maybe build some skills where they don't have it. [LONG PAUSE] And I think the importance there is understanding how these factors are needed and how they are used within the university setting.

Conclusions and Implications

The need to better understand comprehensive merit-based strategies in American higher education is spurred in part by the rapid diversification of the student population by race, class, gender, national origin, and, increasingly, international student status. This chapter provided a systematic review of literature on comprehensive merit-based strategies in higher education with a particular emphasis on selective college admissions, pipeline interventions, and college retention programs. A growing literature on related research, practice, and policy is increasingly supportive of more comprehensive merit-based strategies (i.e., methods that combine traditional SAT/ACT-type assessments with various noncognitive criteria). To date, our literature review revealed that such comprehensive merit-based approaches have been most frequently studied in the context of college admissions with fewer empirical studies of their use in precollege pipeline interventions or college retention programs. It was also interesting to find that the predominant literature on comprehensive approaches to higher education admissions focuses primarily on medical and professional school admissions rather than undergraduate admissions.

The strong emphasis on more comprehensive strategies in medical school admissions has been systematically spurred by the Association of American Medical College (AAMC) Holistic Review Project (https://www .aamc.org/initiatives/holisticreview). In general, the AAMC focus on holistic review emphasizes "a flexible, individualized way of assessing an applicant's capabilities by which balanced consideration is given to experiences, attributes, and academic metrics and, when considered in combination, how the individual might contribute value as a medical student and a future physician" (Supreme Court of the United States, 2003). This new AAMC project is designed to assist medical schools to go beyond the narrow use of the Medical College Admissions Test (MCAT) to develop more holistic review policies, processes, and practices and evaluate their effects and outcomes. This ongoing project may enable medical schools to continue to break new ground in the development of innovative holistic review tools:

> Along with MCAT scores, the admissions committee uses transcripts, and letters of recommendation to gauge applicant's academic preparation. They use information from application forms, personal statements, letters, and interviews to learn about applicants' health-related experience, volunteer and other work, extracurricular activities, future goals, and personal and professional

characteristics, like empathy, integrity, and work habits. (AAMC, 2010, p. 5)

These more comprehensive approaches to admissions have been found to have a wide range of benefits including the promotion of diversity in highly selective programs and elite universities. As Sedlacek (2004) and others suggest, the consideration of dimensions of a student's potential that are complementary to traditional, academic measures of merit is one possible means of ensuring that talented students of all backgrounds have an opportunity to make significant contributions to American society in the 21st century. However, our current knowledge of comprehensive merit approaches is still limited by the shortcomings of related studies on admissions, precollege pipeline, and college retention. Many published articles are either descriptive or evaluation studies, with serious methodological, conceptual, theoretical, and practical limitations.

Findings from intensive interviews with university experts on the *importance* of comprehensive merit approaches, *utilization* of noncognitive factors, and *student development* implications can help to guide future research, practice, and policy. Consistent with the growing empirical literature, the administrators interviewed generally agree with the importance of noncognitive factors in more comprehensive admission, pipeline, and retention efforts in higher education. However, despite positive views of noncognitive factors, administrators could not provide details about their systematic utilization or evidence-based practices. The university experts were still seeking more systematic ways to utilize noncognitive factors in comprehensive decisions within their units and expressed a strong need for better assessment options and additional research. Administrators noted they had no coherent guidelines to follow in their consideration of noncognitive factors, and their units' procedures were more a matter of "art" rather than systematic assessment, program evaluation, or theory-driven intervention research.

Therefore, despite general support, it was difficult for the administrators to specify the details about how noncognitive factors are actually taken into account when making decisions about pipeline, admissions, or retention programs. Admissions administrators expressed an especially strong interest in future research that further clarifies how specific noncognitive factors provide additional, evidence-based information about an applicant's strengths that is not redundant with information about academic strengths. In addition, administrators who oversee precollege pipeline and college retention programs were especially interested in better understanding how their program activities might reinforce or develop noncognitive factors and, in turn, students' future academic and career success. Comments by the program administrators we interviewed indicated an implied student development assumption—that programs positively affect the academic performance and success of students because the programs facilitate and strengthen noncognitive strengths. However, while program administrators could make general statements about how program activities might facilitate the development of noncognitive factors, no one could clearly specify the mechanisms through which students would benefit.

Note

The authors would like to acknowledge Valerie Johnson for her editorial assistance and Jamie Carlisle and Avis Randle for their assistance in transcribing digital audio files of the administrator interviews.

References

Adebayo, B. (2008, Summer). Cognitive and noncognitive factors: Affecting the academic performance and retention of conditionally admitted freshmen. *Journal of College Admission*, pp. 15–21.

Arbona, C., & Novy, D. M. (1990). Noncognitive dimensions as predictors of college success among Black, Mexican-American and White students. *Journal of College Student Development, 31*, 415–422.

Association of American Medical Colleges. (2010). *Using MCAT Data in 2011 Student Selection.* Washington, DC: MCAT Research Office.

Bowman, P. J. (2006). Role strain and adaptation issues in the strength-based model: Diversity, multilevel, and life-span considerations. *Counseling Psychologist, 34*, 118–133.

Bownell, K., Lockyer, J., Collin, T., & Lemay, J. (2007). Introduction of the multiple mini interview into the admissions process at the University of Calgary: acceptability and feasibility. *Medical Teacher, 29*, 394–396.

Brown, S. D., Tramayne, S., Hoxha, D., Telander, K., Fan, X., & Lent, R W. (2008). Social cognitive predictors of college students' academic performance and persistence: A meta-analytic path analysis. *Journal of Vocational Behavior, 72*, 298–308.

Campbell, T. A., & Campbell, D. E. (1997). Faculty/student mentor program: Effects on academic performance and retention. *Research in Higher Education, 38*, 727–742.

Close, W., & Solberg, S. (2007). Predicting achievement, distress, and retention among lower-income Latino youth. *Journal of Vocational Behavior, 72*, 31–42.

Devonport, T. J. & Lane, A. M. (2006). Relationships between self-efficacy, coping and student retention. *Social Behavior and Personality*, *34*, 127–138.

Elam, C. L., Wilson, J. F., Johnson, R., Wiggs, J. S., & Goodman, N. (1999). A retrospective review of medical school admission files of academically at-risk matriculants. *Academic Medicine*, *74*(Suppl.), S58–S61.

Fortson, S. B. (1997). An evaluation of a program to influence academic self-concept among African American male college students. *Journal of Employment Counseling*, *34*, 104–107.

Fuertes, J. N., Sedlacek, W. E., & Liu, W. M. (1994). Using the SAT and noncognitive variables to predict the grades and retention of Asian American university students. *Measurement and Evaluation in Counseling and Development*, *27*, 74–84.

Gibson, P. A., Leavitt, W. M., Lombard, J. R., & Morris, J. C. (2007). Acknowledging the "professional" in a professional degree program: Waiving the standardized exam for in-service applicants to a MPA program. *College Student Journal*, *41*, 872–885.

Gilbert, J. (2008). Application quest: A case study on holistic diversity in admission. *Journal of College Admission*, *199*, 12–18.

Gloria, A. M., Robinson-Kurpius, S. E., Hamilton, K. D., & Willson, M. S. (1999). African American students' persistence at a predominantly White university: Influences of social support, university comfort, and self-beliefs. *Journal of College Student Development*, *40*, 257–268.

Harris, S., & Owen, C. (2007). Discerning quality: using the multiple mini-interview in student selection for the Australian National University Medical School. *Medical Education*, *41*, 234–241.

Hedlund, J., Wilt, J. M., Nebel, K. L., Ashford, S. J., & Sternberg, R. J. (2006). Assessing practical intelligence in business school admissions: A supplement to the graduate management admissions test. *Learning and Individual Differences*, *16*, 101–127.

Hofmeister, M., Lockyer, J., & Crutcher, R. (2008). The acceptability of the Multiple Mini Interview for resident selection. *Family Medicine*, *40*, 734–740.

Hojat, M., Robeson, M., Damjanov, I., Veloski, J. J., Glaser, K., & Gonnella, J. S. (1993). Students' psychosocial characteristics as predictors of academic performance in medical school. *Academic Medicine*, *68*, 635–637.

Keenan, K., & Gabovitch, R. (1995, October). *Evaluating the impact of a freshman seminar program on student development and retention.*

Paper presented at the annual conference of the North East Association for Institutional Research. Burlington, VT.

Kennett, D. J., & Reed, M. J. (2009). Factors influencing academic success and retention following a 1st-year post-secondary success course. *Educational Research and Evaluation, 15*, 153–166.

Kulatunga-Moruzi, C., & Norman, G. R. (2002a). Validity of admissions measures in predicting performance outcomes: A comparison of those who were and were not accepted at McMaster. *Teaching and Learning in Medicine, 14*, 43–48.

Kulatunga-Moruzi, C., & Norman, G. R. (2002b). Validity of admissions measures in predicting performance outcomes: The contribution of cognitive and non-cognitive dimensions. *Teaching and Learning in Medicine, 14*, 34–42

Kyllonen, P. C., Lipnevich, A. A., Burris, J., & Roberts, R. D. (2009). *Personality, motivation, and college readiness: A prospectus for assessment and development* (Educational Testing Service Research Report No: RR-09-xx). Princeton, NJ: Educational Testing Service.

Lemay, J., Lockyer, J. M., Collin, V. T., & Brownell, K. W. (2007). Assessment of noncognitive traits through the admissions multiple mini-interview. *Medical Education, 41*, 573–579.

Lotkowski, V. A., Robbins, S. B., & Noeth, R. J. (2004). *The role of academic and non-academic factors in improving college retention.* Iowa City, IA: ACT, Inc.

Lui, O. U., Minsky, J., Ling, G., & Kyllonen, P. (2009). Using the standardized letters of recommendation in selection: Results from a multidimensional Rasch Model. *Educational and Psychological Measurement, 69*, 475–492.

Mavis, B. E., Shafer, C. L., & Magallanes, B. M. (2006). The intentions of letter writers for applicants to a baccalaureate-M.D. program: Self-report and content analyses of letters of reference. *Medical Education, 11*, 11–16.

Milem, J. F., & Berger, J. B. (1997). A modified model of student persistence: Exploring the relationship between Astin's theory of involvement and Tinto's theory of student departure. *Journal of College Student Development, 38*, 387–400.

Neville, H. A., Heppner, P. P., & Wang, L. F. (1997). Relations among racial identity attitudes, perceived stressors, and coping styles in African American college students. *Journal of Counseling and Development, 75*, 303–311.

Nicpon, M. F., Huser, L., Blanks, E. H., Sollenberger, S., Befort, C., & Robinson-Kurpius, S. E. (2006–2007). The relationship of loneliness and social support with college freshman's academic performance and persistence. *Journal of College Student Retention, 8*, 345–358.

Noble, K., Flynn, N. T., Lee, J. D., & Hilton, D. (2007). Predicting successful college experiences: Evidence from a first year retention program. *Journal of College Student Retention, 9*, 39–60.

Pike, G. R., Schroeder, C. C., & Berry, T. R. (1997). Enhancing the educational impact of residential halls: The relationship between residential learning communities and first-year college experiences and persistence. *Journal of College Student Development, 38*, 609–621.

Pritchard, M. E., & Wilson, G. S. (2003). Using emotional and social factors to predict student success. *Journal of College Student Development, 44*, 18–28.

Rayle, A. D., Kurpuis, S. E. R., & Arredondo, P. (2006). Relationship of self-beliefs, social support, and university comfort with the academic success of freshman college women. *Journal of College Student Retention, 8*, 325–343.

Reiter, H. I., Eva, K. W., Rosenfeld, J., & Norman, G. R. (2007). Multiple mini-interviews predict clerkship and licensing examination performance. *Medical Education, 41*, 378–384.

Reyes, R. (2007). A collective pursuit of learning the possibility to be: The CAMP experience assisting situationally marginalized Mexican American students to a successful student identity. *Journal of Advanced Academics, 18*, 618–659.

Robbins, S. B., Lauver, K., Le, H., Davis, D., Langley, R., & Carlstrom, A. (2004). Do psychological and study skill factors predict college outcomes? A meta-analysis. *Psychological Bulletin, 130*, 261–288.

Rowley, L., & Bowman, P. J. (2009). Risk, protection, and achievement disparities among African American males: Cross-generation theory, research and comprehensive intervention. *Journal of Negro Education, 78*, 305–320.

Sedlacek, W. E. (2004). *Beyond the Big Test: Noncognitive assessment in higher education.* San Francisco, CA: Jossey-Bass.

Sedlacek, W. E., & Sheu, H. B. (2004). Academic success of Gates Millennium Scholars. In E. P. St. John (Ed.), *Readings on Equal Education: Vol. 20. Improving access and college success for diverse students: Studies of the Gates Millennium Scholars Program* (pp. 181–198). New York, NY: AMS Press.

Sternberg, R. (2004). The Rainbow Project Collaborators and the University of Michigan Business School Project Collaborators: Theory-based university admissions testing for a new millennium. *Educational Psychologist, 39*, 185–198.

Stolte, S. K., Scheer, S. B., & Robinson, E. T. (2003) The reliability of noncognitive admissions measures in predicting non-traditional Doctor of Pharmacy student performance outcomes. *American Journal of Pharmaceutical Education, 67*, 129–143.

Streyffeler L, Altmaier E. M., Kuperman S, & Patrick L. E. (2005). Development of a medical school admissions interview phase 2: Predictive validity of cognitive and noncognitive attributes. *Medical Education, 10*, 10–14. Available from http://www.med-ed-online.org

Supreme Court of the United States (2003). Opinion of the Court on *Grutter v. Bollinger*. Available online at: http://law2.umkc.edu/faculty/projects/ftrials/conlaw/gruttervbollinger.html

Ting, S. R. (2000). Predicting Asian Americans' academic performance in the first year of college: An approach combining SAT scores and noncognitive variables. *Journal of College Student Development, 41*, 442–449.

Ting, S. R., & Robinson, T. L. (1998). First year academic success: A prediction combining cognitive and psychosocial variables for Caucasian and African American students. *Journal of College Student Development, 39*, 599–610.

Tracey, T. J., & Sedlacek, W. E. (1984). Noncognitive variables in predicting academic success by race. *Measurement & Evaluation in Guidance, 16*, 171–178.

Urlings-Strop, L. C., Stijnen, T., Themmen, A. P. N., & Splinte, T. A. W. (2009). Selection of medical students: a controlled experiment. *Medical Education, 43*, 175–183.

Walpole, M., Simmerman, H., Mack, C., Mills, J. T., Scales, M., & Alano, D. (2008). Bridge to success: Insight into summer bridge program students' college transition. *Journal of the First Year Experience & Students in Transition, 20*, 11–30.

Watt, K. M., Huerta, J., & Lozano, A. (2007). A comparison study of AVID and GEAR UP 10th grade students in two high schools in the Rio Grande Valley of Texas. *Journal of Education for Students Placed at Risk, 12*, 185–212.

Zhang. Z., & Richards, R. S. (1999, May). *Increasing retention and achievement: A summer transition program at work.* Paper presented at the annual meeting of the Association for Institutional Research. Seattle, WA.

Ziv, A., Rubin, O., Moshinsky, A., Gafni, N., Kotler, M., Dagain, Y., . . . Mittleman, M. (2008) MOR: A simulation-based assessment centre for evaluating the personal and interpersonal qualities of medical school candidates. *Medical Education, 42*, 991–998.

CHAPTER 14

TOWARD A 21st-CENTURY MERITOCRACY: BRIDGING SCHOLARSHIP, INTERVENTION RESEARCH, AND SOCIAL CHANGE

Phillip J. Bowman and Edward P. St. John

There is nothing so practical as a good theory and nothing so theoretical as a good practice. —Kurt Lewin, 1890–1947

There is a growing paradigm shift away from the misuse of SAT/ACT-type test scores as synonymous with merit toward more comprehensive merit approaches that combine such high-stakes testing with other evidence-based merit criteria (e.g., Lemann, 1999; Schudson, 1972; Wrightman, 2003). This paradigm shift guides not only more holistic review in selective college admission but also more comprehensive assessments of merit in other contexts including K–12 pipeline programs, student services in higher education, and employment training, as well as career, leadership, and multilevel talent development interventions within an increasingly diverse nation. In the 21st century, innovative experimentation with comprehensive merit concepts, approaches, and practices can provide the foundation for a more inclusive meritocracy that goes beyond the 20th-century American meritocracy. Lemann (1999) notes that an *inclusive concept of meritocracy* emphasizing "equal opportunity, with rewards to the deserving and careers open to talented" (p. 343) is deeply rooted in the core values of the United States. He also critiques the narrow "one-dimensional" approach to meritocracy that emerged as the American meritocracy in the 20th century:

> Let us say you wanted to design, from scratch, a system to distribute opportunity in the fairest possible way. Would you design the American meritocracy as it now exists? You would only if you believed that IQ test scores, and more broadly, academic performance are the same as merit. That's a defensible position, but it ought at least to show itself openly to be debated, rather than be presumed. If it did, arguments against it would quickly emerge. Merit is various, not unidimensional. Intelligence tests, and also education itself, can't be counted on to find every form of merit. They

325

don't find wisdom, or originality, or humor, or toughness, or empathy, or common sense, or independence, or determination—let alone moral worth (p. 345).

In contrast to the 20th century, a more inclusive 21st-century American meritocracy would provide equal opportunity for talent development to all groups—rather than systematic blocked opportunities to some and nepotism, elite sponsorship, and privileged networks to successful outcomes for others. Despite some strong opposition during the last quarter of the 20th century, deep-seated cultural assumptions continue to result in a common misuse of SAT/ACT-type tests as valid measures of innate ability and as sufficient indicators of merit in education, employment, and other high-stakes decision contexts (e.g., Bowman, Chapter 1, this volume). However, as we move further into the 21st century, a major paradigm shift toward a more comprehensive merit agenda is spurred by five major forces: (1) a need for evidence-based holistic college admissions strategies in response to anti–affirmative action policies; (2) a need for comprehensive approaches to K–20 pipeline interventions that promote higher education, advanced careers, and talent development; (3) a need for comprehensive strategies to close historical race, class, and gender achievement gaps; (4) a need for comprehensive responses to declines in U.S. cross-national educational rankings and related global competitiveness concerns; and (5) a growing body of supportive scientific research conducted by experts at the Educational Testing Service (ETS), American College Testing (ACT), Inc., and university-based scholars.

Most of the past focus on the need for a more comprehensive merit agenda has centered on ongoing experimentation with *"holistic review"* strategies in college admissions and K–12 outreach in response to nationwide opposition to affirmative action policies (e.g., Gilbert, 2008; Pusser, 2004; Sternberg, 2004). In addition, the compelling need for a more comprehensive merit agenda has also grown as the *"multiple achievement gaps"* literature has broadened the focus beyond divisive debates about "racial" disparities toward more inclusive and strategic analyses of complex socioeconomic, gender, and global disparities (e.g., Bowman, Chapter 1, this volume; Darling-Hammond, 2010; Kahlenberg, 2010; Whitmire, 2009; Wiseman, 2010). Perhaps the most compelling case for a new 21st-century merit agenda is a growing recognition that future *"U.S. competitiveness"* in the global economy may well depend on more comprehensive strategies to close cross-national achievement gaps between the United States and higher performing Asian and European nations. The U.S. Department of Education has begun to respond to this crisis with a growing number of national policy initiatives to address cross-national disparities reflected in several international achievement studies including the Program for International Student Assessment (PISA; http://nces.ed.gov/surveys/pisa/), Trends in International Mathematics and Science Study (TIMSS; http://nces.ed.gov/pubsearch/pubsinfo.asp?pubid=2009001), and the Progress in International Reading Literacy Study (PIRLS; http://nces.ed.gov/surveys/pirls/).

Need for Strategic National Action:
The Policy-Relevant Intervention Challenge

The growing debate about cross-national achievement gaps and U.S. competitiveness is reminiscent of educational policy debates over the Russian Sputnik challenge in the 1950s that spurred the National Defense Education Act (NDEA), which provided unprecedented higher education opportunities for underrepresented students. President Barack Obama highlighted the nation's strategic response to this challenge in his 2011 State of the Union address:

> [N]ations like China and India realize that with some changes of their own, they could compete in the new world. And they started educating their children earlier and longer, with greater emphasis on math and science . . . Sustaining the American dream has never been about standing apart. It requires each generation to sacrifice, and struggle, and meet the demands of a new age . . . We need to out-innovate, out-educate, and out-build the rest of the world . . . This is our generation's Sputnik moment.

President Obama went on to recall the strategic national action a half century ago when the Soviet's beat the United States into space with the successful launch of the first-ever satellite called Sputnik in 1957. One year later, the landmark NDEA was signed into law with funding for U.S. educational institutions at all levels. To help America compete with the Soviet Union, the NDEA provided unprecedented opportunities for talented students from underrepresented groups, which were further enhanced by antipoverty and civil rights laws of the 1960s and 1970s. This strategic national action helped to increase higher education enrollment from 15% of college-age youth in 1940 (one half million) to 40% of the age group by 1970 (7.5 million). Further clarifying the current generation's "Sputnik moment," President Obama noted,

Over the next 10 years, nearly half of all new jobs will require education that goes beyond a high school education. And yet, as many as a quarter of our students aren't even finishing high school. The quality of our math and science education lags behind other nations. America has fallen to ninth in the proportion of young people with a college degree.

These concerns were further reinforced by the Committee on Prospering in the Global Economy of the 21st Century in its 2005 report, *Rising above the Gathering Storm: Energizing and Employing America for a Brighter Economic Future*, for the National Academies. The Executive Summary of this comprehensive 500-page report concluded that "without a renewed effort to bolster the foundations of our competiveness, we can expect to lose our privileged position" (p. 13). The 2010 "Gathering Storm" follow-up report concluded that America's relative global position had worsened five years later and that the only promising avenue for sustainable U.S. prosperity was through innovation (Members of the 2005 "Rising Above the Gathering Storm" Committee, 2010). This report noted that the United States ranks only 20th in high school completion, 16th in college completion rates, and even worse in mathematics and science education. To promote innovation in the interests of U.S. competitiveness, the report recommends greater investing in research, attracting more global talent, and multilevel interventions to eliminate cross-national achievement gaps. The report emphasizes the particular challenge of persistent gender, racial/ethnic, and class gaps in science, technology, engineering, and mathematics (STEM):

While the representation of women among those receiving bachelor's degrees in all fields from US universities exceeds 57 percent, less than 20 percent of the degrees in engineering are awarded to women—with the most recent trends slightly worsening. Among sixth graders who received scores above 700 on the mathematics Scholastic Aptitude Test 30 years ago boys outnumbered girls by 13:1. In the more recent tests, the ratio is 4:1—suggesting once again that societal rather than biological issues are at work. Similarly, black and Hispanic representation among those receiving bachelor's degrees in engineering is less than one-half their proportionate share of the overall population. (p. 49)

Several European countries, Canada, and China appear to be more efficacious than the United States in the development of comprehensive policies to reduce national and cross-national achievement gaps and expand higher education access (Altbach & Peterson, 2008; Goastellec, 2008; Li & Lin, 2008). Guided by strategic national policy, these countries have been able to rapidly expand higher education opportunities for all citizens with clear goals of improving national educational rankings and competitiveness in a global economy. For example, Goastellec (2008) notes that 51% of a given age group enters higher education in European Union nations, but the comparative number is over 70% for countries with the highest access (Australia, Finland, Island, Poland, and Sweden). Similarly, China's great leap toward mass higher education has been spurred by a radical expansion policy enacted on June 24, 1999. For example, Li and Lin (2008) note that the rationale for China's impressive higher education expansion is based on the formulation EHE > QQW > MD/EG > NA:

> By this simplified formulation, Chinese leaders assume that the expansion of higher education (EHE), would boost the quality and quantity of the whole workforce (QQW), then lay the foundation for modernization development (MD) and economic growth (EG), and finally fulfill national achievement. (p. 282)

China's strategic national action is a central component of a strong national motivation to catch up with countries such as the United States, Japan, the United Kingdom, France, and Germany.

From Action-Research to Reciprocal Translation Strategies

To ensure U.S. global competitiveness in the 21st century, a growing number of stakeholders have begun to emphasize the importance of comprehensive "action-research" strategies to systematically guide strategic experimentation, innovation, and multilevel intervention. In addition to higher education, the business world as well as the U.S. Department of Education, National Institutes of Health (NIH), National Science Foundation (NSF), the National Academies, and other stakeholders increasingly support more comprehensive approaches that include both evidence-based innovation and related action-research strategies to improve U.S. competitiveness. As suggested throughout this volume, the efficacy of these comprehensive approaches may well require action-research with cutting-edge translational strategies that build on more inclusive concepts of diversity and merit to address ***"multiple achievement gaps,"*** including complex racial, socioeconomic, gender, and global disparities.

Guided by strategic national policy, innovative action-research strategies can help to systematically promote experimentation, a more inclusive 21st-century meritocracy, and talent development in the United States and beyond. Viable action-research strategies can build on the classic work of social psychologist Kurt Lewin to emphasize the logical interdependence of good social theory and good social action: "there is nothing so practical as a good theory—and nothing so theoretical as a good practice" (Marrow, 1969, p. viii). As a "practical theorist," Lewin (1997) viewed action-research as

> comparative research on the conditions and effects of various forms of social action, and research leading to social action. This by no means implies that the research needed is in any respect less scientific or lower than what would be required for pure science . . . progress will depend largely on the rate with which basic research in the social sciences can develop deeper insight into the laws that govern social life. This basic social research will have to include mathematical and conceptual problems of theoretical analysis. Above all, it will have to include laboratory and field experiments in social change. (p. 144)

Over 60 years ago, this early statement by Lewin inspired the development of the University of Michigan (UM)'s Institute for Social Research (ISR), which has become world renowned for promoting basic scholarship and informing public policy. In addition to basic social science scholarship, Lewin's early work also continues to inspire innovative action-research and policy-relevant reciprocal translation approaches. Scholar-activists affiliated with the UM's National Center for Institutional Diversity continue to collaborate with ISR and a growing number of other policy-relevant stakeholders to promote both innovative action-research and reciprocal translation strategies. For example, the Action Inquiry Model (AIM), discussed in the following section, provides a reformation of the action tradition that is compatible with the new demands for research that informs reform efforts to reduce inequalities in education, health and other policy domains. After introducing AIM, we consider how this approach can be integrated with a unique reciprocal translation research agenda that brings the use of strengths-based indicators to scale in reforms that expand educational opportunities and reduce inequalities.

The Action Inquiry Model:
A Unique Approach to Intervention Research

The Action Inquiry Model (AIM) has evolved through over twenty years of research aimed at informing policy development and educational improvement in both K–12 and higher education (St. John, 2009a, 2009b). Consistent with Lewin's (1997) concept of action research, AIM evolved from research that used state of the art methods to inform and support efforts to improve social equity in education. We briefly describe the origins and prior uses of AIM before considering how it can be used to support basic and applied research that aims to build and test comprehensive merit approaches in college admissions, student financial aid, curricular reform, and student support services in higher education as strategies for improving academic success.

Development of the Action Inquiry Model. In the late 1980s, Hank Levin and graduate students at Stanford University adapted John Dewey's concept of inquiry to provide a method for reform of schools serving low income students thought to be at risk educationally (Levin, 1987). The Accelerated Schools Model involved a two-phase process with an embedded emphasis on action inquiry: taking stock of where the school is failing to involve educators in a process of using data to study their school and identify challenges and organizing teams in the school to use an inquiry process of pilot testing alternative approaches to improvement in the schools. While more than 1,000 schools eventually tried the process and there was substantial evidence of changes related to target outcomes, research evidence has been inconclusive (Finnan, St. John, McCarthy, & Slovacek, 1995).

In the late 1990s, Levin's approach was adapted as part of a state-wide reading reform project in Indiana. In this project, there was evidence the approach had a positive impact on reducing retention rates in grade level and improving other school outcomes (St. John, Loescher, & Bardzell, 2003). The main lessons from the original inquiry method were (a) there needed to be more integration of data-based approaches in reform efforts that used action inquiry, (b) an explicit focus on both achievement and equity was needed to guide educational reform, and (c) the emphasis on action inquiry promoted learning within schools and at the policy level. Based on this experience, it appeared evident that with further adaptation it might be possible to develop an alternative to narrow accountability-driven reform that placed a more explicit emphasis on expanding educational opportunity for underrepresented students.

In the 2000s, with support from the Indiana Commission on Higher Education and Lumina Foundation, a research team at Indiana University formalized AIM as a comprehensive action-research method for improving retention and degree attainment in higher education. The Indiana Project on Academic Success (IPAS) undertook comprehensive reform efforts involving several teams from fifteen college campuses. The research team used data from ETS on SAT scores, the student questionnaire that is part of the SAT, and data from state data systems to build the 2000 cohort of high school graduates in Indiana, then tracked them through college. The assessment study examined patterns in academic preparation for Indiana and U.S. high school students, including the relationship between courses completed and test scores using the ETS data and student records, enrollment patterns within the state system of higher education, major choices, transfer, and persistence (e.g., St. John, Carter, Chung, & Musoba, 2006).

The IPAS team provided campuses with technical assistance to assess retention rates and identify challenges to retention for underrepresented students. Based on their own assessment results, campuses organized teams to address the challenges using a range of strategies including orientation, supplemental instruction, learning communities, and revised academic program design. In most instances, the campus teams engaged in formative strategies to evaluate, redesign, or refine existing practices. There was substantial evidence of improvement at several campuses (Hossler, Gross, & Ziskin, 2009; St. John & Musboa, 2010).

Based on the experience with IPAS, the AIM was refined with core elements of the process further clarified (St. John, McKinney, & Tuttle, 2006; St. John 2009a, 2009b). The AIM process (Figure 1) involves

- *assessment* leading to the identification of critical challenges (e.g., challenges related to educational attainment for low-income/first-generation students);

- *organization* of teams to address critical challenges;

- *engagement* in the action reform process to address challenges (e.g., based on an understanding of the challenge, teams redesigned practices and tested the results); and

- *targeted* evaluation of the challenges identified and the solutions proposed and tested to refine and improve interventions.

Figure 1. Action Inquiry Model

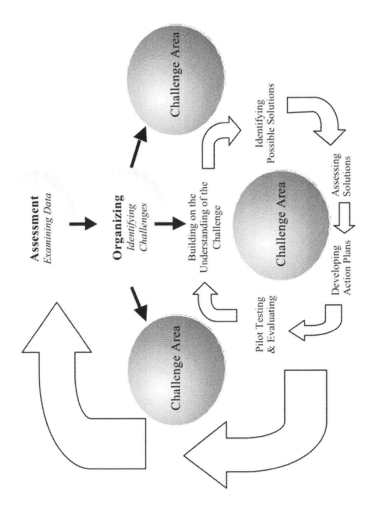

Source: St. John, McKinney, & Tuttle (2006).

Using the logic of AIM has proved as valuable for working with policy makers at a state level on refining policies as it has been in working with campuses to improve access and retention. The keys to success have proved to be (a) use of assessment to identify challenges rather than to identify failures, (b) use of the results from assessments to inform program redesign, and (c) use of formative and summative evaluation to promote organizational learning. In the process of this research, it has been possible to inform policy, improve practice and build workable theories of academic pathways (St. John & Musoba, 2010) and academic capital formation (St. John, Hu, & Fisher, 2010). *Linking to the Comprehensive Merit Agenda.* The comprehensive merit agenda involves finding better ways of providing every student with the opportunity to attain a quality education (Perry, Moses, Wynne, Cortes, & Delpit, 2010) by reducing achievement gaps in the K–20+ pipeline from Kindergarten through higher education and career outcomes based on potential and talent. Bowman's strengths-based approach (Chapter 8, this volume) provides a frame for balancing traditional achievement measures with understandings of the ability of students to navigate educational and social systems, a crucial aspect of improving academic success by underrepresented students (St. John et al., 2010). This multilevel framework also provides a basis for identifying challenges to diversity that merit attention and inform action. AIM provides a three-stage approach to address gaps within a field of action (i.e., a school or school system, a college or department, or a state-level education agency):

1. *Assessment*: Using appropriate quantitative and qualitative methods to track students through the system, discern points of departure or under-achievement that result in gaps, and identify specific features and processes within the current system that appear related to the gap. When systems collect information on strengths-based indicators, it can be used in the assessment process.

2. *Organizing*: There are two organizational approaches for using assessment results to inform reform: (a) an intentional application of AIM involves organizing teams to address the challenges (members of the teams should be drawn as volunteers from the units facing challenges), or (b) if integrating AIM into existing planning and

management strategies within government agencies and educational institutions, the assessment results can be used to inform decision making processes when the researchers provide technical assistance at critical points in the process.

3. *Inquiry Process*: Action inquiry involves thinking through reasons why the current system isn't working as intended, using data analyses as a source of information along with observations and reflections on past experience. It has provend crucial to treat current and past practices as *pilot tests* that can be evaluated and then refined and adapted to fit local circumstances. When an intentional application is used, it helps to go through all of the steps of the inquiry process. Whether the process of change and adaptation is structured or informal, it is crucial that educators routinely evaluate and reflect on the results of their practices with the same indicators used to identify the challenges or gaps.

Using action inquiry provides a means of integrating research into strategies for improving diversity. When we view narrowing of gaps in the pipeline as an intent or outcome along with other educational outcomes, we can use state of the art research methods as forms of support for policy development and educational change (e.g., St. John & Musoba, 2010). In addition, using the logic of action inquiry in consultations and collaborations on applied research with reform-oriented foundations, government agencies, and educational institutions makes basic research possible. For example, a decade of research and collaboration with the Bill & Melinda Gates Foundation and Lumina Foundation including studies of major intervention programs resulted in the testing of "academic capital formation," a new theoretical framework for promoting uplift (St. John et al., 2010).

Toward a Reciprocal Translation Research Approach: Bridging Basic Scholarship and Multilevel Intervention

In addition to the innovative Action Inquiry Model, the development of a 21st-century merit agenda must also translate basic findings from theory-driven scholarship both to clarify complex merit issues in diversifying populations and to inform the development of exemplary interventions. As illustrated in Figure 2, the University of Michigan's National Center for Institutional Diversity (NCID) has begun to bring together scholars in basic disciplines and multilevel partners engaged in policy-relevant intervention research guided by an integrative **Reciprocal Translation Model (RTM).** This unique RTM promotes the *reciprocal benefits* of *exemplary intervention research* and *basic scholarship* for guiding innovation in multilevel intervention to address policy-relevant challenges and opportunities of diversity. Figure 2 highlights how the reciprocal translation of" basic scholarship"←→"intervention research" focuses on both (a) the *"reciprocal translation"* of policy-relevant intervention challenges into opportunities for basic scholarship and theory-development (right oval) and (b) the *"traditional translation"* of basic scholarship to guide innovation in the design or improvement of intervention strategies (left oval).

In an early statement, social psychologist Kurt Lewin (1997) noted that such reciprocal translation research should integrate two types of research questions:

> It is important to understand clearly that social research concerns itself with two rather different types of questions, namely the study of general laws of group life and the diagnosis of a specific situation . . . Problems of general laws deal with the relation between possible conditions and possible results . . . The knowledge of laws can serve as guidance for the achievement of certain objectives under certain conditions. To act correctly, it does not suffice, however, if the engineer or the surgeon knows the general laws of physics or physiology. He has to know too the specific character of the situation at hand. This character is determined by a scientific fact-finding . . . For any field of action both types of scientific research are needed. (p. 145)

The potential scholarly and scientific benefits of translating theoretical knowledge from exemplary intervention research to basic scholarship are reflected in the classic Lewinian adage that there is "nothing so theoretical as a good practice."

Reverse Translation—From Intervention to Scholarship. As suggested in Figure 2, *policy-relevant intervention* research can promote multilevel innovation and inform policy makers, administrators, professional experts, and best practices. The preceding highlights of AIM show how organizational,

Figure 2. National Center for Institutional Diversity
Bridging Basic Scholarship with Policy-Relevant Intervention Research
Reciprocal Translation Model: Scholarship ↔ Intervention

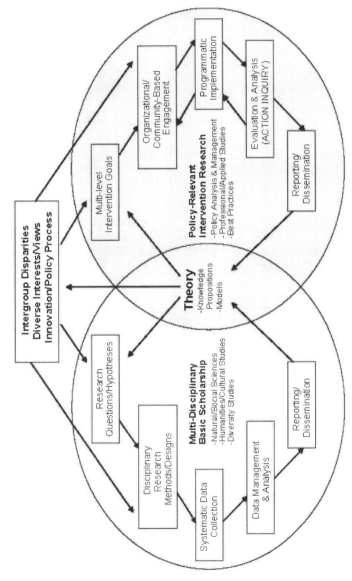

formative, and summative evaluation data are critical for planning, developing, and institutionalizing strategic action and public policy. Figure 2 highlights how AIM can help to systematically identify implementation challenges to promote innovative problem solving among organizational, community-based, and policy stakeholders. Within the comprehensive RTM, AIM strategies can guide a multilevel social change process that focuses on multiple barriers and challenges to a more inclusive American meritocracy. For example, AIM enables the formative evaluation of several concurrent challenges facing multilevel interventions (e.g., educational institutional challenges as well as related policy challenges at the local, state, national, and/or international levels).

In addition to their practical benefits, exemplary interventions can also provide the context for basic scholarship to further test, validate, develop, extend, or reformulate basic theory. In the inductive tradition, the AIM is designed to produce an interrelated set of empirical findings on policy-relevant interventions that provide both specific and general insights. As a heuristic device, the AIM can provide an inductive framework for the reverse translation of intervention research findings into more basic theoretical questions and scholarship. For example, the use of AIM with several innovative higher education pipeline interventions has helped to generate hypotheses and theoretical insights to extend social capital theory to cutting-edge scholarship on "academic capital formation" (St. John et al., 2010).

Traditional Translation—From Scholarship to Intervention. In the classic deductive tradition, the RTM in Figure 2 also promotes the conventional translation or application of basic multidisciplinary scholarship in the natural/social sciences, humanities/cultural studies, and the expanding area of diversity studies (racial/ethnic, gender, class, disability, etc.). The traditional translation of basic scholarship-to-intervention reflects the related Lewinian adage that there is "nothing so practical as a good theory" (Lewin, 1997; Marrow, 1969). This traditional translational paradigm is the foundational pillar for evidence-based professional practice and can help to further apply and extend basic theory by systematically testing core theoretical propositions through interventions within a wider range of natural settings.

Basic scholarship in natural science disciplines is translated into innovative engineering experiments and applications, and basic scholarship in the life sciences is translated into clinical trials, medical practice, and innovative health interventions. Similarly, basic scholarship in the social/behavioral science disciplines (i.e., psychology, sociology, economics, political science, and anthropology) is translated into innovative intervention strategies in education, business, social work, public health, public policy, and other professional practice fields. Multiple methods are needed in theory-driven intervention research to ensure external validity, but randomized and quasi-experimental designs remain the gold standards to maximize internal validity and clearer causal inference about intervention efficacy on policy-relevant outcomes (Cook & Campbell, 1979; Dublin, 1983; Hoye, Harris, & Judd, 2002; Shadish, Cook, & Campbell, 2001; Tierney, 1996).

A growing body of basic social/behavioral science research conducted by university-based scholars and experts at ETS and ACT, Inc. is currently being translated into exemplary intervention contexts with major implications for a comprehensive merit agenda in the 21s century. Bridging such cutting-edge scholarship with multilevel interventions can help to provide the type of evidence needed to address deep-seated conflicts over contested constructs of merit in higher education and divisive debates about merit, diversity, and opportunity (see Bowman, Chapter 2, this volume). The complexity of debates about diversity and merit in higher education calls for theory-driven scholarship within multiple disciplines.

Despite the importance of multidisciplinary research, Table 1 highlights how basic scholarship in psychology continues to be especially salient in translational interventions with significant implications for the development of more comprehensive approaches to merit (e.g., Bowman, 2006; Robbins et al., 2004; Roberts, Walton, & Viechtbauer, 2006; Sedlacek, 2004). Cutting-edge work based at the ETS Center for New Constructs continues to translate basic **personality psychology** scholarship on emotional intelligence, SAT-type assessments and other indicators of "personal potential" into more comprehensive K–16 pipeline interventions (e.g., Roberts et al., 2006; Burrus et al., Chapter 10, this volume). Similarly, cutting-edge work based at ACT, Inc continues to translate basic **counseling psychology** scholarship on psychosocial factors, ACT-type assessments, and other indicators of "student readiness" into more comprehensive K–16 pipeline interventions (Burkum et al., Chapter 11, this volume; Ramos, Chapter 6, this volume; Robbins et. al., 2004).

For over 40 years, Sedlacek and his colleagues at the University of Maryland have translated basic **educational psychology** scholarship on eight noncognitive factors to guide innovative interventions in educational settings (e.g., Sedlacek, 2004, Chapter 9, this volume). This seminal noncognitive approach has proved useful in higher education admissions, counseling, advising, mentoring, retention, curricular, student affairs, career development, and college outreach efforts as well as innovative interventions such as the Gates Millennium Scholars Program. Finally, a new collaborative project based at the University of Michigan's National Center for Institutional Diversity (NCID) builds on the interrelated work by

ETS; ACT, Inc.; Sedlacek; and other university-based experts to promote more comprehensive approaches that combine SAT/ACT-type assessment with additional evidence-based merit criteria. Guided by the RTM, this project extends basic scholarship on the **social psychology** of role strain and adaptation to guide innovation in multilevel interventions to reduce achievement gaps, improve higher education opportunity, support career success, and promote talent development (e.g., Bowman, 2006, Chapter 8, this volume). This comprehensive strengths-based approach also supports the importance of strategic partnerships to integrate insights from studies on a range of critical merit constructs in collaborative research and policy-relevant intervention.

Table 1: Translating Basic Psychological Scholarship Into Exemplary Intervention Research

Basic Psychological Scholarship & Related Interventions based on Comprehensive Merit Constructs	Related Research Programs on Comprehensive Merit Constructs
Personality Psychology: Emotional Intelligence Factors & K–16 Outreach Interventions (e.g., Roberts et al., 2006)	Educational Testing Service Center for New Constructs
Counseling Psychology: Psychosocial Factors & K–16 Outreach Interventions (e.g., Robbins et al., 2004)	American College Testing, Inc. Student Readiness Inventory
Educational Psychology: Noncognitive Factors & Gates Millennium Scholars/ Noncognitive Research Program Other Education Interventions (e.g., Sedlacek, 2004)	University of Maryland
Social Psychology: Role Strain-Adaptation Factors & Exemplary Higher Education/ Career Pipeline Interventions (e.g., Bowman, 2006)	University of Michigan Natl. Center for Institutional Diversity

Conclusions and Future Directions

This concluding chapter further clarifies the challenge of developing a 21st-century meritocracy and calls for a policy-relevant translational research agenda to expand merit considerations by bridging interdisciplinary scholarship with comprehensive, evidence-based, and innovative intervention strategies. There is growing evidence that an inclusive meritocracy that goes beyond SAT/ACT-type testing to consider a broader range of strengths and talents is critical for a number of reasons within a diversifying U.S. population (e.g., Bowman & Betancur, 2010; Friedman, 2005; Gurin, Lehman, & Lewis, 2005; Page, 2007; Perry et al., 2010; Trent & St. John, 2008). For example, compelling business and strategic rationales for a more inclusive meritocracy were clearly articulated in the amicus briefs filed by *Fortune* 500 corporations, military leaders, governmental officials, and many other organizations to support the University of Michigan's 2003 Supreme Court cases to promote diversity in higher education. Hence, a more inclusive meritocracy should be a core component of strategic national action to insure the talent development, multicultural competence, organizational excellence, and sustainable development necessary for global U.S. competitiveness in the 21st century.

The development of a more inclusive 21st-century meritocracy will require strategic exchanges, collaborations, and partnerships to bridge cutting-edge scholarship with multilevel interventions that inspire innovation, public policy, and social change. Since 2008, the National Center for Institutional Diversity (NCID) at the University of Michigan has promoted exchanges between university-based, ETS, and ACT, Inc. experts and a growing number of government, foundation, corporate, nonprofit, and other stakeholders regarding the need to collaborate on a more inclusive merit agenda for the 21st century. Promoting such policy-relevant exchanges is one of several priorities of a new NCID-based National Consortium for Diversity Scholarship and Policy (NCDSP) that seeks to better bridge basic scholarship and policy-relevant intervention to address pressing challenges and opportunities of diversity.

The NCID-NCDSP is explicitly organized around the RTM highlighted in Figure 2 to promote the "reciprocal" translation of "basic scholarship-to-exemplary intervention" and "exemplary intervention-to-basic scholarship." A growing number of consortium initiatives bridge cutting-edge diversity scholarship with strategic exchanges, collaborations, and partnership activities between university-based scholars and policy-relevant stakeholders engaged in innovative interventions in diversifying populations. For example, a series of collaborative exchanges resulted in this current **Volume**

25 of *Readings on Equal Education.* Hopefully, this volume can provide clearer direction for future research on more comprehensive approaches to diversity and merit that systematically inform innovation in holistic college admissions, higher education pipeline programs, and other policy-relevant talent development interventions.

The various experts in **Volume 25** support the importance of a more comprehensive merit agenda to guide strategic national action in the 21st century. At this critical stage of American history, strategic national action can provide the foundation for more proactive intervention research that moves beyond a reactionary focus on "innate minority deficits," "anti–affirmative action," "reverse discrimination," "racial quotas" or "unfair preferences" (e.g., Bowen & Bok, 1998; Bowman & Smith, 2002; Gilbert, 2008; Gurin et al., 2005; Pusser, 2004). Toward this end, both scholars and governmental agencies such as the National Institutes for Health (NIH), National Science Foundation (NSF), and the Department of Education have begun to reframe K–12, higher education, and career pipeline interventions to close multiple achievement gaps as matters of national competitiveness (e.g., Darling-Hammond, 2010; Chubin, DePass, & Blockus, 2009; DePass & Chubin, 2008; Frierson, 1991; Kahlenberg, 2010; Oakes, Rogers, Lipton, & Morrell, 2002; Olson & Fagen, 2007; Whitmire, 2009).

The strategic reframing of merit debates from innate deficits to strengths-based talent development can provide a unique opportunity for collaborative ventures to design comprehensive merit approaches that promote innovation and guide ***exemplary multilevel interventions*** to reduce multiple achievement gaps. Strategic partnerships to promote success among highly talented women and minorities in STEM fields are especially critical as the United States continues to lose ground in both higher education and global economic status (e.g., Chubin, DePass, & Blockus, 2009; DePass & Chubin, 2008; Olson & Fagen, 2007). For example, guided by a growing national alliance of STEM stakeholders, *NIH-National Institute for General Medical Sciences* currently funds a NCID collaborative study to better understand comprehensive strategies to improve interventions that increase the number of talented students from underrepresented backgrounds who excel in undergraduate studies, pursue advanced doctoral degrees, and succeed in biomedical/behavioral science research careers. In addition, NCID is a strategic partner in an impressive *NSF-ADVANCE Institutional Transformation* intervention at the University of Michigan that has become a national exemplar for developing innovative strategies to enhance the advancement of women in STEM fields (Stewart, Malley, & LaVaque-Manty, 2007).

A new 21st-century merit agenda that improves *"U.S. competitiveness"* must also include strategic partnerships to close cross-national gaps by developing comprehensive interventions to reduce especially persistent racial/ethnic and socioeconomic achievement disparities. To reduce such complex racial and class achievement gaps, collaborative ventures on policy-relevant interventions in both community colleges and low-income public schools provide unique opportunities to break new ground with more comprehensive merit approaches. For example, NCID-based scholars are engaged in a new collaboration with a *NSF-Louis Stokes-Alliance for Minority Participation* project to promote experimentation with more comprehensive pipeline strategies to improve opportunities for talented students from segregated urban schools who enter community colleges as a pathway to baccalaureate and advanced degrees in STEM fields.

With funding from the *Ford Foundation* and others, NCID-affiliated scholars are engaged in a growing number of strategic partnership activities with K–12 public school systems to develop more comprehensive approaches to address the disturbing racial and class achievement gaps across urban-suburban schools. At the national level, two emerging national policy initiatives by the *U.S. Department of Education* offer especially unique opportunities. New *Race to the Top* reforms are replacing the top-down *No Child Left Behind* law with more comprehensive and flexible interventions to build on the strengths of local communities, school boards, principals, teachers, and students themselves. Similarly, a comprehensive *PROMISE NEIGHBORHOODS* initiative combines high-stakes SAT/ACT-type testing with collaborative efforts to *strengthen multilevel systemic resources* including teachers, classrooms, schools, families, and neighborhoods. Both of these efforts need to support strategic partnerships guided by a comprehensive merit agenda to address the dramatic achievement gaps in urban schools while also promoting U.S. competitiveness in the 21st century.

In conclusion, as we move further into the 21st century, the challenge of U.S. competitiveness should increasingly push our diversifying nation toward a more inclusive American meritocracy. To respond to this historic challenge, strategic national action can build on policy-relevant translational research guided by the critical issues highlighted in this volume. Strategic partnerships and collaborative efforts must promote a new 21st-century meritocracy that goes beyond long-standing, divisive, and outdated debates about diversity and merit that increasingly threaten the U.S. global position. As we move further into the 21st century, such an inclusive American meritocracy appears to be the most viable strategy for improving U.S. competitiveness by closing multiple achievement gaps and promoting higher education, talent development, and career opportunities within an increasingly diverse nation and global economy.

References

Altbach, P. G., & Peterson, P. M. (2008). America in the world higher education and the global market place. In D .P. Baker & A. W. Wiseman (Eds.), *The Worldwide transformation of higher education* (pp. 313–335). Bingly, England: Emerald.

Bowman, P. J. (2006). Role strain and adaptation issues in the strength-based model: Diversity, multilevel, and life-span considerations. *Counseling Psychologist, 34*, 118–133.

Bowman, P. J., & Betancur, J. J. (2010). Sustainable diversity and inequality: Race in the USA and beyond. In M. Janssens, M. Bechtold, G. Prarolo, & V. Stenius, (Eds.), *The sustainability of cultural diversity: Nations, cities and organizations* (pp. 55–78). Cheltenham, UK: Edward Elgar.

Bowman, P. J., & Smith, W. A. (2002). Racial ideology in the campus community. In W. A. Smith, P. G. Altbach, & K. Lomotey (Eds.), *The racial crisis in higher education: Continuing challenges for the 21st century* (pp. 103–120). Albany: State University of New York Press.

Bowen, W. G., & Bok, D. (1998). The admissions process and "race-neutrality." In *The shape of the river: Long-term consequences of considering race in college admissions* (pp. 15–53). Princeton, NJ: Princeton University Press.

Chubin, D. E., DePass, A. L., & Blockus, L. (2009). *Understanding interventions that broaden participation in research careers: Embracing the breadth of purpose* (Vol. 3). Conference Summary, Bethesda, Maryland, May 7-9, 2009. Available online at:. http://php.aaas.org/programs/centers/capacity/documents/Interventions Report2009.pdf

Committee on Prospering in the Global Economy of the 21st Century. (2006). *Rising above the gathering storm*: *Energizing and employing America for a brighter economic future* (Report prepared for the National Academy of Sciences, National Academy of Engineering, and Institute of Medicine of the National Academies). Washington, DC: National Academies Press.

Cook, T. D., & Campbell, D. T. (1979). *Quasi-experimentation: Design and analysis issues in field settings*. Boston, MA: Houghton Mifflin.

Darling-Hammond, L. (2010). Structured for failure: Race, resources, and student achievement. In H. R. Markus and P. M. L. Moya (Eds.), *Doing race: 21 essays for the 21st century* (pp. 295–321). New York, NY: W. W. Norton.

DePass, A. L., & Chubin, D. E. (2008). *Understanding interventions that encourage minorities to pursue research careers: Building a community of research and practice.* Bethesda, MD: American Society of Cell Biology.

Dublin, R. (1983). Theory building in applied areas. In M. D. Dunnette (Ed.), *Handbook of industrial and organizational psychology* (pp. 17–40). New York, NY: Wiley.

Finnan, C, St. John, E. P., McCarthy, J., & Slovacek, S. (Eds.). (1995). *Accelerated schools in action: Lessons from the field.* Newbury Park, CA: Corwin.

Friedman, T. (2005). *The world is flat: A brief history of the 21st century.* New York, NY: Farrar, Straus and Giroux.

Frierson, H. T. (1991). Intervention can make a difference: The impact on standardized tests and classroom performance. In W. A. Allen, E. G. Epps, E. G., & N. Z. Haniff (Eds.), *College in black and white: African American students in predominantly White and historically Black public universities* (pp. 225–238). Albany: State University of New York Press.

Gilbert, J. (2008). Application quest: A case study on holistic diversity in admission. *Journal of College Admission, 199,* 12–18.

Goastellec, G. (2008). Changes in access to higher education: From worldwide constraints to common patterns of reform?. In D. P. Baker & A. W. Wiseman (Eds.), *The Worldwide transformation of higher education* (pp. 1–26). Bingly, England: Emerald.

Gurin, P., Lehman, J. S., & Lewis, E. (2005). *Defending diversity: Affirmative action at the University of Michigan.* Ann Arbor: University of Michigan Press.

Hossler, D., Gross, J. P. K., & Ziskin, M. (Eds.). (2009). *Readings on Equal Education: Vol. 24. Enhancing institutional and state initiatives to increase student Success: Studies of the Indiana Project on Academic Success.* New York, NY: AMS Press.

Hoye, R. H., Harris, M. J., & Judd, C. M. (2002). *Research methods in social relations* (7th ed.). Florence, KY: Wadsworth.

Jahlenberg, R. D. (2010). *Rewarding strivers: Helping low-income students succeed in college.* Washington, D.C.: Century Foundation Press.

Lemann, N. (1999). *The big test: The secret history of the American meritocracy.* New York, NY: Farrar, Straus, and Giroux.

Levin, H. M. (1987). Accelerated schools for disadvantaged students. *Educational Leadership, 44*(6), 19–21.

Lewin, K. (1997). *Resolving social conflicts and field theory in social science.* Washington, DC: American Psychological Association.

Li, J., & Lin, J. (2008). China's move to mass higher education: An analysis of policy making from a rational framework. In D. P. Baker & A. W. Wiseman (Eds.), *The worldwide transformation of higher education: International perspectives on education and society* (pp. 269–295). Bingley, England: JAI Press.

Marrow, A. J. (1969). *The practical theorist: The life and work of Kurt Lewin.* New York: Basic Books.

Members of the 2005 "Rising Above the Gathering Storm" Committee. (2010). *Rising above the gathering storm, Revisited—Rapidly approaching category 5* (Report prepared for the Presidents of the National Academy of Sciences, National Academy of Engineering, and Institute of Medicine of the National Academies). Washington, DC: National Academies Press.

Oakes, J., Rogers, J., Lipton, M., & Morrell, E. (2002). The social construction of college access: Confronting the technical, cultural, and political barriers to low-income students of color. In W. G. Tierney & L. S. Hagedorn (Eds.), *Increasing access to college: Extending possibilities for all students* (pp. 105–122). Albany: State University of New York Press.

Olson, S., & Fagen, A. P. (2007). *Understanding interventions that encourage minorities to pursue research careers: Summary of a workshop.* Washington, DC: National Academies Press.

Page, S. (2007). *The difference: How the power of diversity creates better groups, firms, schools, and societies.* Princeton, NJ, and Oxford, England: Princeton University Press.

Perry, T. Moses, R., Wynne, J., Delpit, L., & Cortes, E. (2010). *Quality education as a constitutional Right: Organizing to create a movement.* Boston, MA: Beacon Press.

Pusser, B. (2004). *Burning down the house: Politics, governance, and affirmative action at the University of California.* Albany: State University of New York Press.

Robbins, S., Lauver, K., Le, H., Langley, R., Davis, D., & Carlstrom, A. (2004). Do psychosocial and study skill factors predict college outcomes? A meta-analysis. *Psychological Bulletin, 130,* 261–288.

Roberts, B. W., Walton, K., & Viechtbauer, W. (2006). Patterns of mean-level change in personality traits across the life course: A meta-analysis of longitudinal studies. *Psychological Bulletin, 132,* 1–25.

Schudson, Michael (1972). Organizing the "Meritocracy": A history of the College Entrance Examination Board. *Harvard Educational Review, 42*(1), 34–69.

Sedlacek, W. E. (2004). *Beyond the big test: Noncognitive assessment in higher education.* San Francisco, CA: Jossey-Bass.

Shadish, W. R., Cook, T. D., & Campbell, D. T. (2001). *Experimental and quasi-experimental design for generalized causal inference.* New York, NY: Houghton Mifflin.

St. John, E. P. (2009a). *Action, reflection and social justice: Integrating moral reasoning into professional education.* Cresskill, NJ: Hampton Press.

St. John, E. P. (2009b) *College organization and professional development: Integrating moral reasoning and reflective practice.* New York, NY: Routledge Taylor.

St. John, E. P., Carter, D. F., Chung, C. G., & Musoba, G. D. (2006). Diversity and persistence in Indiana higher education: The impact of preparation, major choices, and student aid. In E. P. St. John (Ed.), *Readings on Equal Education: Vol. 21. Public policy and educational opportunity: School reforms, postsecondary encouragement, and state policies on higher education, Readings on equal education* (pp. 341–386). New York: AMS Press.

St. John, E. P., Hu, S., & Fisher, A. S. (2010). *Breaking through the access barrier: Academic capital formation informing public policy.* New York, NY: Routledge.

St. John, E. P., Loescher, S. A., & Bardzell, J. S. (2003). *Improving reading and literacy in grades 1–5: A resource guide to research-based programs.* Thousand Oaks, CA: Corwin.

St. John, E. P., McKinney, J., & Tuttle, T. (2006). Using action inquiry to address critical challenges. In E. P. St. John & M. Wilkerson (Eds.), *Directions for Institutional Research: Vol. 30. Reframing persistence research to support academic success.* (pp. 63–76). San Francisco, CA: Jossey-Bass.

St. John, E. P., & Musoba, G. D. (2010). *Pathways to academic success: Expanding opportunity for underrepresented students.* New York, NY: Routledge.

Sternberg, R. J. (2004). Theory-based university admissions testing for a new millennium. *Educational Psychologist, 39,* 185–198.

Stewart, A. J., Malley, J. E., & LaVaque-Manty, D. (2007). *Transforming science and engineering: Advancing academic women.* Ann Arbor: University of Michigan Press.

Tierney, W. G. (1996). An anthropological analysis of student participation in college. In F. K. Stage et al. (Eds.), *College students: The evolving nature of research* (pp. 280–290). New York, NY: Simon & Schuster.

Trent, W., & St. John, E. (Eds.). (2008). *Readings on Equal Education: Vol. 23. Resources, assets, and strengths among successful diverse students: Understanding the contributions of the Gates Millennium Scholars Program.* New York, NY: AMS Press.

Whitmire, R. (2009). *Why boys fail: Saving our sons from an educational system that's leaving them behind.* New York, NY: American Management Association.

Wiseman, A. W. (2010). *The impact of international achievement studies on national education policymaking.* Bingly, England: Emerald.

Wrightman, L. F. (2003). Standardized tests and equal access: A tutorial. In M. J. Chang, D. Witt, J. Jones, & K. Hakuta (Eds.), *Compelling interest: Examining the evidence of racial dynamics in colleges and universities* (pp. 49–96). Stanford, CA: Stanford University Press.

INDEX